FAMILIES, POLITICS, AND PUBLIC POLICY

A Feminist Dialogue on Women and the State

EDITED BY
IRENE DIAMOND

AFTERWORD BY
MARY LYNDON SHANLEY

Longman
New York & London

Families, Politics, and Public Policy

Longman Inc., 1560 Broadway, New York, N.Y. 10036
Associated companies, branches, and representatives
throughout the world.

Developmental Editor: Nicole Benevento
Editorial and Design Supervisor: Frances Althaus
Production Supervisor: Ferne Y. Kawahara
Manufacturing Supervisor: Marion Hess

Library of Congress Cataloging in Publication Data
Main entry under title:

Families, politics, and public policy.

Includes index.
1. Family—United States—Addresses, essays, lectures. 2. Social change—Addresses, essays, lectures. 3. Women—United States—Social conditions—Addresses, essays, lectures. 4. Social conflict—United States—Addresses, essays, lectures. 5. Women—Government policy—United States—Addresses, essays, lectures.
I. Diamond, Irene, 1947–
HQ536.F334 1983 306.8′5′0973 82-20357
ISBN 0-582-28268-3

Printing: 9 8 7 6 5 4 3 2 1 Year: 91 90 89 88 87 86 84 83

Manufactured in the United States of America

To my mother, Freida, and my children, Adam and Ross

We are deluged with facts, but we have lost,
or are losing, our human ability to feel them . . . .
We know with the head now, by the facts, by the abstractions . . . .
Why we are thus impotent, I do not know. I know only that this
impotence exists and that it is dangerous . . . I know, too, or think
I know, that, whatever the underlying cause of the divorce of feeling from
knowing, that divorce reveals itself most vividly in the strange and
ignorant belief that the life of the imagination lies at an opposite pole
from the life of the inquiring mind--that men can live and know and
master their experience of this darkling earth by accumulating information
and no more . . . . The real defense of freedom is . . . that
feeling-life of the mind which actually knows because it involves itself
in its knowing, puts itself in the place where its thought goes, walks in the body
of the little Negro girl who feels the spittle
dribbling on her cheek . . . .

ARCHIBALD MACLEISH

Contents

Part III Visions and Strategies

Preface

I come to this volume as a mother, feminist, and political scientist; thus the issues I prodded my friends and colleagues to consider were initially framed by some deeply felt questions that, for me, had not been sufficiently explored either in policy discussions of the family or in feminist theorizing. My own experiences as a mother in a male-dominated society and a movement committed to transforming that society made me frustrated with available solutions and prescriptions for family life, whether from mainstream culture or its different critiques. If not totally blind to gender inequality, they often seemed shallow, abstracted, or mechanistic, devoid of much understanding of the needs of children, the importance of nurturance, or the value of holistic perspectives. Could my own discipline, the only social science that was not a participant in the debates on the family, provide some clarity of thought and vision? While I held no brief for the superiority of political science—indeed, it largely accepted the traditional liberal notion of the family as a purely private entity and had become centered on a constricted conception of the political (did this explain its nonparticipation?)—nevertheless it had certain resources. With its ties to the Western tradition of political philosophy and the empirical research generating contemporary public policy analysis there was the possibility of moving beyond the impoverished political analysis that seemed to prevail. As the debates intensified, the intellectual and personal challenges drew me toward a project on politics and "the family."

Not surprisingly, as the project evolved and the political events of the early 1980s brought familial issues to the center of American politics, new questions emerged, and political scientists as well began to take heed of the public debate. My original questions concerning the tensions between individual autonomy and the collective good, the problematic aspects of gender neutrality, and the contradictions of state solutions took on new dimensions and a real immediacy in the context of an ascendant right. I began to see tensions between scientific expertise and human dignity and security that had simply not occurred to me when I began. These new complexities intensified my conviction of the importance of considering public policy within a framework that took a broad view of political life without assuming the immutability of gender hierarchy, yet the new research still reflected the bifurcations between theory and empirical policy analysis that first disturbed me. This collection does not purport to solve this problem, but it does provide a beginning for creating the synthesis essential to more informed action and policy making. Moreover, it demonstrates that family policy matters cannot be considered apart from the question of women's status and existing conflicts between the sexes.

The authors represented here are all persons sensitive to women's experiences and sympathetic to the view that women's subordinate status is changeable, but are not necessarily committed to a particular notion of the nature of that subordination or a particular mode of change. Thus these essays do not hold one point of view on the nature of family life for women, the interrelationships of family life and other institutions, the origins of change, or even what desirable change is. Some take contemporary political and economic structures as a given; others do not. Policy is taken seriously throughout, yet there is no common assumption that policy change is the measure of meaningful change. It is my expectation that the commonality of a feminist perspective together with the range of philosophical assumptions and methodological approaches will reveal issues and problems that many readers had never considered. At a minimum, whether she or he, "expert" or general reader, thinking will be stretched.

The volume is divided into three sections. The first, "Power, Social Relations, and Political Agendas," provides a theoretical and historical context for examining the connections between familial change, the status of women on the one hand, and the political and economic characteristics of the state on the other. The essays also point to the psychological, social, and economic roots of conflict between the sexes and the possibilities for change. The second section, "The Policy Domains: Production, Nurturance, and Sexuality," focuses more intensively on how we re-create ourselves through consideration of selected policy problems. These essays demonstrate how familial change raises new issues, provide background on the competing values in a given area, and examine through a feminist lens commonly suggested reforms. The last section, "Visions and Strategies," picks up themes in the first two sections and explores more directly the concepts that shape how we currently re-create ourselves. By looking both to other societies and the possibilities within our own, the essays here permit the reader to broaden her or his visions about how human dignity and security could be realized.*

*Of course if political visions are to speak to our common humanity, more attention will have to be paid to the particularities of race, age, and physical impairment than is the case in this volume. The latter two are completely blank here. In part this is due to the usual exigencies of time and space, but it also reflects the incomplete visions that infuse much contemporary political thinking about the family as described in the introductory essay.

Acknowledgments

This project could not have been completed without the support, encouragement, and penetrating criticism of a number of dear friends and colleagues. Indeed, early conversations with Molly Shanley, the first person to whom I voiced my interest in a project, permitted me to move forward. Later, in the midst of writing, Martha Ackelsberg, Lee Quinby, and Steve Erie listened sympathetically, yet always pushed me to clarify my thinking and prose. Martha's own essay for the volume provided me with vital inspiration when my spirit was lagging. Robert Browning, Gail Melson, and Dena Targ pointed me toward a number of important resources, while Pat Bidelman and Barrie Thorne took the time to offer careful readings of the introductory essay. At Longman, the editorial support and good humor of Nicole Benevento and Carol Camper ensured that my administrative nightmares did not materialize. And of course without the efforts and commitment of each of the contributors there would be no volume. I am deeply indebted to you all and will always have fond memories of our conversations and letters.

Irene Diamond

Introduction

> Recognizing that our nation was founded on a strong traditional family, meaning a married heterosexual couple with or without natural children, it is imperative and we demand that the President immediately correct by Executive order the name "White House Conference on Families" and let it be further known in all futures as the "White House Conference on the Family."
>
> Minority report, 1980 White House Conference on Families, Minneapolis

"Family" versus "families." Mere wordplay? Or a politically charged battle with the potential for "revisioning"[1] and reconstituting our social relations and political life? In the midst of an explosion of reports and public pronouncements by research institutes, conferences, academics, social welfare professionals, religious leaders, and politicians, it is impossible to fully describe the current discourse on the family, let alone assess its likely outcome. Speculation is further complicated by the fact that familial language is often more readily associated with defenses of the established order than with struggles for the new. One might, as a consequence, initially see this explosion as another instance of the ritual French social historian Jacques Donzelot claims we in Western societies enact at regular intervals. According to Donzelot, we are drawn to this familial ritual "to decipher our destiny, glimpsing in the death of the family an impending barbarism, the letting go of our reasons for living, or indeed, in order to reassure ourselves at the sight of its inexhaustible capacity for survival."[2] Not surprisingly, some feminist interpretations of the current obsession with the family describe it as a dangerous exercise in nostalgia.[3]

Feminists have good reason to be skeptical of a public discourse centered on the family, both because of the historic role of the patriarchal family in the subordination of women and the critical stance toward established modes of discourse that is (or should be) intrinsic to a feminist understanding of the world. At the same time, the contextualism that distinguishes the best feminist scholarship suggests that one-dimensional characterizations falsify more than they reveal. Feminist analysis thus demands an examination of the ambiguities and complexities particular to the current controversies regarding the family and the state. Since this volume, by intent, will become part of this discourse, this introductory essay first examines the origins of the contemporary "family versus families" debate before explaining the particular concerns of the chapters to follow.

Through an examination of the nuances of language in American debates regarding social welfare questions, this essay suggests the inadequacies of the "demographic reductionism" that characterizes many accounts of the current interest in the familial. In contrast, the analysis here stresses the importance of the political context within which these demographic changes have occurred: exploring the interplay of political actors, social movements, bureaucratic and scientific interests, along with the character of political life that shapes how these "events" have become a subject of interest. Because this essay is exploratory, in the process of unraveling the often contradictory trends that infuse the current debate, additional questions emerge. In particular, a number of questions about the operation of power in American society are only touched on. My intent is to be suggestive and to widen the scope of discussion. Toward this end the essay closes by considering how feminist policy analysis might revitalize both the practice and study of politics.

THE ORIGINS OF THE FAMILIAL FOCUS

In October 1976, during a meeting with the National Council of Bishops, candidate Jimmy Carter agreed to hold a White House Conference on the Family if he were elected to the Presidency. This decision followed his announcement, shortly after receiving the nomination, that he had taken the unusual step of appointing a special adviser for family policy. Carter, firmly entrenched in nineteenth-century notions of family sanctity, pronounced that "the family was the first government . . . if we want less government, we must have stronger families, for government steps in by necessity when families have failed."[4] Numerous Washington watchers agreed that family policy became "the new kid on the block" in policy circles in the early years of the Carter administration. But to what extent was this fashion attributable to Carter's campaign promise and the subsequent planning and organizing for the conference? Can a case be made that Carter functioned as the issue entrepreneur without whom a public worry would never have been brought to the governmental agenda? Yet if we were to attribute this shift in concern only to the actions of highly visible elected leaders, what importance should we give to Walter Mondale, Carter's vice-president? Mondale, during his earlier tenure as chair of the Senate Subcommittee on Children and Youth, had used this rather minor committee as a forum for raising the issue of the family and government policy. According to Sidney Johnson, current head of the Family Impact Seminar, a research/advocacy group in Washington, D.C., and former staff director for Mondale's committee—where the idea of family impact statements received its first public hearing:

> Mondale took on an issue that had always belonged to the conservatives . . . started a redefinition of families and that has made families a concern that has spread. Men are now being called upon to be family members and parents and spouses.[5]

Although Mondale, not Carter, was the first in the electoral arena to give voice to this issue (and his hearings did accelerate a trend that was in turn shaped by Carter's conference), in the end the solo entrepreneur or great-leader mode of analysis is inadequate. Although fascinating in terms of political intrigue and ambition, this analysis tends to obscure the location of power and the dynamics of political change in the American welfare state. A great-leader mode of analysis blinds us to the social planners and bureaucratic entrepreneurs who work in the hazy boundaries between the private and public sectors of the economy, to the conflicts regarding the power of such planners, and to the social movements whose demands and revelations help shape all modes of public discourse. In short, a more broadly focused search for origins will demonstrate that the current situation is a product of the convergence of several, often contradictory trends.

From Individual Opportunity and Poverty to the Familial

In the post-World War II period the United States underwent a major growth in federal funding for scientific research. This was followed in the 1960s by a growth in the federal share of social welfare spending. This growth, fueled in part by the 1935 Social Security Act and the more concerted services strategy of the Kennedy-Johnson years (in particular such legislative initiatives as the 1962 Social Security Act Amendments and the Economic Opportunity Act of 1964), expanded the army of professionals directly or indirectly tied to a federally funded services strategy for ministering to persons in need.[6] While a "scientized" services approach to human need certainly did not originate in the 1960s—being more appropriately dated to the turn of the century—a significant transformation in scope did occur in the 1960s. In large part this intensified period of growth was shaped by the political pressures that arose out of the civil rights movement's exposure of the extensiveness of American poverty as the movement shifted its focus from legal inequities to economic injustice. Thus, throughout much of the 1960s, until the ideological retrenchment signaled by the 1968 campaigns of George Wallace and Richard Nixon, social reformers and bureaucratic entrepreneurs promoting the programmatic interests of service providers and the humanistic interests of client recipients often couched their advocacy in terms of eliminating poverty and advancing individual economic opportunity. Dominant intellectual and political currents were oriented toward change, which in the American political tradition typically produces a focus on individual achievement and advancement. With the civil rights movement's evolution into its black power phase, racial consciousness and antagonisms became even more salient. In the context of intensified racial consciousness many social reformers denounced as racist a Labor Department report on the black family in which Daniel Patrick Moynihan suggested that social programs would be more effective if a family policy focus were adopted.

As the black political struggle faded—its vitality in some measure siphoned off by the career opportunities the emergent "social welfare economy" had created—social welfare advocates shifted briefly to language that highlighted social welfare needs through reference to children.[7] In 1971, for example, many poverty reformers joined forces with child development specialists and feminists to support the Comprehensive Child Development Act, a series of amendments to the original Economic Opportunity Act. A more exclusive focus on children was a logical outcome of the "human capital" approach that undergirded the programs of the Great Society, but in the context of struggles over school desegregation and related disputes regarding federal power, this language evoked the specter of heavy-handed state intrusion. Richard Nixon's ringing denunciation that the proposed reforms would undermine the "family centered" approach to childrearing quickly exposed the limitations of the new tack.

In 1973 the Committee on Children and Youth (which had developed the failed child care bill) signaled a shift in focus with its hearings, "American Families: Trends and Pressures." This refocusing continued when the Carter administration in 1976 retitled HEW's Office of Child Development to Administration for Children, Youth and Families. A similar shift from children to families occurred within study groups of the Carnegie Corporation and the National Academy of Sciences. In 1971 the Academy's National Research Council received a grant from the Department of Health, Education, and Welfare to form an Advisory Committee on Child Development that would examine federal programs with respect to children. As Gilbert Steiner observed, none of the tasks given to the committee mentioned the word family, but the final report, issued in 1976, was called *Toward a National Policy for Children and Families*, and, like the Carnegie Council Report, *All Our Children: The American Family Under Pressure*, issued in 1977, called for income supports and social services for families as the best way of serving children.[8]

The Limits of a Scientized Service State

It might be argued that this shift in language represented a defensive effort on the part of providers and advocates to protect social welfare jobs and advance the redistributive policy goals of the 1960s in a period when societal concern with economic and racial justice had diminished. Joseph Featherstone contended that the hope for a family policy on the part of veterans of the civil rights movement was "the direct result of the failure of the civil rights movement to transcend the ideal of individual opportunity . . . . One way to begin linking the old particularistic civil-rights agenda to a new and more inclusive one is to insist on family supports as a universal right for all."[9] From this perspective, the shift was largely tactical and did not represent a philosophical change of heart regarding the state as a mechanism for redistribution. For example, the Children's Defense Fund, an advocacy group that developed out of the civil rights movement, warned in a 1978 report:

> What we have found and detailed in this report is a national disgrace . . . that cannot wait one more day for correction. The daily plight of these children, often left family-less, makes a mockery of our professed belief in family.[10]

At the same time, familial language also provided a vehicle for speaking to the perceived benefits and costs of social welfare rationalization and systematization that had come to constitute the modern welfare service state. Conflicting assessments over the actual and potential benefits of this form of the welfare state increasingly produced divisions among social change advocates who were essentially committed to some degree of redistribution between class and racial groupings. Continuing in the tradition of many Progressive era reformers, some social welfare specialists argued that a focus on families could provide the basis for a more "comprehensive" or "integrated" approach to social problems. For example, Catherine S. Chilman, a social welfare professor and former policy analyst within HEW, writing in *Social Casework*, critiqued as inadequate "partial, inexpensive programs addressed primarily to changing people rather than systems" and bemoaned what she saw as a dangerous trend—"a disbelief in the importance and power of rational planning to deal with problems of our society."[11] Sweden's consciously planned family policy approach to social problems, developed during the 1930s crisis over a declining population, was often cited by such advocates as a model for social policy in the United States.

Other liberal and leftist analysts also used familial language to comment on social problems; but rather than exhortation, their purpose was to sound a note of caution. They revealed the reputed costs of delivering social services through the bureaucratic delivery systems of the state. Elaborating on a line of thought initially developed by the Frankfurt theorists of Germany and made concrete by both the experience of American policy initiatives and the client rebellions of the 1960s, they argued that power had accrued to experts and professionals. This shift in power had occurred at the expense not only of neighborhood, kinship, and friendship modes of dealing with human need but also the dignity and rights of clients.[12] For some, a familial focus was evoked as a way of empowering people against the perceived onslaught of professionals. Christopher Lasch, a neo-Marxist historian and one of the more vocal advocates of this point of view, argued:

> Historians of the family have paid too little attention to the way in which public policy, sometimes conceived quite deliberately not as a defense of the family at all but as an invasion of it, contributed to the deterioration of domestic life. The family did not simply evolve in response to social and economic influences; it was deliberately transformed by the intervention of planners and policymakers.[13]

Lasch pointed to the role of scientific expertise in the construction of the emotional life of the modern nuclear family. Nevertheless, his emphasis on invasion, together with his insistence that Freudian psychoanalysis was not part of that construction, in many ways reinforced the conventional belief that the family had a pre-given "natural" structure. In addition, it reinforced the other popular belief that meaningful caring and self-development take place only within family units.

This "social change" critique of systematization was certainly not a unified whole; nevertheless, the analysis often weakened initiatives for further policy development. Perhaps the most vivid instance was the Carnegie Council's plea for strengthening families through the improved delivery of many of the same social services that it earlier argued had undermined the power of the family. Ultimately, Lasch's version lent itself to manipulation by critics of the welfare state who did not hold a commitment to redistribution and were antagonistic to any form of scientific authority.[14]

During the 1970s, then, social reformers often used familial language to defend, advance, and critique the welfare state. Their attraction to this mode of discourse probably had less to do with the characteristics of the welfare state than the personal and social upheaval generated by the women's movement. But attention to the professionals' discourse also reveals that a "families" focus was often tied to an ecological framework. This language suggests the influence of the other important social movement of the period—the ecology movement—and thus points to the complexity of the interplay between social movements and professionals.

While not new, arguments for ecological thinking, both in theoretical approaches to human development and in the provision of social services, became increasingly common in the 1970s.[15] My hypothesis is that for many ecological/familial advocates this linguistic turn represented an effort to call attention to the contextual and relational aspects of human existence obscured by a reform rhetoric that had focused solely on individuals. Both the women's movement and the ecology movement had emerged from political movements of the 1960s and the contradictions of advanced capitalism in the American political environment. While the American political economy was increasingly centered on a set of simultaneously fragile and interdependent productive relations, personal and political life rested on increasingly atomized and fragmented social relations. Although the explicit goals of the two movements differed, each in its way served to reveal dimensions of social and political life obscured by the economic determinism that had come to dominate many of the social change movements of the '60s. The ecology movement directly concerned itself with threats to the interdependencies of individuals and their physical environment. At the same time, the women's movement's naming of women's nurturance work in families, conjoined with their support of women's sexual freedom and entrance into the paid labor force, uncovered, but in a painful or emotionally threatening way, the importance of such interdependencies. Within this political context, a search for language that spoke to the relational requirements of human existence intensified.

The public familial debate was, on the whole, centered almost exclusively on some version of "what would happen to the children?"—most likely because of the age and health of the activists and spokespersons within the women's movement. Nevertheless, as a consequence of increases in longevity and expansions of the definition of the handicapped, the care of persons other than children concerned providers and researchers involved with the aged and handicapped. Thus, for example, when the Carter administration proposed to merge the promised White House Conference on Families with the scheduled 1980 White House Conference on Children and Youth (because of the political debacle that followed Carter's attempted appointment of a black divorcee with children as executive director of the Families Conference), the Coalition of Family Organizations, a newly formed lobbying organization for human service providers and researchers, objected to the merger. In a letter to the HEW Secretary, COFO argued that the merger would not provide sufficient focus on issues broader than children and youth, such as "the impact of the handicapped on family life" and "the problems of families dealing with their aged members."[16] For some social reformers, familial language provided a very appealing mechanism for addressing the question of services throughout the life cycle. A subject of concern was the charge that the incentive structure of government programs made it difficult for families to care for their incapacitated dependents in their own homes.[17]

THE EVOLUTION OF "FAMILIES"

The descriptive account I have offered does not adequately explain why a familial strategy for advancing social welfare goals took the particular form that it did. This was not the first time that such a strategy had been used. Indeed, social reformers and segments of the feminist movement had used a familial strategy as they struggled to create the modern welfare state at the turn of the century.[18] Today, as in the earlier period, the political-social context is one where there is considerable ferment regarding both woman's appropriate role in society and accepted notions of what citizenship for women involves. At the same time, the new context is significantly different. In the intervening years, three factors had so exploded the historical diversity of familial arrangements in the United States that traditional race, class, and ethnic categories were no longer sufficient. As a consequence of (1) the entrance of middle-class white mothers into the paid labor force, (2) the accelerated separation between reproduction and sexuality, and (3) the continued transfer of power from religious to scientific authority, the familial now included two adults of the same gender, working mothers with young children, and significant numbers of unattached women with children. "Families" became visible through the interplay of the rights rhetoric of sexual movements that emerged and scientific experts who, in their continuing will to reveal the invisible, created new objects of study.[19]

Where earlier male domination was centered in an institutionalized and gender-stratified family, by the last quarter of the twentieth century this was no longer true. Moreover, the growth in scientific consciousness permitted a questioning of assumed linkages between biology and gender roles. Feminism was thus able to challenge and publicly reveal the underside of familial life—the sexual violence and one-sided nurturance—in a manner that would have been impossible for earlier feminists.[20] However limited and circumscribed the alternatives for women within a sex-segregated labor market and an increasingly "phallocentric sexual market," the contemporary context presented a different set of possibilities. The sheer expansion of the human services sector of the economy, together with the expansion of access to abortion and birth control and the increased legitimacy of nonmarriage options, meant that women of all classes and races could at least contemplate some form of economic independence from individual men.[21] As a consequence, areas of life that appeared to be the most personal and immutable—from who could do housework to who could initiate sex to who could leave a marriage—were transformed into questions. Within this larger context some degree of politicization occurred whether women "chose" to take advantage of the alternatives offered, to question their value, or to reject them. Additional complications arose from the fact that the new alternatives affected the attitudes and behaviors of many adolescents, perhaps most visibly the sexual activities of girls. Thus politicization extended to relations between parents and children.

This schematized account of the evolution of "families" remains to be more fully worked out. Public opinion data suggest that rejection of the new alternatives did not occur along gender lines. (I suspect, however, that there are important differences between the genders as to why they were "rejectors," "questioners," or "accepters.") Preliminary evidence also suggests that for "rejectors," many of the "alternatives" appeared to be changes imposed by a welfare state that social reformers had created.[22] Indeed, from the emergence of contemporary feminism until the election of Ronald Reagan, the Equal Rights Amendment, equal employment, and affirmative action policies had been overtly supported by all administrations, regardless of political party. Access to contraception had been facilitated through Supreme Court decisions and the growth of federally funded family planning programs, and access to abortion through these mechanisms as well as through federally funded health insurance programs. Taking account, then, of the impressions of the power of the welfare state and the different experiences of changes in the structure and emotional content of both gender relations and parent/child relations, we begin to gain a deeper understanding of the contemporary battle over "family" versus "families."

Many of the advocates for a "families" focus did not acknowledge the centrality of the feminist movement to the new discourse on social welfare. Nor did they place the same primacy on an individual woman's economic and sexual independence as did spokespersons for explicitly feminist organizations.[23] But in contrast to "family" advocates, "families" spokespersons tended to stress adaptation to familial change and "diversity" of familial needs and forms. Illustrative of this pattern was the definition of the family that emerged from a special 1973 American Home Economics Association Convention called to develop a philosophy appropriate for the 1970s:

> Two or more persons who share resources, share responsibility for decisions, share values and goals, and have commitments to one another over time. The family is that climate that one "comes home to" and it is this network of sharing and commitments that most accurately describes the family unit, regardless of blood, legal ties, adoption or marriage.[24]

With the politicization that developed once Carter's conference was announced, the definitional question was often avoided by simply talking "families,"[25] but on the whole, the "families" agenda was oriented toward legitimating the economic and social claims of adults and children who were members of familial units that deviated from the husband-breadwinner/wife-homemaker/multiple children ideological norm. For example, the National Gay Task Force, Parents Without Partners, and the National Alliance for Optional Parenthood joined with traditional provider groups such as the Family Services Association to form the Coalition for the White House Conference on Families.

Not surprisingly, the promised "Conference on the American Family" became a "Conference on Families" because of pressures for a more "neutral" term.[26] Carter's predilections to the contrary, certain political factors dictated the shift to families. HEW's permanent policy staff had numerous professional ties with human service providers and researchers. Women held more appointive positions in the Carter administration than in any previous administration, even though the advances women had made within the Democratic party did not result in as many appointments as had been desired. Moreover, by this time segments of the women's movement, in particular the segment that saw social change as intimately dependent on policy change within existing institutions, had begun to argue that a families agenda could serve as a vehicle for advancing the feminist agenda. Such issues as child support, the difficulties facing working mothers, the housing problems of women with children, and the poverty of female-headed households could also be pursued through a "families" agenda. One observer of the 1977 Houston Women's Conference noted that the participants "outdid themselves in insistent commitment to the family." And shortly after, the NOW Legal Defense and Education Fund began organizing for its own family conference. The statement of purpose for their November 1979 conference read:

> We believe the future of the family is an overriding feminist issue. Through freeing men and women from old sex-stereotyped roles, feminism seeks to help all people achieve their full potential individually and in responsive relationships with others. Therefore we are confident that feminism will ultimately lead to stronger, more varied, more nurturing and loving families.[27]

There certainly was not unanimity within organized feminism regarding a "families" strategy; the heated criticisms Betty Friedan met in her call for a "second stage" were only one manifestation of this skepticism.[28] Nonetheless, this brief overview of the origins of the "family" versus "families" debate indicates that the turn to familial language in the 1970s cannot simply be laid at the door of persons who would identify themselves as defenders of the established order. Social change advocates and social reformers, many with ties to the welfare state—either as recipients of funds for the provision of social services or as beneficiaries of social research programs—were intimately involved in the process of bringing the familial debate into the federal policy-making arena.

PUBLIC POLICY: WOMEN AND THE STATE

In order to more fully appreciate the confluence of trends shaping today's familial debate we need to pay more attention to another nuance in this familial discourse: the role of the state and more specifically the question of the impact of public policy. At first glance it might appear that this linkage was attributable to the women's movement's declaration that seemingly private areas of life were structured by relations of power in the public world. But upon further reflection one must also take account of the discussion during the 1970s of almost all societal issues with reference to public policy.[29] This centering of political discourse on public policy, when it is even noted, is often attributed to some combination of the expanding role of governmental activity in the twentieth century, the growth in the number of persons trained to do scientific research, the growing influence of such persons, and technological developments such as the increased information processing capacity of computers. Indeed, in the familial arena we have seen a new nexus between the provision of social services and large-scale social research programs.[30] All these trends might be traced back to the shift in consciousness emerging out of the enlightenment that scientific expertise could be used to control and shape events. In the twentieth century the expectation that government can and should have programs based on scientific expertise escalated with the disruptions of the Great Depression and World War II and became institutionalized during the Great Society. In this process programs themselves became objects for systematic study.

Important as this explanation may be for the intensified focus on public policy, I would suggest that it is insufficient. This new political discourse may also have emerged, ironically, out of the social movements of the 1960s and early '70s that were highly critical of the assumptions and values embedded in much social science research. These movements revealed that state programs were not neutral and often had harmful consequences for everyday life. My hypothesis is that their demands for alternative ways of organizing society reoriented the shapers of public consciousness, including the wielders of scientific expertise, to the question of the concrete impacts of the state on ordinary lives.

Criticisms of the limitations of social science and traditional welfare state policies for dealing with social problems have been picked up by "pro-family" forces as well, further contributing to the complexity of today's debate. Mrs. Connaught Marshner, chairwoman of The National Pro-Family Coalition and editor of the "Family Protection Report," explained:

> What we're doing is to try to break the stranglehold that the professional human-service types and the bureaucrats have on family life. The human service types want more government. The way to solve problems they think is to throw more money into government programs. The pro-family people think that the best way to help the family is to get the government out of family life.[31]

The "Family Protection Act," introduced in September 1979, was conceived as "the conservative alternative" to the policy agenda of welfare state reformers who were perceived as the controlling force of the Families Conference. According to Senator Paul Laxalt, the legislative father of this codification of the New Right's social policy agenda: "For years we have been debating on the terms of those who want to remake society. Now those groups will have to explain why they oppose the traditional idea of the family."[32]

The decade had begun with the feminist movement's questioning of the costs for women of the twentieth-century nuclear family. But by the decade's end Ronald Reagan had been elected to the Presidency with the aid of the New Right on a platform that pledged to oppose federal intrusion into family life and its commitment to the traditional role and values of the family in our society. Because the New Right is new, and the available evidence regarding its supporters and organizational structure so thin, any generalizations regarding its origins are necessarily tentative and partial. Preliminary evidence suggests that this movement has been able to build on many traditional right-wing issues regarding federal power, fiscal conservatism, and race.[33] On the other hand, one feature that earned this movement the term "new" was its ability to mobilize around opposition to issues generated by feminism, in particular the Equal Rights Amendment and abortion.

This movement is nevertheless considerably more complex than a mere reaction to feminism. While I do not disagree with the centrality of the reverberations of feminism, I would argue that a more dialectical understanding is in order. My own hypothesis is that this movement, segments of which might be argued to be an alternative women's movement, arose from two sources: (1) the increased legitimacy of political activity by women in the 1970s and (2) the tensions and dislocations that accompanied the previously discussed explosion of familial arrangements. The structural changes common to all advanced capitalist societies, especially the rapidity of alterations in female labor force participation and sexuality, were indeed disruptive of prevailing patterns. Yet these changes did not in themselves create the tensions and dislocations that fed the movement. Instead, one must look to the context within which the structural changes occurred, in particular the ideology of individualism in American political, cultural, and economic life. Although its form may have varied with transitions in the marketplace—one recent commentator has cleverly described a shift from "possessive capitalism" to "permissive individualism" with the transition to advanced capitalism[34]—the ideology's shaping force is still vital. In short, because the ruptures occasioned by profound structural change were experienced in a context where social, political, and economic relations were already infused with strong centrifugal forces (individualism untrammeled by the remnants of earlier notions of community), the resultant ripples were exceedingly complex and disruptive. For the short run, at least, the well-being of women was both advanced and undermined, and in ways that cut across traditional class lines.

American feminism drew on the ideology of individualism to mobilize women to attack all forms of male privilege with a vigor that was not possible in societies without a strong liberal tradition and its rhetorical commitment to individual autonomy.[35] Concomitantly, when feminism turned to the state it focused heavily on the Equal Rights Amendment, abortion, and equal opportunity legislation, policies laden with ideological messages that also reverberated on the lives of women who did not value or were unable to take advantage of the new gender options. Thus, for example, by mid-decade a new category of "displaced homemaker" had emerged as significant numbers of men were able to seize the heightened focus on individualism and sexual freedom to further absolve themselves of responsibilities to sexual partners and children.

While feminism's rhetoric certainly contributed to this focus on sexual freedom, it is important to remember that this occurred within a more general expansion of scientific and commercial discourses on sexuality that predated feminism. This expansion of discourses (what Michel Foucault terms the "deployment of sexuality") through the twentieth century produced an intensified focus on sex as the instrument of truth. In the process sexuality came to be defined as "the very core of being." This new definition, which, according to Foucault, is a product of the scientific will to render the invisible visible, fostered a multitude of cultural changes, not the least of which was the narrowing of human pleasures.[36] In turn, this narrowing facilitated the rupture of normative patterns of responsibility between the genders.

Understandably, women differed over the value of these developments, a difference that does not fall neatly into feminist and antifeminist categories. The crucial point is that women with children confronted many of these dislocations with added difficulty because of the way individualism had shaped the American welfare state in three critical respects: (1) the social policies that produced a limited and often punitive social welfare infrastructure; (2) the housing policies that produced suburban sprawl and isolated domestic workplaces; and (3) the economic policies that produced little or no job security. In view of these dislocations, the active participation of women in a social movement that sought to resurrect divine authority within the family as a counter to scientific authority associated with the state becomes a bit clearer. In fact, one might argue that the more general popularity of the nineteenth-century vision of the family as the only haven of nurturance and security against the contractual, contingent, and competitive relations of the public world was in part attributable to the fact that it had a material base. For example, one consequence of the lack of job security is frequent geographic mobility with the resultant strains on friendship, neighborhood, and kinship ties. Thus, during periods of need and/or emotional disruption, women are often unable to draw on long-standing ties. Nor can they count on being treated with dignity by a means-tested welfare system. As a consequence of the knowledge that few alternatives to a nuclear family exist, there is a strong motivation to seek such a unit. The irony is that the weaknesses of the social welfare infrastructure and friendship ties, together with the heightened emphasis on sexuality, make it difficult for people to find the nurturance that they seek.[37]

A FEMINIST DIALOGUE

The essays in this volume grow out of an awareness of the double-edged nature of much recent social change and a desire to create the possibility for transformatory change. As the last decade has unfolded, and as feminist scholars have begun to uncover the androcentric, time-bound, and individualistic biases in conventional categories of analysis and the will toward domination that appears to infuse existing theories of transformation, the contradictions and the strengths of a feminist perspective have also emerged.[38] Not surprisingly, since feminism seeks to change the physical-cultural world, neither feminist theory nor practice has been completely divorced from the categories of thought and value in the dominant culture. Thus, the strain within feminist movements that has always aspired to a vision of community beyond the satisfaction of individual self-interests did not develop sufficiently to become a part of public consciousness. Yet, as the essays in this volume demonstrate, feminist scholarship is not afraid to reflect on itself and on the world in a manner that does not cringe at engagement. For example, as scholars have explored the creation of human consciousness and the activities of women in daily life, they have revalued and clarified our understanding of the necessity of nurturance activities in human societies. And as these essays demonstrate, because feminist scholars speak with a multiplicity of voices, this scholarship does not create a closed system with its attendant rigidities and doctrinaire solutions. The authors here remain divided over whether the American Capitalist State, or any state, can effect progressive change that is not simultaneously a new mode of social control. Nor are they united on the utility of the concept of the state for understanding power relations.[39] At the same time, their willingness to explore in the messiness of the material world points to questions that often have not been previously posed. They lead us to contemplate, for example, whether a redefinition of human identity might emerge if nurturance were associated with more than one gender. And, if so, whether some of the seemingly intractable resource and administrative problems of advanced capitalist societies might be eased.[40]

Because the contemporary discourse of public policy analysis has on the whole been scientized and therefore depoliticized and dehumanized, the reader may be somewhat jarred by the insistence in these essays on investing public policy analysis with considerations of human nature, historical change, political transformation, and moral vision. Yet, weaving together what has historically been separated is central to the power of feminist inquiry. Feminist policy analysis in turn evolves out of the women's movement's growing recognition of the material vulnerability of the majority of women in contemporary America and out of the radical questions feminist theorists pose regarding the accepted norms of society. The precariousness of women's lives and their intimate involvement in the maintenance of life heightens the importance of an orientation that is applied and solution oriented; at the same time, examining problems from women's vantage point reveals the limitations of existing practices and formulations. Giving serious consideration to the question of gender will not solve all problems. As several of the essays suggest, some forms of sorrow and turmoil will exist no matter what the political order. Feminist analysis can, however, aid in the difficult process of sorting out dilemmas that are attributable to the failure of collective will and political imagination from those that are not. Our objective here is to offer a way of considering public policy that can remind us of the potentialities of politics.

Harold Lasswell's original appeal for a policy orientation in the social sciences derived from a hope that an approach focusing on the "fundamental and often neglected problems which arise in the adjustment of man in society" would realize "human dignity in theory and fact."[41] Nevertheless, as Charles Lindblom and other critics have observed, policy analysis devolved into a generally superficial and conservative orientation.[42] Some might argue that Lasswell's goal was a false one because the analytic method of the social sciences, which decomposes social reality, is destructive of social and political relations that flourish when imbued with shared understandings. From this perspective, the fragmentation of modern life denounced by critics of diverse persuasions is a product of the scientific method that destroys the unity of thinking, acting, and feeling. Yet feminism, which grows out of a scientific world view but has been struggling to create a new unity, challenges us to move beyond this bifurcation. Our hope is that the understanding created by the emergence of a still evolving feminist mode of analysis will provide the impetus for paths out of this impasse.

NOTES

1. The term "revisioning" comes from Adrienne Rich's essay "When We Dead Awaken: Writing as Revision" (1971) reprinted in Rich's *On Lies, Secrets, and Silences* (New York: Norton, 1979).

2. Jacques Donzelot, *The Policing of Families* (New York: Pantheon, 1979), p. 4.

3. See, for example, Sandi Cooper, "Feminism and Family Revivalism," *Chrysallis*, Summer 1979.

4. "A Statement in New Hampshire, August 3, 1976," *The Presidential Campaign, 1976, vol. 1, Jimmy Carter* (Washington, D.C.: Government Printing Office, 1978), p. 462.

5. *Los Angeles Times*, 1 February 1980, part 4.

6. Overall employment trends are discussed in Erie et al. in this volume. What the growth in federal social welfare dollars has meant on an organizational level remains to be more fully documented. Thus, for example, the Family Service Association of America, an organization of private social service agencies formed in 1911, reported that total income from public sources climbed from 13.8% in 1967 to 23% in 1973.

7. For further discussion of the concept of a social welfare economy and its depoliticization of blacks, see Michael H. Brown and Steven P. Erie, "Blacks and the Legacy of the Great Society: the Economic and Political Impact of Federal Social Policy," *Public Policy* 29, no. 3 (Summer 1981).

8. Gilbert Y. Steiner, *The Futility Family Policy* (Washington, D.C.: Brookings, 1981), p. 23.

9. Joseph Featherstone, "Family Matters," *Harvard Educational Review* 49, no. 1 (February 1979): 36.

10. Children's Defense Fund, *Children Without Homes* (Washington, D.C.: CDF, 1978), p. xiii.

11. Catherine S. Chilman, "Public Social Policy and Families in the 1970's," *Social Casework*, December 1973. For another clear example of this perspective see Sheila B. Kamerman and Alfred J. Kahn, "Explorations in Family Policy," *Social Work*, May 1970, pp. 181–86.

12. See, for example, Mary C. Howell, *Helping Ourselves: Families and the Human Network* (Boston: Beacon, 1975); or Peter L. Berger and Richard J. Neuhaus, *To Empower People: The Role of Mediating Structures in Public Policy* (Washington, D.C.: American Enterprise Institute, 1977). I do not mean to imply here that all social change critics of the welfare state invoked familial imagery. Indeed, it did *not* occur among critics who documented that the experts' appropriation and redirection of extended kinship, friendship, and neighborhood modes of dealing with human need had particularly high costs for women. See for example, Barbara Ehrenreich and Deirdre English, *For Her Own Good* (New York: Anchor Press, 1978).

13. Christopher Lasch, *Haven in a Heartless World* (New York: Basic Books, 1977).

14. Thus, for example, Onalee McGraw used Lasch to support her critique from the right in *The Family, Feminism and the Therapeutic State* (Washington, D.C.: Heritage Foundation, 1980).

15. Some might argue that the popularity of the ecological perspective on familial issues

was attributable to Urie Bronfenbrenner's influential book, *The Ecology of Human Development* (Cambridge, Mass.: Harvard University Press, 1970). Bronfenbrenner's work was certainly important in creating linkages between theorists and practitioners (for example, he became an adviser to the Family Impact Seminar). Nevertheless, this shift in thinking was too widespread to be attributed solely to one theorist who, despite his argument for the central importance of the environment, appeared incapable of envisioning nongender-linked modes of childrearing (see his testimony before the Mondale hearings, American Families: Trends and Pressures). In tracing the sources of this shift it is worth taking note of N. C. Hook and Beatrice Paolucci's "The Family as an Ecosystem," *Journal of Home Economics* 62 (1970). This discussion of the evolution of ecological thinking contends that Ellen Swallow Richards's initial definition of home economics was clearly an ecological one, but that the participants at the original turn of the century Lake Placid Conferences (out of which the association was created) had rejected explicit use of the term "ecology" because it had been appropriated by botanists. For a history of what Dolores Hayden has described as "The Lost Feminist Tradition," see *The Grand Domestic Revolution* (Cambridge: MIT Press, 1981).

16. Letter dated October 4, 1977 reprinted in the *COFO Memo* 1, no. 1 (Fall 1977). This organization consists of the American Association of Marriage and Family Counselors, the American Home Economics Association, the Family Service Association of America, and the National Council of Family Relations.

17. Tax credits for parents of handicapped children and families caring for elderly dependents were expanded as part of the 1981 Economic Recovery Act.

18. Donzelot, *Policing of Families*, contends that in France the beginning of the twentieth century marked a turning point with respect to the family being a dividing line between defenders of the established order and those who contested it. "The family became the . . . point of support from which demands were launched for the defense and improvement of the standard of living." Progressive reformers in the United States used a familial strategy in a similar fashion, but this does not answer the question of whether this marked the first time reformers used the family to contest the established order. For example, in the early nineteenth century, abolitionists, as well as defenders of slavery, used familial imagery to argue for their respective causes.

19. For example, the Minnesota Inventory of Marriage and Family Research, which calculated the frequency of publications per year on emergent family issues, found that there were .03 publications on alternative lifestyles during the period 1900–1964; 5.0 for 1965–72; and 31.0 for 1973–78. There were no references to dual career families until 1973–78. Cited in *The Status of Children, Youth and Families 1979* (Washington, D.C.: Department of Health and Human Services, Office of Human Development Services, Administration for Children, Youth and Families), p. 224.

20. For another discussion of why because of women's limited opportunities outside the family nineteenth-century feminism did not confront male power in the family as directly as contemporary feminism, see Barbara Easton, "Feminism and the Contemporary Family," *Socialist Review* 8, no. 3 (May–June 1978). Individual theorists, in particular Elizabeth Cady Stanton and later Charlotte Perkins Gilman, developed insightful critiques that in many ways foreshadowed the critiques that burst forth in the late 1960s. But even here, because neither fundamentally questioned biological determinism, they could not conceive of men as potential nurturers.

21. Several of the essays in this volume discuss a transformation from family-centered to state-centered patriarchy and discuss the fact that with this transformation the sex segregation of the paid labor market has not been appreciably altered. While I would agree with these

authors that the character of male domination has changed markedly within the last 100 to 150 years, to characterize the transformation as a shift from family to state tends to obscure transformations in sexuality that have been central to these changes.

22. An interesting example here is a letter a woman wrote to her senator to express her opposition to the E.R.A.: "Forced busing, forced mixing, forced housing. Now forced women! No thanks!" Cited in *Women's America: Refocusing Our Past*, ed. Linda K. Kerber and Jane Dehart Mathews (New York: Oxford University Press, 1982), p. 417.

23. The Carnegie Council's *All Our Children* was heavily criticized by some feminists, in particular for its recommendation that as a backup system to a full employment policy the government should provide a guaranteed job to any head of household with at least one child. This, in combination with its recommendations that a parent with primary responsibility for raising young children should be guaranteed an income if "she (or he) decides to stay at home," was viewed as sending women back to the kitchen. Yet, what was perhaps most striking about the report was the extent to which it had incorporated a feminist perspective. The notion that the well-being of children was dependent on the effective enforcement of federal equal opportunity laws was in many ways the only recommendation that distinguished this report from the numerous reports dating back to the first White House Conference on Children in 1909 that recommended aid to parents as a way of helping children.

24. This definition, from a May 1977 publication titled "A Force for Families," came out of the American Home Economic return in 1973 to Lake Placid, where it had not held a convention since 1907. This desire to reiterate "its original purpose" (interview, current staff member) appears to have been partially a response to the shock created by a speech Robin Morgan delivered at the 1972 annual meeting of the association. In that speech Morgan charged that the association had become the "enemy." For further discussion of reactions to Morgan's speech, see F. Mannino, "An Ecological Approach to Understanding Family and Community Relations," *Journal of Home Economics* 66 (1974).

25. The National Advisory Committee for the WHCF agreed that the conferences should avoid the issue of defining the family.

26. Steiner, *Futility Family Policy.*

27. *National Assembly on the Future of the Family, Resource Book*, November 19, 1979, p. 7.

28. This ambivalence together with the fact that NOW's energies were focused on ratification of the Equal Rights Amendment probably accounted for why NOW dropped out of active participation on the National Advisory Committee of the WHCF. The centralization of feminist political activity regarding policy matters that had occurred during the 1970s also contributed to the fact that, on the whole, feminist organizations were not very well prepared for the grass-roots organizing phase of the conference. Staff members for the conference observed that the current political strength of the "New Right" grew out of its organizing activities for the conference.

29. For a general discussion of this boom as it was reflected in new journals, the creation of new graduate programs, and the institutionalization of policy analysis positions in government, see William Dunn, *Public Policy Analysis: An Introduction* (Englewood Cliffs, N.J.: Prentice Hall, 1981), pp. 22–23; and Allen Schick, "Beyond Analysis," *Public Administration Review*, May/June 1977, pp. 258–63.

30. For example, Wakefield Washington Associates reports that when asked in 1976 for a five-year forecast of the most promising area in the field of federally funded social science research they concluded that family research offered the greatest promise. They identified 2500 federally funded research projects on the family for fiscal year 1976; 72% of the projects were research demonstration grants whose primary purpose was the evaluation of service

delivery. See *Family Research: A Source Book, Analysis, and Guide to Federal Funding* (Westport, Conn.: Greenwood Press, 1979).

31. *Los Angeles Times*, 1 February 1980.

32. As quoted in Richard A. Viguerie, *The New Right: We're Ready to Lead* (Falls Church, Va.: Viguerie Company, 1981), p. 155.

33. Alan Crawford, *Thunder on the Right* (New York: Pantheon, 1980); Allen Hunter, "In the Wings: New Right Organization and Ideology," *Radical America* 15, no. 1/2 (Spring 1981): 113–38; Rosalind Petchesky, "Anti-abortion, Antifeminism, and the Rise of the New Right," *Feminist Studies* 7, no. 2 (Summer 1981): 187–205.

34. See Timothy W. Luke, "Regulating the Haven in a Heartless World: The State and Family in Advanced Capitalism," *New Political Science*, Fall 1978, pp. 51–74.

35. One might also argue that the receptivity of American women to a feminist critique is in part due to the absence of European-type family policies designed to ease the burden of women's dual roles. Ironically, the absence of these policies is in part attributable to the strength of the liberal tradition.

36. Michel Foucault, *The History of Sexuality*, trans. Robert Hurley (New York: Pantheon, 1978), and Robert A. Padgug, "Sexual Matters: On Conceptualizing Sexuality in History," *Radical History Review*, Spring/Summer 1979, discuss how sexuality became an instrument of truth. In the United States the role of scientific expertise vis-à-vis the commercial discourse was perhaps most visible in the activities of the 1970 Commission on Obscenity and Pornography. See Irene Diamond, "Pornography and Repression: A Reconsideration," *Signs* 5, no. 4 (Summer 1980): 686–701. For a discussion of how the deployment of sexuality facilitated the narrowing of human pleasures, see Irene Diamond and Lee Quinby, "Dionysus Returned: Feminism in the Age of the Body" (paper presented at the 1982 Meeting of the National Women's Studies Association, Arcata, California, 1982).

37. This pattern is in part reflected in statistics on marriage and divorce. The United States has both higher marriage and divorce rates than any other advanced-industrial nation.

38. For an analysis of the first three biases, see Michelle Rosaldo, "The Use and Abuses of Anthropology: Reflections on Feminism and Cross-Cultural Understanding," *Signs* 7, no. 3 (Spring 1980): 389–417; and for an analysis of the will to domination, see Isaac Balbus, *Marxism and Domination* (Princeton: Princeton University Press, 1982); Susan Griffin, "The Way of All Ideology," *Signs* 7, no. 3 (Spring 1982): 641–60.

39. David Easton, in "The Political System Besieged by the State," *Political Theory* 9, no. 3 (August 1981): 303–25, provides a useful overview for why the concept of the state is currently being resurrected by analysts of a variety of different persuasions. At the same time, Michel Foucault, particularly in *Power/Knowledge, Selected Interviews and Other Writings*, ed. Colin Gordon (New York: Pantheon, 1980), argues rather provocatively that the fruitfulness of the concept has been exhausted. His arguments raise serious questions about whether feminists should even engage in developing a theory of the state.

40. This possibility is suggested by the work of Nancy Chodorow, *The Reproduction of Mothering* (Berkeley: University of California Press, 1978); Jane Flax in this volume; and Diamond/Quinby, "Dionysus Returned."

41. Harold D. Lasswell, "The Policy of Orientation," in *The Policy Sciences*, ed. Daniel Lerner and Harold D. Lasswell (Stanford, Calif.: Stanford University Press, 1951).

42. Charles E. Lindblom, "Integration of Economics and the Other Social Sciences Through Policy Analysis," in *Integration of the Social Sciences Through Policy Analysis*, ed. James C. Charlesworth (Philadelphia: American Academy of Political and Social Sciences, 1972); and Laurence H. Tribe, "Policy Analysis: Analysis or Ideology?", *Philosophy and Public Affairs 2*, no. 1 (1972): 66–110.

Part I

Power, Social Relations, and Political Agendas

1

Jane Flax

Contemporary American Families: Decline or Transformation?

Is "the family" declining? Social commentators and political activists from the left and the right seem to agree that it is. On the left, Marxists bemoan transformations in the economy that have made it more difficult for the family to function as a unit of resistance against capitalist exploitation.[1] Social theorists such as Horkheimer, Adorno, and Lasch[2] perceive a decline in patriarchal authority within the family that deeply affects children's psychological development. According to their analysis, social authority is replacing paternal power as the primary socializing force in the child's life. Consequently, the child develops a weak ego and for that reason is less able to exercise autonomy and resist social or political control.[3]

On the right, influential writers like Gilder also discuss a loss of paternal power, which they treat as both symptom and cause of the family's decay. The villain for Gilder is the state; he believes the state is displacing the individual father as provider, thereby making it possible for women to achieve a measure of economic and social independence from individual men.[4] Women are no longer compelled by economic or social pressure to perform their traditional civilizing task—to tame men, to persuade them to sublimate their aggressive energy into a competitive struggle for the economic survival of themselves and their families. Lacking such pressure, men become demoralized, engage in antisocial acts, or both. Divorce increases; worker productivity declines; unmarried women have children; women (married or unmarried) receive welfare or jobs secured through affirmative action

I am deeply indebted to Kirstin Dahl, Heidi Hartmann, and Phyllis Palmer for sharing their ideas with me, and to my therapy patients for permitting me to enter their internal world. This paper was criticized and improved by members of my feminist theory study group. None of these persons is responsible for how their insights have been incorporated into this paper or for its present form. Conversations with Nannerl Keohane about an earlier version of this paper contributed significantly to my own sense of clarity about the central argument and the theoretical work required to support. This article is a revised version of "Tragedy or Emancipation: On the 'Decline' of Contemporary American Families," in *The Future of American Democracy: Views from the Left*, ed. Mark E. Kann (Philadelphia: Temple University Press, 1982).

programs; and men become more discouraged, eventually abandoning their traditional familial responsibilities (and economic risk taking) altogether.

In this essay I treat as problematic what these and similar accounts of the "decline" of the family take for granted: that "the family" as a simple unit exists, that "the family" as such is declining, and that this decline threatens to destroy the very possibility of civilized life. Also implicit in all these accounts is the claim that the family is/was/can be a private realm, a retreat from the power- and interest-motivated activities of the "public" world. Here, it is alleged, the individual can be herself or himself. The individual's moral development and capacity for autonomy is said to be rooted in experiences within this realm. It follows, therefore, that any state or other public interference in the family must be an attack on the individual's freedom and integrity and on the essential civilizing force within society.[5]

Contrary to this cluster of ideas, I argue that "the family" does not exist and that although one form of the family *is* declining, this development presents the possibility of an emancipatory transformation in social relations. Those who bemoan the decline of "the family' are not wrong in assuming that the social relations that constitute it are essential to civilization. They are wrong, however, to assume that the traditional patriarchal family* is essential for a healthy society. On the contrary, these social relations are destructive to individuals of both genders and to social and political life as a whole. This conclusion is supported by a four-part argument that (1) decodes "the family" to reveal its constituent social relations, (2) analyzes data on the present composition and trends in the organization of households, (3) presents a psychoanalytic account of human development within patriarchal family organization, and (4) discusses some of the social and political consequences of that account.

DECODING THE FAMILY

In order to evaluate the claim that the family is declining, we must first clarify what the family is. In doing so, it soon becomes evident that the family does not exist. Rather, what we call "the family" is a series of social relations that crystallize into apparently concrete social structures. These structures become reified into an abstract entity, which is then called "the family."[6]

Reification[7] arises in part from the intense (and often unconscious) emotional investment in particular notions of the family developed precisely because we all grow up in families. We project wishes on to this abstract entity, and the intensity

*By the traditional patriarchal family, I mean a group of related individuals in which the father controls whatever economic resources are available to it and the mother has primary responsibility for caring for children until a socially determined age of maturity. The resources subject to the father's control include the labor of other family members and the childbearing capacity of the wife. In such families the husband, wife, and children may cooperate to ensure their joint survival, but there are also many sources of tension and potential conflicts of interest between them.

of those wishes infuses the abstraction with a false concreteness, making distortions difficult to recognize and overcome.

Three kinds of social relations constitute the family: production, reproduction, and psychodynamics. These relations in turn reflect the family's embeddedness in other social structures, which are also constituted by similar social relations. Analysis is further complicated by the fact that the family is internally constituted by very different sorts of persons and their interrelationships. There are adults and children (but the adults are also partly children since their childhood lives on in the unconscious). There are males and females, both children and adult. There may be a variety of relations governed by kinship and gender rules, and each of these persons engages in a variety of social relations with persons "external" to the family.

Thus, just as Marx uncovered the whole structure of capitalism by decoding the commodity form, a close examination of the family reveals a multiplicity of persons and complex relations behind what looks like, for example, a small unit of four persons. In order to fully decode the social relations within the family, we must understand kinship, sex-gender systems,[8] the constitution of each person's own internal world,[9] the natural history and biology of the species,[10] as well as the culture and relations of production in which the family is embedded. We must also understand the processes by which individuals appropriate and incorporate experience and make it their own. Here, too, some of these processes may vary by age,[11] gender, race, and class and may by specific to the experience or structure immediately involved. The conscious ideas developed about our relationships with others are only one aspect of the total process.

Once this variety of social relations is acknowledged and clarified (see Figure 1.1), it is obvious that families vary by race and class and that experience within the family (as well as outside it) varies by gender and age. Experience in any particular family is overdetermined by all three kinds of social relations as they affect the internal relations of the family members, the internal world of each member, and the relations of its members to the "external" world. Of course the character of internal relations affects how each member acts in the "external world" (in the ability to tolerate anxiety, for example) and external relations invariably affect the character of internal ones (for example, loss of a job).

These rather abstract statements are unified by and are reflections of one underlying thesis: Individual human beings and human history itself are constituted by social relations.[12] These social relations arise out of and must meet material necessities that typify humans as a species. There has been tremendous variation over time in *how* these necessities have been met, yet certain regularities persist. Especially significant is the continuing existence of relations of domination, most importantly those governed by class and gender. Those material necessities are (1) the need to construct environments in order to survive (production), which requires social relations of production; (2) the production of new persons and the transformation of the relatively unformed neonate into a well-behaved member of

FIGURE 1.1 Male-Female Relations of Production.

MALE		**FEMALE**	
Production	**Reproduction**	**Production**	**Reproduction**
(relative) unity of relations		(relative) unity of relations	
PSYCHODYNAMICS / CHILDHOOD		PSYCHODYNAMICS / CHILDHOOD	

CHILD

(differentiating)
relations

Internal Relations of the Family

male/female	female/child
male/child	female/male
female & male/child	male & female/child
male/internal objects	female/internal objects
child/male	
child/female	developing internal objects
child/female & male	

(would have to be expanded for other children and intimate others)

society (reproduction); (3) the need to structure and regulate each person's internal experiences, thereby creating a complex internal world, constituted in part by innate temperament, the interaction of psyche and soma (including sexuality), and internalized object relations.

These material necessities are rooted in the peculiar character of human beings. Referring to (1) above, we must interact with nature to provide food, clothing and shelter for ourselves. Humans rarely have been able to provide all necessary material goods for themselves, even at a subsistence level. Individual survival thus depends upon some form of social cooperation. As for (2), we are both embodied and thinking/communicative animals. This duality makes culture both possible and necessary, but also creates the basis for conflicts between the unmediated demands of the body and those of culture. Organized groups must structure and control sensual experience so that people can live together with a minimum of conflict. A complex system of institutions, such as religion and the state, exist in part to regularize and legitimate such social control, as well as to mediate and disguise subgroup relations of dominance and conflict. Culture also makes sublimation—the creative, socially useful, and mediated expression of thought and feeling—possible (relations of reproduction). As for (3), the relatively extended infancy and slow psychomotor development of *homo sapiens* makes us particularly affected by and dependent on our early relations with others. Partially through relations with others we develop an internal world that is not always accessible to consciousness and is partially resistant to external influence once initial psychological development is completed.

Families are the intersection of the three primary forms of social relations (see Figure 1.2). Given its social location, it is clearly impossible for the family or familial experience to assume one unchanging form. The social location of the family makes possible *both* a moment of autonomy ("privacy") from other institutions and renders it particularly sensitive to them. Whether its resistance or its vulnerability is more evident depends upon the particular character of each form of social relation at the moment of their conjunction.

In any case it is unlikely that change, even in only one form of social relation, will have strictly localized effects. In a period of major change in productive relations, for example, it is likely that a family may be forced to alter its internal relations. A wife may take a paying job to counter inflation, and this in turn may bring unexpected tensions within the psychodynamic balance of the family as a

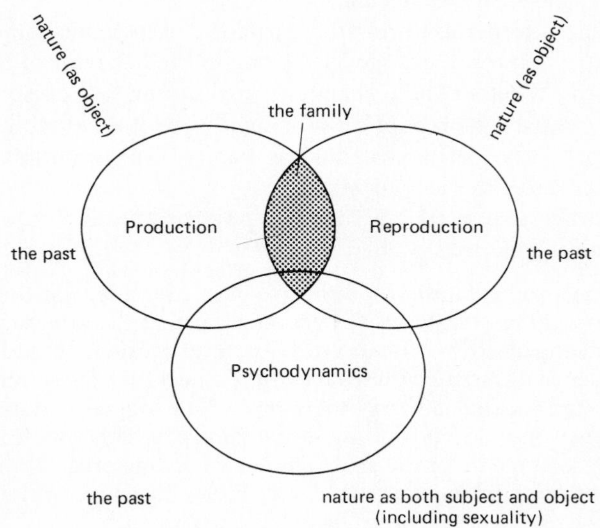

FIGURE 1.2 The Family in "External" Relations.

whole. Fewer women available for volunteer work and who require instead more social services for themselves and their families (e.g., day care) puts increased demands on the state and other institutions within the relations of reproduction. These demands then arouse both psychodynamic and political resistance to changes in women's "traditional" role. Counter pressure is put on the state, and cuts in social services result in additional work for families, especially women. New tensions are created within the family, and the process of adjustment and resistance continues.

THE FAMILY AS CONTESTED TERRAIN: DECLINE OR TRANSFORMATION?

Currently, or so many social commentators and politicians claim, the family's vulnerability is most evident. Leaving aside the already discussed problems of identifying "the family," what is meant by its decline? This is not always clear. Phenomena as diverse as the availability of abortion, teenage pregnancy, drug abuse, sex education, violence in the schools, the juvenile crime rate, the inability of high school graduates to read, the divorce rate, the entrance of women into the labor market, and especially the demands of the feminist movement are offered as evidence for and examples of causes of this decline.

Demographic information on family structure necessitates a more complex diagnosis. There *are* important changes occurring in the behavior of family members, especially women. Whether these changes constitute or will cause a decline of the family depends, in part, on a *political* judgment as to the desirability of one traditional family form, the patriarchal nuclear family. The traditional form is both remarkably stable and experiencing stress.

From a purely structural and demographic perspective, it appears that the family has remained relatively stable:

> As the various family aspects have been presented for the contemporary period (1950–1970), it has become clear that the structure of the family has changed little throughout these three decades. In addition the incidence of most of these structural aspects are fairly similar to the ones reported for the 1850 to 1880 sample. The biggest variation is in the number of children residing in the family, which also accounts for most of the change in family size. These two characteristics, then, are responsible for most of the change in the structure of the American family since 1850. These changes . . . are small.[13]

Nevertheless, four interrelated changes in the *behavior* of family members, especially women, have affected family life. These changes have accelerated since 1970, which is also the period in which the women's liberation movement became a highly visible public presence. They are (1) the increasing divorce rate, (2) the increase in families headed by women, (3) the increase in rates of labor force participation by women, and especially (4) the increase in the number of "working mothers." I suspect that these phenomena are among the most significant elements constituting the perceived "decline" of the family, for they present at least the possibility of less patriarchal control over women and familial relations.

The divorce rate has doubled since 1966. "If present patterns continue, 40 percent of all women in their late twenties currently getting married will end up being divorced."[14] There is a complex relation between women's labor force participation and divorce. "There is now fairly convincing evidence that the higher a wife's earnings, other things being equal, the more likely it is that a couple will separate."[15] Conversely, once divorced, a woman, even if she had not entered the labor market before, will generally be forced to do so because few women receive any form of alimony or child support. In any case, it is clear that women, especially women with small children, are entering the labor force in ever increasing numbers. In 1900 only 6 percent of women in the United States worked outside the home. By March 1980 the figure had risen to 51 percent.[16] Even more remarkable is the increase in "working mothers." By 1980 59.1 percent of women with children aged six to seventeen were in the labor force, as were 45 percent of those who had at least one child under six.[17]

Divorce and labor market participation are related in another way. Women are more likely to appreciate the necessity of knowing how to support themselves, given the likelihood of divorce. Also, if they can support themselves, they are less likely to tolerate an unsatisfactory marriage and more likely to be assertive of their needs within marriage. As Isabel Sawhill argues, these new attitudes can be destabilizing to a marriage:

> We suspect that changing attitudes about women's roles and the fact that more married women are participating in the labor market have combined to create new tensions within marriage while simultaneously decreasing the social and economic constraints which once bound many women to relatively unsatisfactory marriages.[18]

Somewhat similarly, Andrew Hacker argues:

> The view that women are "the major cause of much marital discord" can be interpreted not as assigning blame but as a coolly descriptive statement. What it suggests is that most men still expect deference from their wives, an attitude behooving those inherently inferior. Women are the ones who are changing, asking to be seen as equals . . . men find it difficult, often impossible, to adapt to this new climate. They may say they want wives who are accomplished and independent. But they also want them docile. It is the women, not the men, who are vivid in our present phase of domestic history. They are the force unsettling men, a consequence that can only weaken marriage.[19]

Of course, divorce or the possibility of it is not the only reason women work. Given that currently "only 46 percent of all jobs in the economy pay enough to sustain a family at a 'reasonable' level,"[20] there is a powerful economic incentive both to work and to be married (or to remarry), for the wife's earnings are often essential to family well-being. In 1979 wives who worked full-time during the entire year contributed 34.7 percent of total family income.[21] In 1980 the median income of married-couple families with both partners in the labor force was $26,432. With only the husband working, median family income was $18,799.[22]

Thus the relationship between wage labor and marriage is complex and contradictory: Women are compelled to work by economic necessity, and low wages may encourage the pooling of resources through marriage. On the other hand, the independence gained through working may lead the wife to demand more equality within marriage (including sharing housework and childrearing, which becomes a second and equally demanding job when added to wage labor). The tensions arising from women's changed views of themselves and marriage and the demands of the "double shift" may lead to divorce, but women's inability to earn enough to support themselves and their children provides a powerful incentive for remarriage.

Other trends that some find disturbing are the growth in female-headed households and the increase in the number of unmarried heterosexual couples who are living together. This number tripled between 1970 and 1980. By 1980 1,560,000 individuals were included in this category. In addition, the number of same-sex persons living together is growing.[23]

Do these trends—the increase in the divorce rate, in female-headed households, in female labor market participation, and in the number of unmarried people living together—mean that the family is declining? One definite consequence is that the family of four, with two children cared for by the mother at home while the father is working for a wage is no longer the norm. However, it is certainly an error to equate this particular family structure with "the family" and then to assume that therefore "the family" is declining. As research in anthropology and history has shown, family and kinship systems have varied widely over time; there has never been a single entity called "the family," even within one culture or at one time.[24] Furthermore, rather than bemoan the decline of the patriarchal form of the family, perhaps celebration is a more appropriate response. Although its current stress and potential disappearance is threatening to every aspect of our existence (psychodynamic, economic, and reproductive), the patriarchal nuclear family is itself the source of, or a contributor to, many of our most fundamental social and psychological difficulties. I now discuss why this is so.

HUMAN DEVELOPMENT IN CONTEMPORARY SOCIETY: AN OBJECT RELATIONS ACCOUNT

It is in and through the social relations of the family that we first become persons, who in turn maintain and reproduce capitalist patriarchy.[25] Among the most important factors that make this replication possible is the organization of childrearing within the family. Despite the economic and social changes discussed in the previous section, women of every race and class continue to have a primary responsibility for child care. This fact has far-reaching effects; its consequences reverberate through internal and social life and cannot be reversed merely by increased female participation in the labor force.

This section explores some of the internal psychodynamic consequences of contemporary childrearing arrangements, focusing on why and how general social relations such as gender, class, and race become literally part of our "inner" selves. While gender may seem to be a "natural," fixed biological attribute, closer examination of individual development will show that gender is the socially constructed set of meanings attached to anatomical differences. In and through family relations, by means of the processes of internalization, biological sex is transformed into a gender identity, which then constitutes part of the core self.

My analysis here is derived from object relations psychoanalysis.[26] Object relations theory and psychology generally take for granted that the mother (and/or other women) is the primary caretaker.[27] These theorists do not usually explore the negative consequences women's responsibility for early child care entails (nor would they necessarily agree with my inferences). Although the logic of their theory points to the importance of the character of all social relationships and the determinants of those relations, they generally focus intensively on the mother-child relationship abstracted from its social and historical context.[28] They stress the reciprocity of the mother-child relation from birth, yet tend to describe development from the child's experience, not the mother's or the totality of the interaction of the two. Thus my account of human development in contemporary society is not so much a literal rendering of object relations as an interpretation of it.

The most basic tenet of object relations theory is that human beings are created in and through relations with others.[29] The "psychological birth of the human infant"[30] does not occur simultaneously with physical birth. While physical birth is a distinct event, psychological birth is a complex interpersonal process stretching over roughly the first three years of life. People seek relations with others not only for sheer physical survival or pleasure but out of an innate need for human relationship. Early human development is thus social and interactive in character.

Included within the process of psychological birth is the initial structuring and restriction of the child's sexuality. Initially the human neonate is polymorphous. Sensual pleasure is gained from a wide range of experience, not only between the child and other persons, but between the child and physical objects and natural functions. Because of the demands of most cultures, however, most persons eventually become heterosexual, genitally oriented, and (women at least) relatively monogamous adults.

Children's psychological development is a dialectical process played out in and through a changing relationship between mother and child. Both members of the dyad must learn to be sensitive to the needs and feelings of the other while also attempting to have their own needs met. Early development occurs between two poles: symbiosis and separation-individuation. In symbiosis (one to six months), "the infant behaves and functions as though he and his mother were an omnipotent system—a dual unity within one common boundary."[31] The infant has no sense of its own body boundaries and is extremely sensitive to its mother's moods and feelings. In this state of fusion with the mother, I and not-I are not yet differentiated, and inside and outside the self are only gradually distinguished. This phase is "the primal soil from which all subsequent human relationships form."[32]

The infant must then move from the symbiotic relationship with the mother through the process of separation and individuation, which begins at about six months and continues to about the end of the second year. The child gradually develops an autonomous ego, practices and takes pleasure in its locomotor skills (which allow it to physically distance itself from the mother), and explores the possibilities of being its own separate person. The initial euphoria present in the discovery of the child's own powers and skills diminishes as it discovers the limitations as well as the possibilities of its developing skills. The child learns that not only is it not omnipotent but that the mother, too, is not all powerful. By the end of the third year a "core identity" or a distorted one, is established. In contemporary society, gender is a central element of this core identity.[33]

For adequate completion of all phases of the psychological birth process, the mother should be emotionally available to the child in a consistent, reasonably conflict-free way. She should be able to enjoy the sensual and emotional closeness of the relationship without losing her own sense of separateness or developing a narcissistic overinvestment in the child as a mere extension of her own self. Her infantile wishes for a symbiotic relationship should have been adequately gratified in childhood. If this is not the case, resentment and hostility may be aroused in her by the infant's needs. The mother thus requires adequate support, both emotional and material, from adults who are able to nurture her and reinforce her own sense of autonomy.

Within contemporary society, however, neither adequate emotional nor material support are likely to be available. Moreover, the very fact that only one woman tends to be present for the infant during this period creates difficulties of varying sorts for the mother and the girl or boy child. A closer examination of these problems reveals how the external world enters even the most (apparently) personal and isolated relationship. For many women, basic material resources are scarce. The added expenses of a child put a new burden on family resources, which is most likely to fall on the husband, increasing his resentment of the child and placing additional strains on the marriage.[34] This makes it more difficult for the wife to complain, since she knows how hard he is working.[35]

The newborn child, extremely sensitive to nuances of feeling, may pick up this strained atmosphere, and especially if it is innately less able to tolerate stress, may respond in ways that make the situation even more difficult for the mother (e.g., eating or sleeping difficulties). The stresses in the marriage and finances (compounded if there are other children) make it more difficult for the mother to provide the unhurried nurturance that the child requires. If the mother attempts to work outside the home, she is faced with the lack of good child care and well-paying, flexible jobs; the guilt of "abandoning" her child (according to social ideology); and the exhaustion of performing both household and wage labor. This may provide a material reinforcement for deeply felt unconscious resentment of the infant, stemming from unresolved issues in her own development. The geographical dispersion of extended families and the liberal ideology of "dependence is weakness"[36] make it less likely that trusted older females will be present to help the new mother.[37]

Even if material resources are adequate, the isolation of the mother-child dyad creates other problems. It is difficult for the mother to recognize the child as a potentially autonomous other if it is her primary activity and reason for being. Her own sense of autonomy is eroded by the lack of other work, adult companionship, and the physical and emotional closeness with the child (e.g., breast feeding). The problem of narcissism and overidentification is compounded if the child is female. The sheer physical differences in a gender-stratified society force some recognition of separateness if the child is male.

Deep needs for nurturance are often aroused in women during this period, both because of the demands of the child and because unconsciously the mother's own memories of infancy are evoked. Husbands are often unable to satisfy these needs, both because of the demands of work and because of the suppression of their own relational capacities. The prevalence of homophobia makes the articulation of these needs and their gratification by other women difficult. Female children seem to evoke these nurturance needs most powerfully in their mothers (due to gender identity), but precisely because of the ambivalences aroused, mothers are less likely to provide their daughters with a satisfactory symbiotic relationship or to help them resolve it. The relationship with their mother often leaves women with a deeply felt unresolved wish for symbiosis, which is one of the unconscious roots both of women's relational capacities and their ability and willingness to sacrifice for the sake of having and maintaining relationships (including childbearing and rearing).[38]

Class, race, and gender help determine the particular character of the process of psychological birth in part through the mother's interpretation and control of the child's behavior. What is seen as creative and to be encouraged in a middle-class child may be seen as dangerously willful in a working-class or black child.[39] Learning to control oneself is more important than learning to express oneself in a situation in which survival depends on learning to fit into an existing hierarchy. Encouragement of autonomy can be a cruel hoax, given a realistic assessment of the child's chances to succeed. Thus the working-class mother may have more ambivalent feelings about her child's drive toward autonomy, which may dampen the child's pleasure in and exploration of her own powers, which may in turn lead to a lessening of self-respect and a lowering of expectations, of what one has a "right" to demand from the self and others.

During the process of separation-individuation, the child explores and continually develops its separateness, then returns to the mother for "emotional refueling." The potential presence of this relationship allows the child to leave it. Gradually the relationship is internalized and becomes part of the child's internal psychic reality. The ambivalence present throughout this process gradually intensifies. The child both wants to return to the symbiotic state and fears being engulfed by it. In "good enough" social relations a resolution is achieved in which both members of the dyad come to accept their bond (mutuality) and their separateness. This is the basis of a truly reciprocal relationship between the pair, which creates the possibility for the child to then establish reciprocal relations with others.

In contemporary capitalist and patriarchal society, however, it is often not possible to fully achieve a satisfactory synthesis, nor are other social relationships characterized by reciprocity.[40] Becoming aware of gender means recognizing that men and women are not valued equally, that in fact men are socially more esteemed than women. Becoming engendered, therefore, entails a coming to awareness of and to some extent internalizing asymmetries of power and esteem.

The boy child must identify with the father to consolidate his differentiation from the mother. Given our rigid sex-gender system, this requires him to repress the "female" parts of himself. By age five he will have repressed his memories of his earliest experience and many of his relational capacities. He will have developed the "normal contempt" for women that is a fundamental part of male identity under patriarchy.[41] Depending in part on his class, he will have either suppressed part of his capacity for genuine autonomy or sublimated it into a quest for competitive advantage and/or differential recognition. The boy attempts to resolve the ambivalence inherent in the separation-individuation process by denial (of having been related), projection (women are bad; they cause these problems), or domination. These defenses become part of ordinary male behavior toward adult women and to anything that seems similar to them—the body, feelings, nature. The ability to control (and be in control) becomes both a need and a symbol of masculinity. Relations are turned into contests for power. The desire for reciprocity is distorted into a desire for mastery. In contrast, the girl, precisely because of her continuing ambivalent tie to the mother, cannot so thoroughly repress her early experience and relational capacities. She seeks relationships, even at the expense of her own autonomy.

The two genders come to complement each other in a rather grotesque symmetry. Each gender must repress or only partially develop parts of the self.[42] Such incomplete and distorted development is both one of the roots of the replication of patriarchy and of the psychological suffering within it. In adulthood, males and females are often unconsciously driven to seek out the other gender, to complete the partial development of the self through a relationship with the other, who embodies the aspects one lacks or is unable to express. Yet these relationships are often unsatisfactory; there is a haunting sense of disappointment, of something essential lacking. The reasons for this disappointment are difficult to identify and articulate to the other or even to the self. True reciprocity, while longed for, is resisted (or not striven for) out of fear of domination or a desire for it. Thus while many people are unhappy in the present, as the rate of divorce and the appeal of pop psychologies indicate, they are also afraid to change, in part out of fear of the return of repressed infantile feelings.[43] The temptation is to resolve the conflicts by moving backward to apparently simpler times when each person knew his or her place and the rules governing human relations seemed clearer and universally obeyed.

THE CHILD IN THE PERSON: REVERBERATIONS OF FAMILY LIFE IN WORK AND POLITICAL LIFE

Our early experiences are not lost as we develop, for they are retained in the unconscious and continue to reverberate throughout adult life. We are often unaware of these reverberations since they are expressed in feeling or bodily forms (such as psychosomatic illness), not thought. Their roots are not immediately accessible to consciousness, and their very existence may be so threatening and/or disorganizing that they remain repressed.

The unconscious is not totally ahistoric, however, for it is partially constituted in and through social relations. For example, profound changes, whose dimensions we can only guess at, would occur if the infantile drama were played out in relation to both genders, rather than exclusively with women.[44]

Currently, the oppression of women and the repression of early infantile experience are linked by the fact that *women and only women* "mother." Because the tension between the infant's many desires and its limited capacity to fulfill them unaided is played out in relation to only one gender, women are experienced as both the physical memory of this struggle and the cause of it. Women also embody the residual infantile ambivalence—the wish to be cared for and totally fused with another person and the dangers that this wish poses to the distinctness of self. Both individual male development and patriarchy are partially rooted in a need to deny the power and autonomy of women as experienced and feared in infancy.[45] This experience is literally a part (although repressed) of the self and as such its return to consciousness must be defended against. The experience of maturing in a family in which only women mother ensures that patriarchy will be reproduced, since the child becomes an adult who has a deep wish to replicate the familial division of labor and the emotional characteristics of the same-gender parent.[46]

As a result of these processes, women's primary identity will most typically be bound up in childrearing and maintaining relationships (despite the likelihood they will work for a wage at least at some point in their lives), while men's identity will be bound up in wage work. This split, I would argue, is one of the roots of male resistance to women's entrance into the labor force, especially in positions of authority.

Women's experience of the conflict between nurturance and autonomy is likely to revolve around the deeply felt opposition of being loved or being autonomous. Success in work may be experienced as a threat to the possibility of being loved (a fear often confirmed by male response to female success).[47] This threat may unconsciously lead to self-undermining ambivalence in taking oneself seriously as a worker. This ambivalence is experienced not only in relation to the self but to other women as well. An autonomous woman threatens others because she appears to have rejected her role as nurturer. Women may undermine and/or resent other women's rejection of traditional femininity (e.g., contemporary antifeminism). Women's ambivalence toward work and to other women at work is reinforced by contemporary work relations in which success in professional jobs often requires the suppression of "female" attributes and capacities including childbearing and rearing (or makes enjoyment of them more difficult).

The abstract, instrumental character of work relations has other important consequences. People do not expect to receive erotically infused gratification from their work—either in their relations with co-workers or in the work process itself. These expectations (that work will be alienating, that one can only be one's self at home) decrease militancy for change and resistance to oppressive work situations. In turn, the more abstract and fragmented nonfamilial social relations become with the development of capitalism, the more the need for intimacy intensifies. Intimacy is found now for many people primarily, if at all, in the family. Yet simultaneously, the more instrumental and competitive the "outside" world becomes and the more isolated and insular each family is, the more difficult women find it to succeed at their work—to create and maintain a "haven from a heartless world" for men and children—and the more pressure is put on them to do so. Thus contemporary capitalism both reinforces women's traditional roles as wife and mother and, simultaneously places additional and often contradictory demands on them (e.g., the need to work for a wage).[48] The stress produced by these demands is one of the roots of contemporary feminism.

The split between autonomy and nurturance affects political life as well. Sublimated forms of object seeking (what Freud called libido) provide a powerful bond between members of a community.[49] Libido is a root of compassion and the ability to regard the other as equal to oneself (as ends, not means, in Kantian terms). It provides an unconscious need for social interactions with others and for the other to develop himself or herself fully (to be a pleasurable object for the self). True reciprocity is a basic social condition for participatory democracy and social morality. It bonds people together into a social whole that is simultaneously personal and communal. The capacity to enter into reciprocal relationships must be an integral aspect of the person, for otherwise considerations of selfish interest are likely to be overwhelming, and conflict will be resolved through violence or force. The transformation of another person into an alien other is the first step in the process of domination.

If erotic object seeking is confined to the family, public life is impoverished because the need for autonomy is transformed into the attempt to maximize one's own "privately" conceived ends through "political" and economic action, unbounded by concern for others or the social whole. We become the calculating Hobbesian creatures celebrated (or at least settled for) by rational liberal "democratic" theory. The frequency with which contemporary intimate relations break down is painful evidence of the fact that familial relations alone cannot satisfy the depth of our need for social relations. The turn to the self, unnourished by either public or private life, is bound to end in despair and/or the search for a Great Mother, the guru-leader who finally makes one feel good (loved and valued as a person).

Writers on both the left and the right are not wrong to blame some of our social and individual unhappiness on the social relations of the family. They are wrong to look to the past for a model of the healthy family or to assume that it can exist in isolation from other forms of social relations. My analysis of the family has shown that the only adequate ground for human emancipation is a radical transformation in all forms of social relations (productive, reproductive, and psychodynamic). This emancipation can only occur through a long struggle with our own demons as well as externalized forms of power. New forms of political activity for which both consciousness raising and "speaking bitterness" can serve as partial models must be developed.

The task of political transformation is thus infinitely more complex than conservatism, liberalism, or orthodox Marxism generally comprehend. What is at stake, as Aristotle understood so long ago, is the very possibility of genuine, full human development for both the individual and the social whole. For, as Hanna Pitkin states:

> Accurate self-knowledge and responsible self-government, autonomy rightly understood, have been the dual aspects of human maturity, at least since the Greeks. To be grown up means to understand who you are and what you are doing, and to take competent responsibility for it. Since we are all in fact members of one another, connected to others through the conditions and consequences of our actions in countless ways, being grown up means knowing those connections and taking responsibility for the consequences. Only in interaction with many and diverse other, only in relation to the "we," can we gain that knowledge in a determinate way or make that assumption of responsibility effective. I cannot fully discover who I am, learn public judgment, in exclusively private relationships. And I am not yet fully taking charge of my life and of what I do until I join with my fellow citizens in political action.[50]

It is time to grow up, to discard our fantasies of the all-powerful mother. As long as we unconsciously believe that we can go home to her (or to nature) and she will make everything all right (or that it is all her fault when things go wrong), we can never reach maturity either as individuals or as a (potential) polity. We will be paralyzed in the state of unhappy consciousness in which "actions and its (the self, the species) *own* concrete action remain something miserable and insignificant, its enjoyment pain and the sublation of these positively considered, remains a mere 'beyond.'"[51]

These fantasies grow out of and are nourished by a particular form of the family, which is in turn reinforced by and reinforces other forms of social relations. To transform a set of social relations so deeply rooted within us is a dangerous enterprise that is certain to arouse deep resentment in men and women. Yet an examination of some of the psychological, political, and economic consequences of the patriarchal family provides compelling reasons for celebrating, even working to hasten, its decline.

As women leave home, it is important that they learn to take responsibility for public acts, to confront and transform power relationships. Men need to take responsibility for knowing their own feelings and being responsive to the feelings of others. Domination and submission can be replaced by reciprocity as the governing principle of all social relations. Can two genders—bent and distorted, weighted with conscious and unconscious history—transform and redeem the past, in the name of a future nobody can clearly see? On this question rests not only the future of feminism and the family but perhaps human life itself.

NOTES

1. See, for example, Eli Zaretsky, *Capitalism, The Family and Personal Life* (New York: Harper & Row, 1976); and Elliott Currie, Robert Dunn, and David Fogarty, "The New Immiseration: Stagflation, Inequality, and the Working Class," *Socialist Review* 10, no. 6 (November–December 1980): 10–31. Heidi Hartmann, "The Family as the Locus of Gender, Class and Political Struggle: The Example of Housework," *Signs* 6, no. 3 (Spring 1981): 366–94, provides a critique of some of this literature.

2. See especially Max Horkheimer, "Authority and the Family," in *Critical Theory* (New York: Herder and Herder, 1972); the Frankfurt Institute for Social Research, "The Family," in *Aspects of Sociology* (Boston: Beacon Press, 1972); Theodore Adorno, "Sociology and Psychology II," *New Left Review*, no. 27 (January–February 1968); Christopher Lasch, *Haven in a Heartless World: The Family Besieged* (New York: Basic Books, 1977).

3. See Wini Breines, Margaret Cerullo, and Judith Stacey, "Social Biology, Family Studies and Anti-Feminist Backlash," *Feminist Studies* 4 (February 1978): 43–67, for an excellent critique of Lasch's work.

4. George Gilder, *Wealth and Poverty* (New York: Basic Books, 1981), esp. pt. 2. Gilder's analysis at points is quite close to a radical feminist one, although his conclusions are very different. Compare his argument about welfare, for example, to the notion of public and private patriarchy in Carol Brown, "Mothers, Fathers and Children: From Private to Public Patriarchy," in *Women and Revolution*, ed. Lydia Sargent (Boston: South End Press, 1981).

5. For a classic statement of this position, see G. W. F. Hegel, *The Philosophy of Right*, trans. T. M. Knox (New York: Oxford University Press, 1952), pp. 110–22.

6. See the fine critiques of contemporary scholarship on the family by Rayna Rapp, Ellen Ross, and Renate Bridenthal, "Examining Family History," *Feminist Studies* 5, no. 1 (Spring 1979): 174–200.

7. I am adapting Marx's claim that reification permeates all capitalist social relations by extending it to familial relations, an area generally ignored within Marxist theory. On reification, see Karl Marx, *Capital*, vol. 1 (New York: International Publishers, 1967), pt. 1; and George Lukacs, "Reification and the Consciousness of the Protelariat," in *History and Class Consciousness* (Boston: MIT Press, 1971).

8. This is Gayle Rubin's term, which she develops in "The Traffic in Women: Notes

on a Political Economy of Sex," in *Toward an Anthropology of Women*, ed. Rayna Reiter (New York: Monthly Review Press, 1975).

9. On the constitution of the internal world, see Harry Guntrip, *Personality Structure and Human Interaction* (New York: International Universities Press, 1961), pp. 192–245.

10. The history of human evolution and its continuing influence is little understood and much disputed. See, for example, the essays by Adrienne L. Zihlman, "Women and Evolution, Part II: Subsistence and Social Organization Among Early Hominids," and Donna Haraway, "Animal Sociology and a Natural Economy of the Body Politic, Parts I and II," *Signs* 4, no. 1 (Autumn 1978): 4–20, 37–60.

11. Some of these processes may be age, gender, race and/or class specific. On age, see Jean Piaget, *The Construction of Reality in the Child* (New York: Ballantine Books, 1954). On class and gender, see Lillian Breslow Rubin, *Worlds of Pain: Life in the Working Class Family* (New York: Basic Books, 1976). On race bias, see Bonnie Thorton Dill, "The Dialectics of Black Womanhood," *Signs* 4, no. 3 (Spring 1979): 543–55.

12. An insight I owe to Marx, especially his "Theses on Feuerbach," in *The Marx-Engels Reader*, 2nd ed., ed. Robert C. Tucker (New York: W. W. Norton, 1978).

13. Ruby Ray Seward, *The American Family: A Demographic History* (Beverly Hills, Calif.: Sage, 1978), pp. 170–71.

14. Andrew Hacker, "Divorce a la Mode," *New York Review of Books*, 3 May 1979, p. 26.

15. Isabel Sawhill, "Discrimination and Poverty Among Women Who Head Families," in *Women and the Workplace*, ed. Barbara Reagan and Martha Blaxall (Chicago: University of Chicago Press, 1976), p. 202.

16. *Money Income and Poverty Status of Families and Persons in the United States*, Bureau of the Census, Current Population Reports, Series P–60, No. 127 (Washington, D.C.: Government Printing Office, August 1981), p. 5.

17. Ibid.

18. Sawhill, "Discrimination and Poverty," p. 202.

19. Hacker, "Divorce," p. 24. An additional source of strain may be the unequal division of labor within the household. See note 48.

20. Zillah Eisenstein, *The Radical Future of Liberal Feminism* (New York: Longman, 1981), p. 210. The statistic is taken from *Newsweek*, 6 December 1979, p. 69.

21. Andrew Hacker, "Farewell to the Family?" *New York Review of Books*, no. 4, 18 March 1982, p. 41.

22. *Money Income*, p. 12.

23. *Marital Status and Living Arrangements*, Bureau of Census, Current Population Reports, Series P–20, No. 365 (Washington, D.C.: Government Printing Office, October 1981), p. 4. Due to the persecution of homosexuals, it is impossible to determine precisely how many of these persons are in homosexual relationships.

24. On variations within the family generally, see "Introduction" in *The Family: Its Structure and Functions*, ed. Rose Laub Coser (New York: St. Martin's, 1974), pp. xv–xxvii; and Claude Levi-Strauss, "The Family," in *Man, Culture and Society*, ed. Harry Shapiro (London: Oxford University Press, 1956). On variations within Western Europe, see E. Anthony Wrigley, "Reflections on the History of the Family," in *The Family*, ed. Alice S. Rossi, Jerome Kagan, and Tamarah Hareven (New York: W. W. Norton, 1978).

25. On the concept of capitalist patriarchy, see the essays by Eisenstein and Hartmann in *Capitalist Patriarchy and the Case for Socialist Feminism*, ed. Zillah Eisenstein (New York: Monthly Review Press, 1979); and *Feminism and Materialism*, ed. Annette Kuhn and

Ann Marie Wolpe (Boston: Routledge and Kegan Paul, 1978), esp. pp. 1–67, 254–89. On the patriarchal structure of the family and the centrality of the family to patriarchy, see Rubin, "The Traffic in Home"; and Nancy Chodorow, *The Reproduction of Mothering: Psychoanalysis and the Sociology of Gender* (Berkeley: University of California Press, 1978). On the unequal distribution of work within the home, see note 48 below. For important attempts to delineate some of the layers of fantasy, ideology, and reality that adhere to the concepts and experiences of motherhood, see Dill "Dialectics of Black Womanhood"; Dorothy Dinnerstein, *The Mermaid and the Minotaur* (New York: W. W. Norton, 1976); Adrienne Rich, *Of Woman Born: Motherhood as Experience and Institution* (New York: W. W. Norton, 1976), esp. pp. 56–83; and Sara Ruddick, "Maternal Thinking," *Feminist Studies* 6, no. 2 (Summer 1980): 342–67.

26. My understanding of object relations theory has been immeasurably deepened by conversations with Kirstin Dahl, a child therapist at the Yale Child Studies Center. Harry Guntrip, *Psychoanalytic Theory, Therapy and the Self* (New York: Basic Books, 1971), provides a good introduction to object relations theory. See also D. W. Winnicott, *The Maturational Processes and the Facilitating Environment* (New York: International Universities Press, 1961). See as well the clinical material in Jane Flax, "The Conflict Between Nurturance and Autonomy in Mother-Daughter Relationships and Within Feminism," *Feminist Studies* 4 (June 1978): 121–89; and "Mother-Daughter Relationships: Psychodynamics, Politics and Philosophy," in *The Future of Difference*, ed. Hester Eisenstein (Boston: G. K. Hall, 1980).

27. This fact cannot be adequately explained as merely a "natural" extension of women's childbearing capacities or as a consequence of the institution of private property or of our primate heritage. Indeed, the desire and capacity to mother should be separated from the capacity to give birth. See Alice S. Rossi, "A Biosocial Perspective on Parenting," in Rossi, Kagan, and Hareven, *The Family*. Critics of Rossi's article include Breines, Cerullo and Stacy, "Social Biology"; Chodorow, *Reproduction of Mothering*, pp. 18–21; and the symposium "Considering 'A Biological Perspective on Parenting,'" *Signs* 4 *(Summer* 1979): 695–717. Burton White somewhat reluctantly supports my conclusion. See his *The First Three Years of Life* (New York: Avon, 1975), p. 256. It is indicative of the power of patriarchal ideas that psychologists conclude from the study of child development, not that children need reliable, consistent, and loving relationships (which they obviously do), but that only their *mothers* can provide such a relationship. A recent example of this confusion is Selma Fraiberg, *Every Child's Birthright: In Defense of Mothering* (New York: Bantam, 1977).

28. However, both Winnicott and Guntrip do recognize the barriers contemporary social relations pose to the achievement of true reciprocity. See D. W. Winnicott, *The Family and Individual Development* (London: Tavistock Publications, 1965), esp. pp. 155–69; *Guntrip, Personality Structure*, pp. 15–42.

29. See Guntrip, *Personality Structure*, pp. 276–320.

30. This is Margaret Mahler's term. See Margaret Mahler, Fred Pine, and Anni Bergman, *The Psychological Birth of the Human Infant* (New York: Basic Books, 1975).

31. Ibid., p. 44.

32. Ibid., p. 48. Some of this material first appeared in a different form in Flax, "Nurturance." I use the word "mother" rather than "caretaker" or "parent" because typically women do this work and I wish to emphasize this fact. However, this does not imply that men could not do it. Nor does it imply that the earliest relationship must be dyadic, although the child would probably find it difficult to bond with a larger number of people—perhaps more than three. Definitive evidence on this question is not available.

33. John Money and Anke A. Ehrhardt, *Man and Woman, Boy and Girl* (Baltimore: Johns Hopkins University Press, 1972), pp. 176–94. According to Money and Ehrhardt, the child's sense of gender is firmly established by the age of one and one-half to two years and has little to do with an understanding of sexuality or reproduction.

34. On male resentment of children, see Chodorow, *Reproduction of Mothering*, pp. 189–209. Wife and child abuse as well as incest are likely to begin or increase when women become pregnant.

35. See the interviews in L. B. Rubin, *Worlds of Pain*, esp. Chaps. 7 and 10.

36. On the impact of this ideology on working-class men, see Richard Sennett and Jonathan Cobb, *The Hidden Injuries of Class* (New York: Vintage, 1972), esp. pp. 105–25.

37. This is less true among very poor black women. See Carol Stack, *All Our Kin* (New York: Harper & Row, 1970); and Joyce Ladner, *Tomorrow's Tomorrows* (New York: Anchor, 1972). However, these authors document strategies for survival within a situation of basic powerlessness marked also by the absence of men as reliable wage earners. The costs to both men and women in this situation are quite high.

38. See Flax, "Nurturance," and Chodorow, *The Reproduction of Mothering*, pp. 92–110, on the lack of separation between mothers and daughters and its consequences.

39. Sennett and Cobb, *Hidden Injuries*, pp. 53–90; L. B. Rubin, *Worlds of Pain*, pp. 23–48. Maya Angelou, *I Know Why the Caged Bird Sings* (New York: Random House, 1970) describes some of the contradictions of raising black children in the South.

40. Marx, *Capital*, pp. 71–93, discusses the illusions of "free exchange," which is the capitalist notion of reciprocity.

41. Sigmund Freud discusses this in "Some Psychical Consequences of the Anatomical Distinction between the Sexes," reprinted in *Women and Analysis*, ed. Jean Strouse (New York: Dell, 1974), esp. p. 10; see also Chodorow, *Reproduction of Mothering*, p. 11. Mahler et al., *Psychological Birth*, p. 102, discuss developmental differences between boys and girls beginning at 21 months.

42. Dinnerstein, *Mermaid and Minotaur*, p. 4.

43. Much of the dynamics discussed here arise out of subtle qualities of interaction and interchange of feeling states rather than overt and easily identified behavior. Such dynamics have been most often analyzed by psychotherapists. See, for example, the case studies reported in R. D. Laing and A. Esterson, *Sanity, Madness and the Family* (Baltimore: Penguin, 1964). Children's play as well as clinical material from the psychotherapy of both adults and children is an important source of information on psychodynamics. On children's play, see D. W. Winnicott, *Playing and Reality* (New York: Basic Books, 1971), pp. 38–64. For its use in child therapy, see D. W. Winnicott, *The Piggle: An Account of the Psychoanalytic Treatment of a Little Girl* (New York: International Universities Press, 1977). It should also be evident that the relationship between individual development and the various forms of social relations is never simple and direct, and they cannot be captured by such crude models as the economic determinism of vulgar Marxism or the tendency of "empirical" social science to focus on overt attitudes and cognition, and on correlations between "objective" characteristics (race, income) and these abstracted "beliefs." We are far from an adequate comprehension of the complex overdetermination of each person's experience by the particular qualities of each child/adult or adult/adult relation, innate constitution (including the biochemical processes of the brain) and cognitive capacities, the inevitable permutations and distortions which occur in the incorporation of experience in the preverbal state of infancy, the internalization of and the need to adapt to the demands of productive and reproductive relations, and the ongoing, continuous processes within the psyche (both conscious and unconscious).

44. This is not to imply that changes in childrearing arrangements alone are sufficient

to bring about human emancipation. Obviously there are many preconditions to such change—such as altering the organization of production which would in turn require major political and economic transformations. However, I believe that without altering childrearing arrangements, full emancipation will be impossible. By altering childrearing arrangements, I do not mean merely involving men more fully in childcare within isolated nuclear families, nor do I think the purpose of political action ought to or can be to remove all "external" (socio-economic) impediments so that women can be "perfect" mothers, contrary to the claims of Nancy Chodorow and Susan Contratto in "The Fantasy of the Perfect Mother," in *Rethinking the Family: Some Feminist Questions*, ed. by Barrie Thorne with Marilyn Yalom (New York: Longman Inc., 1982). Indeed, one of the purposes of this chapter is to analyze the roots of this fantasy and to delineate some of its dangerous psychological and political consequences. See also footnote 43 of this chapter. I develop this point more fully in "A Materialist Theory Of Women's Status, "*Psychology of Women Quarterly* 6, no. 1 (Fall 1981): 123–36.

45. Dinnerstein, *Mermaid and Minotaur*, pp. 35–114, 160–97.

46. Chodorow, *Reproduction of Mothering*, esp. pp. 3–10, 173–209. Freud once suggested that what a woman looks for in her husband is her mother. See his "Female Sexuality," reprinted in Strouse.

47. Hacker, "Divorce," p. 27, cites studies which suggest "that as women enter positions once held by men they become either less attracted to marriage or less attractive as marriage partners. Nor is it clear that even open-minded husbands want wives with attainments approaching their own. At this point in only 7.3% of American marriages are the wife's earnings 'perceptibly higher' than her husband's."

48. See Hartmann, "The Family as Locus"; and Eisenstein, *Radical Future of Liberal Feminism*, pp. 206–14. L. B. Rubin, *Worlds of Pain*, cites studies that indicate that "in the aggregate, husbands contribute the same amount of time to the family—about 1.6 hours a day—whether their wives work or not. Furthermore, husbands' family time remains independent of wives' employment when age, class, and number of children are controlled for" (p. 228). See also Ann Oakley, *The Sociology of Housework* (New York: Pantheon, 1974), pp. 135–80. Women spend 40–90 hours a week on the average on housework. Women with paying jobs tend to be on the lower end of this scale (Oakley, pp. 92–99). According to a recent (1972) UNESCO study, the disparity between men's and women's contribution to the family exists cross-nationally. In the countries surveyed, employed men spend no more than one half hour a day on housework and child care, while employed women spend at least an hour and a half a day. See Elise Boulding, "Familial Constraints on Women's Work Roles," in Blaxall and Reagan, *Women and Workplace*, pp. 112–13.

49. Freud and Plato both appreciate the power of sublimated libido. See, especially, Sigmund Freud, *Civilization and Its Discontents* (New York: W. W. Norton, 1961); and Plato's *Symposium.* In Freud, however, libido is originally totally narcissistic. I agree with Guntrip (*Personality Structure*, pp. 69–113) that this idea is tied to Freud's biological mechanism and is contradicted by other aspects of his theory, especially the notion of a superego. In Plato ideal libido is not embodied, a notion permeated by patriarchal assumptions.

50. Hanna Fenichel Pitkin, "Justice: On Relating Private and Public," *Political Theory* 9, no. 3 (August 1981): 349.

51. G. W. F. Hegel, *The Phenomenology of Mind*, trans. J. B. Baille (New York: Harper & Row, 1967), p. 270.

2

Zillah Eisenstein

The State, the Patriarchal Family, and Working Mothers

It is important to understand what is at stake in the present discussions of the so-called crisis of the American family.[1] The New Right is disturbed by what it sees as a challenge to the power and authority of the father by both the feminist movement *and* the interventionist welfare state. Feminists want to develop family forms that recognize the autonomy and reproductive freedom of women as a central tenet of their existence. Given the real conflicts between patriarchy and capitalism, "the" state does not have a cohesive policy on or for "the" family of the 1980s, and as a result, the state itself faces a "crisis."

The purpose of this essay is to explore the family as a social and political unit, with a history to be understood, characterized by relations of power and domination. Instead of assuming that the changing nature of the family today reflects its abnormal functioning, I argue that the family as a product of historical processes has and is always changing. Hence, the important question to be explored here is how and why the family changes and how these changes reflect and at the same time construct power relations. History is defined in terms of economic class struggle, patriarchal conflict, and racial domination, although the present essay focuses primarily on patriarchal conflict. The family reflects these three processes and structures the way they are historically played out. The so-called crisis of the family must be understood as a part of this history.[2] Once one recognizes this, one can understand why the family is at the center of political struggle in the 1980s.

Outside of this historical context it is impossible to understand the (1) patriarchal family as a major element in structuring (2) social patriarchy.[3] The above distinction is between the (1) hierarchical sexual organization for the repro-

This is a much revised and updated version of "El Estado, la familia patriarcal y las madres que trabajan," *En Teoria*, no. 1 (April–June 1979); 135–68; which was subsequently published by *Kapitalistate, Working Papers on the Capitalist State* 8 (1980): 43–66. For a more developed analysis of the state and the "working mother," see my *The Radical Future of Liberal Feminism* (New York: Longman, 1981), esp. Chaps. 8–10.

duction of sex-gender[4] as it exists in the family, and (2) the organization of sex-gender as it exists throughout the society understood as a totality. The two realms are related and structure each other but, I argue, they are not one and the same thing.

For instance, by understanding the family one begins to comprehend the structural relations of power between men and women to the extent the family reflects and defines these relations. But one cannot assume that *all changes* in the organization of the family reflect a parallel change in the relations of power either in the family or in society. Nor can one assume that all changes in patriarchal relations in the family are always paralleled in the system of social patriarchy. In fact, the opposite may occur. I try to show here that as some of the patriarchal relations of the family have been undermined by changes in women's consciousness and position in the economy, the state through the system of social patriarchy is trying to reinforce familial patriarchy. The two domains are utterly related, but they never can be reduced to the activities of the other. Hence, it may appear that changes in the family have given women more power in the system of social patriarchy. Before this can be assessed, however, one must examine how these changes reflect the political needs of social patriarchy itself.

Although it is true that men have less legal power in the family as fathers today (they no longer own women or children outright), one would not say that the base of social patriarchy has eroded if it is still able to reproduce the sex-gender system. Even for those who define patriarchy in more legalistic terms, it does not necessarily follow that the system has been weakened. After all, the particular expression of patriarchal privilege changes with new social relations, and these changes are reflected in the law. We shall see that the particular legal expression of patriarchal privilege is expressed differently with the development of the bourgeois state's separation between politics and economics and the ideological distinction between public and private realms. It becomes more difficult to understand what the patriarchal base of power is as it becomes more mystified through bourgeois law, ideology, and practice.

In order to demystify patriarchy as a system of power, and its use by particular economic modes, one needs to understand that patriarchy is not a static system of power. One cannot look for a static structure to express the relations of patriarchy. The changes and processes one sees are part of the definition of patriarchy. They express its historical formulation[5] and have been ideologically defined and politically structured by different internal relations in the transition from feudalism to capitalism. By understanding this we begin to grasp the real history of patriarchy in relation to the particular economic class needs of a period. We also begin to see the unifying element through history of the sexual division of labor and society for mothering. And we shall see that part of patriarchal history is the attempt to mystify this unity. Therefore, we first must discuss the meaning of the patriarchal family as part of the social and political system for reproducing gender, before we discuss the family's transition from feudalism to capitalism, and before we analyze the state's role in managing the current "crisis" of the family.

THE DYNAMIC OF PATRIARCHY

The patriarchal dynamic of the family involves the hierarchical sexual ordering and differentiation of society that is carried over into each economic period. The following discussion suffers from a sort of abstraction because the patriarchal dynamic, located in the patriarchal family, always is expressed alongside *and through* the economic system of society. But it is important to understand, to the extent that one can, what this patriarchal history and system is unto itself. Only then can we really understand its import to the different economic modes and its total political meaning.

It is interesting to note that some historians believe that because the "form of community in which the father is the supreme authority in the family"[6] no longer exists, it is incorrect to use the term patriarchy for the largely changed present-day relations of legal power. It may be true that male privilege is not protected through as repressive a legal system structured around the male as father and proprietor in familial patriarchy as it once was, but the redefinition of his power both in family and social patriarchy speaks to the changing nature of male supremacy, not its demise.

Patriarchy as a system of sexual hierarchical relations that differentiates male *from* female is not fully embodied within the law to begin with. The law does define and protect particular male privileges through marriage law and the like, but many of the privileges derivative of sexual hierarchy and differentiation remain in practice without laws to define them as such. For instance, there is no specific law that says women will rear children, do laundry, or be the cooks. It is the economic dimension of patriarchy that is openly embodied in bourgeois patriarchal law—woman's relationship is explicitly stated in relation to property, possessions, income. The law more indirectly tries to control her sexual life (abortion law),[7] although there are instances of direct interference (laws against homosexuality). This is part of the way the state, through law, protects the ideological notion that sexual questions are part of the private realm. The law in the bourgeois state is premised on the clear distinction between private and public realms. Laws dealing directly with sexuality in terms of prostitution or homosexuality are developed on the premise that they affect the public realm and hence still operate in terms of the above ideological distinction. As a result, patriarchal privilege is often protected by its indirect presence in the law. Whether a woman chooses to bear a child is supposedly her "private" affair. Whether the law gives her options to do otherwise is not understood as a reflection of indirect patriarchal control. Even with the changes that have occurred in the law from the thirteenth century, there are still many statements of patriarchal privilege within the law today. This is what the struggle for the Equal Rights Amendment attests to. To cut these struggles off from the historical struggle against patriarchal control is to destroy a sense of the *continuous* power relations of patriarchy and the struggle against it. After all, history reflects the process of changing needs, and patriarchy, as it attempts to organize itself in terms of these needs, changes and develops itself.

Patriarchy's dynamic of power is centered in the controls developed to limit women's options in relation to motherhood and mothering. This locates the universal dynamic force of patriarchy within the social relations that define women as mothers and that reproduce within women the need to mother. These relations are defined historically and therefore are always changing, although the need, as such, for the sex-gender system does not change. Women reproduce, and yet changes in contraception change our relationship to that reproduction. Women have constantly borne and reared children as mothers, and this changes as the culture, economics, and medical health of a society change. The mother of ten in the sixteenth century was a different kind of mother than the mother of the eighteenth century. The woman who labored in the fields and in the house in the seventeenth century was different from the mother of the Victorian era. The middle-class mother of the nineteenth century was a different mother than the sweatshop laborer of the early twentieth century, and both differ from the wage-earning mother of the late twentieth century. And still all these women are mothers—responsible for the bearing and rearing of children in many different forms, but responsible nevertheless for the reproduction of a new generation.

The political definition of woman as both childbearer and rearer is used to maintain a system of male privilege that sustains the economic-class arrangements of society. This definition of woman is kept potent by the activity of daily life that reproduces these mental images as reality. The potency of this sexual logic is protected and reproduced through the institution of motherhood and the process of mothering.[8] Because early child care is female dominated, boys and girls alike learn that it is women who rear children. Of course this activity in and of itself is not the problem, but rather it is how this activity becomes sexually assigned within the family and within the larger social, economic, and political setting. Women's biological assignment to bear children and their political assignment to rear them are both part of the life force of patriarchy. The connection between bearing and rearing children is a political one—the logic derives from the patriarchal power relations of the society. The organization of the rearing of children reflects these political priorities.

Patriarchy, then, is largely the sexual and economic struggle (because these are never separated in practice) to control women's options in such a way as to keep primary their role as childbearer and rearer. Power reflects the activity of trying to limit choices. That is why "freedom of choice" is always an inadequate model for those who do not have power. The choices have already been limited and defined for them. For instance, women's choices exist within the political context of the sexual division of labor and society that defines woman's primary role as mother. The priorities of patriarchy are to keep the choice limited for woman so that her role as mother remains primary.

Patriarchy does not merely exist because men hate women. It exists because as a system of power it provides the mothers of society. This involves the caring and love they provide, the children they reproduce, the domestic labor they do, the commodities they consume, the ghettoized labor force they provide. The starting point for all these realities is motherhood itself. Trying to understand the force of patriarchy is basically trying to understand what it does. And what it does in the end is reproduce a new generation of mothers, which reproduces gender, that is, masculine and feminine personality structures.

THE FEUDAL PATRIARCHAL FAMILY

By examining the family in feudal society one sees that there have been significant changes in woman's activity within the family as well as changes in the role of the family in the larger economy. But one also sees that these changes occur while the basic system of patriarchy—the differentiation and separation of male and female life—is maintained. What we need to understand better is how these changes reflect the history of patriarchy itself and not its demise. I argue that with the advent of wage labor we have the fuller differentiation between familial patriarchy and social patriarchy, just as we have the differentiation in bourgeois society between the state and the economy, domestic and wage labor, and the ideological mystification of these realities through the distinction of public and private realms. It is important to note here, however, that the public-private distinction gets redefined in bourgeois society; it does not originate with it. This distinction is not a development of bourgeois society; rather, it is inherent in the formation of state society. The formation of the state institutionalizes patriarchy; it reifies the division between public and private life as one of sexual difference. The domain of the state has always signified public life, and this is distinguished in part, from the private realm, by differentiating men from women. The state's purpose is to enforce the separation of public and private life and with it the distinctness of male and female existence. Bourgeois society has its own particular ways of rewiring this patriarchal reality: the separation and differentiation of men from women.

One needs to clarify how today's ideology about the family differs from both the reality and ideology of feudal patriarchal family life. With the development of the bourgeois patriarchal family and state an ideological distinction arose between public and private life that was based in the actual reorganization of work away from the self-sufficient home of feudalism toward the wage-labor system. Arising from this change came the separation of work and home both in actual terms and its ideological representation. Whereas the feudal patriarchal family was an integral part of the system of production, the capitalist patriarchal family is based on the distinction between domestic and wage labor and hence is represented ideologically as separate and apart from the world of work (wage labor).

One should not assume here that because the economic organization of the family shifted with the development of capitalism that the sexual hierarchy enforced in the family disappeared. While economic systems have redefined and manipulated the patriarchal family, a continuity has remained in the relations of patriarchal power. Practically and ideologically defined by the integration of work and home, the family in feudal society was structured by a hierarchical sexual division of labor and sexual differentiation that maintained a system of female reproduction and mothering. Today, although the role of the family in relation to the wage-labor system has changed, as has the ideology that describes the family, a sexual division of labor and society still exists. In fact, the sexual division of labor developed in a more rigid form in early capitalism as a result of the separation of public and private spheres, which did not exist in feudalism. Today the rigid patriarchal division of public and private, home and work life, is being challenged by advanced capitalism's need for working mothers. Hence, the arguments of the New Right that the (patriarchal) family is in crisis.

Because the feudal patriarchal household was rooted in the unity of capital and labor, with the development of the capitalist wage-labor system the feudal home, as a self-sufficient unit supplying its own needs, disappeared.[9] Capitalism required the destruction of the self-sufficient worker as well as the self-sufficient home. Moreover, the decline of the family and domestic industry and its replacement by wage labor provided the material basis for a redefinition of the patriarchal division of public and private life into one of the home and work. Women's lives, within the family, became redefined as their place in the world of work, and the actual world of work came to be defined in terms of the wage-labor process.

The revolutionary changes that the feudal patriarchal family underwent were related to its place in the process of production and did not reflect challenges to the patriarchal structuring of sexual reproduction and mothering. Although women were an integral part of the work process, their work assignments reflected the sexual division of labor and society related to mothering itself. Women's particular choices in relation to reproduction were limited by a lack of medical knowledge about contraception. Although women, on their own initiative, tried many methods of birth control,[10] they often found themselves pregnant. Given the high infant-mortality rates at this time, the birthrate also needed to be high. Hence, women as reproducers and mothers were necessary to the system of feudalism, as they are, although historically redefined for capitalism.

In summary, the feudal patriarchal family was more a part of the society than the early capitalist patriarchal family in terms of the integration of work and home, in terms of the lack of a child-oriented existence, and in terms of existing before the development of a whole culture of privacy, intimacy, and individualism. The family in this sense was more public both ideologically and practically because its private role had not yet been developed. Patriarchy, as a system of power, manipulates this relationship between what is private and public and what appears to be public and private. During feudal society the family is discussed as public, and as such one does not ask whether there are relations of power other than feudal class relations because no differentiation is made between patriarchal family and feudal economic relations. As such the sex-gender system operates but is totally mystified through the economic relations of society. With the development of early capitalism and the differentiation of the family and the economy, the distinction is manipulated once again to interfere with understanding the patriarchal base of the family. This time it is said that the family is so disconnected from the economy and the public world that it is protected *from* the relations of power in society. Either way, the family is not understood in terms of its patriarchal base, that is, until married women are required to traverse both worlds as we move from early to advanced capitalist society.

THE ADVANCED CAPITALIST PATRIARCHAL FAMILY

After discussing the relations of power that express continuity in the history of patriarchy in feudalism and early capitalism, we need to explore how this unity gets redefined in terms of the needs of advanced capitalism. How are conflicts developing between patriarchy and advanced capitalism as a result of the continued split (both ideological and real) between work (wage labor) and home and the increase of married women wage earners? As capitalism tries to mold patriarchy to its needs, some of the relational and ideological needs of patriarchy have been undermined, and as a result the system of familial patriarchy appears less able to sustain the system of social patriarchy. Capitalism, however, needs the system of social patriarchy[11] (capitalist patriarchy) and therefore cannot afford to undermine it, nor can it sustain the conflicts that arise as a result.

In order to understand the political totality involved here, it is necessary to examine how the priorities of the system of patriarchy (sexual differentiation and mothering) and the priorities of capitalism (the class relations of private property and profit maximization) may come into conflict with one another. By focusing on these conflicts it becomes clearer that we are talking about two systems of power that have to organize in relation to each other. The conflicts are proof of the relative autonomy each must have in order to operate in the interests of the other. Otherwise their respective power bases are undermined. We shall see that today's conflicts reflect the undermining of certain patriarchal relations at the same time that advanced capitalist society needs them. The most important political dimension of these conflicts is the new level of consciousness they are creating among women.

Although the conflicts addressed here are said to lay the basis for the weakening of patriarchal controls, they do not do so by themselves. Even though the family today seems to be undergoing fundamental changes, both structurally and ideologically, the underlying hierarchical power relations between women and men within the system of social patriarchy have not *yet* been challenged. As a matter of fact, there are significant attempts to reassert patriarchal power through antifeminist activity.

The particular conflicts I examine are representative of the tensions between the advanced capitalist economy (and its supportive liberal values of equal opportunity and liberal individualism) and the patriarchal relations of the hierarchically organized sexual division of labor and society and its related protective values. The state's objective is to create cohesion between these systems, for they need to function as one if the advanced capitalist patriarchal order is to be protected. At present, cohesion is disrupted by conflicts between the relations of patriarchy vs. the ideology of liberalism (i.e., the lack of opportunity for women in patriarchy vs. the ideology of equal opportunity); the relations of advanced capitalism and the ideology of patriarchy (i.e., the need for women wage workers vs. the ideology of woman in the home); and between the ideology of patriarchy and the ideology of liberalism (i.e., the ideology of woman's inequality vs. the image of equal opportunity).

The first of the series of conflicts that is appearing today is the contradiction between the dominant liberal ideology of equal opportunity and the reality for most women of continued dependence. The doctrine of equal opportunity has not replaced the patriarchal relation of female dependency;[12] rather, they both exist somewhat antagonistically within the family. More specifically, to the extent women have taken seriously and internalized the individualist values of bourgeois society for themselves, they are in conflict with the patriarchal relations of the family that define females as dependent rather than independent beings. This antagonism becomes amplified when women seek jobs and are still faced with the responsibilities of a family and household organized in terms of a system of male privilege.

Advanced Capitalist Patriarchy

Male Privilege .... Liberal Individualism

Patriarchal Family .... Capitalism

.... Conflict
________ Supporting
.... Potential for both

Given our earlier discussion of the feudal family, the relations between the family and feudal patriarchy do appear to be in greater harmony than those of advanced capitalist patriarchy and the family.

Feudal Patriarchy

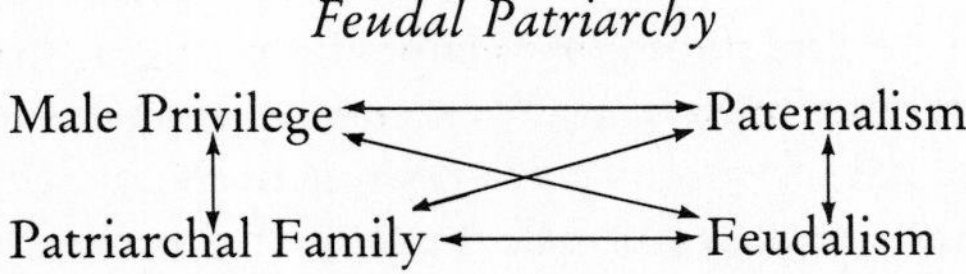

As conflict between the ideologies of liberal individualism and male privilege develops and heightens in advanced capitalism, so do the real needs of both capital and the family in terms of women workers. Within feudalism the male privilege of the family supports the paternalism of the economic order, whereas the male privilege of the family comes into conflict with both the needs of the market and its ideology of "individualism." The transformation of capitalist patriarchy appears to be currently rooted within the conflicts between the patriarchal relations of the family, the relations of the economy, and their respective ideologies.

A second and related level of conflict arises between the patriarchal values of society that define woman's responsibility and place in the home as mother vs. the growing needs of the advanced capitalist economy for women to enter the work force. This conflict has a long history of development and accommodation.

From the 1890s until World War I in the United States, the conflict arose between the reality of women working as wage laborers and the ideology defining womanhood.[13] In this sense women who labored for wages were denied entry into the world of femininity as ideology defined it. The Victorian image of womanliness excluded the wage-earning woman. Woman was defined in terms of the home and motherhood. Women who worked for wages viewed marriage as a way to escape the toil of the factory and for those women, married or unmarried, who remained in the work force, wage work was acceptable as long as they did not attack or question the conventional standards of womanliness. Sarah Eisenstein has stated that "this meant that she did not force others to recognize that she worked and that she did not identify or think of herself as a 'working woman.'"[14]

Although the image of Victorian woman has undergone an update, the rest of this description of pre-World War I women can be accurately applied to women in the twentieth century, specifically during the Great Depression of the 1930s and in the McCarthyite '50s. The ideological shift that has taken place since the '50s is mainly a move from "woman's place is in the home" to the notion of woman as "secondary earner" or "working mother." Hence there have been multiple attempts to reconcile women's labor outside the home with their (still) primary definition as mother. This means that however women enter the labor force (needs of capital), their position within patriarchal relations must be reinforced in order to protect the unity of patriarchal history. The continued existence of patriarchy is reflected in the sexual segregation of women in the labor force itself that simultaneously "allows" women into the realm of wage labor while reinforcing their inequality there and with it their role as mother.[15] It is also reflected in the growing number of part-time and seasonal jobs that "allow" women to maintain their double responsibilities as both wage worker *and* mother.

The sexual ghettoization in the labor force maintains this definition of woman as mother in that it places her in a secondary position within the labor force, which reinforces her primary position within the home. If woman has few options as to job choice in the world of paid work and her wages are low, her dependence upon a man has not *fundamentally* changed, particularly if she is married with children. Only 46 percent of all jobs in the economy pay enough to sustain a family at a "reasonable" level.[16] This may explain why 96 percent of the population eventually marries, and even though 38 percent of these people will get divorced, 79 percent of those who divorce remarry.[17]

Economic dependence, then, is part of the system that maintains marriage, the family (even the single-parent family), and mothering. Besides this ultimate priority, the structuring of these sexual hierarchical relations maintains a system of domestic labor that increases the profit system for individual corporations. In a Chase Manhattan Research Report (1978) it was noted that if a housewife were paid for her household labor, she would be worth $257.73 a week. Each housewife therefore performs a job worth $13,391 a year, whereas the aggregate housewife services would be worth $250 billion a year.[18] This work is done, and it is not recognized as work by the system of capitalist patriarchy as long as woman is defined in relation to motherhood via her biological activity of reproduction.

The accommodation of this conflict between women as wage workers, mothers, and domestics is not as successful as it may appear. As more women enter the labor force, they expect the ideology of equal opportunity to apply to them; but when they see their limited options within the labor force, the conflict between the ideology of equal opportunity and women's real second-class status within the labor force becomes highlighted.

They become more conscious of the work they do in the home against the backdrop of their wage labor. The arbitrariness of the sexual division of labor that assigns them the labor of the home seems less justifiable as they also go off to work each day and come home tired. Women's expectations about a fair division of labor change as they are forced to carry the burdens in both work realms.

The discussion above points to the conflict that arises from the changes women's lives undergo as they enter the labor force while the patriarchal relations and values of dependence both in the home and on the job are maintained. Awareness of this conflict has heightened as women who identify as middle class have entered the world of wage labor, alongside women of the working class. Their participation in the labor force has made the "double day of work" more visible to society, which defines itself as middle class.[19]

This involvement of middle-class-conscious women in the wage-labor force has begun to alter the previously accepted patriarchal view that woman belongs in the home. Liberal patriarchal ideology now speaks about the equal opportunity for women as well as men, although this opportunity is spoken of alongside woman's primary responsibility for childrearing. This is the latest attempt to define the consciousness of wage-working women as inclusive of her responsibilities within the sex-gender system itself, as well as the labor force. Yet this ideological adjustment to protect the reality of the working mother is only partially successful because it heightens the demand and political relations of the two work worlds at the same time that it tries to smooth them over.

The interesting phenomena we are currently experiencing is that the recognition of women as workers in the United States cannot be connected to a recognition of women's equality with men or a fundamental reorganization of the mothering process as women's responsibility. Women who used to work within the home instead of the labor force and now find themselves working in both realms are faced with a new understanding of the sexual division of society and the inequalities connected to it. They become more conscious of the work they do as childbearers and rearers as they have less time in which to do it. Women themselves begin to question the hierarchical organization of their lives as their existence in both worlds crisscrosses. The pressures of the home are exacerbated by the added pressure of the workplace. Boss and husband seem more and more alike.

The argument here hinges on the acceptance that the particular development of a large middle-class consciousness among women is part of the present political reality that helps lay the basis of liberal feminist consciousness. Whether or not one thinks that many of the women who identify as middle class perform working-class jobs (as they have been defined in terms of the particular needs of monopoly capitalism),[20] typists, clerks, waitresses, secretaries, and so forth often identify as middle class. It is true that most women who work in the labor force do wage and salaried work that is alienating and exploitative and can easily be defined as working class in this "objective" sense. But this does not help one understand that these very workers may identify as middle class. This disparity between one's reality and one's consciousness of it is important to understand because it highlights the role of ideology in inverting reality for us.[21] Once one has internalized aspects of the society's ideology, reality is perceived in its inverted or manipulated form. In this process ideas and reality are no longer totally separate.[22] Hence a woman who performs a working-class job and identifies as a middle-class person has to be defined in terms of the totality of these two spheres and must be dealt with politically in these terms. Her feminist consciousness reveals a dynamic particular to her middle-class expectations as it reflects the rhetoric of equal opportunity and the limitations placed on these expectations by the sex-gender system.

There are real economic-class differences among women that cannot be fully explained by speaking of the middle-class woman as merely a reflection of false consciousness (i.e., as a mystification of her true working-class nature). Nevertheless, working-class and middle-class women (especially married women) share much more in reality than their consciousness of their economic class might lead one to believe. The shared experience of the "working mother" cuts across economic class lines, as does the definition of woman as childbearer and rearer and domestic. The fact that 97 percent of the telephone operators are women cuts through traditional economic-class divisions. The way ideology intervenes to distort reality, and the way this becomes reproduced through our consciousness, is highly important in understanding how working-class reality and middle-class consciousness can be reflecting similar relations of the patriarchal system while supposedly representing different political realities.

What are the needs of our society as they currently define working-class and middle-class women? What effect does the acceptance of woman as "working mother" have on the system of male privilege? Will supports for "working mothers" continue in such a way as to protect the basic sexual hierarchy of society, or will they undercut it? While the need (in terms of unemployment) is to limit women's options in the labor force, inflation requires that women remain as "working mothers." As such the conflict that exists has developed out of woman's dual role in the labor force and her life at home—the ideology of liberal individualism and the reality of sexual dependence.

These conflicts are partially reflected in the divorce rate, which has doubled in the last ten years. The number of households headed by women has increased by more than a third in this decade, having more than doubled in one generation.[23]

These changes have begun to challenge the present organization of the family. The question is whether these changes can be guided by feminist priorities or whether the state will retain its control in this latest stage of the historical and political development of the family.

THE ADVANCED CAPITALIST PATRIARCHAL STATE AND FAMILY

How does one begin to understand the state's role in the maintenance and reproduction of patriarchy? Is there an official governmental position on the family that does not necessarily coincide with other interests in the state? Is today's problem for the state that it has not arrived at a cohesive policy on the family but rather has multiple and conflicting ones that reflect the several levels of conflict that have arisen between capitalism and patriarchy?

The question of how the state chooses to deal with the arising conflicts between the needs of capital and the needs of patriarchy has to be understood in terms of the political relations and purposes that define the state in the first place. Instead of thinking of the state as an abstract thing, one needs to understand it as a political relation that grows out of the political need to mediate conflict and to create order. The state intervenes to maintain and reproduce social cohesion[24] of the political totality. In order to do this the state must maintain the hierarchical relations that structure both the relations of capital and the sex-gender system, through a system of social patriarchy.

The state involves the (1) governmental apparatus with its relatively autonomous[25] relation to the (2) economic class structure and (3) sexual hierarchical order of the society via the family. The state represents these interests, but because they often are in conflict with one another today, it must stand apart from the whole, while it sorts through how to promote the totality. The bottom line for the state is always the protection of the capitalist patriarchal system as a whole. However, the choice of *how* to go about this ultimately reflects the relative autonomy of the state. It is within this limited realm of choice that conflicts internal to the state appear.[26] The structural aspects of the state are supported through the system of ideological supports—for example, the media—and through the entire system of law. The ideological apparati[27] involve the media; the church, as it operates as organized religion; and the education system, defined as the formal cultural training structured through the schools. The social relations involved in these networks, which are primarily responsible for the maintenance and reproduction of patriarchal ideology, reflect the state's involvement and investment in patriarchal relations. The system of law organizes the above relations as it regulates all social relations. The legal formulation of the sex-gender system, through marriage law, abortion law, day-care law, and so forth monitors the relations of familial patriarchy. The state oversees the way the law connects the ideology of patriarchy with its practice and with the needs of the political totality.

The institution of marriage through the system of law directly connects the family to the relations of the state and indirectly maintains its ideological justification. From its inception the family is political. Levi Strauss has stated that "... the structure of the family always and everywhere, makes certain types of sexual connections impossible, or at least wrong."[28] Legitimacy of children becomes part of the system of control. "The important thing is that every society has some way to operate a distinction between free unions and legitimate ones."[29] The organization of such relations is most definitely a concern of the political order and as such is dealt with by the state. The question is not whether the state, a representative of the power relations of society, has a policy on the family, but rather what the policies are.

The difficulty in understanding the state's policies on the family is related to the way ideology tries to cloak them. For instance, the family is presented through today's ideology as private and hence unrelated to the public functions of the state. Even discussions like Christopher Lasch's,[30] which accuse the state of invading the privacy of the home, are premised on the division and hence reproduce the mystifications about the family as historically apolitical. This ideological cloaking, which is a part of the political relations of the state in the first place, tries to cover up the fact that the legal system as an arm of the state operates both directly (abortion law)[31] and indirectly (marriage law) to define woman's options as a mother within the family.

Today state intervention is being used for the purpose of smoothing out the conflicts between the ideology of liberal individualism and the ideology and reality of male dominance. Factions within the state are trying to reassert patriarchal control by challenging existing abortion rulings, publicly funded day care, the ratification of ERA, and homosexual rights. These four policy areas during Carter's Presidency represented the arena for conflict between the conservative right and the center liberals, inside and outside the state apparati. The center liberals, represented by Carter, supported the program of stabilizing the patriarchal family while protecting the image and reality of the "working mother." Their problem was to figure out how to do this, given the real conflicts that existed within the state itself between the center and the conservative right headed by Reagan, as well as the new levels of (liberal) feminist consciousness in the country. The state's activity serves to mediate these conflicts and grows out of the irreconcilability of these conflicts.[32]

For instance, Carter's support of the ERA can be understood and hence reconciled with the huge political mobilization against it when one sees that he was trying to reassert some sense of patriarchal order in the family without denying woman's role in the economy. After all, the ERA does not address the question of patriarchal control or sexual hierarchy; rather it legitimizes it in (liberal) equal opportunity terms. Carter's faction of the state realized that women's equality before the law is an adjustment that the state has to make in order to stem the tides of (liberal) feminist struggle, which otherwise might lead to more radical indictments of society. Carter understood that a law cannot make equality or *by itself* change dominant social relations. Representatives of the state know this, although they

disagree among themselves on how best to manipulate the pro-ERA feeling of the liberal feminists, who believe real equality can be won through the law. Carter understood this and therefore could support the ERA (while doing nothing to actually get it ratified) in the hopes of demobilizing the liberal feminist movement and at the same time gain electoral support. Liberals within government knew how large the (liberal) feminist movement and its support was and is. What they did not understand was that Carter's record on the ERA and other women's issues had been so bad that he would not be able to mobilize this feminist support against Reagan in 1980. As a result, antifeminists (who are a minority) voted for Reagan, and feminists (who are a majority of the public) did not vote. Hence Reagan's win.[33]

The important point to recognize is that although profeminist forces may be on the defensive since Reagan's election, they represent the view of a majority of men and women today. Polls reaffirming a woman's right to decide about an abortion and information gathered from polls on the ERA document this majority support. One needs to realize that the New Right developed in large part in order to counter the gains made by the women's movement. The women's movement, which made major gains throughout the 1970s for women, is now forced to devise a workable politics for the '80s—one that takes into account and tries to counter New Right strategy. Not until this happens can the women's movement regain the offensive.

The conflicts that appeared in Carter's administration, in the 1980 election, and now under Reagan reflect the enormous conflict that exists within the state about how patriarchy—the sexual differentiation and hierarchy that maintains the relations between men and women—can be restabilized in an advanced capitalist economy that requires a majority of married women to work in the labor force. Conflict within the state about how to restabilize the family, however this unit comes to be defined for the 1980s, exists between Reagan, New Right forces, center-Republicans, and Democrats of the center, right, and left. They all agree, however, that new family policy is needed and is central to dealing with the present crisis of liberalism and the capitalist patriarchal state.

Although it may appear that the Reagan state is hegemonic, it by no means is unified on a "rightist" position enforcing the traditional patriarchal family. Conflicts reflect different visions of how best to revitalize patriarchal society and with it capitalism. The right obviously believes it needs to reassert patriarchal control by denying many of the feminist gains made by women for abortion since the 1973 Supreme Court ruling legalizing abortion. Those of the "center" within the state know that these gains are related to women's ability to work and remain in the labor force, and they understand that this is a necessity in an economy in which the wages of 46 percent of the jobs are unable to support a family of four.

These issues of patriarchy and the capitalist economy are intimately connected to each other. Jerry Falwell, leader of the evangelical right and Moral Majority (which is neither), documents these dual concerns in *Listen America.* When writing about the rights of children, he states that they should have the right "to have the love of a mother and a father who understand their different roles and fulfill their different responsibilities . . . to live in an economic system that makes it possible for husbands to support their wives as full time mothers in the home and that enables families to survive on one income instead of two."[34] He is angry and critical of the economy and inflation because it has eroded the place of the father in the family. "The family is the fundamental building block and the basic unit of our society, and its continued health is a prerequisite for a healthy and prosperous nation. No nation has ever been stronger than the families within her."[35] According to Falwell, the father's authority must be reestablished and with it the order of society. In this sense, the fight against abortion is the fight to reassert patriarchal control.

I would also argue that President Reagan's economic policies seek to *redefine the relationship between the state and the family* as much as they attempt to deal with the question of inflation. The proposed 1981–83 budgets limit and curtail the responsibilities of the (welfare) state and increase the responsibilities (and supposed freedom) of the family. The real question is which family Reagan and the right are imagining when they propose their budget cuts. How is the single-parent welfare family supposed to absorb the budget cuts? How is the woman-headed, working-class family (which defines a majority of women-headed households) supposed to cope? Perhaps the hope is that choice will be curtailed to none other than the traditional patriarchal family mode.

The two-parent family, with the father earning the income and the mother at home with two children, applied to only 17 percent of all families in 1980. How can one protect the traditional patriarchal family when it no longer exists for a majority of individuals? More disturbing is the question whether this model can be forced on people with no other options, even though it has become anachronistic for the advanced capitalist economy.

By asserting the role and purposes of the family *against* the state, the 'New Right' hopes to reestablish the power of the father in the family. According to Jerry Falwell, government has developed at the expense of the father's authority. "The progression of big government is amazing. A father's authority was lost first to the village, then to the city, next to the State, and finally to the empire."[36] I think the state will have to look beyond the traditional patriarchal family to resolve the contradictions between capitalism and patriarchy. Those representing "center" interests in the state recognize that this is an outworn model and therefore continue to seek a model that can create cohesion for the capitalist patriarchal state.

Because the state does not operate independently of the struggles that take place between conflicting economic class and patriarchal needs, its policies can often be contradictory. The conflicts can reside within the federal government itself, as they do now, between antiabortion forces and those who support population control and hence support abortion. This conflict reflects the tensions between the right and the center that exist in agencies like Health and Human Services (formerly Health, Education, and Welfare). In other words, the state is not unified on a position on abortion or the family in the same way the Trilateral Commission and southern cowboy forces conflict over aid to the flow of capital to the Southwest.

These conflicts within the state both reflect and reproduce the present conflicts in society.

If we are to understand the family as a part of patriarchal history, we have to understand the family as it develops through real struggles with the state. This is part of the present-day politics of the family that needs to be understood so that feminists fight against family policies that seek to reinstitute the traditional family —which no longer exists for a majority of men, women, and children—and not settle for policies that merely seek to adapt the family to the pressures of advanced capitalism. Richard Viguerie of the New Right was correct when he stated that the family will be to the 1980s what the Vietnam war was to the '60s and '70s. Feminists need to ensure that they remain a part of this struggle over the family because it is the same struggle that will make possible women's liberation.

NOTES

1. I wish to thank Beau Grosscup, Miriam Brody, Mary Ryan, and Ros Petchesky for reading earlier drafts of this paper.

2. See Wini Breines, Margaret Cerullo, and Judith Stacey, "Social Biology, Family Studies, and Anti-Feminist Backlash," *Feminist Studies* 4, no. 1 (February 1978): 43–69; and Elizabeth Pleck, "Two Worlds in One: Work and Family," *Journal of Social History* 10, no. 2 (Winter 1976): 178–95.

3. My thanks to Mary Ryan for clarifying this distinction for me.

4. See Nancy Chodorow, *The Reproduction of Mothering: Psychoanalysis and the Sociology of Gender* (Berkeley: University of California Press, 1978); Dorothy Dinnerstein, *The Mermaid and the Minotaur: Sexual Arrangements and Human Malaise* (New York: Harper & Row, 1976); Gayle Rubin, "The Traffic in Women: Notes on the 'Political Economy of Sex," in *Toward an Anthropology of Women*, ed. Rayna Reiter (New York: Monthly Review Press, 1975).

5. The movement from the two-parent nuclear family to the single-parent family is wrongly understood as a move away from patriarchal relations. It is a reflection of the present challenges to the system of male privilege, but it is already being readapted to the needs of patriarchal power.

6. *The Random House College Dictionary* (New York: Random House), p. 974.

7. See James Mohr, *Abortion in America* (New York: Oxford University Press, 1978).

8. Chodorow, *Reproduction of Mothering*.

9. For an excellent discussion of the breakup of the self-sufficient family as a unit of production with the advent of capitalism, see Roberta Hamilton, *The Liberation of Women: A Study of Patriarchy and Capitalism* (London: George Allen and Unwin, 1978).

10. See Linda Gordon, *Woman's Body, Woman's Right* (New York: Grossman, 1976).

11. See my "Developing a Theory of Capitalist Patriarchy and Socialist Feminism," in *Capitalist Patriarchy and the Case for Socialist Feminism* (New York: Monthly Review Press, 1978).

12. See C. B. MacPherson, *The Real World of Democracy* (London: Oxford University Press, 1966) and *The Political Theory of Possessive Individualism* (London: Oxford University Press, 1962), for a full explication of equal opportunity theory and its limitations.

13. My discussion here is indebted to my sister, Sarah Eisenstein. Her dissertation, "Working Women's Consciousness in the United States, 1890-W.W.I" remains unfinished due to her long battle against cancer and her early death. Also see Mary Ryan, *Womanhood in America* (New York: New Viewpoints, 1975).

14. S. Eisenstein, "Working Women's Consciousness," chap. 3, p. 42.

15. See Baxandall, Reverby, and Gordon, *America's Working Women* (New York: Vintage, 1976); Heidi Hartman, "Capitalism, Patriarchy, and Job Segregation by Sex," in Eisenstein, *Capitalist Patriarchy*; and Sheila Rowbotham, *Woman's Consciousness, Man's World* (London: Penguin, 1973) for a discussion of how woman's role as mother is reinforced by her options in the labor force.

16. *Newsweek*, 6 December 1976, p. 69.

17. *Newsweek*, 15 May 1978, p. 67.

18. Gerder Lerner, quoting from Sylvia Porter's "What's a Wife Worth," in Lerner, *The Female Experience: An American Documentary* (New York: Bobbs-Merrill, 1977), p. 110.

19. See Harry Braverman, *Labor and Monopoly Capital* (New York: Monthly Review Press, 1974), for a discussion of the structural changes in the labor force and the effect on clerical labor.

20. Ibid.

21. See Karı Marx and Frederick Engels, *The German Ideology* (New York: International Publishers, 1947), for a discussion of the meaning of ideology and its relation to material forces.

22. See Antonio Gramsci, *Selections from the Prison Notebooks* (New York: International Publishers, 1971); and Nicos Poulantzas, *Classes in Contemporary Capitalism* (New York: Schocken Books, 1974), for a discussion of the importance of ideology and its place within the dialectic.

23. "The Family in Transition: A Challenge from Within," *New York Times*, 27 November 1977, p. 74.

24. See Poulantzas, *Classes in Contemporary Capitalism*, for a discussion of the state's role in social cohesion.

25. See Ralph Miliband, *Marxism and Politics* (Oxford: Oxford University Press, 1977); "The Capitalist State: Reply to Nicos Poulantzas," *New Left Review* 59 (January/February 1970): 53–60; and "Poulantzas and the Capitalist State."

26. I am indebted to Miliband's discussion in *Marxism and Politics* and to Poulantzas for their discussion of the relative autonomy of the state, although neither one discusses the question of autonomy in terms of the needs of patriarchy.

27. See Poulantzas, *Classes in Contemporary Capitalism*, for an intriguing discussion of the role of ideology in relation to the state.

28. Claude Levi-Strauss, "The Family," in *Family in Transition*, ed. A. Skolnick and J. Skolnick (Boston: Little, Brown and Company, 1971), p. 63. Also see Claude Levi-Strauss, *The Elementary Structures of Kinship* (Boston: Beacon Press, 1969).

29. Ibid., p. 57.

30. Christopher Lasch, *Haven in a Heartless World* (New York: Basic Books, 1977).

31. Mohr, *Abortion in America*.

32. See Hal Draper, *Karl Marx's Theory of Revolution, State and Bureaucracy*, vols. 1 and 2 (Moscow: Progress Publishers, 1970), for a discussion of the state, although their understanding of the irreconcilable conflicts stemmed from the relations of the economic class structure of capitalism. Patriarchy has no identity on the state level.

33. Zillah Eisenstein, "Antifeminism in the Election and Politics of 1980," *Feminist Studies*, Summer 1981.

34. Jerry Falwell, *Listen America*! (New York: Doubleday, 1980), p. 148.

35. Ibid., p. 121.

36. Ibid., p. 26.

3

Jean Grossholtz

Battered Women's Shelters and the Political Economy of Sexual Violence

I work in and with and for a battered women's shelter. It is clear to all of us that this is the battlefront; that the women we see are the walking wounded; that others are still held captive by economic, social, and ideological forces; and that still others are dead or will soon be killed. Battered women, sexually abused women and children, victims of rape, women who live in fear and shame simply because they are women—this is the everyday reality of patriarchal power, and each story makes clear the connection between the state and patriarchal power.

Violence against women is a political problem of fundamental importance to the feminist movement. To understand that it is political, that it is deeply rooted in the political economy of the United States, is also to understand that the "state" will not, indeed cannot, act to eliminate this violence. Those who still seek, out of necessity, state support in the form of the criminal justice system, social service agencies, and the legislature must realize the limitations and the dangers of that support. Although the focus of this paper is battered women and the creation and maintenance of refuges and support systems for women who live in daily fear of their lives, the analysis applies in the broader areas of all of our lives whether we are academics or lawyers, waitresses or secretaries. Class and race are not protections. These statuses are not irrelevant to our struggle and our personal security, but they are irrelevant to our fundamental status as objects of men's violence.

What is violence against women all about? We now know that it is extremely common. Sixty to 70 percent of all married women experience some physical violence from their husbands.[1] One in every three women will be raped in her lifetime.[2] Estimates of incestuous abuse of children run as high as 34 percent of all children, and more than 90 percent of these children are female.[3] National statistics show one in four women under the age of eighteen have been sexually abused.[4] The standard statistic of the shelter movement is that one woman is beaten every eighteen seconds in the United States. How have we lived with this knowledge? Why is this not a national disgrace?

We know from studies of rapists and batterers that these are ordinary men, indistinguishable from nonrapists and nonbatterers.[5] They come from every walk of life, from every status in society. And we know that in the case of rape and battering it is most often planned, deliberate, unprovoked, an expression of male power and aggression.[6]

Knowing these things, feminists have understood that such violence is a way of keeping women in their place, that it is functional to patriarchy. Fear of this violence forces us to seek male protection, to restrict our movements, to seek safety in the private sphere of the home rather than engage in an active public life. Although we have known and understood these facts about violence against women, we have ignored their ramifications. To face this reality and make sense of it requires us to understand the role of the state and the requirements of our own liberation.

The state is a set of power relations that has the exclusive right to use force to maintain those relations.[7] These power relations assume the dominance of males in public positions, politics, economic life, and social life—that is, patriarchy. These power relations also assume the dominance of private ownership of property and the private right to make decisions about its use—that is, capitalism. Thus the state maintains a given distribution of power in the society through its actuations, which may include the ultimate sanction of force, and that distribution of power can be described as "capitalist-patriarchy."

It is axiomatic that we live in a patriarchal society. It is also axiomatic that the political economy incorporates and maintains that form of social power. But the economic requirements of capitalism did not create patriarchal power. Capitalism made use of a power structure that already existed.

The male need to dominate women comes out of a deeper, more fundamental concern.[8] Their need to control women rises out of their desire to ensure the availability of women as sexual partners by enforcing on women the absolute requirement of phallic-centered sex. Combined with a desire for control over the reproductive process, and probably anger at the loss of the mother, male aggression has historically been expressed against women. Male determination to control and define women's sexuality and reproduction as reflections of phallic-centered sexuality has taken the form of imposing compulsory heterosexuality and mandatory motherhood on women.[9]

Patriarchal power is maintained by socialization into sex roles that support compulsory heterosexuality, that decree motherhood and wifehood for women, and that encourage all of us to believe that this is natural and therefore unchangeable—indeed, unchallengeable. We are rewarded for conformity and punished for stepping outside these roles. Violence against women is a means of hammering home the message that women belong to men, that women's bodies are men's property. Living with this violence, women have come to understand the need to circumscribe their behavior. We no longer ask why or how or what for. We are accustomed to being told, after reports of rapes, not to go out alone, to lock our doors, to remain in lighted areas. No one suggests that there should be a curfew for men until the rapist is found. No one suggests restraints on men's freedom. Women are expected to, and do, accept the responsibility for this violence. The fear of such violence that women internalize is essential to the maintenance of the power structure of patriarchy. After all, no social group can define half its members as the property of the other half and as not fully persons without some ultimate form of coercion.

The power relations of sexuality and reproduction are not simply social forces but are integrated into the economic system and enforced and maintained, in part, by the political system. These relations take different forms and perform different functions depending on the needs of the economic system. Kinship patterns and inheritance, for example, are deeply integrated with economic needs.

Capital accumulation is the base requirement of capitalism. An important aspect of capitalism that we often ignore is the need for the aggregation of capital through inheritance. In a patriarchal society, male control of property is critical. Under capitalism, the need to ensure large accumulations of wealth for investment ties the question of inheritance directly to the economic system. Women's reproduction must be controlled in order to allow property to pass along the male line. Men must know their sons, estates must pass intact from generation to generation. Marriage contracts among the poor are of little importance; among the wealthy, they are vital. Under capitalism, the state becomes the agent for enforcement of the property relations of marriage and inheritance.

The accumulation of capital imposes other requirements that lend themselves to patriarchal exploitation. Inequality is fundamental to the creation of surplus labor and a cheap labor force. The exploitation of the labor of others, the impoverishment of many, the misuse of the land and natural resources—these are part of capitalism. Therefore it serves capitalism to divorce concern for human life, childrearing, nurturance, and a good quality of life from public affairs. The divorce of those assigned those tasks from participation in economic decisions is necessary to keep what are, in effect, contradictory values and motives out of those decisions. By the same token, those who are assigned participation in those decisions must be divorced from those concerns or convinced that they are less important or not relevant. Think of the contradiction of a human person assigned and committed to mothering and rearing a child making decisions to pollute a river, possibly the town water supply, in order to accumulate profit. To divorce men from these feelings, from these concerns, to convince them that self is more important than other, that man-made creations are more important than natural, that successful human development is measured by material success, is vitally important to capitalism's existence. Without the willing participation of most of the population in behavior consistent with the needs of capitalism, the state's coercive role would have to be expanded with the attendant diversion of some profits to pay the cost of such coercion.

Capital accumulation requires that the goods produced bring a return beyond the cost of labor used in their production. Keeping the cost of labor as low as possible is a central aim of the economy. Capitalism needs a population that is disciplined and ready to report for work each morning, to do whatever job is assigned them, motivated to strive as hard as possible to produce as much as possible during the workday and willing to accept the least amount of wages in return.

How is that labor force created, trained, and made ready to go to work every morning at the least cost? One half the population is assigned roles labeled "wife" and "mother" with the unpaid task of bearing and rearing children and nurturing them and the men currently in the work force. Through its control of birth control information, abortion rights, and support for medical research on reproduction, the state imposes mandatory motherhood when it suits the needs of the economy and allows some alternatives when the economy requires a cutback in population. And the system assures that men will stay firmly in control of women's reproduction, of women's bodies.

In another area, that of organizing society and socializing its members to accept the behavioral requirements that are imperative to the political economy, the nuclear family is a key structure. The family maintains the sex-role stereotypes so essential to the provision of a labor force. The family also allows for power to be exercised, to be played out in ways that provide catharsis for men who are powerless in their workplace and in their polity. Denied meaningful participation outside the home, they are assured of power within the home. The family teaches and disciplines children to these power relations.

The maintenance of the family unit depends on the acceptance by women of the self-effacing, submissive roles of wife and mother. It depends on women identifying themselves with men as secondary beings, as of less importance in the public world, as requiring male protection. It depends on a socially enforced insistence on heterosexism, on the unchallenged expectation that women are economically, socially, and sexually dependent on men. Even when the economic position of men is undercut by poverty, unemployment, or racist exclusion, men's control of women is assumed.

Controlling the availability of child care, creating pressures on mothers to stay with their children, keeping wages for women low, defining women's work outside the home in terms of the jobs they do inside the home, sustaining the normative assumption that women are wives and mothers and not part of the labor force—these are evidences of state control of women's lives in support of the economy and male dominance. That this ideology is maintained in the face of clear evidence that most women work, that many head families, and that very few families fit the model of a working husband and a wife at home is evidence of its power. The film *Rosie the Riveter* lays out with great clarity the manipulation of women by the state. When women are needed in the work force, as in wartime, child care is provided, the media message changes to encourage women to work, and the insistence that children need their mothers at home is forgotten.[10] When women are no longer needed in the labor force, reversion to the norm is explicit and immediate.

One of the more devastating requirements of this set of power relations has been the imposed separation of women by race and class. The deadly silence about women's lives generally applies even more forcefully when black women are concerned. Only as sex objects or as "mammies" do they appear in the ideology of patriarchy. Black women have always worked, have always headed families, have never been on pedestals (although there is a notable similarity between the pedestal and the slave block), and have never been regarded as weak and in need of protection.

The silence about black women's lives is devastating in its impact and most ironical in discussions by white women that implicitly assume that all women are white. In this way we cooperate in our own oppression. Consider also the imposed divisions of women by class when class itself is determined by the status of males we are assigned to. It is important to the economic and political order that we identify with our class and its privileges and not with our sisters. I think of this often as I open boxes of precleaned, precut, prepackaged chicken for supper and realize that this was brought to me by the nearly slave labor of black women at such places as the Sanderson chicken plant in Laurel, Mississippi, and that huge corporate profits are made out of providing me this convenience. The systematic exploitation in which I participate extends to the women of Asia, Africa, and Latin America whose labor fashions my running shoes, sews together my softballs, assembles my wonder electronic watch—in short, provides for luxury consumer goods at cheap prices. These contradictions we ignore at our own peril. Our identification with the world of consumption, with our class privilege and not with our sisters, is critical for the maintenance of capitalism *and* patriarchy.

The historical betrayal by white women of their sisterhood and ties to women of color is a reality that cannot be denied and will not disappear. The ramifications of that betrayal for our struggle to create a truly feminist politics that will embrace the oppression of all women are painfully and continuously present. That historic experience of identification with white male power has embedded in white women's consciousness and behavior rejection and disempowerment of black women. White women's struggle to transform themselves into feminists will have to be fought out against the racist requirements of the capitalist patriarchy. The structure of the society and the economy is such as to actively reward conformity and punish deviance. The handful of women who have been accepted into the higher ranks of the legal, academic, and business professions have learned to mold their behavior to be tough-minded and male-like and at the same time feminine enough to meet male needs for women as subordinate human beings. These adaptations are most often conscious and deliberate, understood as survival skills among the oppressed.

Violence is the ultimate means of curbing women's attempts to break away from the roles assigned to them by the capitalist patriarchy. By allowing men to be, as Kathy Barry puts it, "out of control with permission," by imbedding in male and female personality the idea that women's sexuality is the property of men, in the marriage bed and in the streets, the state acting through the laws, the police, the courts, and even the medical establishment has made women take the responsibility for the violence done to them.[11] It is her fault if she goes to his dormitory room with him, or does not give him what he wants when he wants. And "it" is any number of violent acts.

Knowing this, living with this fear, women consciously and unconsciously circumscribe their lives to take on the responsibility for protecting themselves from the arbitrary sexual violence of men. Assured that her place is in the home, that she cannot raise her children alone, that her work will never be paid sufficiently to support those children, she accepts her need to stay in a relationship with a man, regardless of his violence. Bombarded with the message that women are only fulfilled in relation to a man, she manipulates her body and face to attain a model of beauty that will meet male ideas of proper womanhood. Cut off from her sisters, encouraged to deny her own sensibilities, a woman becomes a nonperson, little more than the appendage to the man she has attracted.

Political scientists have developed theories of terrorism to account for the fact that entire populations appear to accept and conform to oppressive systems. Terrorism, they say, disorients people because terrorist acts are arbitrary, unpredictable violence. There appears to be no pattern, no clear cause, no direct understandable link between the victim's behavior and what happens to him or her. In such situations human beings become extremely cautious, conformist. Such is the reality and effect of violence against women; it is political terror.

Consider what happens when a woman is raped. Consider what happens when a woman calls the police because her husband is beating her. Consider what happens when a female child tells someone her father has molested her. The criminal justice system appears most often to have tried the victim. They have not aimed to punish the male violater. They have colluded in the violence.[12]

The struggle of women to force change in laws, court procedures, and police reaction, and to provide care and aid for the victims, has been long and difficult. How does one account for the resistance we have encountered? The enormity of the task in the face of the heart-stopping statistics on violence against women indicates the functionality of this violence for the political economy. The state is not simply a difficult mechanism to work with to accomplish our goals — it is antagonistic to those goals.

At the most basic level of human services we have seen this resistance in practice. The battered women's movement, the attempt by women to create safe shelter for women unsafe in their own homes, has met enormous resistance, has had to fight hard for funding, and has been constantly buffeted by forces that would distort and misdirect the goals. State agencies are concerned with keeping the family together at any cost—at the cost of woman's mental health, of a child's self-esteem, even of physical survival. The needs of women and the basic requirements for an adequate support system to help women out of these dangerous situations contradict the state's purposes.

It is not easy to get a woman to leave the dangerous situation. This in itself—the fact that many women stay in living situations where they are regularly beaten, stomped, cut, raped, and abused—is testimony to the effectiveness of the social system in training persons for their roles in life. Women who have been persistently abused, mentally and physically, have lost their self-esteem and have come to regard themselves as valueless. Such women fear that they cannot provide for themselves or their children, that they cannot make it on their own. Most often they believe that somehow what is happening is their fault. Relatives and the churches very often encourage them to believe that they should stay and make the best of it.

Unless a man is willing to undergo therapy to work out his problems, to radically change his behavior and his view of his wife and family, there is little hope the battering will cease.

Battered women's shelters were initially created by women for women, although in recent years, as the need has grown more apparent, city and state agencies have contributed to the creation of shelters. But the state, acting at every level, sees shelter as temporary, an interlude in a couple's life together. Marital disputes, as they are euphemistically called, are none of the state's business. But rarely is the violence occasioned by a dispute. Most often it has no understandable cause. Women often report confusion, a lack of understanding of what is happening to them. It can be triggered by a burned meal, a sharp word, a crying child, an expressed desire to get a job or go to school, or simply being in a room. The terminology "marital dispute" implies a disagreement between husband and wife, an argument in which both are participants. Incidents of violence rarely have that character; yet the courts, the police, and the social service agencies would have us believe in that designation, would have us think these were understandable and extraordinary conflicts. In reality, we are discussing a crime called assault and battery, often assault with a deadly weapon. It is a crime that leaves the victim wounded, often hospitalized. Batterers act as if such assault was no crime, was of no great import. They expect forgiveness. Often they turn from battering to wanting sexual intercourse with their wives; rape is frequently part of the battering incident. From all sides the woman is encouraged to believe that the incident is "normal," and in fact for many women it becomes just that—a normal, expected part of their lives. The pressure to stay in the home and in the marriage is tremendous; the pressure to return after a cooling-off period is equally great.

It is important to understand that the state does little to help such women, provides little hope for them if they choose to leave their husbands. Such services as the state provides may only exacerbate the extreme self-deprecation these women suffer after years of beating and violence. Governmental bureaucracies at federal, state, and local levels are constructed to create a necessary separation between client and administrator, between the person needing help and the giver of help. This is part of the control system of bureaucracies. Inherent in this system is the idea, implied or expressed, that the client is somehow responsible for the problem. Somehow the client has been unable to cope and is therefore less successful, or less of a human being, than the person behind the desk. The client has few rights in the situation; she is not an individual but a "case," and cases have explicit requirements. Such a system automatically destroys self-esteem and self-worth in the individual who seeks help. The operation of human service agencies, from welfare offices to unemployment offices, tends to follow this model. Partly this is to make sure that selling one's labor to capitalist enterprises remains more attractive than the alternative. Frequently, individuals hired by these agencies attempt to operate differently, to treat the people they serve as valued persons with rights. Such individuals often make a difference to the people they serve, but they rarely survive.

A battered women's shelter cannot operate on this basis. It would be a contradiction in terms. The physical abuse a woman has suffered is necessarily accompanied by emotional and psychological abuse. A shelter's purpose is to give women the strength to demand that they not have to live in fear of violence. To do this a woman must come to value herself, to grow in self-esteem, to understand her rights, to honor her individuality.

Help for battered women requires some very special qualities that are alien to state-run human service agencies. First, the shelter staff cannot separate themselves from the women in shelter. In a fundamental sense we are all battered women; the experiences of one woman match the experiences of all. The separation of shelter persons into staff and client is contradictory. What is required is mutual understanding, bonding between women, and a sense of common problems and common experience. Such an atmosphere is necessary for a battered woman to find solace, support, and strength to renew her confidence in herself. That woman's connection with all women must be validated by the shelter staff. This requires that the shelter embody a clear, unequivocal understanding of the causes and effects of violence against women, that any hint of women as the cause of their physical endangerment be eliminated. One of the basic requirements of shelter staff, paid or volunteer, is a commitment of one's self beyond the simple job assigned. The qualifications and credentials that one could list for a staff person are not those of degrees or administrative experience. An effective battered women's shelter is one with a basic total commitment to women and to helping women take control of their lives and their children's welfare. This means an ongoing commitment to helping battered women understand that what has happened to them is not unusual or self-inflicted and, most important, that they need not and should not live in fear. In a sense shelters bring women "through the looking glass," allowing them to understand that the violence is not "normal," not acceptable, that it is an outrage. The shelter staff seeks to help women take themselves and their skills and capacities seriously and take charge of their own lives.

The administration and organization of a shelter also differs from that of state agencies. Administration and rules can never be more important than the needs of women. Hierarchies and chains of command place barriers between women that continue patterns of control. Hegira, a battered women's shelter in Westfield, Massachusetts, began life as a program administered by a large human services agency along with a number of other government funded agencies.[13] Within weeks, conflicts developed between the umbrella agency and the shelter. The shelter staff did not create a hierarchy, so it was hard to hold one individual accountable. The shelter staff developed a collective process and a weekly support group to talk about intrastaff problems. This seemed strange, if not ludicrous, to the host agency. Issues arose over hiring and firing, over community outreach forums that limited attendance to women, over evaluations of staff performance, over what appeared to the staff to be too much paperwork. In truth, the human services agency was acting out of well-established processes for bureaucracies. Hegira was acting out of different motives. The goal had redefined the structure, and the structure did not fit with the expectation of the state definition. This was an inevitable conflict. The end result was Hegira, Inc., a separate, nonprofit corporation that runs a shelter for battered women through methods and with manners that would turn any government bureaucrat purple.

The operation of the shelters assumes a form and structure out of step with societal ideas of structure and power. The shelters embody, consciously or unconsciously, a feminist politics. Shelters are radical forces in the midst of human service agencies and radical threats to the ongoing political economy of violence. A battered women's shelter cannot take the maintenance of the nuclear family or sex-role stereotypes as its goal; it must by its nature work against the agenda of the political economy. It is no wonder that shelters have difficulty finding adequate funding, that they are almost entirely private or voluntary organizations, and that they are castigated as hotbeds of man-haters and marriage wreckers. These are attempts once again to deny the reality of violence against women, to blame the victim and those who would assist the victim rather than confront the set of power relations that such violence sustains.

The ideology of patriarchy, expressed through academic, economic, and social mechanisms and enforced through rewards provided by these structures and punishments meted out for deviance from them, is so well integrated into our personal world views as to be invisible. Thousands of women have lived and still live in constant fear and danger; they accept their lot as punching bags for their husbands. The fact is the willing participation of the population in the basic sexual dominance of males over females allows for, and even encourages violence. Definitions of human personality, individual purpose, and life expectations in terms coherent to patriarchal power, on the one hand, and capitalist power, on the other, are powerful social facts that have shaped our lives. The ideology asserts in many shapes and forms that this distribution of power is natural; like economic man, like greed and materialism, male dominance is natural. Because it is natural, it is also assumed to be unchangeable, necessary. That, too, is part of the ideology.

The only models for change available within this context are models that prevent change, that only hold out the possibility that women (or other excluded persons) can, if they adopt the right behavior, follow the right stream, achieve the position that white men have held. But the woman corporation president can still be raped, is still one with the pornographic images of women on billboards, is still an alien in the language, and is still a silent figure in history and literature. Divorced from her sisters, isolated in an individualistic philosophy, she has won the dubious privilege of living part of her life "just like a man." To see change through these means is to become part of the resistance to change.

To develop strategies of resistance that will change these power relations requires a clear understanding of the forces maintaining the system and their interests. Violence against women is not a haphazard, unrelated phenomenon that has simply been overlooked by the criminal justice system. It is no accident that the response to rape is to sweep women, not rapists, off the streets. Patriarchal power requires random violence as the means of compelling women, through fear and endangerment, to submit to self-depreciation, heterosexuality, and male dominance in all spheres of life. Capitalism has integrated this historic set of relations into its relations of production. The economic system rests squarely on male dominance, and the political system that supports and maintains that economy also supports and maintains male dominance. It is important to understand that this is the case. We must no longer allow these relationships of power to be invisible. The first step to change is to recognize reality.

NOTES

1. Murray Straus, "Wife Beating: How Common and Why?" *Victimology* 2, nos. 3–4 (1977–78): 443–58; Murray Straus, "A Sociological Perspective on the Prevention and Treatment of Wifebeating," in *Battered Women*, ed. Maria Roy (New York: Van Nostrand Reinhold, 1977); and Del Martin, *Battered Wives* (San Francisco: Glide, 1976), pp. 11–15; these summarize the statistics. Lenore Walker, *The Battered Woman* (New York: Harper & Row, 1979), asks, "Who are the battered women?" and answers, "If you are a woman there is a 50% chance it could be you" (p. 19).

2. Allen Griswold Johnson, "On the Prevalence of Rape in the United States," *Signs* 6, no. 1 (Autumn 1980): 136. Johnson found that "a conservative estimate would be that 20–30 percent of girls now 12 years of age would suffer a violent sexual attack during the remainder of their lives." This statistic excludes infant and child sexual abuse, which many experts place even higher. Johnson, in response to a male critic of his article, replied that he had himself disbelieved the statistics but had reexamined his data, checked his methods with demographers, and was left with the inescapable conclusion that sexual violence is pervasive and that "the normal functioning" of the social system entails violence against women. *Signs* 6, no. 2 (Winter 1980): 349.

3. Florence Rush, *The Best Kept Secret: Sexual Abuse of Children* (Englewood Cliffs, N.J.: Prentice-Hall, 1980), pp. 4–5 *passim*; Ann Wolbert Burgess, *Sexual Assault of Children and Adolescents* (Lexington, Mass.: Lexington Books, 1978); Louise Armstrong, *Kiss Daddy Goodnight* (New York: Hawthorn Books, 1978); Sandra Butler, *Conspiracy of Silence: The Trauma of Incest* (San Francisco: New Guide Publications, 1978).

4. As reported at the National Conference on Child Abuse and Neglect, Milwaukee, Wisconsin, 7 April 1981. *See New York Times*, 8 April 1981.

5. Stanley Brodsky, "Sexual Assault: Perspectives on Prevention and Assailants," in *Sexual Assault*, ed. Stanley Brodsky and Marian J. Walker (Lexington, Mass.: Lexington Books, 1976), pp. 1–7; A. Nicholas Groth, "The Rapist's View," in *Rape Crisis and Recovery*, ed. Ann Wolbert Burgess (Bowsie, Md.: R. J. Brady, 1979).

6. Duncan Chappell, Robley Geis, and Gilbert Geis, eds., *Forcible Rape: The Crime, the Victim and the Offender* (New York: Columbia University Press, 1977), esp. Chap. 14.

7. I use the term "state" because it denotes a broader conceptualization of power than either government or political system. Both of the latter terms have come to have limited scope of concerns. In this paper "state" refers to the authoritative allocation of values and the authority to exact conformity to rules by means that can include the threat or actual use of force. The state can act at local or national levels.

8. I am aware that academic readers would feel more comfortable if I stated these ideas as propositions, as hypotheses. By distancing myself from them and avoiding direct

responsibility for my thoughts I could be considered more academic. I take the risk of being dismissed in order to take the responsibility for what I think is true.

9. I have been enlightened and influenced by Adrienne Rich, "Compulsory Heterosexuality and Lesbian Existence," *Signs* 6, no. 1 (Autumn 1980); and Marilyn Frye, "To be and Be Seen: Metaphysical Misogyny," *Sinister Wisdom* 17 (1981).

10. See, for example, Francine D. Blau, "The Data on Women Workers, Past, Present and Future," in *Women Working*, ed. Ann Atromberge and Shirley Harkness (Palo Alto: Mayfield, 1978), esp. p. 37: "Between 1940–45 the female labor force expanded by 5.5 million and 38% of all women 16 and over were working. But the 1947 figures indicate that considerable ground was lost in the immediate postwar period." See also U.S. Department of Labor, Women's Bureau, *Handbook of Women Workers, 1979*.

11. Kathleen Barry, Female Sexual Slavery (New York: Avon 1981).

12. The likelihood of a conviction for rape increases when the defendant is black or is a member of another racial minority, particularly if the victim is white. The political economy is heavily invested in racism and the need to keep nonwhite men under control.

13. As was the case for most shelters, the early financing often included Community Development block grants and CETA staff positions. The Reagan administration has all but eliminated these sources.

4

Eileen Boris
Peter Bardaglio

The Transformation of Patriarchy: The Historic Role of the State

The 1980s opened with a new sense of the American family in crisis. Much of this sense of crisis had its roots in the revived political struggle over the family, a struggle that has engaged a wide range of forces. Feminists and gay activists, on the one hand, have sought self-determination within the family or autonomy from it. On the other hand, church fundamentalists and political conservatives of the New Right have tried to restore the traditional patriarchal family in which the father reigned supreme. In either case, the central focus of the political conflict has been the role of the state in families. This essay explores the historical evolution of this role and concentrates on the transformation of patriarchy from the power of men within families to the power of men through the state—a change facilitated by innovations in public policy and the law and accompanied by profound social tension.[1]

THE ARGUMENT

The historical relationship among families, the status of women, and the formulation of laws and public policies for governing the household remains largely unexamined.[2] Yet if social scientists and policy makers are to comprehend fully current issues involving families, these issues need to be put in historical perspective. History provides a way of thinking about the past that helps us understand and define the present; it serves to expand our sense of how the past becomes the present and what alternatives exist as a result.[3]

In this essay we argue that American families, the status of women, and the laws and public policies regulating the household underwent significant changes over the course of the nineteenth and early twentieth centuries, but at the same time certain key continuities remained. Alterations in laws and public policies left many men with less legal power in the family by the end of the period. This does not mean, however, that patriarchy was destroyed; instead, it was transformed. The

The authors wish to thank Carl Degler, Irene Diamond, Jim Gilbert, and Heidi Hartmann for their comments and criticisms on earlier drafts of this essay. Responsibility for the final product, of course, belongs solely to the authors.

long-run impact of this process was to preserve the subordinate status of women in American society in a new form.

Before proceeding to the historical analysis, we should clarify the terms central to our argument: patriarchy, law, public policy, the state, and the family. In particular, the current use of the concept of patriarchy is far too general and vague. We need to examine the specific means by which male domination of women has been maintained during various historical periods. The source of women's oppression has not been biological differences as such, but the social relations constructed around these differences. And, clearly, these relations and the sexual conflict and struggle that have resulted from them have varied over time and place.

More specifically, patriarchy can be viewed as the struggle between women and men to control women's labor power. Controlling women's labor power allows men to restrict women's options primarily to childbearers and rearers. As Zillah Eisenstein notes, however, it is important to distinguish between the roles of childbearer and rearer. While it is the biological assignment of women to bear children, it is the political assignment of women to rear them. The role of the woman as mother, then, is both a universal condition and a historically created one.[4]

The law has played a central historical role in expressing and shaping patriarchy. If patriarchy is defined in its strictest terms as the reduction of the wife to the status of property owned and controlled by the husband, it is true that patriarchy has never existed in the Anglo-American legal tradition. Yet because patriarchy has not existed in this absolute sense does not mean that it is incorrect to use the notion of patriarchy as defined above to describe the relations of legal power in American families during the nineteenth and early twentieth centuries.[5]

The concept of law employed here is not the conventional one of an institutionalized system of jurisprudence. We would argue that the law deals with social relations and that changes in the law cannot be considered apart from society. The law, as E. P. Thompson insists, is an ideology that expresses social relations in a peculiar form that both serves and legitimizes the power of dominant groups. Legal change, in this sense, is the product of conflict between dominant groups and those that seek to share power with them or replace them entirely. In either case, the ability of a group to influence the institutions of social control or the system of social relations is obviously at stake.[6] Yet patriarchy as a specific system of hierarchical relations is not fully embodied in the law. While the law does define and protect many male privileges, others exist without laws to define them as such. There is no particular law, for example, that says women will rear children. By defining what is law and nonlaw, though, the law historically has limited women's options and roles largely to those concerned with childbearing and rearing.[7]

In the United States the law has provided the foundation for the multistoried building of public policy. Chief executives—presidents, governors, and mayors—further define policy when they announce executive orders, propose legislation, and send enacted legislation to appropriate agencies for enforcement. Ultimately, of course, public policy is forged in the minute decisions made by those directly involved in translating statutes into rules and regulations, and in interpreting them on a daily basis. Here we focus on the broad policy decisions of federal and state governments because we are concerned with public policy as a means to maintain male power.

The state has been the arena for the operation of public policy and the consequent transformation of patriarchy. By the state, we mean the structure of society through which those with power rule. The state acts, in other words, to legitimize the structures of dominance and subordination in society. For feminists, in particular, this means that we must consider how the state both reinforces and extends the structures of male dominance.[8] Thus it becomes crucial to examine historically the ways in which the state has initiated social control over women, especially control over their labor power and sexuality, both in the family and outside of it.

Finally, in considering the family, we focus on its historical rather than its biological dimensions. Instead of viewing the family in universal terms, we regard the family as a kinship unit composed of various ages and sexes whose structure varies over time and among classes, races, and cultures. In this sense, as far as the American past is concerned, it is more accurate to speak of "families" rather than "the family." Yet people in the past spoke of "the family," not "families," when formulating public policy. Moreover, by the 1830s, the state sought to maintain a particular family norm: the nuclear family of domestic mother, children, and breadwinner father. For this reason, we refer to "the family" throughout the remainder of this essay.

Given these definitions, it is now possible to frame our argument in more specific terms. During the nineteenth and early twentieth centuries, the state through changes in law and public policy increasingly intervened in relations between husbands and wives, parents and children. The growth of state intervention occurred especially in families deemed to have failed in some way, such as families that lacked the economic resources to be self-sufficient. Yet the rise of the liberal welfare state shaped even middle-class families. Although these families were preserved as economically private units with the evolution of the modern state, this evolution also led to the recognition of the individual rights of women and children within self-supporting families. The recognition of these legal rights posed a serious challenge to the previously undisputed power of husbands and fathers. Hence, the emergence of the welfare state did not erode the family as such, but it did begin to undermine the patriarchal structure of relations between women and men within many families.

The decline of familial patriarchy, however, did not lead to the destruction of male dominance in society at large. Instead, the state moved to replace the family as the main force that structured patriarchy in the broader society. In other words, as the state eroded familial patriarchy, it became the new linchpin of social patriarchy—the organization of hierarchical gender roles and relations throughout society. The nineteenth and early twentieth centuries thus saw not the decline of patriarchy but its transformation from a familial to a state form.[9]

An important reason for this transformation was the change during the 1800s in the status of children. As industrial capitalism developed, children became less valued for the immediate, unskilled labor they had provided in older, agrarian societies. Instead, children became increasingly valued for their future skilled labor as members of the industrial labor force. For this reason, children—and the labor required to raise them—changed in the 1800s from a property that men wanted to control to individuals who required a great deal of attention and training.

To assist women in this newer mode of childrearing, a system of state patriarchy emerged, and through the process of rationalization, increasingly took over childrearing itself. Laws and public policies—as well as governmental institutions and professional supervision by doctors, educators, social workers, and other so-called family experts—developed as part of a larger support system that reproduced patriarchal social relations. Consequently, male-dominated—even male-headed—families became less important to the maintenance of male domination in the social arena outside the family. Of course, despite changes in law and public policy, patriarchy persisted in many families. More important, increasingly egalitarian legal relations in families were counterbalanced by the continued economic exploitation of women at home and in the workplace.[10]

FAMILY LAW IN THE NINETEENTH CENTURY

American family law underwent a profound shift in the nineteenth century. Important changes took place in laws relating to property rights of married women, divorce, child custody, and adoption. These nineteenth-century legal developments expressed alterations not only in relations between husbands and wives, and parents and children, but also between the state and families. As wives and children won certain individual rights and as relations between family members became more egalitarian, the relationship between families and the state grew more unbalanced in favor of the latter. In this way, the basis was laid during the 1800s for a new form of patriarchy, one that centered on the state rather than the family.

The main function of family law in nineteenth-century America, in terms of patriarchal dominance, was to reinforce and maintain the ideological distinction between the public and private realms as one based on gender differences. This distinction was certainly not new in American culture, but with the rise of the factory and wage labor it was increasingly justified on the basis of the reorganization of work away from a previously self-sufficient home. This redefined separation between public and private, then, provided the foundation on which a transformed patriarchal power structure was erected in the late 1800s. Most importantly, the state—through the law and other institutions—assisted in the restriction of women's roles primarily to childbearing and rearing within the home as the norm, while it legitimized men's participation in economic and political activities outside the home.[11]

The crucial transformation was accomplished during the nineteenth century in two overlapping but distinct stages, with the dividing line being roughly the Civil War. Between about 1790 and 1860, as Michael Grossberg observes, family law was refashioned to promote the rights of individual family members at the expense of the patriarchal family. The traditional model of patriarchy derived from English common law in which the male head of the family was considered supreme; it was replaced with an updated version in which wives and children possessed interests and rights recognized by the law. With this new concept of the family, theories of individualism and distinctive legal identities were substituted for the older, more organic view, and the contract became the central metaphor for describing relations between family members.[12]

Antebellum family law, however, did not eliminate paternal superiority. Married women and children before the Civil War did not achieve equal legal footing with husbands and fathers in either the courts or statute books, and women and children remained subordinate members of the family. In this sense, antebellum legal shifts functioned to preserve patriarchalism by bringing it more in line with bourgeois notions of individual rights and humanitarianism.

Following the Civil War, the focus of American family law shifted from an assertion of rights for individuals in families to an effort to exert greater public control over family life. What was new in the second half of the nineteenth century was the attempt to link individual family members directly to the state rather than through the male head of the family. The division of the household into separate legal personalities, which characterized the first half of the nineteenth century, made use of government authority in the second half much easier because this division had begun the process of breaking down the older patriarchal family, which had acted as a buffer between individuals and the state.[13] Hence the achievement of individualism and some degree of autonomy for women and children was part of a larger social and political process that led to the ascendancy of the state in American families.[14]

Christopher Lasch has pointed out that the course this transformation took was one of the central ironies of nineteenth-century America. Because state intervention in family life undermined traditional patriarchal authority, women accepted state and professional assistance when it was offered. But in the long run the state expanded its control over domestic life "not only at the expense of patriarchal authority but also at the expense of the authority formerly exercised by women over childbirth, child rearing, and domestic economy."[15] This change, however, did not result from a conspiracy perpetrated on women. Indeed, some women took an active part in this transformation of family life in the nineteenth century. Middle-class women—and a few immigrant women—consciously allied themselves with professional experts such as doctors, lawyers, educators, and social workers to help carry out these legal and political changes.[16]

The loosening of the individual husband's power—a fundamental precondition in the replacement of the family with the state—could be seen especially in the alterations of family property laws during the mid-1800s that gave married women property rights for the first time. The significant restrictions placed on these rights even after the passage of the early married women property laws reflected the fact that state patriarchy during the nineteenth century was only emerging and that the husband still held sway to a significant degree over the family.

Under English common law, elaborate rules and regulations governed the property rights of married women. But underlying these rules was one central doctrine: marital unity. Essentially this doctrine stated that upon marriage, men and women merged into one legal personality, with the husband acquiring absolute ownership of the wife's personal property and lifetime ownership of her lands. The wife had no legal personality; thus, for all intents and purposes, she became legally invisible. The law did allow a father or other relative to establish a separate estate for the woman, either by a premarital settlement or by way of a trust.

In colonial America, these English doctrines and practices were recognized and to some extent followed. Different social and economic conditions—in particular, the shortage of women and labor and the abundance of land—helped enlarge the legal powers of married women in several significant respects. All in all, however, married women before the American Revolution gained only limited advances in their capacity to own property.[17]

The first major reforms in married women's property rights came with state statutes passed in the mid-nineteenth century. These early statutes granted married women greater latitude to deal autonomously with their property in certain situations. They did not, however, grant married women full legal equality in economic matters. No antebellum statute, for instance, clearly provided that the wife was entitled to money or property that she earned during the marriage.

The major motive behind much of the legislation granting married women some property rights was to rationalize land transactions and codify colonial precedents, not to effect any radical changes in relations between spouses. Nevertheless, as Norma Basch contends, this systematization had important implications for the legal contours of the patriarchal family because the legal recognition of women as individuals within American families eroded the doctrine of marital unity.[18] Most important, these changes in the law of family property brought married women into contractual relations with the state, making it easier for the state in the late nineteenth century to encroach further on familial patriarchy as it moved toward a new construction of male domination in the broader society.

This same process could also be seen in the reform of divorce laws during the nineteenth century. As in England, divorces in colonial America were difficult to obtain, and consequently they were rarely granted.[19] Following the American Revolution, divorce remained uncommon, but laws regarding divorce varied widely from state to state. South Carolina, for example, remained a divorceless society until the Civil War, and New York granted divorces only for adultery. But most states during the early nineteenth century expanded on the limited precedents of the colonial era in two ways: They enlarged the range of legal grounds for divorce, and they implemented judicial divorce. Indiana, in particular, went further than any other state before the Civil War in broadening the grounds for divorce. Besides traditional grounds such as adultery, bigamy, and desertion, Indiana's statutes recognized cruelty, habitual intoxication, and conviction for a felony. An open-ended "omnibus clause" also allowed divorce for "any other cause for which the court shall deem it proper that divorce shall be granted."

In addition to this expansion of grounds for divorce, the change in legal procedure for divorce marked a significant development in antebellum American law. While most states before 1800 granted divorces through private bills passed by the legislatures, during the early nineteenth century many courts gained the power to grant divorces as a result of new general statutes. These changes in divorce law reflected important changes in the nineteenth-century concept of the family rather than a sign of family breakdown. The underscored an increasing awareness of the wife's legal personality with the family, as well as crucial gains in individual rights for women. This growing legal equality of men and women within families created enormous pressures, and as William O'Neill observes, divorce became "the safety valve that [made] the system workable."[20] But it was a peculiar kind of safety valve, for it led to a rapid accumulation of power in the hands of the state to determine the internal dynamics of families.

Specifically, as Jane Turner Censer notes, nineteenth-century divorce was "above all an adversary proceeding. To obtain a divorce, the plaintiff not only had to prove the spouse's 'guilt' but also show his or her own 'innocence.'" In other words, one party had to demonstrate that he or she was "worthy" of divorce. For a woman, this involved showing that despite provocation from the husband, she had preserved her fundamental virtue. In this way, members of the bench in deciding whether to grant divorce to a woman measured her against a standard of behavior constructed by the paternalistic state apparatus. Domesticity, propriety, and submissiveness thus all played a critical part in determining whether a divorce would be granted to a woman.[21]

Divorce reform also developed out of the desire to protect women from being victimized by their husbands. As Lasch argues, "it was not the image of women as equals that inspired the reform of divorce laws but the image of women as victims." The typical female image of women in nineteenth-century divorce cases was that of a wife abused by her drunken husband, deserted and left with children to rear and support. In short, as far as divorce was concerned, the achievement in the 1800s of some legal equality for women stemmed from a paternalistic attitude toward them that undermined the notion of equality as readily as it strengthened it.[22] The patriarchal responsibility for women shifted, however, from the male head of the family to male judges.

Child custody was another area of American family law in which changes during the nineteenth-century strengthened the position of women (and children as well) within families but not necessarily in the larger social arena. Under English common law, the father as the unchallenged head of the family possessed almost unlimited right to the custody of his minor offspring. Custody law treated children as little more than pieces of property in which fathers had a vested interests, rather than as individuals whose welfare and interests were legitimate legal issues. The lack of custody rights for married women, like the lack of property rights, rested on the doctrine of marital unity.

In America, colonial law made few inroads into the paternal orientation of custody rules.[23] But after the revolution, American courts undercut the father's absolute custody rights in several important ways. While English courts for the most part refused to deny the father's paramount right to custody, American courts during the early nineteenth-century developed an expanded authority to use judicial discretion in deciding child-custody disputes, and hence to modify the paternal custody right. The outlines of a distinctively American law of child custody began to appear in the early 1800s as courts in this country increasingly declined to enforce the father's custody right as absolute.

In custody disputes between parents, American courts began to consider the welfare of the child, an examination closely linked to the concept of parental fitness. Thus in exercising their discretion courts began to pay attention to the needs of the child and to evaluate the ability of the parties in the dispute to supply the child with the special nurture required to develop fully. This evaluation led to the development of the "best interests of the child" doctrine, which took into account such factors as the age, gender, and health of the child, as well as psychological and material considerations.

Despite some resistance among conservative judges to the loss of the father's paramount custody right, by the late nineteenth century state courts had come to recognize the equal rights of mothers to custody. American courts in the late eighteenth century had begun to grant mothers custody of their illegitimate children, and during the mid-nineteenth century married women began to gain certain custody rights in disputes involving legitimate children. In part, this was due to the growing woman's movement of these years, but more important was a growing belief in domesticity. That is, the judiciary increasingly considered women as uniquely suited to childrearing. It was this apparently natural maternal instinct, the courts agreed by the turn of the century, that most strongly supported women's claims to custody. The development of the "best interests of the child" doctrine had the effect, then, of improving the mother's probability of gaining custody since the courts generally assumed that giving custody to the mother best served the child's interests. By the early twentieth century, mothers had not only equal rights to custody under the law but superior rights in practice. Mothers gained these rights not because they possessed greater power than the father but because the courts viewed them as better able to meet the obligation of childrearing that the state wanted fulfilled.[24]

During the second half of the nineteenth century, courts also exhibited an expanded willingness to acknowledge that biological parents did not always have custody rights paramount to those of third parties. The development of a more child-oriented theory of guardianship reflected in this shift led to a greater emphasis on emotional and psychological ties and away from the traditional patriarchal stress on blood ties. This new theory of guardianship recognized the child as a legal individual and reformulated the parent-child relation in contractual terms. The courts stressed that custody involved not only rights but also responsibilities for the child.

The impact of this new contractual notion of the parent-child relationship was particularly apparent in the development of legal adoption. English common law had refused to recognize the legality of adopting children as heirs and had insisted that parental authority could not be transferred to third persons. But with the development of a voluntary transfer doctrine and a growing emphasis on the welfare of the child that accompanied changes in American child custody law, statutes legalizing adoption began appearing, first in Massachusetts in 1851 and then in many other states within the next quarter-century.[25]

The courts (and behind them the state) gained in the 1800s, then, the power to deny the traditional common law claims to custody on the part of both fathers and natural parents. This development played a central role in the growth of state intervention in American families. While mothers and third parties gained rights at the expense of fathers and natural parents, they all lost power to an increasingly paternalistic state.

Clearly, the "cult of domesticity" played a central role in undermining familial patriarchy. For the demands for the recognition of married women's property rights, along with demands for divorce and child-custody laws favoring the wife, all arose out of the logic of domesticity itself. As far as women's overall status in society was concerned, however serious limitations were inherent in this logic. Granting married women custody rights to their children, for instance, on the basis of their special capacity as mothers to provide nurture did not challenge gender roles in the larger society. Instead, it reinforced the development of separate spheres along gender lines and confined the elevation of women's status to within the family. But the "cult of domesticity" did make women responsible for the protection of the family's moral interests. By taking advantage of this ideology, as Carl Degler suggests, women not only gained more autonomy within marriage but also launched social movements to eradicate prostitution, reduce the level of alcoholic consumption, and protect women from sexual abuse. Thus middle-class women actively altered the outlines of the patriarchal family in pursuit of their own interests. They turned the "cult of domesticity" against itself, and in the process contructed the foundation of modern feminism.[26] Yet men's continued control over female labor at home and in the workplace undermined the victory of these middle-class women.

REGULATING REPRODUCTION

The battle over family limitation in the nineteenth century further demonstrated the shift from familial to state patriarchy.[27] Before the Civil War, legislators and judges were noticeably reluctant to interfere with parental efforts to control the size of their families. Adhering to the dominant ideology of the family as a private sphere, antebellum courts and legislatures made only halting efforts to regulate childbirth.

By the end of the 1800s, however, most states had declared abortion and contraception obscene and illegal. Over the course of the century, then, the state dramatically increased its power over women's efforts to control reproduction.[28]

By and large, pre-Civil War legislation and litigation upheld the common law view that abortion before quickening was acceptable.[29] In *Commonwealth* v. *Bangs* of 1812—a case that gained wide attention—the Massachusetts bench embraced the common law of abortion and thus removed the threat of prosecution from most women who decided to terminate their pregnancies. Subsequent statutes in Massachusetts and New York in 1845 strengthened state control of abortion, but largely by punishing its procurers rather than its users.

The medical establishment spearheaded the nineteenth-century drive against abortion, depicting abortion as a direct assault on the family and the natural function of women. In response to the new statutes and pressure from antiabortionists, the courts in the mid-1800s began to turn abortion into a crime regardless of the stage of fetal development. Repeatedly, judges justified the restriction of abortion on the basis of a desire "to guard the health and life of the mother against the consequences of such attempts" to terminate pregnancy. While they criminalized abortion, antebellum judges shied away from punishing a woman who ended her pregnancy. As Chief Justice Green of the New Jersey Supreme Court argued, "The statute regards her as the victim of crime, not as the criminal, as the object of protection, rather than of punishment."[30] The duty of the state, in short, became the paternalistic protection of women and motherhood.

Laws restricting the availability of contraception, and the court cases upholding them, reflected a similar paternalistic reasoning. Anthony Comstock, head of the New York Society for the Prevention of Vice, led the drive against contraception, which resulted in the passage of a federal act in 1873 that labeled all forms of contraception and abortion "obscene" and banned them from the federal mails. With the "Comstock Law," the state attempted to impose Victorian mores on an increasingly ethnic working class. Although the federal act became the central weapon of the middle-class purity crusade, state laws along the same lines were also passed in the late 1800s.[31]

More than class values were involved in these efforts to regulate contraception. Bans on the dissemination of birth control proposed "to protect purity, to preserve chastity, to encourage continence and self-restraint, to defend the sanctity of the home, and thus engender in the state and nation a virile and virtuous race of men and women," according to Massachusetts Chief Justice Samuel Rugg in the celebrated case of 1917, *Commonwealth* v. *Allison*.[32] The legal attack on contraception, in other words, involved an attempt to uphold the Victorian notion of womanhood. Courts and legislatures attempted to take control of reproduction from women and place it with the state. In contrast, challengers to this repressive sexual order—both free-lovers and feminists—sought a woman-centered means to limit reproduction. While their solution of "voluntary motherhood" rejected mechanical devices and frowned upon abortion, it emphasized the power of women to control their own bodies by saying "no" to men.[33]

After the Civil War, the courts continued to perceive women as victims rather than accomplices in abortion. But the antiabortion crusade of the late nineteenth century succeeded for the most part in convincing judges and legislators to abandon the quickening doctrine. The elimination of this doctrine underscored the end of legal tolerance for abortion. By the turn of the century, an impressive arsenal of laws existed with which to convict abortionists.[34] Nevertheless, the new legal ban on abortion did not stop its use or end the debate on the power of the state to regulate reproductive rights.

Laws on prostitution, like those on abortion and contraception, punished the providers of services and rarely their clientele. Police linked regimentation of prostitutes to the preservation of domestic purity; they even sought to prevent "pure" women (who might be morally soiled) from trying to reform "fallen" women.[35] A similarly paternalistic concern to protect motherhood, as we have seen, motivated judges to prosecute abortionists. Thus the state moved during the nineteenth century to control both female sexual behavior and reproduction.

THE FAMILY WAGE

By the late nineteenth century, changes in family law had loosened the power of fathers within families, allowing increased individual rights for wives and children. Yet the impact of expanded government intervention was more complex than these developments suggest. Formal equality outside the home was tenuous in large part because by the turn of the century the state actively sought to codify the ideal of the family wage as the norm. Certainly, the family wage—a wage for the male breadwinner adequate to support the entire family—became a reality for only a small number of highly skilled and organized workers. But during the Progressive era (1890–1920), the state encouraged this ideal by limiting participation of women and children in the work force through protective labor legislation, child labor laws, and compulsory education.

Social reformers, many of them women and supporters of unionization, helped push public policy in this direction. The push was part of a broader strategy to maintain social order in a period of intensified conflict between workers and employers. In addition, it was a response to the increased assault by capital on the family, for these years saw a significant growth in the numbers of women working. This growth in female employment made it impossible to ignore the contradiction between women as individual wage workers and as moral bulwarks of the home. Support for the family wage, then, became part of an effort to reinforce the domestic roles of women as mothers, wives, and housekeepers.

The emergent state patriarchy that child labor laws, compulsory education, and protective legislation helped create was incomplete and did not necessarily conflict with the interests of employers. Immigrant wives and daughters, whose numbers swelled with fresh recruits from southern and eastern Europe, remained contributors to the family economy, although often as workers in sweated industries in the home rather than in factories. Large numbers of black women also earned wages.[36] Nonwage-earning wives became a reserve army of labor, and wage-earning wives formed a labor pool for low-pay, sex-segregated employment. Thus the family wage had a dual function: It bolstered men's power over women and children, and it facilitated the efforts of capital to segment the labor force along gender lines.

It should be pointed out that the move toward the family wage and protective legislation was seen as a way not only to weaken the economic power of women but to relieve mothers from arduous work. At a time when unregulated industrial capitalism posed a serious threat to worker safety and health, female reformers, trade unionists, and much of the working class viewed the protection of women and children as a positive goal.

But the demand for a family wage took the form of a bargain between fathers: capitalists and their employees.[37] The capitalist father would pay the working-class father enough so that the working-class child could go to school, where class relations became reinforced and children were socialized for their place in society. Employers also indirectly benefited from the services that the wife performed to reproduce the labor power of the husband/employee. Moreover, male unionists, like printers and cigarmakers, could more easily restrict the supply of workers in their trades if state-sponsored disincentives curtailed employment of daughters and wives. As Heidi Hartmann has contended, the inequalities women faced in the labor market pushed them back to the security of the family wage, that is, to dependence on men for economic support even though women's unpaid labor at home made it possible for men to earn a livelihood.[38]

Disincentives to female employment took two forms: male resistance on the shop floor and laws regulating female and child employment. As Ava Barron and Ruth Milkman have pointed out, male resistance to women entering the trades was neither inevitable nor merely a consequence of patriarchal attitudes.[39] Male printers and other craft unionists rejected working with women more because women were semiskilled operatives than because they were women. But as Milkman reminds us, the ideology of domesticity was strongly embedded in craft-union efforts to restrict the supply of workers. This ideology mirrored the reality of married women's labor force participation; even in 1900, merely 14 percent of all working women above the age of ten were wives.[40] Yet these mothers supplemented wages of fathers and children through close budgeting (consumption work), by keeping boarders (domestic labor), or by taking in piecework (sweated industry), while their daughters entered manufacturing. In general, skilled craftsmen were unsuccessful in preventing daughters from labor force participation (if only because many families needed the income), just as they failed to control the introduction of new technologies or halt the deskilling process. Shop-floor resistance never fully determined the sexual composition of the labor force, and yet it helped shape the conditions under which women were relegated to a secondary, lower-paid labor market.

Protective legislation was crucial to the creation of this secondary labor market.[41] Such legislation—in the form of maximum-hour laws, minimum-wages laws, and sanitary requirements—restricted the hours and conditions under which women worked. At a time when no health or safety regulations existed, when few women were in unions, and increasing numbers of daughters were entering the work force, such legislation seemed necessary. But why were men not covered? And why did branches of organized labor, like the Wisconsin Federation of Labor and the Building Trades Material Council of Chicago, actively promote the prohibition of women from trades? "National" interest and male self-interest merged as protective legislation defined all women as potential mothers. Women were seen as a class apart from men; like children, they were "wards of the state," requiring state protection. This assumption seemed logical to the judges in the first major protective legislation case, *Commonwealth* v. *Hamilton Manufacturing* (1876). The court rejected protective legislation for men because such legislation interfered with the so-called sanctity of contract. But freedom of contract, the judges reasoned, could hardly apply to dependent women.

Trade unionists also based their justification of protective legislation on the ideological identification of woman as mother and dependent. In the words of one AFL spokesperson, "it is to the interest of all of us that female labor should be limited so as not to injure the motherhood and family life of the nation."[42] The most influential statement of this argument appeared in the 1908 Supreme Court decision *Muller* v. *Oregon*, which upheld protective labor legislation for working women. Agreeing with the assumption of the famous Brandeis brief, that industrial conditions weakened women's health, the justices codified a new form of state paternalism. They justified state intervention in the labor contract because, "as healthy mothers are essential to vigorous offspring, the physical well-being of woman becomes an object of public interest and care in order to preserve the strength and vigor of the race."[43] Here was sex discrimination in the guise of protection; anatomy became destiny, and that destiny led to the home. As Alice Kessler-Harris has put it, "protective legislation recognized that women had two jobs, one of which had to be limited if the other were to be performed adequately. Yet legislation institutionalized the primary place of the home by denying that women were full-fledged members of the working class."[44]

Women's exclusion from jobs meant that men faced fewer competitors. During World War I, molders, coal miners, and other industrial workers successfully protested the introduction of women workers. Middle-class women in government agencies, while they sought to expand female employment opportunities and secure equal pay for equal work, also supported protective legislation. Whatever the impetus behind the laws—whether to lessen competition from skilled workers, as male craftsmen advocated, or to regulate and improve the workplace for unorganized women, as female reformers urged—limiting women's work options bolstered the power of men as a group. In short, like the family wage, protective legislation had its humanitarian side, but its benefits for women were ambiguous.[45]

Moreover, the state's assumption of familial authority only partially impeded the needs of industrial capitalism. If women had formed a greater proportion of the labor force in manufacturing, then protective legislation would have revealed a more serious contradiction between the needs of patriarchy and those of capitalism. But most women worked as domestic servants and agricultural laborers—sectors not covered by the law—in the early 1900s, and by the 1920s, they were filling clerical and other unprotected white-collar jobs. While laundries, canneries, restaurants, department stores, and the like eventually fell under the law, weak enforcement and legislative loopholes allowed employers to continue to exploit cheap female labor in these sectors. Protective legislation not only helped to restrict women to the domestic sphere, then, it also sustained labor market segmentation.

INSTITUTIONALIZING FAMILIES

We have focused so far on how alterations in law and public policy affected families headed by middle-class and skilled workers. We need, however, to explore in more detail the way in which the development of patriarchal state power varied with class over the course of the nineteenth and twentieth centuries. As pointed out, during the first half of the 1800s, judges and other officials were reluctant to interfere with the internal governance of middle-class families. Instead, they viewed the role of the state as restricted to the recognition of individual rights of family members and to the encouragement of familial autonomy.

While women and children from economically self-sufficient families gained individual rights before the Civil War, members of indigent families found themselves subjected to harsher and more repressive legislation. Stripped of all effective power during the antebellum years, they were brought into a dependent relationship with the state. The family law of the poor, as Maxwell Bloomfield observes, sought to regulate this dependency "through various forms of public relief that respected neither domestic privacy nor individual rights." The connection between the state and poor families, then, was coercive rather than contractual. At the very time that middle-class wives gained at least some increased power over their persons and property, poor women had their freedom of movement curtailed and their children taken away by public officials.[46]

As David Rothman and Michael Katz have demonstrated, the insitutionalization of the dependent and "deviant" was one of the most significant innovations in nineteenth-century public policy. By the end of the 1800s the older poor-law system of almshouses, outdoor relief, and apprenticeships had been replaced by a series of new asylums: penitentiaries, reformatories, mental hospitals, orphan asylums, and public schools. Except for prisons, many of these institutions began as private corporations, but the state increasingly took over and expanded them. The state thus played a major role in the transfer of responsibility for the poor and other dependent groups from the family and community to asylums. This governmental initiative in the sphere of social welfare created the basis for the flowering of the welfare state in the twentieth century.[47]

During the nineteenth century in particular, specialized institutions arose to rehabilitate and reform children from indigent and deviant families. Although colonial Americans had placed some children in institutions, apprenticeship had provided the primary means to deal with poor, neglected, and delinquent children. The spread of child-care institutions in the new republic drastically undercut the authority of lower-class parents and marked the most significant shift before the Civil War in the balance of power between the state and families. State statutes incorporating child-care institutions granted them broad authority to intervene in families, and when contested, the courts generally supported the legality of these powers.

The institutional undermining of parental authority did not necessarily mean that the state intervened to weaken the family. On the contrary, as Eli Zaretsky contends, reformers modeled their orphan asylums and reform schools after the "well-regulated family." The aim of these institutions was not to dismantle dependent or deviant families, but rather to reconstruct the character of individual members in terms of the middle-class norm. Of course, asylums and reformatories often fell far short of their declared goal of rehabilitation, and contemporary critics claimed that abuse and exploitation flourished behind institutional walls.[48]

The emergence of a national child-saving movement following the Civil War intensified the assault on the authority of lower-class parents. Beginning with the establishment of the New York Society for the Prevention of Cruelty to Children in 1874, child savers formed societies to aid abused or neglected children throughout the country. In addition, they joined with legislators, judges, and professional child-care experts to strengthen state controls over childrearing. These efforts on the part of child savers, which reaches their climax at the turn of the century, were especially directed at the offspring of the immigrant poor to foster their resocialization to middle-class, Protestant values and habits.

The appearance of juvenile courts in the early twentieth century represented the most far-reaching achievement of the child savers' movement. The Illinois legislature created the first juvenile court in 1899 for Chicago, and by 1920 all but three states had a juvenile court system. The policies of the juvenile courts aimed at keeping families together, but they commonly had just the opposite effect. The courts monitored parents and children under a broadly defined set of statutory guidelines and removed delinquent or neglected children from families that did not conform to reformers' notions of proper domestic life.[49]

The state in its role as parent drastically reduced the legal rights of those falling under the jurisdiction of juvenile courts. For instance, probation officers did not need a search warrant to enter a probationer's home. As a juvenile court judge explained, "With the great right arm and force of the law, the probation officer can go into the home and demand to know the cause or delinquency of a child. . . . He becomes practically a member of the family and teaches them lessons of cleanliness and decency, of truth and integrity." This paternalistic vision of the officer as family member led reformers to overlook the coercive nature of the newly created courts.[50]

The reformers' greatest hope for buttressing gender roles among the lower class lay in the public school system. As noted previously, compulsory education removed working-class children from the labor market and reinforced the function of the father as breadwinner. Moreover, in preparing children for their future place in society, the schools served as agents of cultural standardization. Public schooling reinforced the sexual division of social life central to the society as a whole. Not only did teachers and textbooks promote domesticity and feminine values for girls, but the curriculum itself differentiated along gender lines. Girls learned sewing, cooking, and other domestic tasks; boys, metalworking, carpentary, and other potential industrial skills.[51]

The expanding government intervention in social welfare, then, revealed much less respect for the individual rights of women and children in lower-class families than for those in middle-class families. This heritage of unequal treatment in terms of class—as well as gender—helped shape the welfare state that emerged in the twentieth century.

THE WELFARE STATE: STATE PATRIARCHY TRIUMPHANT

Initiated by the social reforms of the Progressive era and coming to full bloom under the New Deal, the welfare state institutionalized the power of men over women even as it helped to free women from the confines of the nuclear family. The state maintained—even extended—men's superior control over material resources by providing unequal benefits to male and female recipients of entitlement programs. New Deal reformers continued to pursue the goal of Progressive era "social housekeepers," to "clean" the world in order to protect their homes. In essence, the welfare state became the power behind the persistence of the family norm, although it intervened directly only in the lives of the poor or deviant.

The major programs of the Progressive era intended to shore up the nuclear family with its male breadwinner and domestic mother. Workingmen's compensation, for one, allowed the disabled father to receive a wage; federally supervised wage arbitrations placed the ideal of the family wage at their center. Tenement-house reform, pure food and drug laws, and other health measures were to permit mothers to fulfill their duties in safe, clean domestic environments. Social purity legislation, antivice campaigns, censorship, and prohibition became the moral equivalent of tenement cleansing.[52] In most of these areas, it should be noted, women were the rank and file as well as the leaders of reform. They would protect the uniqueness of womanhood just as they would save the special character of childhood (through compulsory education, child labor laws, and a higher age of sexual consent). These female reformers assumed the moral superiority of women and, in this culture-bound manner, worked to make it possible for immigrant and poor women to be true to woman's nature within a familial setting. Nonetheless, as the writings of Jane Addams and Charlotte Perkins Gilman make clear, the fight for better conditions for women and children was also a fight against paternalism as they understood it: the arbitrary power of the father in the family and of the superior in other social relations (such as between employer and employee). But paternalism was assuming a different form in this period, one in which the loosening, if not breakdown, of familial patriarchy coexisted with the emergence of state patriarchy. They very social measures supported by women ironically helped create that new order.

The Mothers' Pension Movement illustrated this irony. Pushed by women reformers as a protection for widows, it reflected the general commitment to the private family. Forty states enacted aid to mothers, widows' pensions, or mothers' pensions between 1911 and 1919. Rather than support child care, legislatures solved the problem of widows with children by paying women to remain at home. Motherhood, in a sense, became a civic function for the state. Women received cash subsidies as payment for service to the state. According to one welfare worker in 1915, "The system of Mothers' Assistance rests upon the theory that a competent child trainer is of greater value to the state than a woman wage earner handicapped by the care of young children."[53] But only mothers lacking the support of husbands qualified. As with protective legislation, eligibility rules and enforcement actually narrowed the options of women, forcing many mothers with small children to work. Rather than subsidize motherhood, Mothers' Pensions promoted female employment in the marginal labor market. Furthermore, the apparatus necessary to enforce the system—inspectors to check that a woman never worked more than one to three days away from home or at night, and to see that no male boarders resided in her home—enmeshed recipients in a net of state paternalism that interfered on a long-term basis with the individuality of welfare mothers.

The New Deal continued to promote motherhood without fundamentally altering the segmentation of the labor market.[54] Instead, its program codified the sexual division of labor within the society, helping to reinforce sexual inequality. Works Progress Administration (WPA) nurseries, for example, provided work for unemployed teachers, mostly women, and gave the children of the unemployed what social workers judged a better environment for family life. Once mothers went off relief, however, they no longer qualified to send their children to government day care. Moreover, married women workers in the public sector particularly felt the budget-cutting knife through implementation of Section 213, "the married persons clause," of the 1932 Economy Act. This law mandated the dismissal or furlough of married people first if their spouse also worked for the government. Ambiguity in the law left decision making in the hands of bureau chiefs; those opposed to the employment of married women discharged rather than furloughed such women even if it meant loss of the woman's retirement benefits. Not until 1937 were enough votes mustered in Congress to repeal an act passed with the deliberate idea of keeping wives at home.

Penalizing working mothers encouraged the domestic norm; so did New Deal relief programs. Under the National Youth Administration, young men constructed highways and built buildings; young women assisted at nursery schools and libraries, performing services once associated with the home. They typed, filed, and carried out other clerical tasks. They also learned sewing. Their jobs simply replicated the major areas of female employment. Black women were placed in domestic service training programs, again a reflection of existing labor market divisions. The WPA displayed a similar pattern. Women found themselves predominantly in canning and sewing or assigned to housekeeping aid projects. Only 12 to 19 percent of workers under WPA were women; specific eligibility requirements—that the recipient be the principal breadwinner, that there be only one recipient per family, and that the recipient prove she or he was truly in the labor market—worked against women. New York City's relief program typically would give aid only to male household heads. Few programs recognized women as a special category, and when they did, as with the 1937 WPA Household Service Demonstration Project, they bolstered traditional sexual divisions.

New Deal labor legislation either excluded women from benefits or reinforced the existing structure of the market. Wage codes under the National Industrial Recovery Act (NIRA) legislated sexual differentials; a full quarter of 465 codes set forth in 1933 put women's wages 14 to 30 percent lower then men's. The "July 1929" clause, enabling employers to pay persons below the minimum wage if their wages as of July 1929 were lower than the code, created a business loophole. So did the exemption of "light and repetitious work," otherwise known as "female work." The NIRA codes also excluded domestic servants and exempted clerical workers at insurance companies with the result that many women were not covered. Yet, while many codes were never enforced, nearly a quarter of women in manufacturing came under them. Improved working conditions may have resulted, along with the right to organize, but women still experienced workplace inequality.[55]

The Social Security Act of 1935 also codified the sexual divisions of the day. By excluding domestics, farm workers, and educational, charitable, and hospital personnel, Social Security left uncovered at least one-third of all married women workers. As conceived, the act provided more benefits to men than women; when in 1939 it redefined the recipient as the worker and his family, Social Security assumed the male family wage as the norm. It actually discriminated against working wives because such women received the same amount as nonworking wives—unless their primary income benefit was more than 50 percent of their husbands'—and they still had to pay taxes on their income.

New Deal welfare programs thus responded to the economic crisis, but through a viewpoint shaped by the domestic ideal. Programs for children especially projected the state as a protective father. Here, too, views of the family reinforced the sexual division of labor, with girls coming out of the Great Depression trained for domesticity or with few skills suitable for anything beyond the marginal female labor sector. Regulation of child labor removed one crucial contributor to the family economy; mothers responded by finding jobs. Their daughters left school on special work permits to stay at home while their mothers worked outside the home. But in later years these daughters clung to the domestic ideal and disapproved of women working, rather than follow their mothers as role models.[56] Daughters acting as mothers and mothers acting as fathers appeared as an aberration of the depression period rather than a product of advanced capitalist patriarchy. By maintaining the domestic ideal and keeping needy families together, New Deal welfare measures supplemented economic programs that were reorganizing capital. Mothers worked because of conditions created by the economic crisis; while the state, as father, prohibited child labor. These results foreshadowed the contradictions between patriarchy and capitalism that would plague the postwar years.

THE PATRIARCHAL STATE AND WOMAN SUFFRAGE

By the outset of World War II, then, patriarchy had undergone a thorough transformation and the state had become the father. Even as it had assisted women in undermining the patriarchal family, the state had institutionalized the power of men over women in the wider social arena. Yet women had also gained the vote well before this time. Did not this significant political victory offset, or at least undercut to some extent, male dominance outside the family?

We agree with Ellen DuBois that the nineteenth-century feminist demand for suffrage directly challenged the ideological distinction between the public and private spheres, especially the male monopoly on public power. Furthermore, as William Leach shows, feminists did not simply embrace the conservative position that suffrage merely extended woman's role as moral arbiter in the family to all of public life. Instead, feminists viewed suffrage, like the recognition of married women's property rights and demands for divorce and child-custody laws favoring the wife, as a means to equalize relations between women and men. Indeed, in an important sense, the demands for reform of domestic relations laws built a bridge between the private sphere of the home and the public sphere of political power. For where middle-class women persuaded paternalistic lawmakers to grant women greater protection in the home, militant suffragists soon followed, demanding the vote for women.[57]

Yet the fact remains that even after women gained the right to vote in 1920, they continued to occupy a subordinate position in society. The radical promise of the demand for woman suffrage failed to materialize, and men still maintained a strong hold over public power. To understand why this happened, we must look not to the strategy and tactics of the woman suffrage movement, but to the timing of the movement's victory.

The demand for the female vote had undeniably radical potential when it first appeared during the mid-nineteenth century as a mass phenomenon. In particular, it posed a serious threat to male dominance outside the family because men had not yet constructed a viable alternative to the patriarchal family for structuring gender relations in society at large. If female suffrage had been achieved during this early period, it might actually have given women the leverage necessary to head off the efforts of men to turn to the state as they were being challenged within the family. We will never know for certain. But we can be sure that after decades of struggle and delay the ratification of the Nineteenth Amendment in 1920 came only once the foundation of state patriarchy was firmly in place. At this point, the far-reaching threat that female suffrage originally posed to the power of men over women was little more than a frustrated cry down the long corridor of the bureaucratic state.

NOTES

1. For general surveys of the current political scene, see Zillah Eisenstein, "Antifeminism in the Politics and Election of 1980," *Feminist Studies* 7, no. 2 (Summer 1981): 187–205; Rosalind Pollack Petchesky, "Antiabortion, Antifeminism, and the Rise of the New Right," in ibid., pp. 206–46; Allen Hunter, "In the Wings: New Right Organization and Ideology," *Radical America* 15, nos. 1, 2 (Spring 1981): 113–38; Christine R. Riddiough, "Women, Feminism, and the 1980 Elections," *Socialist Review*, no. 56 (March–April 1981): 37–54; and Linda Gordon and Allen Hunter, "Sex, Family and the New Right: Anti-Feminism as a Political Force," *Radical America* 11, no. 6; 12, no. 1 (November 1977-February 1978): 9–25.

2. In addition to historical studies on the role of law, public policy, and governmental institutions in families cited below, see Arthur W. Calhoun, *A Social History of the American Family*, 3 vols. (Cleveland, 1917–19); Howard Gadlin, "Private Lives and Public Order: A Critical View of the History of Intimate Relations in the United States," in *Close Relationships*, ed. George Levinger and Harold Rausch (Amherst: University of Massachusetts Press 1977), pp. 33–72; George E. Howard, *A History of Matrimonial Institutions*, 3 vols. (Chicago, 1901); Stanley N. Katz, "Legal History and Family History: The Child, the Family, and the State," *Boston College Law Review* 21 (July 1980): 1025–36; Barbara Laslett, "The Family as a Public and Private Institution: An Historical Perspective," *Journal of Marriage and the Family* 35 (August 1973): 480–92; and Eli Zaretsky *Capitalism, the Family and Personal Life* (New York: Harper & Row, 1973).

The most thorough examination of American family law to date is Michael C. Grossberg "Law and the Family in Nineteenth Century America" (Ph.D. dissertation, Brandeis University, 1979). Other important discussions of state intervention in families include Carol Brown, "Mothers, Fathers, and Children: From Private to Public Patriarchy," in *Women and Revolution: A Discussion of the Unhappy Marriage of Marxism and Feminism*, ed. Lydia Sargent (Boston: South End Press, 1981); pp. 239–68; Jacques Donzelot, *The Policing of Families* (New York: Pantheon, 1979); Zillah Eisenstein, "The State, the Patriarchal Family and Working Mothers," *Kapitalistate* 8 (1980): 43–66; Christopher Lasch, *Haven in a Heartless World: The Family Beseiged* (New York: Basic Books, 1977); Christopher Lasch, "Life in the Therapeutic State," *New York Review of Books* 27 (12 June 1980): 24–31; and Eli Zaretsky, "The Place of the Family in the Origins of the Welfare State," in *Rethinking the Family: Some Feminist Questions*, ed. Barrie Thorne with Marilyn Yalom (New York: Longman, 1982), pp. 188–224.

3. Carl N. Degler, "Remaking American History," *Journal of American History* 67 (June 1980): 22–24.

4. Joseph Interrante and Carol Lasser, "Victims of the Very Songs They Sing: A Critique of Recent Work on Patriarchal Culture and the Social Construction of Gender," *Radical History Review* 20 (Spring/Summer 1979): 25; Heidi Hartmann, "The Unhappy Marriage of Marxism and Feminism: Towards a More Progressive Union," in Sargent, *Women and Revolution*, pp. 13–19; and Eisenstein, "The State, the Patriarchal Family and Working Mothers," pp. 45–9.

5. Norma Basch, "Invisible Women: The Legal Fiction of Marital Unity in Nineteenth-Century America," *Feminist Studies* 5, no. 2 (Summer 1979): 346–47.

6. E. P. Thompson, *Whigs and Hunters: The Origins of the Black Act* (New York: Pantheon, 1975), pp. 262–65; Michael E. Tigar and Madeleine R. Levy, Law and the Rise of Capitalism (New York: Monthly Review, 1977), pp. xiii–xiv; and Eugene D. Genovese, *Roll, Jordan, Roll: The World the Slaves Made* (New York: Vintage 1974), pp. 26–27.

7. Eisenstein, "The State, the Patriarchal Family and Working Mothers," pp. 45–46.

8. David A. Gold, Clarence Y. H. Lo, and Erik Olin Wright, "Recent Developments in Marxist Theories of the Capitalist State," *Monthly Review*, October 1975, p. 36; and Mary McIntosh, "The State and the Oppression of Women," in *Feminism and Materialism*, ed. Annette Kuhn and AnnMarie Wolpe (London: Routledge and Kegan Paul, 1978), pp. 254–89.

9. Brown, "Mothers, Fathers, and Children," p. 240. See also Eisenstein "The State, the Patriarchal Family and Working Mothers," p. 44. Unlike Christopher Lasch, we do not see the growth of state intervention leading to the destruction of the family. Instead, we agree with Eli Zaretsky that such intervention helped to create a new form of family. Zaretsky, however, succumbs to the mistaken view of the family as a monolithic unit in which the interests of men and women coincide. We, in contrast, see state intervention in families as part of the transformation of patriarchy. Changes in family structures, in other words, were inextricably linked with changes in the form of patriarchy. See Lasch, *Heaven in a Heartless World*; and Zaretsky, "The Place of the Family in the Origin of the Welfare State."

10. Brown, "Mothers, Fathers, and Children," p. 242–47; and Hartmann, "The Unhappy Marriage of Marxism and Feminism," pp. 20–27.

11. Eisenstein, "The State, the Patriarchal Family and Working Mothers," pp. 49–52.

12. Grossberg, "Law and the Family," pp. iv, 18–19.

13. Ibid., pp. 338–40.

14. For a comparative perspective on this process, see Donzelot, *The Policing of Families*, pp. 82–106.

15. Lasch, "Life in the Therapeutic State," p. 27.

16. Grossberg, "Law and the Family," pp. 325–28.

17. Basch, "Invisible Women," pp. 347–49; Lawrence M. Friedman, *A History of American Law* (New York: Simon & Schuster, 1973), pp. 184–85; Maxwell Bloomfield, *American Lawyers in a Changing Society, 1776–1876* (Cambridge: Harvard University Press, 1976), pp. 95–96; Richard B. Morris, *Studies in the History of American Law* (New York, 1930), pp. 126–31, 135–55; Mary Sumner Benson, *Women in Eighteenth-Century America: A Study of Opinion and Social Usage*, pp. 232, 234–36; and Julia Cherry Spruill, *Women's Life and Work in the Southern Colonies* (New York: Norton, 1972), pp. 356–66.

18. Bloomfield, *American Lawyers*, pp. 112–17; Friedman, *History of American Law*, pp. 185–86; Linda K. Kerber, "From the Declaration of Independence to the Declaration of Sentiments: The Legal Status of Women in the Early Republic, 1176–1848," *Human Rights* 6 (Winter 1977): 118–20; Albie Sachs and Joan Hoff Wilson, *Sexism and the Law: A Study of Male Beliefs and Legal Bias in Britain and the United States* (New York: Free Press, 1978), pp. 77–78; Carl N. Degler, *At Odds: Women and the Family in America from the Revolution to the Present* (New York, 1980), pp. 332–33; and Basch, "Invisible Women," pp. 349–50.

Other discussions of married women's property rights in the nineteenth and early twentieth centuries include Peggy A. Rabkin, *Fathers to Daughters: The Legal Foundation of Female Emancipation* (Westport: Greenwood, 1980); Joan Hoff Wilson, "The Legal Status of Women in the Late Nineteenth and Early Twentieth Centuries, *Human Rights* 6 (Winter 1977): 125–34; and Suzanne D. Lebsock, "Radical Reconstruction and the Property Rights of Southern Women," *Journal of Southern History* 43 (May 1977): 195–216.

19. Friedman, *History of American Law*, p. 181; Bloomfield, *American Lawyers*, p. 97; Benson, *Women in Eighteenth-Century America*, pp. 233–34; Spruill, *Women's Life and Work*, pp. 341–44; and Nelson M. Blake, *The Road to Reno: A History of Divorce in the United States* (New York: MacMillan, 1962), pp. 34–47. See Eighteenth-Century Massachusetts," William and Mary Quarterly 33 (October 1976): 586–614.

20. Blake, *The Road to Reno*, pp. 50–148; Bloomfield, *American Lawyers*, pp. 120–21; Friedman, *History of American Law*, p. 182; and William L. O'Neill, *Divorce in the Progressive Era* (New Haven: Yale University Press, 1967), p. 7.

21. Jane Turner Censer, "'Smiling Through Her Tears': Ante-Bellum Southern Women and Divorce," *American Journal of Legal History* (January 1981): 37.

22. Christopher Lasch, "Divorce and the 'Decline of the Family,'" in *The World of Nations: Reflections on American History, Politics, and Culture* (New York: Knopf, 1973), pp. 39–40. See also Michael S. Hindus and Lynne E. Withey, "The Law of Husband and Wife in Nineteenth-Century America: Changing View of Divorce" (paper delivered at the meeting of the American Society for Legal History, Chicago, October 1978); Karen White, "A Study of Baltimore City Divorces, 1853–1860" (graduate seminar paper, University of Maryland at College Park, December 1980); and Elaine Tyler May, *Great Expectations: Marriage and Divorce in Post-Victorian America* (Chicago: University of Chicago Press, 1980).

23. Grossberg, "Law and the Family," pp. 257–59; Benson, *Women in Eighteenth-Century America*, pp. 239–40; Spruill, *(Women's Life and Work*, pp. 344–45; and Brown, "Mothers, Fathers, and Children," p. 251. See also Lorena S. Walsh, "Child Custody in the Early Colonial Chesapeake: A Case Study" (paper delivered at the meeting of the Fifth Berkshire Conference on the History of Women, Vassar College, June 1981).

24. Jamil S. Zainaldin, "The Emergence of a Modern Family Law: Child Custody, Adoption, and the Courts, 1796–1851," *Northwestern University Law Review 73 (February 1979): 1052–74; Andre P. Derdeyn, "Child Custody Contests in Historical Perspective," American Journal of Psychiatry* 133 (December 1976): 1370–74; Marylynn Salmon, "'Life Liberty, and Dower': The Legal Status of Women After the American Revolution," in *Women, War, and Revolution*, ed. Carol R. Berkin and Clara M. Lovett (New York: Holmes & Meir, 1980), p. 104; Grossberg, "Law and the Family," pp. 231–38, 260–69, 561–69, 589–625; Brown, "Mothers, Fathers, and Children," pp. 252–57; and Bloomfield, *American Lawyers*, pp. 118–19.

25. Grossberg, "Law and the Family," p. 288–96, 642–60; Zainaldin, "Modern Family Law," pp. 1075–84; Bloomfield, *American Lawyers*, p. 120; and Stephen P. Presser, "The Historic Background of the American Law of Adoption," *Journal of Family Law* 11 (1971): 443–516.

26. Degler, *At Odds*, pp. 26–29, 144, 174–75, 279–327; Nancy F. Cott, *The Bonds of Womanhood: Women's Sphere in New England, 1780–1835* (New Haven: Yale University Press, 1977), pp. 5–9, 194–206; and Lasch, "Life in the Therapeutic State," p. 24.

27. Grossberg, "Law and the Family," Chaps. 5 and 12, have the best summary of the battle.

28. See the now standard work, Linda Gordon, *Women's Body, Women's Right* (New York: Penguin, 1977).

29. For an account of this legislation, see James C. Mohr, *Abortion in America: The*

Origins and Evolution of National Policy (New York: Oxford, 1978), pp. 3–45; 119–46.

30. As quoted in Grossberg, "Law and the Family," pp. 196–97.

31. Ibid., pp. 491–96.

32. Ibid., p. 511.

33. Gordon, *Women's Body*, pp. 95–115.

34. Grossberg, "Law and the Family," pp. 536–37, 540.

35. David J. Pivar, *Purity Crusade: Sexual Morality and Social Control, 1868–1900* (Westport: Greenwood, 1973), p. 28. For another discussion of prostitution in America, see John S. Haller and Robin M. Haller, *The Physician and Sexuality in Victorian America* (Urbana: University of Illinois Press, 1974), pp. 235–70.

36. For a study of women's employment, see Alice Kessler-Harris, *Women Have Always Worked: A Historical Overview* (Old Westbury, N.Y.: Feminist Press, 1981).

37. For more positive interpretations of the family wage, see Louise Tilly and Joan Scott, *Women, Work, and The Family* (New York: Holt, Rinehart and Winston, 1978), and the articles of Jane Humphries, especially "The Working Class Family, Women's Liberation and Class Struggle: The Case of Nineteenth Century Britain", *Review of Radical Political Economics* 9 (Fall 1977): 25–41.

38. Heidi Hartmann, "Capitalism, Patriarchy, and Job Segregation by Sex," *Signs: Journal of Women in Culture and Society* 1, no. 3, pt. 2 (Spring 1976): 137–69.

39. Ava Barron, "Women and the Making of the American Working Class" (paper presented at the OAH, Detroit, April 2, 1981); and Ruth Milkman, "Organizing the Sexual Division of Labor: Historical Perspectives on 'Women's Work' and the American Labor Movement," *Socialist Review* 49 (January-February 1980): 95–150.

40. Milkman, "Organizing the Sexual Division of Labor," p. 123.

41. The best summary of protective legislation is Ann Corinne Hill, "Protection of Women Workers and the Courts: A Legal Case History," *Feminist Studies* 5, no. 2 (Summer 1979): 247–73.

42. As quoted by Alice Kessler-Harris, "Where Are the Organized Women Workers?" *Feminist Studies* 3, nos. 1/2 (Fall 1975): 101.

43. As quoted in Hill, "Protection of Women Workers," p. 253.

44. Alice Kessler-Harris, *Women Have Always Worked*, p. 94.

45. Maurine Weiner Greenwald, *Women, War, and Work: The Impact of WWI on Women Workers in the United States* (Westport: Greenwood, 1980), p. 137.

46. Bloomfield, *American Lawyers*, pp. 99, 122; Mason P. Thomas, Jr., "Child Abuse and Neglect; Part I: Historical Overview, Legal Matrix, and Social Perspectives," *North Carolina Law Review* 50 (February 1972): 299–303; and Judith Areen, "Intervention Between Parent and Child: A Reappraisal of the State's role in Child Neglect and Abuse Cases," *Georgetown Law Journal* 63 (March 1975): 899–902.

47. David Rothman, *The Discovery of the Asylum: Social Order and Disorder in the New Republic* (Boston: Little, Brown, 1971); and Michael B. Katz, "Origins of the Institutional State," *Marxist Perspectives* 1, no. 4 (Winter 1978): 6–22.

48. Grossberg, "Law and the Family," pp. 306–8, 312; and Zaretsky, "The Place of the Family in the Origins of the Welfare State," pp. 202–3.

49. Areen, "Intervention Between Parent and Child," pp. 903, 907–8; Michael Zuckerman, "Children's Rights: The Failure of 'Reform,'" *Policy Analysis* 2 (Summer 1976): 382–83; and Grossberg, "Law and the Family," pp. 625–29. Other studies of the juvenile court system include Anthony Platt, *The Child Savers: The Invention of Delinquency* (Chicago: University of Chicago Press, 1969); Joseph Hawes, *Children in Urban Society: Juve-*

nile Delinquency in Nineteenth-Century America (New York: Oxford, 1971); and Robert M. Mennel, *Thorns and Thistles: Juvenile Delinquency in the United States, 1825–1940* (Hanover, N. H.: University Press of New England, 1973).

50. David J. Rothman, "The State as Parent: Social Policy in the Progressive Era," in *Doing Good: The Limits of Benevolence*, ed. Willard Gaylin, et al. (New York: Pantheon, 1978), pp. 78–79. See also David J. Rothman, *Conscience and Convenience: The Asylum and Its Alternatives in Progressive America* (Boston: Little, Brown, 1981); and Steven L, Schlossman, *Love and the American Delinquent: The Theory and Practice of "Progressive" Juvenile Justice, 1825–1920* (Chicago: University of Chicago Press, 1977). Peter L. Tyor and Jamil S. Zainaldin, "Asylum and Society: An Approach to Institutional Change," *Journal of Social History*, 13 (Fall 1979): 23–48; and Susan Tiffin, *In Whose Best Interest? Child Welfare Reform in the Progressive Era* (Westport: Greenwood, 1982).

51. Michael B. Katz, "The Origins of Public Education: A Reassessment," *History of Education Quarterly* 16 (Winter 1976): 381–407. For other discussions of the development of the American public school system, see Michael B. Katz, *The Irony of Early School Reform: Education Innovation in Mid-Nineteenth Century Massachusetts* (Cambridge: Harvard University Press, 1968); David B. Tyack, *The One Best System: A History of American Urban Education* (Cambridge, 1974); and David Nasaw, *Schooled to Order: A Social History of Public Schooling in the United States* (New York: Oxford, 1979). For an example of how the schools replicated gender divisions, see Eileen Boris, "Social Reproduction and the Schools: 'Educational Housekeeping,'" *Signs: Journal of Women in Culture and Society* 4, no. 4 (Summer 1979): 814–20.

52. Zaretsky, "The Place of the Family in the Origins of the Welfare State," pp. 188–224; see also his paper, "The Family and the Welfare State, 1890–1920," presented at the OAH, April 1981.

53. Lynn Weiner, "Subsidized Motherhood: The Mothers' Pension Movement in the U.S." (paper presented at the AHA, Washington, December 1980), esp. p. 9; and Mark H. Leff, "Consensus for Reform: The Mothers' Pension Movement in the Progressive Era," *Social Science Review* 47 (September 1973): 397–417.

54. Much of the detail on the New Deal comes from Lois Scharf, *To Work and to Wed: Female Employment, Feminism, and the Great Depression* (Westport: Greenwood Press, 1980), pp. 43–65.

55. Ibid., pp. 110–38; and Winifred D. Wandersee, "Who Should Work: Government Policies Toward the Employment of Women and Youth During the Great Depression" (paper presented at the AHA, Washington, December 1980).

56. Glen H. Elder, Jr., *Children of the Great Depression: Social Change in Life Experience* (Chicago: University of Chicago Press, 1974), esp. pp. 281–83.

57. Ellen Carol DuBois, *Feminism and Suffrage: The Emergence of an Independent Women's Movement in America, 1848–1869* (Ithaca: Cornell University Press, 1978); William Leach, *True Love and Perfect Union: The Feminist Reform of Sex and Society* (New York: Basic Books, 1980), esp. pp. 3–15; Basch, "Invisible Women," p. 355; and Bloomfield, *American Lawyers*, p. 117. See also Aileen Kraditor, *Ideas of the Woman Suffrage Movement, 1890–1920* (New York: Columbia University Press, 1965); and Degler, *At Odds*, pp. 328–61.

5

Steven P. Erie
Martin Rein
Barbara Wiget

Women and the Reagan Revolution: Thermidor for the Social Welfare Economy

In the 1980 presidential election, the New York Times/CBS News exit poll revealed an eight percentage point gap between men and women voters in their support of Ronald Reagan. By a margin of 54 to 46 percent, men supported Reagan over Jimmy Carter and John Anderson. By the same margin, women voted for Carter or Anderson.[1] This difference was the largest ever observed between men and women in their choice of presidential candidates. After the election, what has been called the "gender gap" widened considerably. According to a Harris poll conducted in late 1981, only 49 percent of women surveyed thought Reagan was doing a good job versus 62 percent of American men.

What accounts for the growing gender gap? In 1980 the conventional wisdom was that much of Reagan's lack of appeal to women reflected the peace issue. In this view, the differences between men and women in presidential voting since 1920, minimal as they generally have been, have resulted from the greater sensitivity of women to the dangers of war.[2] Reagan's massive defense buildup and his administration's anti-Soviet bellicosity undoubtedly have contributed to fears of war.

One suspects, however, that there are domestic as well as foreign policy sources accounting for the widening political gap between the sexes. In the 1980 election, the candidates' stands on the Equal Rights Amendment represented a salient issue for many women.[3] This essay explores an alternative domestic policy source for the political gap between women and men. Since the days of the New Deal, and particularly since those of the Great Society, millions of women have been integrated into the domestic political economy in ways fundamentally different from men. Specifically, as the number of women in the labor force nearly doubled between 1960 and 1979 (from 20 million to 37 million) and as changing norms regarding sexuality, marriage, and divorce propelled the growth of female-headed families, the American welfare state was concomitantly expanding. The welfare state became economically intertwined with the fortunes of many working-age women, who were either service providers or indigent cash transfer and service recipients in a federally funded social welfare economy. In two important sectors of this economy to be examined in this essay—employment and welfare—working-age women constitute over 70 percent of the more than 20 million participants (17.3 million human services workers and 4 million welfare family heads).

Thus the gender gap (i.e., the differential support of the present administration by women and men) also needs to be understood in terms of the Reagan welfare and budgetary policies. The welfare state structures that have economically incorporated millions of working-age women are now being challenged. For fiscal year 1982, the Reagan administration reduced federal social program outlays by $35.2 billion relative to the Congressional Budget Office's "baseline" budget. Between 60 and 70 percent of the social program savings were achieved in programs primarily serving the poor and near-poor. Low-income women and their children make up 60 to 80 percent of the recipients of the federal welfare programs affected.[4] As evidenced by the administration's FY 1983 budgetary proposals, the FY 1982 budget reductions represent only the first round in a substantial pruning of federal social welfare responsibilities. Human services workers as well as welfare recipients will be adversely affected.

Organized into three sections, this essay explores the welfare state dismantlement hypothesis. The first section traces the process of economic incorporation of women into the welfare state between 1940 and 1980, in particular since the early 1960s. It examines the growth of federal social programs during this period and assesses their economic impacts (i.e., cash and in-kind (nonmonetary) transfers and jobs) on two somewhat overlapping groups of working-age women—those heading families and those in the labor force. In addition to estimating the relative numbers of working-age women incorporated into the federal social welfare economy, we attempt to explain their involvement in the welfare and employment sectors. Because the Reagan program so far has focused on those in the labor force, no attempt is made to assess the involvement of elderly women in Social Security and Medicare programs. Programs for the elderly, however, form an important component of the overall social welfare economy.

The second section examines the character of the Reagan welfare and social budget policies and assesses their likely economic impacts on women heading families or in the labor force. The third section considers the likely political impact on women of the Reagan policies. Will the tandem budgetary and welfare policies produce a political alliance among displaced state-sector workers and clients? Will the administration's "profamily" social policies produce cross-cutting cleavages among women, pitting more traditional homemakers against women in the labor force? The study concludes by considering how women might shape employment as a political issue in the 1980s.

THE GROWTH OF THE SOCIAL WELFARE ECONOMY AMONG WOMEN, 1940–1980

The Welfare Sector: Federal Programs and Female-Headed Families

One way in which working-age women have become involved in the federal social welfare economy is as participants in one or more of the major federal welfare programs—Aid to Families with Dependent Children (AFDC), food stamps, and Medicaid. AFDC, a joint federal-state cash-assistance program enacted in 1935, provides financial support to needy children in the case of the death, incapacity, or absence from home of a providing parent. Enacted at a time when few women were in the labor force and most of the adult recipients were "deserving" white widows, the original Aid to Dependent Children program was renamed Aid to Families with Dependent Children in 1962, signaling a shift in policy objectives from the long-term provision of cash assistance to needy children to the provision of rehabilitative social services to "multiproblem" families in order to get them off the dole.

By the late 1960s, as the welfare caseload grew and increasingly became the repository of divorced and unmarried mothers rather than the widowed or disabled, and included black as well as white women, the crucial policy objective became the employability of this new group of welfare mothers. Thus in 1967 welfare mothers were encouraged to mix work and welfare by the "$30 and one-third" rule, whereby the recipient could retain the initial $30 and one-third of additional earnings without a proportionate reduction in welfare payments. Congress also passed a mandatory work registration and training program for adult welfare recipients.[5]

Concomitant with these program developments, there was a dramatic increase in the number of female-headed welfare families. Table 5.1 compares growth rates between 1961 and 1979 for female-headed families with minor children and for female-headed AFDC families. During this period, the number of AFDC families headed by women (over 80 percent of the entire welfare caseload consists of such families) more than quadrupled, from 635,000 to 3,000,000. Part of this welfare increase reflected changing societal norms regarding sexuality, marriage, and divorce, which affected the number of female-headed families. Between 1961 and 1979, the number of such families more than doubled, from 2.2 to 5.9 million. Yet not all of the increase in the number of welfare mothers can be attributed to cultural factors affecting family structure. During this period the welfare participation *rate* among female-headed families with minor children rose from 29 to 50 percent.

Explaining Welfare and Work Patterns. What accounts for the sharp rise in the welfare participation rate among these women? Welfare policy combined with the structure of the labor market to encourage welfare participation *and* the mixing of work and welfare. Regarding program eligibility rules, AFDC is a means-tested program for categorically eligible families, that is, those with needy minor children deprived of the financial support of a parent. Owing to the greater incidence of poverty among female-headed families than among other families, means testing favors greater rates of welfare receipt among such families. Because of more limited job opportunities and skills and because of the burdens of childbearing by a single parent, women heading families were far more likely than others to be poor. In 1979, 39 percent of female-headed families with minor children were below the poverty threshold (as defined by the Census Bureau) compared with 6 percent of all other families.[6]

TABLE 5.1
Growth in the Number of Female-Headed AFDC Families, 1961–1979

	Female-headed Families with Related Children (in thousands)		
Year	*AFDC Families* (*N*)	*All Families* (*N*)	*AFDC Participation Rate* (%)
1961	635	2194	28.9
1969	1298	3374	38.5
1979	2956	5918	50.0
Percent increase, 1960–79	366	170	—

SOURCES: Female-headed AFDC families: 1961, U.S. Department of Health, Education, and Welfare, *Study of Recipients of Aid to Families With Dependent Children, November–December 1961: National Cross-Tabulations* (Washington, D.C.: HEW, August 1965); 1969, HEW, *National Cross-Tabulations from the 1967 and 1969 AFDC Studies* (Washington, D.C.: HEW, December 1971); 1979, unpublished data supplied by the U.S. Department of Health and Human Services. Female-headed families with related children: U.S. Bureau of the Census, *Statistical Abstract of the United States, 1961* (Washington, D.C.: Government Printing Office, 1962); U.S. Bureau of the Census, *24 Million Americans: Poverty in the United States, 1969* (Washington, D.C.: Government Printing Office, 1970); U.S. Bureau of the Census, *Current Population Reports, Characteristics of the Population Below the Poverty Level, 1979* (Washington, D.C.: Government Printing Office, 1981).

During the 1960s AFDC participation also was encouraged by rising benefit levels relative to earnings. Between 1960 and 1970, the average payment per recipient in the AFDC program increased by 75 percent while the average earnings of nonfarm workers rose by only 48 percent. Equally important, owing to a more liberal political climate and to the activities of poverty lawyers, the administrative practices of many welfare agencies were liberalized during the 1960s, resulting in an increase in acceptance rates on AFDC applications from 56 percent in 1960 to 80 percent in 1970.[7]

The launching of federal in-kind programs, notably Medicaid, further encouraged welfare participation, as well as the mixing of work and welfare. Owing to the presence of small children, health care coverage is especially important to women heading families. For many of these women, Medicaid is the only available medical coverage. In a significant number of states, Medicaid eligibility depends upon participation in cash-assistance welfare programs such as AFDC. Because working welfare mothers either work part-time or full-time in low-wage retail and service industries generally without medical coverage, Medicaid coverage depends upon continued welfare eligibility. Not surprisingly, by the late 1970s most AFDC families also participated in the Medicaid program.

The mixing of work and welfare was also facilitated by the work incentives fashioned in AFDC policy. The 1967 welfare amendments, which featured the "$30 and one-third" earned income disregard as well as itemized deductions for work-related expenses such as transportation and child care, created a gap between welfare "entry" levels (the income level at which families could qualify for welfare) and "exit" levels (the income level at which families could earn and still remain on welfare). In 1967, the entry and exit levels were the same—$3300. By 1971, the nationwide entry level had increased by 25 percent (to $4140), while the exit level had risen by 85 percent (to $6132).[8]

As a result of work incentives, the labor force participation rate for welfare mothers rose 28 percent in the 1967–73 period. Data from the Panel Study of Income Dynamics indicate that by the early 1970s about 40 percent of females heading welfare families worked at some point during a given year. For their years on welfare, most women heading families depended nearly as much on their earnings (up to one-third of family income) as they did on public aid (one-third) or on all other sources (another one-third).[9]

Deteriorating labor market conditions in the 1970s sharply affected the number of women applying for welfare and mixing work and welfare. Between 1970 and 1979, the number of women heading families who were in the work force doubled —from 1.7 million to 3.5 million—owing to the dramatic increase in the number of such families and to a rise in their labor force participation rate (66 percent in 1979, up from 59 percent in 1970). These women were more subject to economic vicissitudes than other family heads because of their limited education (30 percent had not completed high school and only 9 percent had completed college) and job skills. Between 1970 and 1978, the unemployment rate for women heading families rose from 5.6 to 9 percent compared with a slight increase among men heading families from 2.6 to 3.6 percent. Rising unemployment sharply reverberated on the AFDC program. In the late 1970s an increase of one percentage point in the unemployment rate for these women was associated with an increase of 38,000 families on the AFDC basic caseload.

The character of the labor market for women encouraged welfare receipt and the mixing of work and welfare. Outside of human services employment, job growth in the 1970s for women largely has been in retail and business services rather than in the goods-producing manufacturing sector. These new jobs generally are in the secondary labor market. Such employment tends to be part-time or seasonal, nonunion, paying subsistence-level wages, featuring few fringe benefits such as health care, and offering limited promotional opportunities. Workers in the secondary sector often are unable to support their families from earnings alone, and thus turn to supplemental forms of assistance such as welfare.[10]

Racial Differences in Welfare Participation. Families headed by black women have become more active participants in federal welfare programs than have families headed by white women. In 1979, 66 percent of the nation's 2 million female-headed black families received welfare at some point in the year compared with 44 percent of the 3.8 million similar white families. Compared with white women, black women stayed on welfare longer and had higher participation rates in federal in-kind programs.[11]

The causes of these racial differences in welfare participation are rooted in interrelated family, marriage, and economic patterns. For many black women, the welfare cycle starts early in the teenage years with an out-of-wedlock birth. With education interrupted and with little work experience, welfare receipt for these women tends to be long-term, especially if a second child follows. For many white women there is a different welfare pattern. Typically, a divorce or separation in the twenties or thirties leads to the use of welfare as a temporary financial safety net pending a job or remarriage.

These racial differences in patterns of pregnancy, marriage, and age of initial welfare receipt partially reflect the bleaker economic environment faced by less educated, young, urban black women and men. Urban lower-class blacks, as Ross and Sawhill and others have noted, generally have the same attitudes and values toward marriage and family as do lower- and middle-class whites.[12] However, the economic environment in which they live prevents them from behaving in similar fashion. Unemployment rates are far higher for black than white teenage women, making welfare an important income source. In addition, less educated black males increasingly do not have the jobs or income enabling them to be stable providers or marriage partners. Frank Levy has shown that between 1964 and 1978 the unemployment prospects for young black males became increasingly uneven. The better educated were becoming more secure in their employment prospects, while the less educated were experiencing greater joblessness.[13]

Reinforcing Welfare and Work Structures. Overall, then, significant numbers of women heading families have become participants in the Aid to Families with Dependent Children program. As mentioned, in 1979, 3 million of the nation's 5.9 million such families were receiving AFDC payments. Many of these women also participated in federal in-kind welfare programs. In 1979, 2.9 million of them received Medicaid; 2.6 million, food stamps; and 2.3 million were enrolled in school lunch programs.[14]

In the welfare sector of the social welfare economy, federal policy reinforced the private-sector secondary labor market for women, thus helping to produce a large-scale work and welfare class. There are both primary and secondary "welfare" systems corresponding to and reinforcing the primary and secondary private-sector labor markets along gender lines. Unemployment compensation represents the primary welfare system. This program enables covered workers (predominantly men, considered to be primary family earners) to move from job to job without impoverishing themselves or their families. Aid to Families with Dependent Children represents a secondary welfare system. Dominated by women (considered to be supplemental earners), AFDC provides minimal support to meet basic family needs. The program acts to subsidize low-wage industries and occupations dominated by women in the secondary labor market by providing cash supplements, fringe benefits such as health care, and supportive services such as day care.[15]

These interlocking secondary welfare and work structures have been contributory factors to what some observers have termed the "feminization" of the poverty population.[16] Before 1969, the increase in the number of female-headed families was accompanied by a decline in the proportion of such families in poverty. Thus the number of poor families headed by women neither rose nor declined. In 1969, 1.8 million such families were below the poverty threshold, roughly the same number as in 1959. Beginning in 1969, the number of female-headed families in poverty increased sharply—to 2.6 million in 1979. The increase reflected both the growing number of such families and the fact that a high proportion persistently remained below the low-income threshold. Among male-headed families, however, the proportion in poverty continued to decline through the 1970s. As a result, the number of low-income families headed by males dropped from 3.2 million in 1969 to 2.7 million in 1979. Thus there has been a sharp shift in the female-male ratio in the poverty population. Between 1959 and 1979, the proportion of all low-income families headed by women dramatically increased from 23 to 48 percent. The National Advisory Council on Economic Opportunity noted ominously that if these trends were to continue, by the year 2000 the poverty population would be entirely composed of women and their children.[17]

While much more needs to be known about the factors accounting for the "feminization" of poverty (including those factors reducing the number of men in poverty), large numbers of women are trapped in poverty by the complex interplay between federal welfare policy and the low-wage labor market. It is not an exaggeration to say that federal and state welfare policy is a de facto labor policy for women in the secondary labor market—regulating labor supply by benefit levels, eligibility rules, and the availability of supportive services such as day care; regulating wages by what is in effect a wage-supplement allowance; and regulating hours by earnings ceilings on welfare eligibility.

Yet the expansion of federal welfare programs, particularly since the mid-1960s, is not the only way in which working-age women have been incorporated economically into the social welfare economy. We now turn to a consideration of the human service job opportunities for women generated by federal funding.

The Employment Sector: Federal Social Programs and Employment Opportunities for Women

Estimating the Employment Generated by Federal Social Outlays. Federal expenditures for social welfare purposes grew dramatically in the post-World War II era. In 1979 federal social outlays amounted to $264 billion, up from $10.5 billion in 1950. As a proportion of GNP, these federal outlays rose from 4 percent in 1950 to 11.5 percent in 1979. Much of the growth in federal social welfare expenditures was concentrated in the period 1965 to 1976. During these years federal social outlays accounted for 17 percent of the nation's GNP increase compared with only 7 percent between 1950 and 1965.

It is difficult to estimate the employment generated by federal social funding, let alone the share received by women. In order fully to grasp the impact of federal outlays in the labor market, one must realize that jobs are created not so much directly at the federal level as indirectly in state and local governments, the private nonprofit service sector, and even in the private profit (particularly health) sector. This is so because federal social outlays are primarily in the form of grants-in-aid to states and localities, contracts to private entities, or income transfers to individuals.

Surprisingly, the federal government is not primarily a direct employer of human services personnel. Of the nation's 17.3 million human services workers, fewer than 3 percent are directly employed by the federal government. Of the 2.9 million federal civilian employees in 1980, only 16 percent (458,000) were in social welfare areas. Instead, federal employment is heavily defense related. Since World War II, national security has accounted for one-third to one-half of all federal civilian employment.

Yet there is evidence that federal social outlays may have generated sizable indirect employment opportunities in other sectors of the economy. In state and local government, federal social welfare grants-in-aid and general revenue sharing (available since 1972) used for these purposes rose from $5.6 billion in 1964 to $55.9 billion in 1979.[18] As a proportion of total state and local social welfare expenditures, federal revenues rose from 14 percent in 1964 to 26 percent in 1979, accounting for nearly one-third of the overall increase. During the same period state and local government human services employment nearly doubled, from 4.9 million to 9.3 million.

In terms of the private nonprofit sector, a substantial (though undetermined) proportion of the revenue of service agencies comes from governmental sources, which subcontract for services. Though most of the public funding of the nonprofit sector appears to come from state and local governments, there is an important indirect federal role. Title XX, for example, is a multibillion-dollar federal grant program to the states for social services. States, in turn, often subcontract to the nonprofit sector for the provision of day care and another social services. In FY 1979, 33 percent of the $3.5 billion in Title XX funds involved purchase of services from the private sector.[19] Federal formula and project grants for manpower and training, alcohol and drug abuse, and mental health also generate a considerable number of jobs in nonprofit agencies. Overall, between 1964 and 1980 human services employment in the nonprofit human services sector rose from 2.2 million to 5.0 million.

Finally, federal funding appears to have played an important (albeit even more indirect) role in the private sector. In addition to grants and contracts, the federal government provides cash and in-kind assistance to eligible individuals. Medicare and Medicaid have significantly expanded the demand for private health services. The creation during the 1970s of a large private nursing home industry primarily came about because of the federal government's indirect role as a financier of Medicare and Medicaid. In this sector, social welfare employment (primarily in health) increased from 700,000 to 2,500,000 between 1964 and 1980.

In these same years total social welfare employment in all sectors rose from 8.1 million to 17.3 million, accounting for 28 percent of the overall increase in the nation's labor force. How might we more precisely estimate the federal government's direct and indirect share of this employment? Two approaches have been used: input-output analysis and federal agency estimates. Lester Thurow has used input-output analysis to estimate the private-sector employment indirectly generated by federal service expenditures. In 1976, 13 percent of private-sector professional services employment (mostly in health, education, and welfare) was indirectly generated by federal outlays.[20] The *National Journal* has used federal agency estimates of indirect employment generated by their programs. For FY 1978, the three major federal social welfare agencies (HEW, HUD, and Labor) estimated 2.7 million indirect federal employees, nearly all in state and local governments as teachers in inner-city schools, welfare caseworkers, community development and housing specialists, or employees in programs designed to reduce unemployment.[21] Together these approaches yield a rough estimate of 4.2 million direct and indirect federal human services personnel in 1980, one-quarter of all social welfare employment.

These approaches underestimate the indirect federal employment role, particularly in the private sector, because neither includes transfer payments. Most of the growth in federal social outlays since World War II has occurred in transfer payments. Whereas in 1952 federal transfer payments were 32 percent larger than service outlays, by 1979 they were 50 percent greater. The one input-output analysis of the effects of federal transfer payments on gross industry outputs is suggestive. For 1972 it is estimated that nearly 20 percent of all direct federal transfer payments were spent in nongovernmental "medical, educational services, and nonprofit organizations."[22] In 1979 federal transfer payments amounted to $206 billion. We can thus surmise that if the industry input-output relationship remained stable between 1972 and 1980, approximately $40 billion in transfer payments flowed into the private human services sector in 1980, generating perhaps an additional 1.5 million to 2 million jobs. Considering as well transfer payment impacts, federal social outlays may have created 5.7 million to 6.2 million human services jobs in 1980, 33 to 36 percent of all social welfare employment. Thus the federal indirect employment role is ten times as great as its direct employment role.

Yet the number of jobs indirectly generated by federal social funding still may be underestimated. As of 1979, the federal share of total social welfare expenditures (private as well as public) was 57 percent, up from 45 percent in 1952. Even if the upper bounds cannot be gauged more precisely, it is evident that federal social funding has generated a startling amount of indirect employment.

How Women Have Fared in Social Welfare Employment. We have chosen to examine employment patterns, particularly for women, in *all* sectors of the social welfare economy—public, private nonprofit, and private profit—that are dependent in some important degree upon federal funding.

Overall employment trends in the human services industry can be briefly characterized as follows: Between 1940 and 1980, the industry grew from 7 to 18 percent of the labor force, thus accounting for one-quarter of the nation's net job increase. During these years the internal composition of the industry changed. In terms of the functional mix—education, health, and welfare—jobs in education no longer dominate as employment growth has shifted to health. With the functional hift, the industry is becoming increasingly "privatized" (but not necessarily with respect to funding source). In 1979, 45 percent of all social welfare jobs were in the private sector compared with 38 percent in 1952.

The expanding social welfare economy has been an important and underrecognized source of job opportunities for women. As Table 5.2 shows, in 1980 nearly one-third of the 37 million women in the labor force worked in human services compared with only 10 percent of the men in the work force. Comparing patterns of job growth for women and men between 1940 and 1980, the social welfare industry created jobs for more than one out of every three women entering the labor force compared with only one out of every six men.

Social welfare employment was especially important for black women. As Table 5.2 shows, 37 percent of all nonwhite women in the labor force in 1980 were employed in the human services sector compared with 30 percent of white women, 13 percent of nonwhite men, and 10 percent of white men. In terms of job growth between 1940 and 1980, 49 percent of all new employment for nonwhite women occurred in social welfare fields compared with 34 percent for white women, 17 percent for nonwhite men, and 16 percent for white men.

Great Society programs in the 1960s heightened the importance of social welfare employment for all groups, particularly women. Between 1960 and 1980 human services accounted for 41 percent of the job gains for women compared with 21 percent for men. Among women, there were significant differences in the importance of human services employment for whites and blacks. For white women, the social welfare economy accounted for 39 percent of the job gain between 1960 and 1980; for black women, an even more dramatic 58 percent.

As Table 5.3 shows, women in the professions are more than twice as dependent as men on social welfare employment. In 1970 (the latest year for which we have data), nearly 80 percent of the 4.6 million female professionals worked in the human services sector—as teachers, nurses, and social workers—compared with 35 percent of the 6.9 million male professionals.[23]

Not only can we estimate the relative importance of the social welfare industry in job gains for women and men, blacks and whites, and professionals, we can also examine the changing demographic composition of the human services work force. While the sector's labor force historically has been heavily female, it has become even *more* feminized during the 1940–80 period, thus raising the question whether the stimulation of labor demands by the federal government has resulted in channeling women ever more intensively into traditional female occupations.[24] In 1940, women comprised 59 percent of the industry's 3 million workers. By 1980, 70 percent of the nation's 17.3 million human services workers were women.

In the 1968–80 period, we can detect the industry's distinct countercyclical role for women. Human services is a peripheral sector of the economy, less affected than many others by major business cycles (though clearly affected by political funding cycles). The National Bureau of Economic Research estimates monthly economic turning points (peaks and troughs), identifying six in the period 1968 to 1980. Social welfare employment was more important for women as economic

TABLE 5.2
Social Welfare Employment Gains by Sex and Race, 1940–1980

	Nonagricultural Civilian Employment (in thousands)[a]											
	Females						*Males*					
	White		*Nonwhite*		*All*		*White*		*Nonwhite*		*All*	
	%	(*N*)	%	(*N*)	%	(*N*)	%	(*N*)	%	(*N*)	%	(*N*)
1940												
Social welfare[b]	17.8	(1,655)	7.2	(95)	16.4	(1,750)	4.7	(1,133)	4.9	(87)	4.7	(1,220)
Other	82.2	(7,668)	92.8	(1,225)	83.6	(8,893)	95.3	(22,834)	95.1	(1,689)	95.3	(24,523)
Total		(9,323)		(1,320)		(10,643)		(23,967)		(1,776)		(25,743)
1980												
Social welfare	29.6	(9,623)	37.3	(1,749)	30.6	(11,372)	9.7	(4,185)	12.9	(659)	10.0	(4,844)
Other	70.4	(22,874)	62.7	(2,943)	69.4	(25,817)	90.3	(38,936)	87.1	(4,454)	90.0	(43,390)
Total		(32,497)		(4,692)		(37,189)		(43,121)		(5,113)		(48,234)
Increase, 1940–80												
Social welfare	34.4	(7,968)	49.0	(1,654)	36.2	(9,622)	15.9	(3,052)	17.1	(572)	16.1	(3,624)
Other	65.6	(15,206)	51.0	(1,718)	63.8	(16,924)	84.1	(16,102)	82.9	(2,765)	83.9	(18,867)
Total		(23,174)		(3,372)		(26,546)		(19,154)		(3,337)		(22,491)

SOURCES: 1940, U.S. Bureau of the Census, *Sixteenth Census of the United States, 1940, Population*, vol. 2, *The Labor Force, Pt. 1: U.S. Summary* (Washington, D.C.; Government Printing Office, 1943); 1980, U.S. Bureau of Labor Statistics, *Current Population Survey, 1980*, unpublished tables.

[a] Annual average employment.
[b] Includes medical, hospital, education, welfare, and religious employment.

TABLE 5.3

Professional and Technical Social Welfare Employment by Sex and Race, 1970

	Nonagricultural civilian employment (in thousands)											
	Female						*Males*					
	White		*Nonwhite*		*All*		*White*		*Nonwhite*		*All*	
Professional and Technical Employment, 1970	%	(*N*)	%	(*N*)	%	(*N*)	%	(*N*)	%	(*N*)	%	(*N*)
Social welfare	79.0	(3264)	82.4	(365)	79.3	(3629)	34.6	(2261)	46.8	(163)	35.3	(2425)
Other	21.0	(869)	17.6	(78)	20.7	(947)	65.4	(4267)	53.2	(185)	64.7	(4451)
Total	100.0	(4133)	100.0	(443)	100.0	(4576)	100.0	(6528)	100.0	(348)	100.0	(6876)

SOURCE: U.S. Bureau of the Census, *Census of Population, 1970, Subject Reports, Occupational Characteristics*, PC(2)-7A (Washington, D.C.: Government Printing Office, 1973).

troughs approached and less important during peaks, when private-sector job growth absorbed greater numbers of women seeking work. In the late 1960s, when the economy was robust, social welfare contributed 35 percent of the job increase for women. In the early to mid-1970s, as the economy experienced a severe recession and women lost a disproportionate number of private-sector jobs in male-dominated industries such as manufacturing where they were only beginning to make inroads, social welfare accounted for 42 percent of the employment increase for women as federal social outlays continued to grow. In the late 1970s, however, as the economy partially recovered and as fiscal strains slowed public-sector employment growth, the contribution of social welfare employment gains declined to 28 percent.

Explaining Women's Employment Gains in the Social Welfare Economy. Several different (though complementary) explanations can be advanced to account for the heavy representation of women in human services employment. These can be summarized as the welfare state, gender socialization, and patriarchal domination interpretations.

The welfare state interpretation is a job-supply model. Women were drawn into the labor force in large numbers because of the "takeoff" in governmental social welfare employment since the days of the New Deal. Expanding welfare state responsibilities took such varied forms as Social Security, welfare, housing, and employment programs in the 1930s; sharply expanded state and local health, education, and welfare services after World War II to meet the needs of growing urban and suburban populations; and the Great Society federal programs for minorities, the poor, and the elderly.

This interpretation seems to be rejected by analysts like Emma Rothschild, who seeks to explain job gains for women in the 1970s primarily in terms of the private-sector shift from manufacturing to services. Three service industries in particular loom large in the employment of women—eating and drinking establishments, health, and business services—having grown in response to the twin "crises" of the family and the corporation. According to Rothschild, the family is increasingly incompetent as an institution for reproducing the labor force, and industries such as food and health care have correspondingly grown to meet these needs. With the decline of the extended family and the aging of the population, the nursing home industry has grown. As for the corporation, it is ill equipped to meet the needs of women employees for social services or for part-time work, preferring to subcontract out such business services as data processing to smaller firms that can manage a part-time and largely female labor force.[25]

James O'Connor's tripartite model of the structure of the labor market—state, monopoly, and competitive sectors, each roughly employing one-third of the labor force—captures more of the complexity of economic life for women than does Rothschild's dualistic model of the private-sector market—retail and service industries versus goods-producing manufacturing.[26] Most of the job gains for women have been in service industries, but in two dissimilar sectors—the retail and business services sector and the human services sector. Most of human services employment (upward of 60–70 percent) is directly or indirectly generated by state-sector social outlays (including state and local as well as federal expenditures).

Yet aspects of a job-supply model to account for human services employment gains for women are troubling. Controlling for differences between the sexes in the numbers entering the labor force since 1960, why were women still more likely than men to secure human services employment? One possible policy explanation for this gender employment effect might be that federal equal employment opportunity legislation, particularly Title VII of the 1964 Civil Rights Act, was earlier and more effectively implemented in the public than private sector, thus creating a demand for women's labor in a sector dominated (at state and local levels) by human services employment. While plausible, this hypothesis is weakened by the fact that Title VII was only belatedly extended in 1972 to cover state and local governments (employing 63 percent of all human services workers in 1970), while sizable female job gains in social welfare clearly predate 1972. Moreover, the few studies of the economic impacts of federal equal employment opportunity legislation, although confined to black rather than women workers, generally have been inconclusive.[27]

More convincing explanations of the crowding of women into the expanding social welfare economy may be found in broader cultural patterns and even in power relationships between the sexes. A gender role or socialization interpretation addresses the question why women would disproportionately enter the "helping" professions. A patriarchal domination or power interpretation addresses the question how and why men have kept women out of traditionally male-dominated industries.

In terms of the socialization hypothesis, both socialist feminists and Marxists have stressed the similarity of the character of the work performed in the social welfare economy to women's traditional roles in the family. In the family women have been socialized into supportive and nurturing roles. Thus their nonmarket activities involved the social reproduction of labor. As women moved into the paid labor market, many continued to perform these traditional women's roles in service industries such as social welfare.[28]

Regarding the patriarchal interpretation, it can be argued that while men need the earnings of women in order to improve the family's economic position, men also have a stake in not altering their position of power, both in the workplace and family (as the primary breadwinner). Thus the segregation of women into lower-paid and less desirable jobs in the services sector (including human services), away from better-paid and more desirable male-dominated corporate or unionized jobs, provides the material foundation permitting the continued dominance of men in work and family life. As Steven Dubnoff notes, "while the emphasis within this perspective is on the maintenance of patriarchal traditions within capitalism, it is clear that this perspective requires a focus on process, in the active agency of men, predominantly through their unions, in excluding women from desirable and higher paid jobs."[29]

In summary to this point, the first element of the welfare state "dismantlement" hypothesis appears confirmed. Millions of working-age women have been integrated into the domestic political economy in ways different from men—as either service providers or as indigent cash-transfer and service recipients in the social welfare economy. This is especially true for black women. Compared with whites, black women are more likely to be welfare recipients or human services workers. Among women generally, those at the top and bottom of the class structure—professionals and welfare recipients—are most heavily involved in human services. Moreover, we have seen the considerable (albeit indirect) role of federal funding in generating social welfare jobs and cash transfers for women.

Yet as one considers how the economic fortunes of many women became intertwined with those of the welfare state, a question that has troubled the women's movement is raised again. Many of the political and legal efforts of the movement were directed at breaking the stranglehold of family-centered patriarchy by encouraging women to play a greater role in economic life outside the family. The expansion of the welfare state has allowed many women to gain economic freedom from men, for human services jobs and welfare cash transfers provide an economic base outside of marriage. The woman's movement has tended to accept the expansion of the service state as freedom from familial patriarchy without adequately considering whether its expansion has increased their dependence on the state. As a form of social organization whereby men control women's labor for the benefit of men, patriarchy has a state-centered as well as a family-centered dimension. Within the human services sector, men continue to dominate top decision-making positions and the most prestigious occupations (e.g., the medical profession). As the human services bureaucracies have expanded, their policies increasingly have structured women's activities, especially those of minority women. Growing uncertainties within the women's movement in the late 1970s (though less evident in the electorate) perhaps reflected this uneasiness with the service state's contradictory emancipatory and control functions.[30]

THE REAGAN SOCIAL POLICIES: ESTIMATING THE IMPACTS ON WORKING-AGE WOMEN

Interpreting Reagan's Attack on the Welfare State

An important interpretation of the origins and character of the Reagan social policies has been offered by Frances Fox Piven and Richard A. Cloward in *The New Class War*. Piven and Cloward argue that Reagan and his big business allies have launched a sudden and massive attack on the federal entitlement programs, designed to force workers receiving cash or in-kind benefits back into the labor market, thereby depressing wages and increasing business's share of profits relative to labor. The expansion of federal income maintenance programs in the late 1960s and early '70s increased the bargaining power of workers relative to employers because it gave workers extra-market means of subsistence, reducing their need to enter the labor market (and drive down wages) during periods of high unemployment. As the entitlement programs grew, they broke the traditional inverse relationship between unemployment and wage levels.[31]

How might federal social programs affect the leverage of transfer recipients in the labor market? As Piven and Cloward note, income maintenance programs (like labor markets) are differentiated. Depending on the character of the beneficiaries, the programs may or may not affect labor market dynamics. Cutbacks in programs such as unemployment compensation and trade adjustment assistance clearly affect (largely male) workers in the industrialized and unionized monopoly sector, weakening their bargaining power. Most federal income maintenance programs, however, cater to dependent populations outside the labor market—the elderly, disabled, or needy children—or to indigent women with limited educational attainments and job skills at the periphery of the market. In the case of the elderly, disabled, and mothers with preschool children, it is hard to imagine how income security programs increase their bargaining power vis-à-vis employers. In the case of mothers with school-age children, the AFDC program does little to increase their market leverage. The program functions as a wage-supplement allowance and may even encourage lower wages in sex-segregated occupations and industries. Other welfare programs—Medicaid, day care—also act as a subsidy to employers of low-wage female labor. If anything, these programs increase the profit margin of affected businesses. Given the character of the beneficiaries of most federal entitlement programs, it becomes difficult to discern how the expansion of income maintenance programs increased the bargaining power of significant numbers of workers in private-sector labor markets.

Yet Piven and Cloward fail to appreciate the important ways besides entitlement programs in which the welfare state affects the labor market. After all, the welfare state is itself a labor market, generating most of the nation's social welfare employment. Thus Reagan's attack on the welfare state represents far more than the "old class war" of the 1930s between capital and labor—this time waged for control of the "new" instrumentalities of federal means-tested entitlement programs: AFDC, food stamps, Medicaid, low-income energy assistance, or public housing. It is a *new* class war precisely because it is being waged against the "new classes" benefiting from the expansion of the welfare state—human services workers and the poor. The new classes largely are composed of women.

In order to shed further light on the domestic policy sources of the gender gap, we now examine the character of the Reagan welfare and social budget changes, estimating their economic impacts upon working-age women. While our analysis of Reagan's impact on the welfare sector of the human services economy is confined to the AFDC program, it should be noted that because of the "feminization" of the poverty population, most of the adult recipients of the major in-kind federal welfare programs now under attack—food stamps, Medicaid, public housing, and rent subsidies—are women.

The Reagan Welfare Policies and Female-Headed Families

In a series of sweeping policy proposals, the Reagan administration has commenced its campaign to radically restructure the AFDC program. The two major thrusts of the new welfare policy for FY 1982 are the elimination of work incentives and the implementation of a workfare program. In the minds of their designers, these two strategies share a common goal of reducing welfare costs. Altering work rules supposedly reduces benefits paid to working welfare recipients. Work relief stigmatizes welfare recipients and drives them from the rolls.[32] Yet the consequences of these policy changes, we argue, may be opposite those the administration intends. Welfare caseloads and costs may increase rather than decrease.

Work Rules. The Reagan administration has dramatically changed AFDC work rules. The disregard for earned income, the "$30-and-one-third" rule, is to be terminated for welfare recipients after four consecutive months of employment. In place of the current itemized deductions for work-related and child-care expenses, the new regulations place ceilings on such disregards. As for work-related expenses, the $75 a month ceiling is substantially below actual average monthly expenses of $123, and the gap will widen each successive year with inflation.

What are the likely effects of these new AFDC work-related policies on welfare receipt and work and welfare patterns among women heading families? The Department of Health and Human Services estimates that these policies would drop 400,000 families—10 percent of the total caseload—from the AFDC rolls, resulting in federal savings of $1.1 billion a year. Yet the new eligibility rules undermine the work incentives that Congress has built into the welfare system over the past fifteen years, and may force many women to *choose* between welfare and work. Many women will choose welfare. As a study of the working poor by the Center for the Study of Social Policy reveals, under the new rules working welfare mothers can wind up with less disposable family income than nonworking welfare mothers.[33] Many women also will choose welfare if, as is the case in one-half the states, AFDC disqualification means the loss of Medicaid eligibility.

While we do not have national estimates of how women will react to the new work rules, a recent survey of Wisconsin's working welfare recipients conducted by that state's Department of Health and Social Services is instructive. The department estimates that over three-quarters of the state's working welfare recipients will decide to forego work entirely because of the new federal work rules. By falling back entirely on AFDC, these families would add $38 million, or 11 percent, to Wisconsin's program costs.[34]

Workfare. Reacting to the possibility of unanticipated rising welfare caseloads and costs attributable to its own policies, the administration has proposed for FY 1983 (as it had done in FY 1982) that states be required to operate community "workfare" programs—a misnomer for work relief—for able-bodied welfare recipients. Rejecting the administration's mandatory workfare scheme for FY 1982, Congress instead gave the states the option of instituting the program. The federal workfare program is generally modeled after the nation's oldest and best-known state-financed work relief program, Utah's Work Experience and Training Program (WEAT), which was started in 1974. The program would require able-bodied welfare recipients not otherwise working at least 80 hours per month (the new earned-income disregard and income-ceiling rules make sure of that) to "work off" in human services agencies, at the minimum wage, the family's monthly AFDC payment.

Workfare is a compulsory work-for-benefit program that provides neither training nor jobs to get women off AFDC. Training and jobs clearly are ideas whose time has *not* come for this administration. Federal funding for demonstration and work-incentive programs in twenty-six states, which encouraged and trained AFDC mothers to work, has been severely curtailed. CETA public-service jobs for welfare recipients also have been eliminated, and CETA job-training programs are scheduled for substantial funding reductions in FY 1983.

In addition to not creating jobs that move women off welfare, workfare programs have high administrative costs and do not prevent welfare abuse. Their true function is to placate middle-class taxpayers and to so stigmatize the doleful state of the truly needy that would-be applicants are induced to find jobs in the private sector, thus reducing welfare caseloads and costs. However, with unemployment on the rise and with the largest federal public-service job program terminated, it is next to impossible for disadvantaged, low-skilled welfare recipients to find full-time jobs in the private sector. The Reagan administration thus may confront the disquieting "unintended consequences" of conservative social experimentation: millions of indigent women toiling in state work relief programs.

Other Policy Changes Affecting Welfare Receipt. The "work disincentives" in the new AFDC regulations are not the only aspects of the administration's economic recovery program forcing women heading families to choose welfare and workfare over work. A sharp cutback in extended unemployment benefits may force thousands of laid-off workers onto AFDC or other forms of public assistance. Of the 300,000 CETA public-service workers terminated, approximately 100,000 were women with little education or few job skills who had moved off welfare because of CETA jobs. Lacking private-sector job opportunities (only 18 percent of the first wave of CETA layoffs have found permanent private-sector employment[35]), many CETA former welfare recipients will be forced to reapply for public assistance.[36] Reductions in federal day-care assistance may also force other working mothers to give up their jobs and fall back on welfare.

Most important, women heading families are likely to be among the first unemployed victims of the administration's tight-money and high-interest anti-inflationary zeal, and thus may be forced onto welfare. As mentioned, women are more subject to economic vicissitudes than other family heads. Given the tightening of the unemployment/welfare caseload linkages in the 1970s, additional unemployment generated by the Reagan economic policies may force even more women onto welfare.

Countering the prospects of its own policies creating a large-scale workfare class among women heading families, the administration in its "new federalism" proposal seeks to devolve AFDC responsibilities onto the states in FY 1984. If AFDC divestiture were implemented, the plan would pressure many states to reduce their care for indigent women and their children.[37]

Estimating the Employment Impacts of the Reagan Social Budget Cutbacks

Working-age women in the labor market are also confronted by the administration's dramatic alteration of federal spending patterns. From 1982 to 1984, $140 billion is slated to be cut (relative to the Carter budget projections) from social programs. The administration plans additional multibillion-dollar social program reductions in 1983 and 1984 to counter the soaring federal deficit.

If enacted in anything approaching its entirety, the Reagan four-year social budget promises to have substantial impacts on women employed in the social welfare economy. At the federal level, the Office of Management and Budget estimates that the budget cuts for FYs 1981 to 1984 will slim the 1.9 million federal nondefense work force by 150,000 (8 percent) by 1987. Of the initial 75,000-person job reduction to be accomplished by 1984, nearly one-third is slated to occur in the four major federal social welfare agencies—Health and Human Services, Housing and Urban Development, Education, and Labor. By 1984, employment in these four agencies will be pared by one-eighth.[38]

Women, particularly those in higher-level professional and managerial positions in the social welfare agencies, have been disproportionately affected by the first round of federal reductions in force (RIFs). Of the 12,000 RIFs as of January 1982, nearly one-half have been in upper-echelon positions (GS 12 and above). Women administrators at these levels have been laid off at a rate 150 percent higher than male administrators—175 per 10,000 federally employed women versus 70 per 10,000 men.[39]

The greatest effects of retrenchment will be felt in state and local governments or in the private nonprofit and profit sectors. At state and local levels, federal grants-in-aid for social welfare purposes totaled $57 billion in 1980. If the administration succeeds in implementing its budget priorities, federal social welfare grant outlays will drop to $34 billion 1984.

The federal government estimates that the termination of CETA public-service employment, the 25 percent reduction in most federal social welfare grants, and the consolidation into block grants of many federal categorical grants would result in an immediate 700,000 jobs lost in state and local governments by the end of FY 1982.[40] These estimates, however, do not tell us how women working in human services areas might be affected. From other sources we learn that the job losses are disproportionately concentrated in the human services sector. Reporting on a survey of one hundred major cities conducted in November 1981, the U.S. Conference of Mayors claims that nearly three-quarters of the responding cities planned to lay off workers, with the sharpest job reductions to occur in health and human services for the poor and in parks and recreation.[41]

Nor is private-sector social welfare employment immune from the Reagan social budget cutbacks. Federal social service and health grants to the states, totaling nearly $5 billion in FY 1981, have been consolidated into several block grants, and their funding levels have been reduced by 25 percent. Previously, states had taken federal grant funds and subcontracted to community-based organizations for the provision of services. Not only will social welfare agencies in the private sector be competing for significantly reduced federal funding but the more flexible block grant arrangement may encourage financially beleagured states to divert funding to governmental rather than nongovernmental agencies.

We cannot estimate more precisely how deep the inroads of the Reagan social budget reductions will be into the various sectors of the human services economy. By a reverse multiplier effect, the reductions in the entitlement programs will also significantly affect social welfare employment.

Yet it is clear that the Reagan welfare and social budget policies have the potential to adversely affect the lives of millions of working-age women. The new welfare rules may remove large numbers of indigent women from marginal private-sector work to state-sponsored work relief programs in human service agencies. The social budget reductions may force countless other women out of human services jobs and into the low-wage private-sector retail and service labor market. In this seeming job rotation of human services providers and recipients, there is a twofold downgrading of the economic condition of many working-age women: from better-paying social welfare jobs to poorer-paying private-sector retail and service jobs and, for women heading families, from marginal private-sector work to workfare.

In this section we have explored a second aspect of the welfare state dismantlement hypothesis. Because the Reagan attack centers on the service and entitlement programs that fund a substantial portion of the social welfare economy, working-age women—over 70 percent of the "new classes"—bear the brunt of retrenchment.[42]

BEYOND REAGANISM

To this point we have examined two aspects of the welfare state dismantlement hypothesis to help explain the growing political estrangement of women from the Reagan administration: the manner and extent to which the economic fortunes of working-age women became intertwined with those of the expanding welfare state, and the character and impact on working-age women of the tandem Reagan welfare and social budgetary policies.

What have been the political impacts on women of the Reagan economic and social policies? Working women clearly see themselves as disadvantaged by the Reagan policies. In December 1981, as the Reagan program was being implemented, the Democratic National Committee commissioned a survey of a sample of 1265 registered voters. In response to the question how Reagan's economic policies had personally affected them, working women saw themselves adversely affected by a nearly two-to-one margin (46 percent negatively versus 27 percent positively). Working men, on the other hand, generally saw themselves favorably affected (40 percent positively versus 34 percent negatively).[43]

Far more work is needed to test hypotheses about the political impacts on women of the Reagan domestic policies. Ideally one would examine the full range of domestic policies, hypothesizing about their possible differential impacts on working-age men and women. Additional public opinion surveys would need to be conducted, asking more specific questions about particular Reagan policies—for example, budget cutbacks, tax cuts, or relaxation of affirmative action enforcement—and about the respondent's relationship to the human services economy and to other state-sector programs. In this manner one could test alternative policy hypotheses—for example, military, environmental, and affirmative action—being offered to account for the gender gap.

In the absence of such data collection and analysis, we must speculate about the likely political impacts on women of the Reagan domestic policies. Will the budgetary and welfare policy retrenchment produce a political alliance among threatened state-sector human services workers and clientele, as James O'Connor suggests?[44] Certain factors encourage such an alliance. Women state workers are more politicized and liberal than women working in other industries. Their voting turnout rate in national elections is typically fifteen to twenty percentage points higher than that of other women in the labor force. For example, in the 1976 presidential election, the turnout rate for female government employees was 77 percent compared with 59 percent for women working in the private sector.[45] Moreover, human services workers and clients share the bonds of womanhood. Other factors, however, hinder the development of a state-sector coalition among women. Racial and class differences divide service providers and recipients. Ninety percent of all female human services professionals in 1970 were white. Fifty-seven percent of all female AFDC recipients are black or Hispanic. Notwithstanding the greater politicization of women working in the state sector, female heads of households display significantly lower levels of political mobilization. In 1976 their turnout rate of 49 percent was ten percentage points lower than that of women as a whole. Will Reagan's attack raise the stakes of political action sufficiently to mobilize dormant clientele groups?

Even if such a worker-client alliance were forged, it must be remembered that the Reagan welfare and budgetary policies are intertwined with a broader conservative social program. The administration's stand on sexual and familial issues, such as abortion, is supported by many women in traditional familial roles outside the labor market. It might be argued that as political differences between men and women are now emerging with respect to economic issues and policy, differences *among* women may soon sharpen with respect to family and sexual issues. To date, this difference between women has been muted by the administration's reluctance to confront the New Right's social-issue agenda. The varying role of the state in family and economic life may soon heighten a different set of tensions among women. While an interclass and interracial alliance between an increasingly proletarianized cadre of human services workers and clientele may be forged, other tensions may heighten between women who have achieved some measure of economic or sexual independence and women in traditional homemaking roles.

To the extent that capital currently is engaged in an investment strike designed to reduce both its tax burden and governmental regulation of economic activity, women must renew the fight for affirmative action and join other political groups seeking greater public and worker control over private investment decisions. In the coming years, these decisions will significantly affect women, not only in terms of domestic job loss due to overseas investment, but also in terms of the introduction of new technologies such as the word processor into "pink collar" occupations employing large numbers of women. Compared with the 1970s, the labor force will grow more slowly in the next ten years. The supply of private-sector jobs may grow at an even slower rate, signaling the need to redefine the meaning of full employment. Women and men thus may need to explore such alternatives as job sharing.

There are limits, however, to interest group politics and to "economism" for women—job leveraging strategies in a slow-growth economy as employment opportunities increasingly move into the private sector. If the historical tensions both within and between the sexes are to be diminished, feminists cannot limit their political energies to contesting the gender allocation of jobs in expanding and declining sectors. The larger issue is the moral vision that women might supply to direct political life to questions broader than economic and military purposes. The sexual division of labor gives women a unique vantage point for critiquing the ways in which men have conducted public life. Nurturing roles in private and public life—the rearing of children, working in the helping professions—heighten the sensitivity of many women to the denial of human dignity that plagues not only this administration but the political communities that men in general have constructed. In this broader context, it would be a mistake for women to halt their political labors at either preserving the social welfare economy from Reagan's Thermidor or assuring a quota of jobs for women in the private sector. The danger is that the Reagan policies may lead women to organize narrowly as economic claimants and as little more. Women must doubly constitute themselves politically—as economic claimants to be sure, but also as challengers to the established male-dominated sociopolitical order.[46]

NOTES

1. *New York Times*, 9 November 1980.

2. For the conventional wisdom, see Martin Gruberg, *Women in American Politics: An Assessment and Sourcebook* (New York: Academia Press, 1968), pp. 13–14; Susan and Martin Tolchin, *Clout: Womanpower and Politics* (New York: Coward, McCann and Geoghegan, 1974), p. 238; Sandra Baxter and Marjorie Lansing, *Women and Politics: The Invisible Majority* (Ann Arbor: University of Michigan Press, 1980), pp. 57–59. During the late 1960s and early '70s the Harris polls revealed a consistent ten percentage point difference

between men and women regarding the pace of the Vietnam withdrawal, with women saying the pace was "too slow." Louis Harris, *The Anguish of Change* (New York: W. W. Norton, 1973), pp. 90–92.

3. According to the New York Times/CBS News exit poll, 66 percent of the women opposing ratification of the ERA voted for Reagan compared with 32 percent of those favoring ratification. *New York Times*, 9 November 1980.

4. "Millions of Poor Face Losses Oct. 1 as Reconciliation Bill Spending Cuts Go Into Effect," *Congressional Quarterly Weekly Report* 39 (26 September 1981): 1833. The Congresswomen's Caucus estimates that 80 percent of the 4 million AFDC households are headed by women. Women head at least 60 percent of the households receiving food stamps or Medicaid assistance. Two-thirds of all households in publicly owned or subsidized housing are headed by women. See *Congressional Record* 127 (2 April 1981): E 1539–40, 1565–68.

5. Laurence E. Lynn, Jr., "A Decade of Policy Developments in the Income-Maintenance System," in *A Decade of Federal Antipoverty Programs*, ed. Robert H. Haveman (New York: Academic Press, 1977), pp. 73–75.

6. U.S. Bureau of the Census, *Current Population Reports*, Series P-60, No. 130, *Characteristics of the Population Below the Poverty Level: 1979* (Washington, D.C.: Government Printing Office, December 1981), pp. 79–80, Table 18.

7. Heather L. Ross and Isabel V. Sawhill, *Time of Transition* (Washington, D.C.: Urban Institute, 1975), pp. 98, 104–6. Welfare policy may have influenced AFDC receipt in even more indirect ways by encouraging the formation of female-headed welfare households. There is some evidence for small program-induced effects on family formation, primarily among nonwhite women. See Ross and Sawhill, pp. 106–20.

8. Ibid., p. 103.

9. Martin Rein and Lee Rainwater, "Patterns of Welfare Use," *Joint Center for Urban Studies Working Paper*, No. 47 (Cambridge, Mass.: Joint Center for Urban Studies of MIT and Harvard University, November 1977), pp. 19–27.

10. Emma Rothschild, "Reagan and the Real America," *New York Review of Books* 28, no. 1 (5 February 1981): 12–14. Econometric studies reveal that welfare receipt is affected by the quality as well as the quantity of jobs. Using data for 1967 and 1971 from the Panel Study of Income Dynamics, Bennett Harrison and Martin Rein have found that for women, holding a poor job (defined as one paying below the national average for that occupation coupled with the national occupational average wage itself paying less than the lower level budget standard as defined by the Bureau of Labor Statistics), all other things being equal, increased the likelihood of going on welfare by 12 percent. Harrison and Rein, "Some Microeconomic Relations Between Work and Welfare," *Working Papers of the Joint Center for Urban Studies*, No. 40 (Cambridge, Mass.: Joint Center for Urban Studies of MIT and Harvard University, October 1976), p. 11.

11. Welfare participation rates for whites and blacks calculated from the sources mentioned in Table 5.1. In terms of the length of welfare receipt, in 1977 41 percent of the black females on welfare had been on four or more years compared with 27 percent of white female AFDC recipients.

12. Ross and Sawhill, *Time of Transition*, pp. 74, 86.

13. Frank Levy, "Labor Force Dynamics and the Distribution of Employability," *Urban Institute Working Paper*, No. 1269–02 (Washington, D.C.: Urban Institute, January 1980), pp. 42–46.

14. U.S. Bureau of the Census, *Current Population Reports*, Special Studies Series P-

23, No. 110, *Characteristics of Households and Persons Receiving Noncash Benefits: 1979* (Washington, D.C.: Government Printing Office, 1981), pp. 3–8.

15. Diana M. Pearce and Harriette McAdoo, "Women in Poverty: Changes in Family Structure, Welfare and Work" (paper prepared for the National Advisory Council on Economic Opportunity, April 1981), pp. 28–32.

16. The term seems to have originated with Diana Pearce. See her "Women, Work, and Welfare: the Feminization of Poverty," in *Working Women and Families*, ed. Karen W. Feinstein (Beverly Hills, Calif.: Sage, 1979), pp. 103–24.

17. National Advisory Council on Economic Opportunity, *Twelfth Report: Critical Choices for the 80's* (Washington, D.C.: Government Printing Office, August 1980), p. 19.

18. U.S. Department of Commerce, *National Income and Product Accounts of the United States, 1929–1976* (Washington, D.C.: Government Printing Office, 1977), Tables 3.16, 3.17; idem, *National Income and Product Accounts, 1976–1979* (Washington, D.C.: Government Printing Office, 1980), Tables 3.16, 3.17. These accounts do not include general revenue sharing funds devoted to social welfare purposes. In 1976–77, for example, 36 percent of state/local revenue sharing funds of $6.6 billion went toward social welfare activities. See U.S. Bureau of the Census, *Expenditures of General Revenue Sharing and Antirecession Fiscal Funds: 1976–77*, Series GSS, No. 91 (Washington, D.C.: Government Printing Office, 1979), Table 8.

19. U.S. Department of Health and Human Services, *Annual Report to the Congress on Title XX of the Social Security Act, FY 1979* (Washington, D.C.: Department of Health and Human Services, February 1980) p. 34, Figure 16.

20. Lester Thurow, *The Zero-Sum Society* (New York: Penguin Books, 1981), pp. 165–66.

21. Barbara Blumenthal, "Uncle Sam's Army of Invisible Employees," *National Journal* 11, no. 18 (5 May 1979): 730–33.

22. See Irving Stern, "Industry Effects of Government Expenditures: An Input-Output Analysis," *Survey of Current Business* 55, no. 5 (May 1975): 9–23, esp. 12–13. For an attempt to use the I–O technique to generate industry employment estimates for selected federal social program expenditures, see U.S. Bureau of Labor Statistics, *Manpower Impact of Federal Government Programs: Selected Grants-in-Aid to State and Local Government*, Report 424 (Washington, D.C.: Government Printing Office, 1973).

23. For further evidence of the role of government expenditures in generating employment opportunities for women, see Thurow, *Zero-Sum Society*, pp. 162–64.

24. See Ralph E. Smith, "Women's Stake in a High-Growth Economy in the United States," in *Equal Employment Policy for Women*, ed. Ronnie Steinberg Ratner (Philadelphia: Temple University Press, 1980), pp. 358–62.

25. Rothschild, "Reagan and the Real America," Rothschild includes health services —in our definition an element of the social welfare economy—in the private-sector service industries.

26. See James O'Connor, *The Fiscal Crisis of the State* (New York: St. Martin's Press, 1973), pp. 13–18.

27. For a summary of studies assessing the effectiveness of equal employment opportunity programs, see Phyllis A. Wallace, "A Decade of Policy Developments in Equal Opportunities in Employment and Housing," in Haveman, *Decade of Antipoverty Programs*, pp. 337–47.

28. Carol G. Brown, "The Political Economy of Women's Liberation," (manuscript, University of Lowell, July 1980), pp. 9–11.

29. Dubnoff, "Beyond Sex Typing: Capitalism, Patriarchy and the Growth of Female Employment, 1940–1970" (paper prepared for the Rockefeller Conference on Women, Work and Family, New York, 21 September 1978), p. 3. Dubnoff's work appears based on Heidi Hartmann's. See Hartmann, "Capitalism, Patriarchy and Job Segregation by Sex," *Signs* 1, no. 3, pt 2 (Spring 1976): 137–69.

30. Brown, "Political Economy of Women's Liberation," p. 32.

31. Piven and Cloward, *The New Class War: Reagan's Attack on the Welfare State and Its Consequences* (New York: Pantheon, 1982), Chap. 1, "Capitalism Against Democracy," pp. 1–39.

32. For a more complete analysis of Reagan's current and proposed welfare policy changes, see Steven Erie and Martin Rein, "Welfare: The New Poor Laws," in *What Reagan Is Doing to Us*, ed. Alan Gartner et al. (New York: Harper & Row, 1982).

33. Cited in Linda E. Demkovich, "Reagan's Welfare Cuts Could Force Many Working Poor Back on the Dole," *National Journal* 14, no. 1 (2 January 1982): 21. Also see Tom Joe et al., *The Poor: Profiles in Poverty* (Washington, D.C.: Center for the Study of Welfare Policy, University of Chicago, March 1981).

34. Cited in Burt Schorr, "Will Reagan's Welfare Plan Work?" *Wall Street Journal*, 24 June 1981.

35. The administration claims that 60 percent of the first 131,000 CETA workers laid off had found jobs or were receiving job training. However, 16 percent of those workers who found jobs were actually transferred to other CETA positions, while another 26 percent were hired by state and local governments and may find those jobs threatened by federal grant-in-aid cutbacks. Joann S. Lublin, "Business Slow to Hire from CETA, Frustrating 'Reemployment' Plans," *Wall Street Journal*, 17 September 1981.

36. Congressional Budget Office, *Effects of Eliminating Public Service Employment*, Staff Working Paper (Washington, D.C.: Government Printing Office, June 1981), pp. 5–6.

37. For a more in-depth analysis of the likely impact of AFDC divestiture, see Erie and Rein, "Welfare."

38. Laura B. Weiss, "Fiscal 1983 Budget: President Proposes Cutting 150,000 from Federal Payroll," *Congressional Quarterly Weekly Report* 40, no. 7 (13 February 1982): 257–59.

39. Lawrence Meyer, "RIFs Hit Women Executives and Minorities," *Washington Post*, 31 December 1981.

40. Estimates supplied by the federal government to the International Labor Organization.

41. U.S. Conference of Mayors, *The FY82 Budget and the Cities: A Hundred City Survey* (Washington, D.C.: U.S. Conference of Mayors, 20 November 1981).

42. For other assessments of the impacts on women of the Reagan social policies, see "Sisterhood Is Braced for the Reaganauts," *New York Times*, 10 May 1981; Lynn Hecht Schafran, "Reagan vs. Women," *New York Times*, 13 October 1981; "Reagan's Women," *New Republic*, 28 October 1981; Patricia Schroeder, "A Sorry Record on Women's Rights," *Los Angeles Times*, 3 November 1981; Mary Fainsod Katzenstein, "Public Policy and the Inequality Between Poor and Non-Poor Women" (paper presented at the 1981 annual meeting of the American Political Science Association, New York City, 3–6 September 1981), pp. 14–25; and budget impact analyses by the Congresswomen's Caucus, *Congressional Record* 127, no. 54 (2 April 1981): E 1539–40, 1565–68.

43. Data supplied by the Democratic National Committee. Note that the question addresses economic policy in general—presumably including the tax cuts as well as the

budget reductions—and thus registers the concerns not only of women in social welfare fields but also of women in nonsocial welfare industries. The latter women are more vulnerable than men to the business cycle because they have less seniority in male-dominated industries such as manufacturing. Women in the social welfare economy, less affected by business cycles, are vulnerable to political funding cycles. See Smith, pp. "Women's Stake," 358–62. Also see Bill Peterson, "Women Shifting Sharply from Reagan," *Washington Post*, 29 March 1982; Everett Carl Ladd, "Does Reagan Have a Problem with Women?" *Public Opinion*, December/January 1982, pp. 48–49.

44. O'Connor, *Fiscal Crisis of the State*, pp. 236–56.

45. U.S. Bureau of the Census, *Current Population Reports*, Series P-20, No. 322, *Voting and Registration in the Election of November, 1976* (Washington, D.C.: Government Printing Office, March 1978), p. 61, Table 11.

46. See Irene Diamond and Nancy Hartsock, "Beyond Interests in Politics: A Comment on Virginia Sapiro's 'When Are Interests Interesting?' The Problem of Political Representation of Women," *American Political Science Review* 75, no. 3 (September 1981), pp. 717–21.

Part II

The Policy Domains: Production, Nurturance, and Sexuality

6

Margaret C. Simms

Women and Housing: The Impact of Government Housing Policy

Women's housing needs and housing problems arise out of a number of factors. Some are directly related to the operation of housing markets, and some are not. One set of housing problems is related to household income, which is in turn related to the race, sex, and age of the householder.

The median income of minority families is significantly lower than that of their white counterparts. Yet, within all ethnic groups, female-headed families have lower incomes than either male-headed or dual-headed families. And women predominate among the elderly, another group that is disproportionately poor. In many cases these income problems are compounded by discrimination and other market practices that further limit the housing choices of women because of their age, family situation, or the race and/or sex of the household head. Racial and sex discrimination by real estate agents and mortgage-lending institutions have been factors limiting access to suitable housing for many families. Although laws and regulations have been implemented to prevent the continuation of racial and gender discrimination, there is evidence that it still plays a role in housing markets. This discrimination has been joined by a more recent form—discrimination against families with children.

Housing is an important commodity not only because of its shelter service but because it provides access to employment services and social and cultural amenities. This essay reviews government housing policies and their impact on the availability, adequacy, and affordability of housing.

HOUSEHOLD COMPOSITION

The typical American household has changed tremendously over the past twenty years, a change that has accelerated over the past decade. The number of households in the United States increased 50 percent between 1960 and 1980. More than one-half of the increase took place between 1970 and 1980, even though the population grew at only a fraction of that rate (see Table 6.1). Most of the growth

TABLE 6.1
Composition of Households: 1960–1980

Type of Household	*1960*	*1970*	*1980*
All households (thousands)	52,799	63,401	79,080
Percent	100.0	100.0	100.0
Nonfamily households	14.7%	18.8%	26.2%
Persons living alone	13.1	17.1	22.6
Other nonfamily households	1.6	1.7	3.6
Family households	85.3	81.2	73.8
Married couple, no children	30.3	30.3	29.9
Married couple with children	44.1	40.3	31.1
One parent with children	4.4	5.0	7.5
Other family households	6.4	5.6	5.4

SOURCES: U.S. Bureau of the Census, P–20 Series, *Households and Families by Type* (Washington, D.C.: Government Printing Office, various years).

has occurred as a result of the formation of new households by young adults and newly separated or divorced couples. These changes can be seen in the increase in the proportion of nonfamily households relative to family households and the growth of households consisting of one-parent families with children. Households consisting of a married couple with children dropped from 44 percent to 31 percent of all households between 1970 and 1980.

In 1980 approximately 8 percent of all households consisted of one-parent households with children, nearly double the proportion of ten years earlier. Family composition varies by race, with minority households more likely to be female-headed than majority households. Among households that consisted of families with children under age eighteen, 15.2 percent of white families were one-parent families in 1979, 13.5 percent headed by a woman. For black and Hispanic families the figures were much higher. Nearly 49 percent of black families were single-parent families in 1979, 45.6 percent of them headed by a woman. Among Hispanic families with children under age eighteen, 23.5 percent were single-parent families, 21.6 percent maintained by a woman.[1]

Among all family households with children, the proportion in which the woman works has increased dramatically. Fifty-three percent of all children under age eighteen had mothers in the labor force in 1980 compared with 39 percent a decade ago. The rate was 51 percent for two-parent families and 60 percent for one-parent families. For black children the rates are higher in two-parent families but lower in one-parent families.

The income available to these families varies by household type, and this has implications for the ability to obtain adequate housing. Women's weekly earnings are only 60 percent of the earnings of their male counterparts, a ratio that has changed little over time. This fact, combined with their lower labor force participation rates and higher unemployment rates, means that they have lower annual incomes. The economic position of these families is unlikely to be improved by child-support payments.[2] In 1975, only one-fourth of all divorced, separated, remarried, and never married women with dependent children received child support. For those women who received payments, the average amount was $2433, with the median payment less than $1500. Two-earner households, on the other hand, have higher incomes than dual-headed single-earner couples. In 1980, the median income for two-earner couples was $26,879 compared with $18,972 for single-earner households.

Overall, minority families have lower income than white families. In 1980, white families had median earnings of $21,904 compared will $12,674 for black families and $14,717 for Hispanic families. Part of the difference is due to the much higher incidence of female-headedness in minority households. Even within categories, however, black and Hispanic families have less household income than white families. The minority-white income ratio is the lowest for female-headed families (see Table 6.2).

The changes that have taken place in the American household have implications for housing markets. Two-earner households have different needs in terms of housing location and neighborhood services since both husband and wife have journey-to-work considerations, with the wife frequently having dual responsibilities at work and home. Women who head households with children have similar responsi-

TABLE 6.2
Family Income in 1980
(current dollars)

	All Races	*White*	*Black*	*Hispanic*
All families	$21,023	$21,904	$12,674	$14,717
Married couples	23,141	23,501	18,593	17,361
Wife in labor force	26,879	27,238	22,795	21,649
Wife not in labor force	18,972	19,430	12,419	14,050
Male householder	17,519	18,731	12,557	13,302
Female householder	10,408	11,908	7,425	7,031

Minority Family Income as a Percent of White Family Income

	Black	*Hispanic*
All families	57.9	67.2
Married couples	79.1	73.9
Wife in labor force	83.7	79.5
Wife not in labor force	63.9	72.3
Male householder	67.0	71.0
Female householder	62.4	59.0

SOURCE: U.S. Bureau of the Census, *Money Income and Poverty Status of Families and Persons in the United States: 1980*, P. 60, No. 127 (Washington, D.C.: Government Printing Office, 1981).

bilities, complicated by the fact that they usually have fewer economic and human resources available to them. The needs of these new family types often come into conflict with those of the growing proportion of single-person households, both elderly and nonelderly. Without government intervention these conflicting needs would be resolved by the private housing market, a market in which the product is largely fixed in location and composition. Because of its long useful life, the stock is only marginally affected by new construction. The balance of the change must come from adaptation of existing units, a procedure that is not without negative consequences in the form of displacement and dislocation.

In the past, government policy has focused primarily on the physical attributes of housing and not on access and locational issues. After a brief review of past policies, our discussion will return to the importance of these aspects of housing.

GOVERNMENT HOUSING POLICY

The federal government has established as one of its policy goals "a decent home and a suitable living environment" for all Americans. The policies and programs that the government has pursued over the years have been aimed primarily at the physical aspects of housing—plumbing, structure, maintenance, and overcrowding. For the most part, these objectives have been fulfilled. The programs have not succeeded in providing equal access for all groups, and some have had negative effects on other stated policy goals.

Federal policy in housing has had two foci: encouraging home ownership and improving the housing of the poor.[3] The government's initial move into housing came during the 1930s with the establishment of two completely different programs. The first was the creation of the Federal Housing Administration (FHA) with its mortgage insurance program (1934). This program changed the nature of home ownership by reducing down payments and extending the repayment period. FHA insurance, in combination with the fact that mortgage interest payments were tax deductible, was a major factor in the dramatic growth in home ownership.[4] It also contributed to the development of suburban communities and in various ways may have contributed to racial segregation. By 1957 the concept of mortgage insurance was so well established that it became privatized, leaving FHA with the relatively high risk cases.

The second development of the 1930s was the establishment of the public housing program. As originally legislated, the program provided for federal payments to repay bonds issued to cover the capital costs of constructing public housing. The local housing authorities were to cover operating costs out of rents and other revenues. Income ceilings and other factors combined to create a clientele consisting disproportionately of minority and female-headed households.[5] By 1969 the pressure of rising operating costs had led to relatively high rent burdens. At that time Congress put a cap on the percent of income tenants were required to pay in rent with the federal government paying the difference between rent revenues and operating costs.[6]

In the past thirty years a variety of other federal programs that have had improved housing and neighborhood conditions as their main objective have been established (and dissolved). One set of programs commonly called "urban renewal," has involved extensive land clearance to remove slums and blight with the expectation that the end result would be better housing for the poor. A second group of programs consists of various interest-subsidy programs that have provided below-market rate mortgages to builders to construct rental housing for low-income households and to moderate-income households for home ownership. A third program group consists of demand-side programs that allow renters to choose their housing units with the federal government paying the difference between a fair market rent (FMR) and 25 percent of household income.

What has been the net effect of these programs on housing opportunities and living environments? As mentioned, the FHA insurance program was instrumental in opening up home ownership opportunities for a broad section of the U.S. population. However, some of its regulations served to reinforce certain discriminatory practices in the housing industry. In the past, emphasis was placed on the neighborhood in which an insured house was located, with "stable, homogeneous neighborhoods" preferred. This reinforced racial segregation because racially mixed neighborhoods were considered unstable; this policy made the federal government a partner to redlining.

Another FHA practice that had a negative effect on women and their families was the practice of discounting a woman's income when calculating loan-income ratios. Until 1973 both FHA and VA supported the practice of discounting a woman's income based on her age and reproductive capacity. The assumption was that women had only a casual attachment to the labor force and would drop out if they married or became pregnant. The practice often had the effect of denying home ownership to families in which the woman made a substantial contribution to family income and virtually ruled out home ownership for women except through inheritance or divorce settlements. Since black families have historically depended on the wife's earnings for a significant proportion of total family income, this practice was especially harmful to them. Although these practices have been outlawed, there is evidence to suggest that mortgage discrimination on the basis of household type, race or ethnicity, and location of property still exists.[7]

Mortgage discrimination, in combination with lower household income, has affected home ownership rates. While 65 percent of all households are homeowners, only 44 percent of black households and 42 percent of Hispanic households own their homes. Forty-seven percent of female-headed households are occupying homes owned by the head.

The public housing and housing subsidy programs have allowed a large number of families to improve their housing conditions. However, not all subsidized housing is physically adequate, and the location of the housing may not provide the "suitable living environment" federal housing policy seeks to promote. Subsidized housing units are frequently located in isolated central-city areas that have few support services or shopping areas. Access to jobs can also be a problem with residents forced to make long commutes or subsist on transfer payments.[8] Another serious drawback is that the programs serve only a fraction of the eligible population. It is estimated that only about 10 percent of the eligible population is served by housing programs, compared to 75 percent served by the food stamp and medical programs.[9] This creates major inequities among households with the same income. In some programs this is exacerbated by the fact that more is sometimes spent on moderate-income groups than is spent on low-income groups.[10]

While most of the funds for housing programs have come from the federal government, local governments have had a strong impact on housing conditions in a number of ways. Through their decision to participate in federal programs they determine whether or not residents or potential residents will have access to housing subsidy programs.[11] Through their execution of federal programs local governments decide which residents will benefit from these programs.

The largest impact on housing that local governments have, though, is through their legislative and enforcement powers. Local ordinances on housing codes and standards, antidiscrimination requirements, and rent control determine the environment in which the housing industry operates. Enforcement of these laws can affect the quality of housing available to local residents. The most powerful weapon, however, is the zoning power that most local governments have. Zoning laws can serve to protect households from undesirable elements such as heavy industry, but they can also be used to exclude low-income families or multifamily rental housing from the community. This denies low- and moderate-income families and renter households access to desirable housing and neighborhood services.

HOUSING CONDITIONS IN THE UNITED STATES

The key issues in housing can be categorized as availability, adequacy, affordability, and accessibility. As indicated, the government has used various programs to help expand the supply of adequate housing. The Bureau of the Census has recorded the increases in the housing stock that have taken place over time, and it has documented the steady decline in the proportion of the population living in substandard and/or overcrowded conditions. By 1976 the proportion of the population that lived in nonstandard housing had dropped to less than 10 percent of all households. However, the percent living in inadequate housing varied by household type. Black and Hispanic households were twice as likely to live in substandard housing in 1976, and large households were one and one-half times as likely to occupy inadequate housing (Table 6.3).

Income is a major reason for the higher proportion of minority and female-headed families living in substandard housing. A HUD study that compared the cost of standard housing in urban areas with the income of various household groups showed that while 80 percent of all U.S. households would have been able to obtain standard housing at costs below 25 percent of their income, the proportions for black, Hispanic, and female-headed households were 63, 71, and 53 per-

TABLE 6.3
Adequacy of Housing, 1976

			Hispanics						
	Total	*Blacks*	*Total*	*Mexicans*	*Cubans*	*Puerto Rican*	*Central & South Am.*	*Female*	*Large*
Units without flaws (thousands)	66,906	6,008	2,689	1,362	212	313	144	15,705	4,386
Percent of all units	90.3	78.6	81.5	79.8	93.4	67.3	78.7	88.0	83.1
Units with flaws (thousands)	7,174	1,632	609	344	15	152	39	2,149	893
Percent of all units	9.7	21.4	18.5	20.2	6.6	32.7	21.3	12.0	16.9
Severely flawed (2 or more) (thousands)	1,890	605	173	77	1	29	7	544	265
Percent of all units	2.6	7.9	5.3	4.5	0.4	6.2	3.8	3.1	5.0

SOURCE: *How Well Are We Housed?* U.S. Department of Housing and Urban Development (Washington, D.C.: Government Printing Office, 1979).

cent, respectively. If 35 percent of income is used as the housing cost cutoff, the proportion of all households that could have obtained standard housing increased to 88 percent, with black, Hispanic, and female-headed households trailing with only 76, 83 and 78 percent able to obtain standard housing. Since this study was based on a comparison of median housing costs and median household income, it does not reveal what households actually paid for housing in 1976. In fact, nearly one-half of all renter households paid more than 25 percent of their income for housing, and both renters and homeowners with a mortgage who had incomes under $7000 were likely to pay more than 35 percent of their income on housing.

ACCESSIBILITY

Housing is a service that, by its location, provides access to other services, such as education, child care, and shopping. It also provides access to employment opportunities. Within metropolitan areas, housing opportunities and services are unevenly distributed. Land costs, zoning restrictions, and transportation networks have led to a spatial distribution that has placed low-income and rental housing close to the central business district and middle-income owner-occupied housing in outlying suburban areas. It has been argued that this arrangement has denied inner-city residents access to employment as blue-collar jobs have moved to the suburbs over time and has also had an effect on the quality of public services available to these households.

An examination of population statistics shows that the spatial location of households is highly dependent on the race and sex of the householder. Although there have been shifts away from central cities and metropolitan areas during the past decade, blacks and Hispanics are still more likely to be in metropolitan areas than whites, and they are over twice as likely to be inside central cities. Within each ethnic group, female-headed households are more likely to be in central cities than the population as a whole (Table 6.4).

While lower family income is a factor in spatial segregation, the impact of limited economic resources is reinforced by discriminatory practices in the housing industry. Although discrimination on the basis of race or sex is illegal, discrimination continues to be a substantial factor in urban housing markets. Recent studies on the rental and sale of housing reveal that minorities are more likely to be denied mortgage credit and are treated less favorably with regard to housing availability.

A fairly recent phenomenon, discrimination against families with children, has placed additional restrictions on the ability to secure suitable rental housing. During the past ten years apartment owners and managers have used a number of restrictive rules to limit or eliminate families with children from rental units. These practices include an outright ban on children, limits on the number and/or ages of children, and limits on the number of children per bedroom or the sharing of bedrooms by children of opposite sexes. A nationwide survey of restrictive rental practices estimated that they exclude families with one child from one-third of all rental units, those with two children from one-half of the rental units, and families with

Table 6.4
Population Distribution by Metropolitan–Nonmetropolitan Residence, 1979

	Total Population[a] *(percent)*	*Female-Headed Families (percent)*
All Races		
Metropolitan	67.5	73.2
Central city	28.1	41.1
Suburban	39.4	32.2
Nonmetropolitan	32.5	26.8
White		
Metropolitan	66.1	70.8
Central city	24.1	32.0
Suburban	42.1	38.9
Nonmetropolitan	33.9	29.2
Black		
Metropolitan	76.1	79.5
Central city	56.4	64.0
Suburban	19.8	15.4
Nonmetropolitan	23.9	20.5
Spanish Origin[b]		
Metropolitan	84.2	89.2
Central city	50.2	63.9
Suburban	34.0	25.2
Nonmetropolitan	15.8	10.8

SOURCES: P–20, No. 350, p. 26; P–23, No. 107, p. 11.

[a] Numbers may not total to 100 percent due to rounding.
[b] Persons of Spanish origin may be of any race.

three or more children from six of every ten units.[12] These practices are more prevalent in newer housing complexes and in white neighborhoods, thereby making it harder for families with children to find housing in the newer (and better) sections of a metropolitan area. Although the practices are usually applied to all families with children, the fact that minority and female-headed families are more likely to be renter households makes the effect of the practice more severe for these households. Unlike racial or gender discrimination, discrimination against families with children is illegal in only a few jurisdictions.

These two factors–low income and discrimination–would not create locational hardships for families if the central city was the preferred location for these households. Evaluations of location and access to employment, services, and social and cultural amenities are divided on this issue.

A key issue for housing accessibility is access to employment. While this point has always been considered important for men, with the increased labor force participation of women over the past decade the relationship between housing location and female employment opportunities has become a subject of interest. Most women who work do so out of economic necessity. Nearly one-half of the women in the labor force in 1979 were single, separated, divorced, or widowed. And for married women with husbands present, wives' earnings are frequently a substantial contribution to household income.

The research on the effect of housing location on women's employment has not been extensive. Most of the economics literature in this area has dealt with the effect of racial segregation on employment opportunities, and it has been inconclusive. Research completed by John Kain seems to point to substantial job losses by blacks as a result of housing segregation. Other studies have contradicted these conclusions, however, pointing out that proximity to jobs does not necessarily increase the likelihood of employment. When unemployment rates are disaggregated by residence, black-white differentials remain.[13]

Within racial and gender groups, labor force participation is higher and unemployment rates are lower in the suburbs than in central cities (Table 6.5). However, the direction of causation is not clear. Since housing in the suburbs is more expensive and consists primarily of owner-occupied units, people who live in the suburbs are more likely to be economically secure.

Table 6.5
Labor Force Participation and Unemployment Rates by Area of Residence, 1980

	Black		*White*		*Hispanic*	
	Male	*Female*	*Male*	*Female*	*Male*	*Female*
Central city						
Labor force participation	69.0%	52.5%	77.2%	51.6%	80.9%	46.2%
Unemployment rate	16.1	14.5	6.8	6.3	10.5	10.3
Suburbs						
Labor force participation	76.2	59.6	80.6	52.9	83.1	51.9
Unemployment rate	11.8	11.8	5.6	6.1	9.0	10.6
Nonmetropolitan						
Labor force participation	68.2	48.8	76.3	49.0	81.3	44.6
Unemployment rate	12.6	15.0	6.4	7.2	8.8	12.4

SOURCE: Bureau of Labor Statistics Report No. 652.

Some recent research by Madden and White on housing location and women's work trips provides further insight into the link between housing and employment opportunities.[14] Statistics show that in all types of households, women live closer to work than men. What is not clear is the way in which these work and housing location decisions are made. Madden and White formulated three hypotheses to explain this phenomenon. One explanation would be that housing decisions are made on the basis of the work trips of both spouses. In this case, housing location is based on a minimization of joint transportation costs. Madden's empirical work (1980), however, reveals that husbands with working spouses have longer work trips than other males. This would suggest that the joint minimization does not involve a housing location decision that places both spouses closer to work. It is possible that the two-earner household locates closer to the wife's job because of her extra household responsibilities, with the male assuming a greater transportation cost. This outcome can also result if "women's" jobs are spatially segregated from "men's" jobs.

An alternative explanation for the shorter trips women make is that they choose their job location after the housing location decision is made. In this scenario, women conduct a job search from a fixed housing location. In addition to added household responsibilities, women may not search far for jobs because the wage gradient is very low. Since the added returns in terms of higher pay are small, it does not pay to travel farther from home.

This hypothesis is consistent with Madden's findings on unmarried women. Unmarried women have shorter work trips than their male counterparts. Since they live closer to the central city than two-earner couples with children, this would imply that unmarried women and married women have different employment locations. Unmarried women with children, however, had longer work trips than unmarried women without children. This finding would seem to indicate that this group of women either had a different set of preferences from women in other situations or they had more limited work and/or housing options. Madden also found that blacks in two-earner and traditional families with children had longer work trips, indicating that race may also limit work and housing options.

In addition to access to employment, housing location has other advantages and disadvantages. In the past it was thought that the suburbs provided better services and amenities. This may not be the case for all households. One recent study of women in suburbs notes that the view of suburbs as a pleasant place to live is based on outsider observations, especially the appearance of physical adequacy.[15] In reviewing four dimensions of urban life—housing environment, community service, social patterns, and psychological well-being—researchers found the suburbs less than ideal in a number of areas. While the physical structures tend to be well-constructed, these homogeneous communities of large, single-family homes tend to preclude singles, widows, and divorced women. The spacing of homes frequently does not provide for gathering places, limiting the ability to socialize in the neighborhood. Their study showed that single and divorced women were more likely to be unhappy in the suburbs, finding travel time and household maintenance burdensome. As others have noted, these women tend to prefer the entertainment, daycare facilities, and other amenities of the central city.[16] This information would tend to suggest that these households live in the central city by choice. However, interviews with women involved in marital dissolution indicate that newly separated and divorced women do not move out of a preference for central-city living. These women have a set of needs that are in conflict with the present spatial distribution of housing. The desire to maintain social status and school settings for the children would suggest that middle-income wives would want to remain in suburban locations. On the other hand, these communities may not provide child-care facilities, social contacts, or a reasonable commute to work.

In the final analysis the locational decision is usually made on the basis of economics. Since women tend to have lower incomes, they find themselves forced out of the suburbs because they cannot afford to live there. If they are unable to maintain the single-family home, there are often no viable alternatives. Therefore, the movement into the central city that takes place after divorce or separation is as likely to be the result of a search for affordable rental housing as a vote for central-city living.[17]

CONCLUSIONS AND RECOMMENDATIONS

The federal government of the United States has had the stated policy goal of providing decent housing and a suitable living environment for all Americans since 1949. Programs to facilitate the achievement of that goal have been in existence since 1934. As a result of FHA programs to promote home ownership, the United States has moved from a nation of renters to one in which the majority of homes are owner-occupied. The national public housing program has provided affordable housing to a large number of low-income families. These two programs, in combination with those instituted after World War II, have been very successful in terms of raising housing standards in the United States. However, they have not been without their negative consequences.

FHA and VA programs accelerated the decentralization of urban areas and facilitated the creation of homogeneous suburban communities. Policies that made "neighborhood stability" an important factor is evaluating loan risk reinforced local zoning practices, which limited the types of housing that could be built. Consequently, most suburban communities were racially segregated and had few multi-family rental units. Public housing programs concentrated a large number of low-income families in a small geographical area, often far from job opportunities and desirable services.

Minority and female-headed households have not shared in the full benefits of housing improvements. They are more likely to be inadequately housed, more likely to be renters, and more likely to live in the older, less desirable sections of central cities. Their spatial isolation creates hardships for them in terms of transportation costs, inferior schools and health services, and inadequate child care.

Government policies to improve the housing position of these households should focus on two things: increasing locational options and reintegrating the use of urban space. Since women have shorter work trips and greater household responsibilities (in both married-couple and single-parent households), access to employment and services is crucial. While households with large incomes can usually bid for the housing services they desire, those with lower incomes cannot do so. A number of policies can be used to increase the housing options available. Housing voucher programs like Section 8 provide families with low incomes greater locational flexibility than public housing, but choice is still limited by housing availability. Any move toward "demand" approaches such as Section 8 or housing vouchers must ensure the enforcement of antidiscrimination laws in order to increase options for minorities.

One set of policies that would increase the diversity of housing available in various locations is a revision of zoning laws. Inclusionary zoning requirements that provide waivers on density if developers include low-income housing in their plans is one approach. Another would be greater zoning flexibility that would permit unrelated individuals to share a dwelling unit. This would allow one-parent families to join together to rent or buy a "single-family" house in a suburban community, a practice that is currently illegal in many jurisdictions.

A reintegration of urban space would not only provide a diversity of housing options in a given area but would also provide comprehensive services such as child care, job counseling, and health care. Some housing communities in the United States already do this, though the practice is much more prevalent in Europe.

Policies must also be developed to counter the effects of recent trends in home ownership and rental housing. The growing number of two-earner and single-individual households seem to have a preference for housing closer to the center of the metropolitan area. This is the result of a desire to reduce commuting time and be closer to cultural and social activities. These preferences, in combination with higher discretionary income, have the effect of increasing the cost of housing traditionally occupied by renter households—a group that is disproportionately minority, female, and elderly. Government policy should be directed toward minimizing the dislocational impacts of central-city revitalization through subsidies and regulatory measures. Restrictive rental practices that discriminate against families with children also decrease the available supply of housing and have a significant impact on minority and female-headed families. Careful thought should be given to possible legislative action that can prevent or control the use of these practices.

The "traditional" family with a wage-earning husband, a full-time homemaker wife, and two children represents only a small portion of all U.S. households. Two-earner couples, one-parent families, and unrelated individual households will be growing as a percent of all households. These facts require a reassessment of federal, state, and local government housing policy. Only by taking account of changing household structure can policy be responsive to the needs of the people.

NOTES

1. The Census Bureau has changed its terminology in recent years, recognizing that "many households and families are no longer organized in accordance with autocratic principles" (Series P–23, No. 107, p. 1, 1980). As a result, the new term for "female-headed families" is "families maintained by female householders with no husband present." For ease of exposition, that term is not used in this essay. "Male-headed families" are those with a male

householder (no spouse). "Female-headed families" are those with a female householder (no spouse). Husband-wife households will be referred to as "dual-headed" or two-parent.

2. U.S. Department of Commerce, Bureau of the Census, *Divorce, Child Custody, and Child Support*, Current Population Reports, Special Studies Series P-23, No. 84 (Washington, D.C.: Government Printing Office, 1979).

3. For a more detailed review of the history of federal involvement, see John C. Weicher, *Housing: Federal Policies and Programs* (Washington, D.C.: American Enterprise Institute, 1980).

4. In FY 1981, mortgage interest deductions reduced federal tax revenues by $19.8 billion. Property tax deductions cost the government $8.9 billion. Over one-third of the benefits went to households with over $20,000 in income. The effect of these two programs was to generate tax savings of 24 to 38 percent of housing costs for families in these brackets. See Congressional Budget Office, *Tax Treatment of Homeownership: Issues and Options* (Washington D.C.: Government Printing Office, 1981).

5. A 1976 survey of 22 large-city public housing authorities revealed that blacks constituted 73 percent of the tenant population while female-headed families constituted 49 percent of the population, percentages far in excess of their representatives in the eligible population. See Raymond J. Stouyk, *A New System for Public Housing* (Washington, D.C.: The Urban Institute, 1980).

6. In 1980 the percentage was raised from 25 to 30 for new tenants. In 1981 the higher limit was extended to all tenants.

7. Margaret C. Simms, *Families and Housing Markets, Obstacles to Locating Suitable Housing* (Washington, D.C.: U.S. Department of Housing and Urban Development, 1980).

8. The tendency to rely on transfer payments is increased when earned income pushes household income over the eligibility ceiling for a subsidized unit.

9. Sue Marshall, "An Evaluation of the Community Development Block Grant Program and the Housing Requirements of Low Income Communities" (paper presented at the Allied Social Sciences Association meetings, Denver, Colorado, 5–7 September 1980).

10. Frank deLeeuw, et al., "Housing" in *The Urban Predicament*, ed. William Gorham and Nathan Glazer (Washington, D.C.: The Urban Institute, 1976).

11. Virtually all white suburbs like Parma, Ohio and Warren, Michigan have turned down federal grants instead of committing themselves to building low-income housing that might attract poor blacks from Cleveland and Detroit. In 1981 Congress changed housing plan requirements making it easier for cities to receive funds without having to make such commitments. See Nicholas D. Kristof, "Congress Redraws Plan on Housing Grants," *Washington Post*, 24 August 1981, p. A–15.

12. Robert W. Marans et al., *Measuring Restrictive Rental Practices Affecting Families With Children: A National Survey.* (Washington, D.C.: Department of Housing and Urban Development, 1980).

13. Margaret C. Simms, *Families and Housing Markets: Obstacles to Locating Suitable Housing* (Washington, D.C.: Department of Housing and Urban Development, 1980).

14. Janice F. Madden and Michelle J. White, "Spatial Implications of Increases in the Female Labor Force: A Theoretical and Empirical Synthesis," *Land Economics* 56 (November 1980): 432–46; and Janice F. Madden, "Why Women Work Closer to Home," Manuscript of University of Pennsylvania, January 1980.

15. Donald N. Rothblatt, et al., *The Suburban Environment and Women* (New York: Praeger, 1979).

16. Gerda R. Wekerle, *A Woman's Place is in the City* (Cambridge, Mass.: Lincoln Institute of Land Policy, 1979).

17. Susan Anderson-Khleif, *Strategies, Problems and Policy Issues for Single Parent Housing* (Cambridge, Mass.: Joint Center for Urban Studies of MIT and Harvard, August 10, 1979).

BIBLIOGRAPHY

Anderson-Khleif, Susan. *Strategies, Problems and Policy Issues for Single Parent Housing*. Cambridge, Mass.: Joint Center for Urban Studies of MIT and Harvard, 10 August 1979.

Clay, Phillip L. "Managing the Urban Reinvestment Process." *Journal of Housing* 36 (October 1979): 453–58.

Congressional Budget Office. *Tax Treatment of Homeownership: Issues and Options*. Washington, D.C.: Government Printing Office, 1981.

deLeeuw, Frank, et al., "Housing." In *The Urban Predicament*, ed. William Gorham and Nathan Glazer. Washington, D.C.: The Urban Institute, 1976.

Goodman, John L., Jr. "Reasons for Moves Out Of and Into Large Cities." *APA Journal* 45 (October 1979): 407–16.

Green, Robert L., et al. *Discrimination and the Welfare of Urban Minorities*. East Lansing: Michigan State University, 1979.

Hapgood, Karen, and Getzels, Judith. *Planning, Women, and Change*. Washington, D.C.: American Society of Planning Officials, 1975.

Madden, Janice F. "Why Women Work Closer to Home." Manuscript, University of Pennsylvania, January 1980.

———, and White, Michelle J. "Spatial Implications of Increases in the Female Labor Force: A Theoretical and Empirical Synthesis." *Land Economics* 56 (November 1980): 432–46.

Marans, Robert W., et al. *Measuring Restrictive Rental Practices Affecting Families With Children: A National Survey*. Washington, D.C.: Department of Housing and Urban Development, 1980.

Marshall, Sue. "An Evaluation of the Community Development Block Grant Program and the Housing Requirements of Low Income Communities." Paper presented at the Allied Social Sciences Association meetings, Denver, Colorado, 5–7 September 1980.

Roncek, Dennis, and Bell, Ralph. "Female-Headed Families: An Ecological Model of Residential Concentration in a Small City." *Journal of Marriage and the Family* 42 (February 1980): 157–69.

Rothblatt, Donald N., et al. *The Suburban Environment and Women*. New York: Praeger, 1979.

SIGNS: Journal of Women in Culture and Society. Special Issue on Women and the American City 5 (Spring 1980).

Simms, Margaret C. "A Housing Agenda for the Eighties." Paper prepared for the National Urban Coalition, December 1980.

———. *Families and Housing Markets: Obstacles to Locating Suitable Housing*. Washington, D.C.: Department of Housing and Urban Development, 1980.

Smith, Ralph E., ed. *The Subtle Revolution*. Washington, D.C.: The Urban Institute, 1979.

Struyk, Raymond J. *A New System for Public Housing*. Washington, D.C.: The Urban Institute, 1980.

U.S. Department of Commerce, Bureau of the Census. *Families Maintained by Female Householders 1970–79*. Current Population Reports, Series P-23, No. 107. Washington, D.C.: Government Printing Office, 1980.

———. *Households and Families by Type* (Advance Report). Current Population Reports, Series P-20, No. 357. Washington, D.C.: Government Printing Office, 1980.

———. *Money Income and Poverty Status of Families and Persons in the United States: 1980*. Advance Data from March 1981 Current Population Survey, Series P-60, No. 127. Washington, D.C.: Government Printing Office, 1981.

———. *Population Profile of the United States: 1979*. Current Population Reports, Series P–20, No. 350. Washington, D.C.: Government Printing Office, 1980.

U.S. Department of Housing and Urban Development. *How Well Are We Housed? Large Families*. HUD-PDR-543. Washington, D.C.: Government Printing Office, 1980.

———. *How Well Are We Housed? Female-Headed Households*. HUD-PDR-344(2). Washington, D.C.: Government Printing Office, 1979.

———. *How Well Are We Housed? Blacks*. HUD-PDR-366. Washington, D.C.: Government Printing Office, 1979.

———. *How Well Are We Housed? Hispanics*. HUD-PDR-333(2). Washington, D.C.: Government Printing Office, 1979.

U.S. Department of Labor, Bureau of Labor Statistics. "Employment in Perspective: Minority Workers." Bureau of Labor Statistics Report No. 652, 1981.

———. "Half of Nation's Children Have Working Mothers." News Release, 15 November 1981.

———. *Handbook of Labor Statistics*. Bulletin No. 2070. Washington, D.C.: Government Printing Office, 1980.

———. *Perspectives on Working Women: Highlights*. Washington, D.C.: Government Printing Office, 1980.

——— "Weekly Earnings of Workers and Their Families: Second Quarter 1981." Bureau of Labor Statistics New Release, 26 August 1981.

———. *Young Workers and Families: A Special Section*. Special Labor Force Report No. 233, 1979.

Voices for Women: 1980 Report of the President's Advisory Committee for Women. Washington, D.C.: Government Printing Office, 1980.

Vroman, John and Greenfield, Stuart. "Are Blacks Making It in the Suburbs? Some New Evidence on Intrametropolitan Spatial Segmentation." *Journal of Urban Economics* 7 (March 1980): 155–67.

Weicher, John C. *Housing: Federal Policies and Programs*. Washington, D.C.: American Enterprise Institute, 1980.

———. "Urban Housing Policy." In *Current Issues in Urban Economics*, ed. Peter Mieskowski and Mahlon Strasheim. Baltimore: Johns Hopkins Press, 1979, pp. 469–508.

Wekerle, Gerda R. *A Woman's Place Is in the City*. Cambridge, Mass.: Lincoln Institute of Land Policy, 1979.

7

Shelah Gilbert Leader

Fiscal Policy and Family Structure

The actual versus the proper role of the state in family life is the subject of heated debate between liberals concerned with individual rights and conservatives who place paramount importance on the family as the basic social unit. If we understand that the conservative norm for the family is patriarchy, then it is clear why the individualism of liberals is labeled "antifamily" by conservatives. Feminism as a women's rights movement is clearly in the liberal tradition and opposes the "pro-family" goals of conservatives.[1] This clash of values pits patriarchal marriage against the feminist goal of marriage as an economic partnership of equals. Conservatives and feminists are each convinced that state policy is in fact inimical to their family norm.[2]

We can shed light on some of the actual effects of state policy on the family by examining a basic state activity: raising and spending money through the power of taxation. Specifically, two policies with nearly universal effect are examined: the current Social Security Act and the Internal Revenue Act of 1978. Do these laws favor traditional marriage in which the male is the sole earner and the wife is economically dependent on her husband; or do they favor nontraditional, two-earner married couples?

The effect of these laws on one- and two-earner married couples has recently been criticized by women's rights advocates, and proposals for changing the laws have been considered by Congress on numerous occasions. Ironically, in its rush to reduce taxes, the conservative 1981 Congress enacted an income tax reform that effectively responds to feminist criticisms of the income tax law (see the Economic Recovery Tax Act of 1981). This essay examines the nature and basis of these criticisms.

Before considering how these two laws actually treat one- and two-earner couples and various proposals to change these laws, we must remind ourselves of demographic trends that have sparked the debate over the fairness of these fiscal policies.

I would like to thank Heidi Hartmann and Martha Philips for their careful review of an earlier draft of this paper. Their thoughtful comments are most appreciated.

BACKGROUND

The traditional American concept of marriage and family was based on four assumptions: (1) marriage lasted until one spouse died; (2) the wife was a full-time homemaker; (3) the husband was the sole earner; (4) the wife's work in the home had no economic value. Public policy has reflected these assumptions.

This model has become or is rapidly becoming obsolete. A 1980 government report noted that "the recent rapid rise in the American divorce rate, to heretofore unprecedented levels, must be counted among the major demographic changes in the United States since World War II."[3] If current trends in divorce continue, marriage will be as likely to end in divorce as in death.[4]

Even more dramatic is the shift from one-earner to two-earner married couples. So many married women are entering the paid labor force that by 1990, it is predicted, only 25 percent of married women under age fifty-five will be full-time homemakers.[5]

At first glance, there is a tendency to assume that many of these women are working for reasons of self-fulfillment and/or to pay for luxuries. In fact, families depend very heavily on the wife's wages. In 1978 married women working full-time contributed almost 35 percent of the total family income.[6] Even more significant, almost 30 percent of the women who worked in 1979 were married to men who earned less than $15,000 a year.[7] This suggests that at least one ingredient of traditional patriarchal marriage—the total economic dependence of wives on their husbands—is now missing from most marriages. Indeed, income contributed by wives is often essential to a family's financial well-being.

State fiscal policy does not reflect this new reality. In fact, fiscal policy has the effect of rewarding traditional marriages. To illustrate this, we turn first to an examination of the so-called marriage penalty tax of the Revenue Act of 1978.

THE MARRIAGE PENALTY

The "marriage penalty" refers to the increased total amount of income taxes two workers must pay when they marry. Although married workers face lower tax rates than single workers, married workers are taxed on their combined earnings. Therefore, when two workers marry, their combined earnings place them in a higher tax bracket and increase their tax burden. In contrast, when a single worker marries someone not in the paid labor force, the income tax paid by the worker is lowered because the same income is then taxed at the lower rate for married couples, and the number of deductions increases.

The marriage penalty arises partly because the tax law attempts unsuccessfully to balance several competing equity considerations. The law is gender neutral, but it is not neutral with respect to marital status. There are different tax rates for married and unmarried persons; the tax rate for single persons is higher than the rate for married persons. The underlying principle guiding the tax treatment of married couples is derived from community property laws. Marriage is treated, for tax purposes, as an economic partnership in which both partners share equally ownership of the couple's wealth. Married couples with the same taxable income pay the same rate of taxes, regardless of who earned the income. A final equity principle is that the income tax is progressive; the tax rate increases as income rises.

It must be stressed that one- and two-earner couples with the same taxable income pay the same tax, but this seemingly fair and equitable treatment is deceptive. Actually, one-earner couples are rewarded by the income tax law, and many two-earner married couples are penalized. The most favorable tax treatment is received by the one-earner couple with the highest income; the law most penalizes less affluent two-earner couples (i.e., the majority of married couples today).

Not all two-earner couples pay the marriage penalty. It applies to couples where the lower-earning spouse earns at least one-fifth of the couple's total income. About 6 million two-earner couples do not pay a penalty because the second earner's contribution to total family income is very small. On the other hand, 19 million two-earner couples do pay the penalty.[8]

The marriage penalty falls on millions of struggling two-earner couples. In 1974, for example, about 70 percent of all joint income tax returns filed by married two-earner couples included a marriage penalty. Fifty-four per cent of the couples who paid the penalty in that year had combined incomes between $10,000 and $20,000.[9]

But the true inequity in treatment of one- and two-earner couples with the same taxable income arises from the hidden costs of labor force participation. One study estimates that at least 15 percent of the second earner's paycheck is spent on transportation to work, Social Security, and clothing.[10] As Clair Vickery points out: "More than 70 percent of the increased expenditures of the working wife family are for transportation and for retirement funds. The additional expenditures for retirement by the working wife are accounted for by her family's larger total contribution to Social Security."[11] Thus, one- and two-earner couples with the same taxable income end up with different amounts of disposable income. The equal income tax rate for these couples does not adequately compensate for the second earner's work-related expenses. The one-earner couple also has more disposable income than a two-earner couple because the latter pays more Social Security taxes.

Some argue that an equal income tax rate for one- and two-earner couples is unfair because the dollar income of the one-earner couple does not include the economic value of the services provided by the homemaker.[12] A similar argument is often made by advocates of extending Social Security disability coverage for married homemakers.

The problem with this argument derives from the assumption that married working women purchase services in the home that are provided free by homemakers. Available data indicates, however, that employed wives do not stop providing free services. Time-use studies comparing two-parent, two-child, urban families found that homemakers not in the paid labor force perform about 58 hours of household work a week compared with 42 hours of weekly housework performed by employed wives. There was no statistically significant increase in the amount of housework performed by the husbands of employed wives.[13]

Time-use studies conducted by the Survey Research Center, University of Michigan, did not match family characteristics but nevertheless found that married women with full-time employment averaged 25 hours a week of housework; full-time homemakers averaged 41 hours of housework weekly. Employed married women worked a total of 64 hours a week compared with 44 hours a week worked by homemakers. To perform their double duties, employed married women slept less.[14] In general, working wives did not purchase all the services performed by homemakers.[15]

SOCIAL SECURITY

In contrast to the income tax law, which treats alike couples with equal amounts of income, the Social Security Act is blatantly unfair in its treatment of one- and two-earner couples. In fact, two-earner couples and single workers actually subsidize a higher benefit for one-earner couples.

A major difference between the income tax law and the Social Security Act is that the former treats marriage as an economic partnership in which all income is jointly owned, while the latter is based on more traditional assumptions about marriage. The law is now largely gender neutral, but not marriage neutral. Dependents of workers covered by Social Security are entitled to benefits, which are pegged to the earnings of workers. The contributions of a covered married worker produce higher benefits than do those of single workers because of the added dependent's benefit. The dependent's benefit is automatically awarded, and two-earner couples get lower retirement and survivor benefits than do one-earner couples with equal average earnings.

Working wives who contribute to Social Security can receive an amount equal to Social Security benefits based either on their own earnings record or their dependent's benefit, not both. Thus, many working wives who contribute to Social Security are no better off at retirement or widowhood than they would have been had they never worked for pay.

Finally, since the law does not recognize marriage as an economic partnership, divorced or widowed women are not entitled to receive the husband's benefit, either by splitting the benefit equally at divorce or by inheriting the deceased spouse's full benefit in addition to their dependent's benefit.

The adverse effect of this law on working wives can be clearly shown. Table 7.1 indicates that as of September 1979, 2,270,000 retired women who had worked and contributed to Social Security were no better off financially than they would have been had they never worked for pay. Their contributions purchased nothing for them except disability insurance. Given current and projected labor force participation rates for married women, the percent of future retired couples who will be adversely affected by the continued existence of a dependent's benefit will become even larger.

TABLE 7.1
Retired Women Age 62 and Over, September 1979

	Number	*Percent*
Currently married	3,485,000	
Former workers no better off	845,000	24
Widows	4,095,000	
Former workers no better off	1,425,000	35
Total retired (including never married)	8,713,000	
Total former working wives no better off	2,270,000	26

SOURCE: Unpublished data, Social Security Administration, Fall 1979.

The fact that the two-earner couple subsidizes the higher benefits one-earner couples receive has been acknowledged by the Social Security Administration and can be clearly demonstrated.[16]

We can, for example, compare fairly typical one- and two-earner couples in which both had $12,000 average annual family earnings at retirement (see Table 7.2). Despite the fact that the two-earner couple paid the *same amount* into the system as did the one-earner couple, the retirement and survivor's benefits paid to the one-earner couple are higher than they are to the two-earner couple.

The Social Security Act further penalizes marriages that depart from traditional norms. Until 1977, for example, divorced homemakers were deprived of all dependent's benefits if the marriage lasted less than twenty years. The Social Security Act of 1977 reduced the duration of marriage requirement to ten years. Yet even when a marriage ends after many years, the divorced dependent spouse cannot receive any benefits until the ex-spouse who was the covered worker dies or retires. Thus, the economic dependence of wives is reinforced by the act.

TABLE 7.2
Retirement and Survival Benefits:
One-Earner Versus Two-Earner Couples

	One-Earner Couple		*Two-Earner Couple*
Worker benefit	$5093		$3173 (worker)
Spouse benefit	2547		3173 (worker)
Total annual benefit			$6346
difference	$7640	< $1294	
Survivor's benefit			$3173
difference	$5093	< $1920	

SOURCE: Testimony of Hon. Martha Keys before the House Ways and Means committee, subcommittee on Social Security, 1 November 1979.

REFORM OPTIONS

As we have seen, both the Revenue Act of 1978 and the Social Security Act, as amended, have the effect of financially rewarding marriages in which one spouse (usually the husband) is the sole wage earner, and the other spouse (normally the wife) is a full-time homemaker and the economic dependent of the wage earner. Demographic data show that this form of marriage is no longer the norm and will probably characterize a minority of marriages in the near future.

Congress has begun to recognize the inequity of this situation and to consider various remedies. For the first time, the Social Security Subcommittee of the House Ways and Means Committee held hearings in November 1979 on the treatment of one- and two-earner couples under Social Security. Similar hearings were held by the House and Senate committees on Aging. In April 1980 a special report on "The Income Tax Treatment of Married Couples and Single Persons" was prepared by the Joint Committee on Taxation for use by the House Ways and Means Committee and the Senate Committee on Finance.

One leading proposal for eliminating the marriage penalty involved making the income tax law neutral with respect to marital status. This proposal would do away with the community property principle of marriage as an economic partnership and would tax earners on their own incomes, regardless of their marital status. This goal could be accomplished in two stages. First, married two-earner couples would be permitted to be taxed on their own earnings using the tax rate for unmarried persons. In the second phase, all earners would be taxed as individuals on a single tax rate. The Action Group of the Marriage Tax Penalty of President Carter's Interdepartmental Task Force on Women supported this approach.

Other reform proposals attempted to end or reduce the marriage penalty without abandoning the community property principle of taxation of couples. In August 1980 former President Jimmy Carter submitted to Congress an economic revitalization program that included a proposal to allow, for purposes of computing tax liability, a deduction from a working couple's taxable income equal to 10 percent of the earnings of the spouse with the lower earnings, up to a maximum income tax deduction of $3,000. This option would have eliminated the marriage penalty for some 4.2 million couples and would have reduced it for most other couples.

At the time, President Carter's proposal was rejected because of its estimated cost—about $4.7 billion in CY 1981. Ironically, it was the Reagan administration's rush to cut taxes in 1981 that created the political opportunity to correct the marriage penalty. The Economic Recovery Tax Act of 1981 provides that, starting in 1982, the lower-income spouse can take a tax deduction of 5 percent up to $1500. In 1983 the deduction will be 10 percent, with a maximum deduction of $3000. Thus the marriage penalty will be reduced for couples earning up to $50,000 where one spouse earns 70 percent of the family income and the other earns 30 percent. Where the income split is nearly equal, the penalty will still occur. Given the lower earnings of most working wives, two-earner couples will usually benefit from this tax reform.

The importance of basing fiscal policy on a view of marriage as an economic partnership is clearly advanced by advocates of reform of the Social Security Act. This principle has been adopted by the Social Security Advisory Council in its 1979 report, by the former Social Security Commissioner Stan Ross, by the National Organization for Women, and by the National Commission on the Observance of International Women's Year. The principle was adopted unanimously by the delegates to the National Women's Conference held in Houston in November 1977 as part of a package of rights for homemakers and was seen as the key to reform of support, property, divorce, and inheritance laws that adversely affect married women.

The leading proposal for reforming the Social Security Act is some form of earnings sharing in which the dependent's benefit would be replaced by an equally shared ownership record of one or both employed spouses. Earnings sharing would rectify most of the present inequities in the law and would enshrine the principle of marriage as a bond of equals rather than of dependency.

Not surprisingly, earnings sharing is vehemently opposed on ideological grounds by many right-wing groups. Phyllis Schlafly's *Eagle Forum* newsletter has charged that the government report *Social Security and the Changing Roles of Men and Women* represents an attack on the social and economic integrity of the traditional family."[17] Schlafly attacked earnings sharing as "antifamily" and falsely charged that the government proposed to deprive homemakers of benefits to which they were entitled.[18]

Schlafly was correct, however, in her understanding that Social Security was originally designed to protect the dependent spouse in the traditional one-earner couple. As long as the marriage fits the traditional mold and remains intact a woman is protected. What Schlafly fails to mention is how vulnerable women are to loss of protection. Dependent homemakers do not have control over the possible early death, desertion, or divorce by their husbands, and these events reveal how fragile is their economic security.

Despite the fact that political conservatives dominated federal politics at the end of 1981, patriarchal ideology is less an impediment to enactment of earnings sharing in the future than is economic pressure on the Social Security program. In order to eliminate the current advantage enjoyed by one-earner couples, either dependent's benefits would have to be reduced or benefits for two-earner couples would have to be raised. President Reagan is strongly opposed to any increase in Social Security benefits, and it is politically too costly to cut existing benefits. If the Republicans increase their hold on Congress after the 1982 election, then it is conceivable that they will attempt to cut dependent's benefits without rectifying the structural bias against working wives. In the interim, Congress is faced with the prospect of inadequate Social Security reserves to cover current operating costs. While Congress scrambles to pass stopgap measures, such as interfund borrowing, to cover operating costs, advocates of earnings sharing find themselves fighting to retain current benefits. In this political climate, it will be very difficult to press for reform of the system as it affects women. Furthermore, with inflation and unemployment expected to continue, payroll taxes will continue to be inadequate to cover current outlays unless Congress agrees to use general revenues and/or raise payroll taxes, as well as improve the investment practices of the trustees.[19]

CONCLUSION

Clearly, the Social Security law and, until recently, the income tax law have had the effect of rewarding traditional marriages at the expense of two-earner couples. Both policies leave the traditional married couple with more disposable income than a similarly situated two-earner couple. Two-earner couples actually subsidize higher Social Security benefits for one-earner couples.

Ironically, some feminists have espoused mutually exclusive principles for reforming both laws. For generations, reformers of marriage laws advanced the community property view of marriage as an economic partnership. Yet some who sought to end the marriage tax penalty would have done so by abandoning this principle in order to tax married workers as individuals. Even more ironic is the fact that the economic policies of Reagan's administration have led to reform of the marriage penalty and the death of earnings sharing (at least for the present).

Feminists have long understood that the vulnerability derived from women's total economic dependence on men often leads to the victimization of women. The feminist pursuit of women's legal rights has been coupled with efforts to reduce the economic dependence of women. Indeed, both goals are inextricably entwined. Experience has clearly taught us, I would argue, that married women are most protected by laws that both recognize women's rights as individuals and view marriage as an economic partnership of equals. Fiscal policies affecting marriage should therefore be based on community property principles. In this way, the dignity, independence, and rights of both homemakers and employed wives will be best protected.

NOTES

1. The goal of full equality for women in the home and society was adopted by attendees at the 1848 Seneca Falls women's convention and has been reiterated by every Presidential Commission since 1963. See "*. . . To Form a More Perfect Union . . . ,*" Report of the National Commission on the Observance of International Women's Year (Washington, D.C.: Government Printing Office, 1976. Equality for women is also the avowed goal of the National Organization for Women).

2. Howard Phillips, national director of the Conservative Caucus and an associate of Richard Viguerie, conservative organizer and fund raiser, stated: "A second major result of policies that have been anti-family, that have begun not just in this decade or even in this century, but have extended for many years, have been the liberation of the wife from the leadership of the husband. It has been the conscious policy of government to liberate the wife from the leadership of the husband and thus break up the family unit as a unit of govern-

ment" (transcription of a taped speech given at Long Beach, California, before a "profamily" rally sponsored by the Citizens for Biblical Morality, 12 July 1980).

The conservative goal of using the state to support patriarchy is embodied in Senator Jepson's (R-Iowa) Family Protection Act, S1378, parts of which are before the Senate Finance Committee. The stated purpose of the bill is to promote the virtues of the American family. Among other provisions, the bill affirms states' rights in spouse abuse and prohibits the Legal Services Corporation from handling divorce and abortion cases. A clear feminist statement on this issue can be found in *The Spirit of Houston, The First National Women's Conference*, by the National Commission on the Observance of International Women's Year (Washington, D.C.: U.S. Government Printing Office, 1978), p. 57.

3. James Weed, "National Estimates of Marriage Dissolution and Survivorship: United States," *Vital and Health Statistics*, Series 3, no. 19 (Washington, D.C.: National Center for Health Statistics, Department of Health and Human Services, November 1980), p. 1.

4. Ibid., passim.

5. Ralph F. Smith, ed., *The Subtle Revolution* (Washington D.C.: Urban Institute, 1979), p. 18.

6. *Money Income of Families and Persons in the United States: 1978* (Washington, D.C.: Department of Commerce, Bureau of the Census, June 1980), p. 130.

7. Women's Bureau, U.S. Department of Labor, unpublished data.

8. "The Marriage Tax Penalty" (study prepared for the Interdepartmental Task Force on Women, Washington, D.C., September 1979). To give the problem some perspective, consider a man who earns $15,000 (about the average for one-earner couples) and marries a full-time homemaker. His income taxes will be reduced by $710. In contrast, when two earners marry and have a combined income of $20,000 (about the average for two-earner couples), their income tax will increase $300 if the lesser earning spouse contributes 35 percent of the couple's income (example is from an April 1980 report of the Joint Committee on Taxation, U.S. Congress).

9. *The Tax Lawyer,* vol. 31, p. 1455.

10. Smith, *Subtle Revolution* p. 161.

11. Clair Vickery, in ibid., pp. 182–83.

12. "The Marriage Tax Penalty." Also, see Ferree's chapter in this volume on the difficulties involved in computing this value.

13. Kathryn E. Walker, "Time Use in Families, A New Study: Implications for Understanding Everyday Life" (paper presented August 1979, Cornell University Research paper, Ithaca, New York).

14. "Empirical Patterns of Time Use" (unpublished paper, 27 April 1979).

15. Smith, *Subtle Revolution,* p. 192.

16. *Social Security and the Changing Roles of Men and Women* (Washington, D.C.: Department of Health, Education, and Welfare, February 1979).

17. "Don't let the Libs and the Feds tear up the Homemaker's Social Security Card," *Eagle Forum*, undated.

18. Testimony by Phyllis Schlafly before the House Ways and Means Committee, Subcommittee on Social Security, 1 November 1979.

19. See my article, "Social Security's Poor Portfolio," *Newsday*, 23 July 1981, for a fuller treatment of these investment practices.

8

Myra Marx Ferree

Housework: Rethinking the Costs and Benefits

To many people, housework is like sunshine: reliable, natural, and free. In such a context, housework seems to be a trivial and static subject. Yet, as feminists take the responsibility for hearing and articulating the point of view of women, who provide the world's housework, it becomes clear that the definition of housework, its relation to the economy, and its role in establishing the social and economic status of women need drastic evaluation. Feminist social theory has produced the belated recognition that housework is the point of connection between two central organizational systems of human life: the economy, or the system of production, and the family, or the system of reproduction.

Concern with housework has also come from less abstract interests. Feminist demands for equality have raised many people's awareness of who does the housework in their own families. As family members struggle over who is responsible for what work, justifications for change and for the status quo have been eagerly sought and fiercely disputed. Not as a matter of theory but as a matter of practice, housework has become a major concern in many households. The practical implications of domestic labor have also become a matter of concern to policy makers. Questions about training programs for "displaced homemakers" and benefits full-time housewives receive under programs such as Social Security have become increasingly prevalent. It is not clear whether the government has consistent policy regarding housework and those who perform it or what policy, if any, would be desirable.

This chapter reviews some of the literature that has developed on the economic and political meaning of housework with an eye toward connecting the abstract theoretical concerns with their practical implications for public policy. To this end we look first at the labor involved in housework and the expectation that women are responsible for this work. Second, we consider the problem of assigning a value

My thanks are extended to Piers Bierne, Christine Bose, Irene Diamond, and Katherine Jones-Loheyde for their careful and critical reading of an earlier draft. Many of their insights and suggestions have been incorporated in the present version.

to this work and the related questions of what it is that housework actually produces. Finally, we consider two aspects of practical social policy: the proposal that women should be paid for housework, and the nature and level of benefits that currently exist for housework. The central argument of the paper is that housework is particularly significant for women because of the dependence and subordination it demands rather than the nature or size of the contribution women make to society in performing housework. This contribution is nonetheless substantial, and it is to this aspect of housework that we turn first.

HOUSEWORK IS WORK

To get a realistic picture of housework in modern society it is first necessary to clear away several layers of myth and misconception. A number of empirical studies done in the past ten years have contributed greatly to this process of demystification. The basic misconceptions that have prevented people from even beginning to look seriously at housework are that housework is not really work, that the work associated with maintaining a home has declined to the point of triviality, and that whatever work remains is shared equally by husband and wife.

The most fundamental myth is that housework is not work. The development of industrialization, which created workplaces away from the home, also created an apparent unity between work and waged work. Work that did not bring in an income and that did not take place in a discrete workplace was no longer seen as work at all. What women did at home was seen, not as work, but as nonwork. In many sociology texts, for instance, the home is portrayed as a place of leisure and rest where one "recovers" one's energies to return to the workplace (the "one" in question being, of course, male). That this process of recovery does not happen of its own accord but needs to be produced by someone's labor (meals prepared, beds made, etc.) is rarely acknowledged. Because the housework that creates a home life is not conceptually distinguished from it, housework itself becomes sociologically invisible. Research on the work that goes on within homes and descriptions of the work process that generates home life help to rescue housework from this invisibility.[1]

A second level of myth recognizes that housework was work in the nineteenth and early twentieth centuries but maintains that such work has all but disappeared today, leaving women with time on their hands and causing women to seek paid employment to fill their idle hours. The "disappearance" of productive work from the home was already taken as fact at the turn of the century.[2] In reality, the high levels of necessary home production in the nineteenth century probably were incompatible with full-time wage work, but among working-class women it was more likely to be housework that was not provided. The family wage, that is, a wage for male earners sufficient to support dependents and allow for the provision of unwaged housework, was a major aim and accomplishment of union organizing in this period.[3] While housework changed in style and content with the increase in single-family homes, plumbing and electricity, and domestic appliances, it is not at all clear that the total amount of housework declined. Today, larger homes, more extensive wardrobes, and more elaborate meals contribute not only to the standard of living but also to the amount of housework characteristic of modern society.[4]

Empirical research on the time spent in housework tends to support this view. The amount of time spent doing housework has not significantly changed over the past fifty years, hovering in the range of 50 to 56 hours per week.[5] The belief that technology has liberated women from housework seems ironic in view of the fact that it appears to have for the most part substituted for the labor of nonwives (servants and other family members).[6] Wives' burden of housework is still substantial. Time budgets, in which a person's activities are recorded at fixed intervals (e.g., every 10 minutes for a day), show that wives' housework time varies from a low of about 25 hours per week for employed wives with no children to a high of about 67 hours per week for housewives with a child less than a year old. The number and ages of children are the major determinants of variation in time spent.[7]

The third level of myth acknowledges the continued existence of a substantial burden of housework but asserts that this burden is evenly divided between husband and wife. There are two versions of this myth. The first holds that the husband does the exterior and/or heavy work and the wife does the interior and/or light work, resulting in a roughly comparable division of labor. The second version admits that women do most of the housework of whatever sort but considers this balanced by the husband's contribution of paid work time. Neither of these arguments is supported by time-use data. Although the wife's employment leads to some decrease in her housework hours, and thus to a higher *proportion* of the housework being done by the husband, his actual hours have not increased.[8]

Even though husbands do not contribute as much unpaid labor to the household as their wives contribute in paid work, Walker and Woods' data show the current share of housework done by men to be approximately 20 percent, an amount too large to be ignored. Particularly if one goal of social policy is to eliminate the automatic equation of women with housework, the participation of men, both husbands and sons, in domestic labor is a matter of some concern. Unfortunately, we still lack essential data to examine differences in the share of housework done by men in different social classes or historical periods. Although more recent data show little sign of any substantial increases since Walker and Woods' 1967–68 study, some systematic changes have occurred in the type and timing of housework done by men. These studies suggest that who does the housework is a social norm rather than an economically rational division of labor and that housework resists reallocation even when the family standard of living suffers as a result. Apparently many families would rather do without certain household services than have them provided by a family member of the "wrong" sex, but the sex specification of tasks varies.[9] Men's domestic labor, however, continues to be regarded as "help" rather than a fundamental responsibility.

In sum, one result of the empirical attention directed toward the home has been the belated discovery that it remains a workplace and consumes a considerable amount of women's time and energies. While work within the household might be done by either men or women, in reality it is largely done by women, even when they also hold full-time paid employment.

In the next section, attention turns to a consideration of housework as the point of connection between the family and the economy. At this point such an analysis is necessarily tentative. The conceptualization of housework as an important but unwaged part of the economy and as a significant but variable component of women's lives establishes only the starting point from which empirical and theoretical questions can be asked.

The Value of Housework

The fact that housework as work exists outside the market economy but within a society chiefly shaped by the requirements of the market system gives it a peculiarly ill-defined status. One such poorly defined attribute is the value to be assigned to housework.[10] In a capitalist economy, work that does not enter the market does not have a cash value set on it. From the standpoint of the producer, such work is unwaged; from the standpoint of the consumer, goods and services available outside the market are "free." Because housework does not have a direct cash value, one must make certain assumptions and argue by analogy to estimate the cash value of housework.

One argument is that the work should be valued at the wage that could be obtained if the producer put an equivalent amount of time into waged work instead. This so-called shadow wage assumes that persons and families are economically rational and will invest their time in the work that will bring the greatest return. The estimated value of housework is then the estimate of wages foregone. This creates a class bias, as the housework done by educated women, who can earn more in the market, is more highly valued. Another difficulty is in specifying the unit that is "investing": the woman, the married couple, or the multigenerational family. For the individual woman and other family members, the costs and benefits may differ; an advantage to the family as a unit may be gained at women's cost, as women have often found when the family breaks up.

The shadow wage argument also assumes a market that is capable of employing people at whatever times of day and whatever periods of time they are available to work. Policies affecting the availability of paid employment change the apparent "value" of housework without altering its intrinsic contribution to the family or the economy. Even when housework would be considered less valuable than paid work, it may be done when paid work is not available; alternatively, housework may be considered more valuable than an additional hour spent in paid work, but employees may not be able to reduce working time without losing their jobs entirely.

Although the shadow wage concept may be of some help in explaining the choice process that leads to a decision to work full-time, part-time, or not at all for pay (assuming that an appropriate decision-making unit can be determined), it does little to establish the value of housework done by persons already fully employed, or those who would be otherwise unemployable, or to establish the marginal value of additional hours put in or taken out of housework. Wage estimates are also unreliable because, in practice, were all full- and part-time housewives to enter the labor market, real wages would probably drop. In short, the shadow wage is an artificial convention that yields little practical information about the social contribution of housework.

A second approach to setting a value on housework involves taking the number of hours put into particular tasks and the value each of these jobs would carry if they were brought into the market and then computing an overall value for the work done. The well-known Chase Manhattan study and its update by the American Council on Life Insurance followed this methodology.[11] Their analysis combined wages for dieticians, practical nurses, chauffeurs, babysitters, maids, cooks, and so forth to arrive at a value of $352 a week (at 1977 wage rates) based on an estimated 100 hours a week. Although this figure and its annual equivalent are widely cited in the popular press, the calculations are based in part on double-counting time (e.g., cleaning and minding children could be carried on simultaneously but were counted separately) as the inflated time estimate clearly shows. Also, only women's housework time was estimated.

Even though these particular estimates are badly flawed, the approach in general could be illuminating if up-to-date time-use data and wage-rate information were used.[12] The assumption that families could or would purchase these services in the market is artifical, however, as is the assumption that individuals do not vary in their productivity per hour or the skill level that they bring to particular jobs.[13] Such artifical assumptions may make little difference to an estimate of the contribution of housework to the GNP or the average standard of living,[14] but such assumptions clearly cannot be applied at the individual household level either to analyze household decision making or to set appropriate wage or benefit levels for housewives.

Types of Production in the Home

Value estimates for housework take into account only the purely economic contributions of housework to the family; in fact, housework has two major productive functions, subsistence and status production.

Some analysts have argued that housework provides goods and services more cheaply than the market and that this is a factor enabling capitalists to keep wages low.[15] In this view the difference between the cost of maintaining a family member who contributes nonmarket labor and the higher cost of this labor if each worker had to provide for his or her own subsistence through the market is an indirect subsidy that housewives offer the capitalist economy as a whole. The assertion that it would be manifestly impossible to pay prevailing market wages to all persons doing unwaged housework is seen as illustrating the magnitude of this subsidy. Capitalism as a system, therefore, is said to derive a benefit from the family wage, even though individual employers might prefer to pay wages only to cover individual subsistence costs.

On the other hand, it can be argued that market goods and services might be cheaper, not more expensive, than home-produced goods and services if they were designed to be provided to a mass market. The choice, for example, may not be between doing a wiring repair oneself or hiring an electrician to do it; one may simply buy a plug to be snapped into place. Similarly, the choice between making one's own clothes and hiring a seamstress is largely circumvented by the availability of ready-to-wear apparel.[16] The problem here is that housework does not disappear entirely but changes form; instead of wiring or sewing, housework becomes shopping for the desired item and using or maintaining it.[17] Services once provided in the home (e.g., medical care) are now also provided in the market; whether on the whole they are cheaper or more expensive is difficult to estimate without reliable values to assign to home production. The mass availability of services as well as consumer goods is well established in advanced capitalist economies[18] and this process also can be seen as beneficial to the capitalist economy; but the two tendencies—to keep housework in the home and to bring it into mass production—are contradictory. It remains unclear when one should expect one tendency or the other to be dominant.

Even though a considerable number of goods and services must still be produced in the home, the widespread availability of mass-produced goods and services means that a significant proportion of housework time is spent in consumption activities. Such activities are work, not leisure. Specifically, they are the work that replaces the service component of merchandising—pickup rather than home delivery of foodstuffs, home assembly of furniture and toys, self-service in stores and gas stations, and the like.[19] As the economy changes to make more of the service work fall on the consumer rather than the producer, such consumption activities become part of the necessary and inevitable work of family subsistence ("we can't eat until someone goes to the store") at all economic levels.

Physical care for dependent family members, both the very young and the very old, is also clearly still a major component of subsistence production within the household. Such personal physical care is expensive to provide because of the labor-intensive nature of the work; in fact, group care for infants, the infirm, and the elderly may never be genuinely less expensive to provide than family care. Fluctuations in the availability and cost of such services in the market reflect the level of subsidy from the rest of society to families needing direct physical care for dependents. Such subsidies may be greater in good times than in bad or for some classes of dependents than for others (the elderly rather than infants, for example). Personal physical care may also be provided for some family members who could provide it for themselves, with probably no net gain in the family standard of living.

Given the present economic system, most families could not have the market supply all of their subsistence needs. Working-class family members in particular may use their own labor to provide goods and services that could not be afforded at market prices; barter with friends and extended family may be a source of other goods and services at less than market costs.[20]

The second major contribution housework makes to the family is in family status production. Family status production is work above and beyond that required for subsistence which serves to maintain and enhance the position of the family vis-à-vis other families in a hierarchy of social prestige.[21] Although family status production has indirect economic consequences, its contribution cannot be measured in narrowly economic terms.

Child-care activities are a major part of the status production process; a parent often does not want merely to have a child, but to have one who will take his or her appropriate place in the social community. Inculcating the values and skills to make the child a respected member of the community involves labor: teaching children manners, training them in physical and/or intellectual skills, maintaining their physical appearance, and so on. But the entrusting of children to babysitters, day-care centers, or schools involves accepting the possibility that the child will be maintained and prepared for adulthood at a different status level (or with a different set of values) than one's own. This may be desirable if it is believed the child will rise in status as a result; it may be resisted if it is believed that the child will be in any way competitively disadvantaged.[22]

Family status production is by no means limited to child care, but includes wives' activities designed to maintain or enhance their husbands' careers[23] and activities that more directly affirm and advance the family's position in the community, such as preparing meals for guests, managing gift exchanges, and preparing family living quarters for inspection by others. Such activities have both a competitive and a cooperative aspect.

The competitive aspect may be the best explanation of why standards for housework have historically risen, keeping the amount of time that has had to be spent on housework relatively constant. Once subsistence needs are met, family needs appear to be defined in terms of advantages relative to other families and therefore escalate as the standard of living in the society rises. Housewives thus do not have a free choice of what technologies to utilize or what standards of performance to adopt, for there are productivity pressures on housework. Capitalism, insofar as it contributes to social hierarchy, also contributes to these productivity pressures.

Even when women take on a substantial burden of paid work, housework still has to be performed at a level appropriate for their class (or class aspirations). The need to provide both paid work and housework constitutes a form of speed-up and brings with it the characteristic fatigue and sense of always being rushed.[24] One can see additional consequences of this competitive aspect of status production work in housewives' need to remain informed about new products and to monitor the level of performance that other housewives of their class have achieved. Consider, for example, the appeasement gestures in housewives' social interactions—calling attention to trivial deficiencies in performance to defuse the competitive tension, having labored strenuously beforehand to conceal or correct any real flaws. Maintaining a visible standard of living and engaging in social display, particularly within the home, not only means that there are more rooms and things to be taken care of than a family would need merely to survive but also that the level of maintenance is higher than would otherwise be the case. A shirt without a button may still be functional, but it is nonetheless "disgraceful."[25]

Status production activities are not solely competitive, however. They also serve to maintain and reinforce connections between those of the same family or class. Food preparation may be especially important here. The pleasure given by a homemade rather than store-bought cake may be experienced by all family members, including the baker. The desire to create and maintain solidarity and belongingness shapes family activities and extends from the family outward to ethnic and friendship ties.[26] Eating together, for example, builds up a relation of affection rather than economic calculation, whether in the family or among friends. Being able to "do for" people one cares about affirms a social relation explicitly not tied to profit and loss. This is an important and rewarding aspect of social life that finds expression in housework and is one reason some housewives resist the idea that housework could be a paid job.

The fact that status production activities carry competitive and cooperative tendencies simultaneously means that housework resists rationalization. The affirmative, cooperative aspects of housework as a social activity are not only personally gratifying but also serve to cement one's membership in a family or in an ethnic, civic, or professional group. In times of crisis, these ties may be economically as well as emotionally crucial, but such social supports are not achieved through careful economic calculation. As Davidoff notes, "there is a constant tension between the aims of hospitality, generosity, lavish display (or 'wilful waste') on the one hand, and the aims of economy, rational planning and careful forethought (or 'meanness') on the other."[27]

In sum, housework is not just a form of economic production that satisfies subsistence needs, whether at, above, or below market costs. While it is a form of production of goods and services to meet strictly economic needs, it is also a form of status production. While the competitive aspect of status production creates productivity pressures on housewives, the cooperative aspect offers personal and social rewards not available in the market.

HOUSEWORK AND THE ECONOMY

Although it is clear that housework is important for the family's subsistence and status, the question remains: To what extent is it important that housework be provided by women rather than men? The obvious corollary is: Important to whom?—Capitalism as a system? Individual employers? Men as a group?

The relationship between a worker's subsistence needs and the economic system as a whole can be seen to be partially expressed in what is sometimes called the reproduction of commodity labor power.[28] Workers sell their labor power for a wage, thus making labor a commodity, and this ability to work needs to be re-created on a day-to-day basis (by being rested, fed, etc.) and on a generation-to-generation basis (by raising new workers to replace the old). The lower the cost of subsistence, the more cheaply a worker can afford to sell his or her labor. If employers pay less than subsistence wages, the difference either has to be made up from somewhere else in the system (e.g., government subsidy to the "working poor" or pooling of incomes between high-wage and low-wage workers in units called families) or the labor power of the workers will gradually be extinguished. When wages are very low, housework and child care may be cut back to levels that endanger social reproduction.[29] Government regulation (e.g., a minimum wage) is one way of ensuring that individual employers do not pay below-subsistence wages in order to increase their current profits at the cost of future generations.

Dalla Costa and others[30] have emphasized the reproduction of labor power as a description of housework because it suggests to them that the benefits of housework do not actually accrue to the husband and children for whom the housewife believes she is working but are instead passed through to employers in the form of lower wages. This suggests that women could withhold their labor (strike) without thereby injuring their families; working-class women in particular are urged to demand a fair wage for their housework from those who benefit from it (employers). Though it is not clear whether Dalla Costa believes that such a demand could ever be met (she implies that housework is the root of all profitability of labor and capitalism would collapse if employers had to pay for this work), some feminists were influenced by her argument and proposed demanding pay for housework as a practical goal.[31]

Although they do not draw this conclusion, the logic of their argument would suggest that capitalism would benefit even more by large households in which one person engaged in domestic production could lower subsistence costs of as many workers and future workers as possible. In other words, if household production is indirectly profitable, as suggested, there should be indirect pressures for economies of scale. The tendency, if any, seems to be in the opposite direction; smaller households are increasingly the norm. This trend benefits the economy as a whole by directly increasing markets for household goods (furnishings, appliances, etc.) and indirectly increasing the amount of housework demanded (more rooms to clean, more individual meals to prepare) and consequently also creating a demand for market services to replace some of this increased housework (e.g., frozen dinners).[32] Such smaller households, however, may only be possible at higher income levels. Thus there may be conflicting pressures toward larger or smaller households from different segments of the economy, and the argument that capitalism as a whole benefits from housework oversimplifies what is evidently a very complex relationship.

Dalla Costa's argument also does not make clear whether there is any economic advantage to be gained for the system as a whole by having individuals provide housework for the family *rather than* work directly for wages, in comparison to having individuals provide housework *in addition to* working for wages. If the latter case were more advantageous, then it is not obvious what additional advantage is derived from having the burden of housework fall disproportionately on women. Some have hypothesized that flexibility between the two arrangements is actually what the system needs to cushion the jolts in the normal functioning of the economy and that the existence of families creates this flexibility.[33] In other words, it is advantageous to have a reserve labor force (of women) that could rely on other income (from men) to survive prolonged unemployment and could then be drawn into paid employment when demand increases,[34] or could be employed in marginal industries which pay sub-subsistence wages. If this is the case, as dual-economy theory suggests it would be,[35] then the *productive* functions of housework may be of little direct benefit to capitalism in comparison to its interest in the continued existence of the family as a mechanism for *redistributing* incomes and providing some "social security" to workers at the fringes of the economy.

The critical function of housework, then, may be in legitimating and supporting the family system. Indeed, the benefits to the family system may be sufficient to outweigh even very considerable economic costs involved in keeping housework privatized. While the family system that housework supports may benefit capitalism, men benefit as well.

HOUSEWORK AND PATRIARCHY

The focus on the benefits or costs to capitalism or individual employers of having a significant portion of the population engaged in unwaged labor tends to ignore the relationship between the wage laborer and the houseworker within the family. Marxists as well as mainstream social scientists have been willing to assume that whatever benefit male workers obtain by having their housework done for them is exactly balanced by their greater cash contribution to the family welfare.[36] This hypothetically fair exchange has had only limited empirical examination, but the evidence there is suggests serious inequity. Income distribution within families is far from equal; women experience a lower level of subsistence, enjoy less leisure, and have little control over discretionary income.[37] While it is difficult to argue that housework provides a direct economic profit for men,[38] it can readily be shown that it contributes to the continued subordination of women to men from which men enjoy an economic advantage both in the labor force and in the family.[39] This subordination takes a variety of forms.

In the first place, housework is economically subordinate to paid work in a cash-based economy. Housework is contingent upon the prior provision of an income and the market goods and services it can buy. One cannot sew without thread, clean without soap, or cook without food; in an urban industralized society such basic necessities cannot be economically produced at home.

The extent and nature of housework required is also dependent on the size of wage the income earner can and does bring home. When the housework provider and income earner are not the same person, it may be that not all income earned is brought home; secretiveness about salary or earnings, holding back part of one's income from the common pot, and demanding a close accounting of money spent are all ways of exercising financial control that are the prerogative of the income earner(s).[40] Housework is thus an intrinsically dependent form of production in a cash economy.[41]

The economic dependence of housework is most fully realized in the occupational role of housewife. Housewives are faced with occupational role requirements that closely approximate those of domestic servants, an otherwise virtually obsolete role.[42] The job provides no separation between home and work, no limit on the number of hours to be worked, and no bounds on the extent and nature of the demands that can be made. In addition, the high level of intimacy in the home allows the possibility of betrayal and creates a need to foster loyalty by isolating the worker from nonhousehold members and making rewards derivative or vicarious.[43] The ideology of the privacy of the home exacerbates the vulnerability of servants and housewives to psychological, economic, or physical abuse and makes "kindness" a quality much to be valued in husbands and employers.[44] Like domestic service, housework continues to be controlled in a manner consonant with traditional (partiarchal) authority: diffuse, particularistic, and global demands met in return by loyalty, diffidence, and repressed hostility.[45]

Being a housewife, then, regardless of how well rewarded or kindly treated, is essentially a subordinate role. In addition, housework tasks are generally seen as most appropriate for lower-status persons to carry out; dealing with dirt and disorder is foremost among these.[46] This function of establishing order extends beyond the physical into the realm of social relations. Housework is often assigned as a means of enforcing discipline in institutions other than the family, as in the case of KP in the armed forces.[47] Doing housework, therefore, can be seen as a means of putting not only things but people in "their" places. Who does the housework is important in part because of the power and status positions it articulates. Who wears the apron is not just a statement about who does the chores.

The subordinate and dependent character of housework does not seem to have interfered with the development of a mythology of housework as a sphere of autonomy and self-development, particularly when contrasted to the paid jobs available to working-class women.[48] Is housework actually more autonomous or skilled than clerical or factory work? The control exercised on housewives is less direct, universalistic, and impersonal than industrial control, but like the traditional control exercised over domestic servants, it may be experienced as even more degrading and oppressive. Servants, after all, left their jobs for factory work as soon as it became available.[49]

In sum, housework is a major factor establishing and expressing the subordination of women to men in the household. This subordination of women to men in the family has meant enormous income advantages for men in the labor market. Women's "prior responsibility" for housework forces many women to compromise their paid labor force participation and accept home-based, part-time, or sporadic work. As a result, women are pushed into the peripheral labor market, which offers characteristically low wages, and employers are provided a pretext for direct discrimination in the better paying monopolistic core.[50]

Concern about women's economic vulnerability has led to pressures and policies for equal opportunity in the labor force, but for the most part these have addressed the problem of overt discrimination in access, pay, and promotion rather than the structural consequences of holding women responsible for housework. The question arises more and more as to whether government policy can effectively address the economic inequities arising from the gender-political division of labor in the household.

PROGRAMS AND POLICIES

Feminist policy on housework currently appears to be mired in a contradiction. Two related but not identical problems are at issue: On the one hand, the poverty of women who are or were engaged in full-time or part-time housework appears to need some immediate and direct remedy; on the other hand, the sex typing of housework and the associated segregation of the paid labor force calls for some fundamental restructuring of the economy as a whole. Unfortunately, ameliorative programs aimed at the economic disadvantages under which housewives currently labor may tend in the long run to reinforce rather than eliminate sex segregation by making full-time housework a more attractive option for women who continue to be at a disadvantage in the paid labor force.

Pay for housework proposals have been caught on the horns of this dilemma. On the one hand, all such proposals, however various in detail, are commonly income-transfer programs. Whether all women, married women, women with children, or full-time housewives would be recipients of the benefits, the cash-transfer aspect of the programs would tend to put a little more money into the hands of women and might help to alleviate some women's poverty. This, plus the consciousness-raising function mentioned above, makes pay for housework programs seem desirable to some feminists.[51] The example of AFDC payments and children's allowances in Europe, however, suggests that the size of the benefit would not be a living wage.[52] The need for paid employment and/or a husband's income would not be changed; housework or motherhood still could not really be considered an independent career.

On the other hand, payment to women for housework would tend to legitimate and institutionalize the idea that housework is women's work. This would tend to undermine women who are struggling, with varying degrees of success, to change the division of labor in their own households. Unless the paying agency closely supervised who performed which tasks and paid accordingly, the money would be allocated on the basis of a sex-stereotyped norm, to housewives rather than for housework. Also, without control over the work process being formally in the hands of the paying agency, what is offered is not really a wage for housework but a transfer payment. As others have pointed out in more detail, this transfer payment would probably not be progressive in its income effects.[53] A transfer payment, however generous, also does not create the potential for a strike or other job action.

Similarly, existing rewards for housework tend not to be proportionate to the amount of work done or the size of the contribution to the family's level of well-being. This structural problem was apparent even at the turn of the century when Gilman denounced the sentimentalizing of housework as a "career."[54] The income tax and Social Security systems that have been introduced since then have preserved this problematic characteristic. What is actually rewarded in the role of housewife is the status of dependent rather than the productivity achieved or time put into the job.

Two provisions in Social Security make it essentially pay for dependency rather than for housework: It cannot be combined with benefits based on one's own earnings record, and in most instances, it is payable without regard to the duration of the marriage. Duration of a marriage is only a rough indicator of the amount of housework done, but the fact that the size of the benefit is exactly the same whether one has been married a week or forty years makes it clearly unrelated to the real costs incurred in housewifery.[55]

Benefits also do not reflect the fact that women who hold paid employment usually do so in addition to continuing to do the bulk of the housework. A person, on retiring, may choose the higher benefit—one based on earnings or on dependency on an earner—but not combine the two. Thus the financial costs of carrying the responsibility for housework are imposed entirely on the woman, rather than shared by other family members who have benefited from having housework done.

An alternative is to base Social Security on a shared earnings record for married couples.[56] The rationale offered for pooling earnings records is that the decision for a marriage partner to limit or increase his or her labor force participation (and to accept jobs congruent with these limits) is a joint decision, and its costs, like its rewards, should be shared by husbands and wives. It should be noted that this makes having a wife engaged solely in household production no longer "free" to husbands, since earnings penalties assessed for reductions in labor force participation are levied against both rather than against the wife alone.[57] Husbands might be less willing to see their wives drop out of the labor force when half the costs of doing so would be borne by each spouse. It also means that being married at the point of retirement would no longer be crucial. Pooled benefits would reflect the duration of the marriage, and these could be combined with benefits based on the earnings record compiled in prior or subsequent years. Additionally, the wife's covered earnings during the marriage would always contribute to a higher level of benefits calculated for both husband and wife. Since lower-income families, especially blacks, depend more on the earnings of women to establish their family standard of living, this would have a progressive effect on the income distribution postretirement.

Note that while the existing system clearly discriminates against couples in which both spouses are employed, since the ratio of benefits collected in retirement to taxes paid is lower than for single-earner couples, it is not housewives who derive the benefit from this arrangement. Housewives are penalized under the present system because they bear the entire cost of their restricted labor force participation in their personal earnings record and, particularly in cases of divorce, can be left in poverty as a result. In addition, women who have spent most of their lives in full-time housework are still likely to have spent some time in part-time or part-year work, yet will see no increase in retirement benefits to reflect their additional efforts and taxes. Husbands, however, receive benefits for their wives and ex-wives at no cost to themselves, either in terms of higher taxes or lower personal benefits. The housewife's benefits under this system are vicarious, and rest upon continued dependency on a generous spouse.[58]

The income tax system, by taking into account the *costs* of supporting a dependent spouse but not the *benefits* provided by housework, indirectly subsidizes families that adhere to a traditional division of labor.[59] Because the system rewards only the family with a *full-time* housewife, it is rewarding income inequality between husband and wife rather than recognizing the value of housework. The subsidy goes to families that maintain one spouse out of the labor market or peripherally attached to it. Again, it is female dependency and the maintenance of a reserve labor force that the system encourages. In addition, there are indirect income effects of this tax system. The tax advantage goes to husbands with high enough incomes to maintain a full-time housewife; the higher tax costs are borne by dual-earner families, single individuals, and unmarried heads of households.

The Reagan administration's recent modification of the "marriage tax" actually gives a tax benefit to dual-earner families with large income differences, while leaving a substantial penalty for many couples with roughly equal earnings. Instead, if couples were able to choose between filing as two single people or as a couple, dual-earner households would be able to avoid the marriage penalty and select the option that reflects their lower ability to pay.[60]

Mandatory individual filing would completely eliminate the current subsidy to single-earner couples, but this would probably make some families no longer able to afford the luxury of full-time housework.[61] If the income tax system remains progressive, mandatory individual filing would also encourage an even division of earning capacity between husband and wife, because increasing the earnings of the higher earner would have less after-tax utility than increasing the earnings of the low-earning spouse, who would have additional earnings taxed at a lower rate. Whether this would in turn create more pressure to share housework more equitably or would simply increase existing pressures for women to combine paid work with housework would remain to be seen.

Additionally, it is becoming clear that some sort of direct intervention is needed now to assist women who counted on continued dependency on their husbands to ensure their financial security but who, through divorce or death, find themselves independent and thus poor.[62] Displaced homemaker programs, which provide "transition benefits," job training, and counselling, can offer some relief to these women and mitigate the risks assumed in lifelong financial dependence.[63]

Such targeted relief, like unemployment compensation, offers less stigma than other welfare programs and may also help prevent some women, especially those with middle-class backgrounds, from falling into poverty-wage employment, drug dependency, or suicidal despair. Displaced homemaker programs, however, do not constitute structural reform, for they offer only temporary support to individuals whose confidence in the present system has been disappointed. Because they mitigate some of the financial risk involved in economic dependency on a man, one might think that displaced homemaker programs would make such dependency seem more attractive, but the fact that such programs are even needed seems to raise consciousness about the risks involved and encourage independence.[64]

The combination of shared earnings records for Social Security and mandatory individual filing for income tax, improbable as such reforms may be in the present political climate, would go a long way toward redistributing the real costs and benefits of housework more equitably, both between husbands and wives within individual families and between richer and poorer households in the economy as a whole. To some extent, the revisions in the Social Security System could help alleviate women's poverty, especially among divorcees and widows. Additionally, these reforms, unlike pay for housework schemes, tend to reduce the implication that housework is women's obligation and to encourage sharing housework and wage-earning work between husband and wife.

Such reforms nonetheless merely touch the surface of deeply imbedded structural assumptions about sex-appropriate roles and responsibilities in the family economy as well as in the labor market. Official policies to create equal opportunities for men and women in paid work will remain without fundamental effect as long as they are contradicted by policies that continue to assert that women's place in life is domestic and dependent.

NOTES

1. Major studies include Ann Oakley, *The Sociology of Housework* (New York: Random House 1974); Sarah F. Berk and Richard Berk, *Labor and Leisure at Home* (Beverly Hills: Sage, 1979); and Helena Lopata, *Occupation: Housewife* (New York: Oxford University Press, 1971).

2. See, for example, Charlotte Perkins (Stetson) Gilman, *Women and Economics* (New York: Source Book Press, 1970; originally published 1898); or Clara Zetkin, "Women Workers and the Woman Question of Today" (1889).

3. Jane Humphries, "The Working Class Family, Women's Liberation and Class Struggle," *Review of Radical Political Economics* 9 (1977): 25–41; Heidi Hartmann, "Capitalism, Patriarchy and Job-Segregation by Sex," *Signs* 1 (1976): 137–70.

4. Christine Bose, "Technology and Changes in the Division of Labor in the American Home," *Women's Studies International Quarterly* 2 (1979): 295–304; Ruth Schwartz Cowan, "A Case Study of Technology and Social Change: The Washing Machine and the Working Wife," in *Clio's Consciousness Raised*, ed M. Hartman and L. Banner (New York: Harper & Row, 1974), pp. 245–53.

5. Joann Vanek, "Time Spent in Housework," *Scientific American* 231 (1974): 116–

20; and Ruth Schwartz Cowan, "The Industrial Revolution in the Home," *Technology and Culture* 17 (1976): 1–23.

6. Bose, "Technology and Changes"; and David Katzman, *Seven Days a Week* (New York: Oxford University Press, 1978).

7. Kathryn Walker and Margaret Woods, *Time Use: A Measure of Household Production of Family Goods and Services* (Washington D.C.: American Home Economics Association, 1976). Also reported in K. Walker, "Time patterns for household work related to homemakers' employment" (National Agricultural Outlook Conference, Washington, D.C., 1970).

8. The classic study by Walker and Woods, ibid., shows that husbands of both employed and nonemployed wives do 1.6 hours of housework a day compared with the 8.1 hours a day of nonemployed wives and the 6.8 hours a day or 4.8 hours a day of wives with part-time or full-time employment, respectively.

9. Recent data on men's share of housework and the failure of families to allocate labor "rationally" are available in Joann Vanek, "Household Work, Wage Work and Sexual Equality," in *Women and Household Labor*, ed. S. F. Berk (Beverly Hills: Sage, 1980); Richard Berk and Sarah F. Berk, "A Simultaneous Equation Model for the Division of Household Labor," *Sociological Methods and Research* 6 (1978): 431–68; Joseph Pleck, "Men's Family Work: Three Perspectives and Some New Data," *Family Coordinator*, October 1979, pp. 481–88; John Robinson, "Housework Technology and Household Work," Berk, *Women and Household Labor*; and J. Robinson, *How Americans Use Time* (New York: Praeger, 1977).

10. In theory, socialist societies assign value and thus wages to jobs on the basis of individual and social need. Their failure to recognize and reward housework is based on considerations other than the difficulty of assessing value, particularly on their premises that housework is nonproductive, that it is private rather than social enterprise, and that it contributes to reactionary or "backward" social relationships between husbands and wives in particular and women and men in general. These issues will be dealt with later in the chapter. Suffice it to note that existing socialist societies have been far more successful in abolishing the role of full-time housewife on these grounds than they have been in reducing women's actual burden of housework or eliminating the social norm that assigns responsibility for housework to women.

11. Both studies are reviewed at length in R. K. Armey, "The Relative Income Shares of Male and Female Homemakers," in *Economics and the Family*, ed. S. Bahr (Lexington, Mass: Heath, 1980).

12. This argument is made in a proposal for national income accounting of household work formally endorsed by the American Home Economics Association and prepared and presented by Kathryn Walker to the Joint Economic Committee, U.S. Congress, 15 August 1973.

13. Richard Berk, "The New Home Economics: An Agenda for Sociological Research," in S. F. Berk, *Women and Household Labor*.

14. Kathryn Walker and William Gauger, "Time and Its Dollar Value in Household Work," *Family Economics Review*, Fall 1973, pp. 8–13.

15. The classic statement is in Maria rosa Dalla Costa and Selma James, *The Power of Women and the Subversion of the Community* (Bristol: Falling Wall Press, 1975). See also Margaret Benston, "The Political Economy of Women's Liberation" *Monthly Review* 21 (1969): 13–27; and Jean Gardiner, "Women's Domestic Labor," *New Left Review*, 116 (1979): 3–27.

16. A detailed comparison of the costs of home and market production of clothing is made in Robert Steadman, "The Economics of Domestic Garment Making," in Bahr, *Economics and the Family.*

17. Batya Weinbaum and Amy Bridges, "The Other Side of the Paycheck: Monopoly Capital and the Structure of Consumption," in *Capitalist Patriarchy and the Case for Socialist Feminism*, ed. Z. Eisenstein New York: Monthly Review Press, 1979).

18. Harry Braverman, *Labor and Monopoly Capital: The Degradation of Work in the Twentieth Century* (New York: Monthly Review Press, 1975).

19. Weinbaum and Bridges "Other Side of Paycheck"; see also John Kenneth Galbraith, *Economics and the Public Purpose* (Boston: Houghton Mifflin, 1973).

20. J. Morgan, I. Sirageldin, and N. Baerwaldt, *Productive Americans* (Ann Arbor: Institute for Social Research, 1966).

21. Hannah Papanek, "Family Status Production: The 'Work' and 'Non-Work' of Women," *Signs* 4 (1979): 775–81.

22. A society such as ours that emphasizes cross-generational occupational mobility may make this the overriding consideration in determining women's occupational roles. Families that accept the premise that a mother at home is essential to a child's social development may limit women's labor force participation and reduce the family's income, requiring them to accept home production of goods and services that might be cheaper or of better quality in the market, or to spend more time in consumption work ("bargain-hunting"). Alternatively, a belief that family status is enhanced by a child's care or education by others may require women's employment to pay tuition bills and force the family to accept less home production or lower-quality market substitutes. Compare Ann Ferguson and Nancy Folbre, "The Unhappy Marriage of Patriarchy and Capitalism," in *Women and Revolution*, ed. L. Sargent (Boston: South End Press, 1981), who argue that the demand for a woman to remain at home to care for infants explains the "inefficiency" of keeping laundry, for example, in home production.

23. Hannah Papanek, "Men, Women and Work: Reflections on the Two-Person Career," *American Journal of Sociology* 78 (1973): 852–72; also Mary Taylor and Shirley Hartley, "The Two-Person Career: A Classic Example," *Sociology of Work and Occupations* 2 (1975): 354–72.

24. See recent data and discussions in Walter Gove and Michael Hughes, "Beliefs vs. Data: More on the Illness Behavior of Men and Women," *American Sociological Review* 46 (1981): 123–28; and Myra Marx Ferree, "Housework and Happiness" (paper presented at Eastern Sociological Society Annual Meeting, 1980).

25. Lenore Davidoff, "The Rationalization of Housework," in *Dependence and Exploitation in Work and Marriage*, ed. D. Barker and S. Allen (New York: Longman, 1976).

26. For a strong position on the role of women's work in the creation of social solidarity, see Max Haller, "Marriage, Women and Social Stratification: A Theoretical Critique," *American Journal of Sociology* 86 (1981): 766–95.

27. Davidoff, "Rationalization of Housework," p. 141. Gardiner, "Women's Domestic Labor," argues for the difficulty of rationalizing housework because of its relational, emotional content, but this is a somewhat different argument. See also Ferguson and Folbre, "Unhappy Marriage," for a discussion of what they term sex-affective production.

28. The classic statements are Dalla Costa, *Power of Women*, and Peggy Morton, "A Woman's Work Is Never Done," in *From Feminism to Liberation*, ed. E. H. Altbach (Cambridge, Mass.: Schenkman, 1971).

29. Ellen Malos, "Housework and the Politics of Women's Liberation," *Socialist Revolution* 37 (1978): 41–72. Malos also provides a good overview of the so-called domestic labor debate.

30. Nona Glazer-Malbin, "Housework," *Signs* 1 (1976): 905–21; Wally Secombe, "The Housewife and Her Labor under Capitalism," *New Left Review* 83 (1974): 3–24.

31. Adele Liskov, "The Valuation of Housework: A Problem of Conceptualization and Measurement" (paper presented at ASA, 1977); Nicole Cox, "Counterplanning from the Kitchen: Wages for Housework" (New York: Wages for Housework Committee, 1976); Lisa Leghorn and Betsy Warrior, *The Houseworker's Handbook* (Cambridge, Mass.: Women's Center, 1975); W. Edmond and S. Fleming, *All Work and No Pay: Women, Housework and the Wages Due* (Bristol: Falling Wall Press, 1975).

32. Barbara Ehrenreich and Deirdre English, *For Her Own Good: 150 Years of Experts' Advice to Women* (New York: Doubleday, 1978), Chap. 5; See also Weinbaum and Bridges, "Other Side of Paycheck."

33. Natalie Sokoloff, *Between Money and Love* (New York: Praeger, 1981); Heidi Hartmann, "The Family as the Locus of Gender, Class and Political Struggle: The Example of Housework," *Signs* 6 (1981): 366–94.

34. Valerie K. Oppenheimer, "Demographic Influence on Female Employment and the Status of Women," in *Changing Women in a Changing Society*, ed. J. Huber (Chicago: University of Chicago Press, 1973).

35. Natalie Sokoloff, "Patriarchial Relations in the Labor Market: Are Things Getting Better or Worse for Women?" (paper presented at Johns Hopkins, April 1981, and discussions in Women and Work Theory Group).

36. Armey, "Relative Income"; Secombe, "Housewife and Her Labor"; John Harrison, "The political economy of housework," *Bulletin of the Conference of Socialist Economists*, Winter 1973.

37. Laura Oren, "The Welfare of Women in Laboring Families in England, 1860–1950," *Feminist Studies* 1 (1973): 107–25; Michael Young, "The Distribution of Income within the Family," *British Journal of Sociology* 3 (1952): 305–17; see also Morgan et al., *Productive Americans*.

38. Nonetheless, it has been attempted. See C. Delphy, *The Main Enemy* (London: Women's Research and Resources Centre, 1977), and the discussion of this position in Maxine Molyneux, "Beyond the Domestic Labour Debate," *New Left Review* 116 (1979): 3–27.

39. Heidi Hartmann, "Capitalism and Women's Work in the Home, 1900–1930" (Ph.D. dissertation, Yale University, 1974); and "The Unhappy Marriage of Marxism and Feminism," in Sargent, ed., *Women and Revolution*; also, Carol Brown, "Mothers, Fathers and Children: From Private to Public Patriarchy," in ibid.

40. Jan Pahl, "Patterns of Money Management within Marriage," *Journal of Social Policy*, 9 (1980): 313–35.

41. Harrison, "Political Economy of Housework."

42. Lewis Coser, "Servants: The Obsolescence of an Occupational Role," *Social Forces* 52 (1973): 31–40; see also Katzman, *Seven Days a Week*.

43. Coser, "Servants."

44. Katzman, *Seven Days a Week*.

45. Colin Bell and Howard Newby, "Husbands and Wives: The Dynamics of the Deferential Dialectic," in Barker and Allen, *Dependence and Exploitation*; Lenore Davidoff, "Mastered for Life: Servant and Wife in Victorian and Edwardian England," *Journal of*

Social History, Summer 1974; Lenore Davidoff, J. L'Esperance, and Howard Newby, "Landscape with Figures: Home and Community in English Society," in ed. *The Rights and Wrongs of Women*, Juliet Mitchell and Ann Oakley (London: Penguin, 1976).

46. Davidoff, "Rationalization of Housework"; and Mary Douglas, *Purity and Danger* (London: Routledge & Kegan Paul, 1966).

47. Davidoff, "Rationalization of Housework," p. 123. Compare Judith Wittner, "Domestic Labor as Work Discipline: The Struggle over Housework in Foster Homes," in S. F. Berk, *Women and Household Labor*.

48. An example of an article that attempts this mythology is James Wright, "Are Working Women Really More Satisfied?" *Journal of Marriage and the Family* 40 (1978): 301–13. The rewards of child care also often seem central. Ferguson and Folbre, "Unhappy Marriage," cite Phyllis Schlafly's claim that "most women would rather cuddle a baby than a typewriter." What Schlafly and many others ignore is that clerical workers also cuddle babies; the issue is what one does with the rest of one's work time.

49. Coser, "Servants"; Katzman, *Seven Days a Week*.

50. E. M. Beck, Patrick Horan, and Charles Tolbert, "Industrial Segmentation and Labor Market Discrimination," *Social Problems* 28 (1980): 113–30.

51. Leghorn and Warrior, *Houseworker's Handbook*; Cox, "Counterplanning"; Liskov, "Valuation of Housework."

52. Carolyn Adams and Kathryn Winston, *Mothers at Work* (New York: Longman, 1980). For further discussion of the marriage penalty and how it arose, see the chapter by Leader in this volume and Nancy Gordon, "Institutional Responses: The Federal Income Tax System," in Smith, *Subtle Revolution*.

53. Carol Lopate, "Pay for Housework?" *Social Policy*, September/October 1974, pp. 27–31; Malos, "Housework and Women's Liberation."

54. Gilman, *Women and Economics*, esp. Chap. 1. As Gilman noted, "The working power of the mother has always been a prominent factor in human life. She is the worker *par excellence*, but her work is not such as to affect her economic status. Her living, all that she gets—food, clothing, ornaments, amusements, luxuries—these bear no relation to her power to produce wealth, to her services in the house, or to her motherhood. These things bear relation only to the man she marries, the man she depends on—to how much he has and how much he is willing to give her" (p. 21).

55. The only exception to this rule is for divorced spouses, who are only eligible for benefits after ten years of marriage, recently reduced from twenty. Even in this case, benefits are an all-or-nothing affair, not prorated, to reflect time spent in housework as ordinary pensions and social security benefits reflect time spent on the job. See Gordon, "Institutional Responses."

56. For details of the system and its impact on women, see ibid. and U.S. Department of Health, Education and Welfare, *Report of the HEW Task Force on the Treatment of Women under Social Security* (Washington, D.C.: Government Printing Office, 1978).

57. For example, years without earnings are averaged into the earnings record if there are fewer than 21 years of covered employment; this minimum will increase to 35 years by 1994. This provision serves to further depress women's benefits, which are already low. See Gordon, "Institutional Responses," and the HEW Task Force report for additional details.

58. The Reagan administration's attacks on the Social Security System and his insistence that it was never intended to provide a full retirement income highlight the even greater inequities women face under private pension systems. Working women under many private plans have to make higher contributions to receive the same level of retirement income.

Dependents' benefits are insecure: A worker can choose an annuity with no joint/survivor benefits without notifying the dependent spouse; if the worker dies even a day before retirement, there are typically no benefits for the spouse even when the joint/survivor option is taken; divorced wives typically have no rights to pension benefits at all, as the Supreme Court recently affirmed in the case of military pensions. See U.S. Department of Labor, Women's Bureau, "Employment Goals of the World Plan of Action" (report for the World Conference on the UN Decade for Women, July 1980).

59. Note also that a single parent with a child is judged to be better off than a one-earner married couple; the former is allowed only a tax deduction for the additional dependent, the latter family is allowed both the tax deduction and the lower tax rate applied to married couples.

60. See the chapter in this volume by Leader; also Gordon, "Institutional Responses." Maintaining the option of joint filing would be a way of helping families that have already made a substantial investment in the traditional sex-segregation of paid work and housework by continuing the subsidy to which they have grown accustomed.

61. Under mandatory individual filing a dependent spouse would be treated the same as any other dependent and entitle the filer to a single additional exemption; tax rates would not vary depending on marital status. It would thus appear to be the most effective way of equalizing the treatment of one- and two-parent households. The fact that elimination of the subsidy that joint filing offers is often seen as making it impossible for many working-class families to maintain a wife out of the labor force should make one question whether housework is subsidizing capital or capital is subsidizing housework.

62. The term "displaced homemaker" was coined by older-women's advocate Tish Sommers in 1975 in setting up a model counseling program in Oakland, California. The term was rapidly adopted by government agencies. See Cynthia Marano, "Displaced Homemakers: Critical Needs and Trends" (paper presented to Agricultural Outlook Conference, U.S. Department of Agriculture, Washington, D.C., November 1979). See also Joann Crabtree, "The Displaced Homemaker: Middle-Aged, Alone, Broke," *Aging*, January–February 1980, pp. 17–20.

63. Such programs are currently funded through CETA and state vocational education departments. As of the end of 1978, 28 states had some form of displaced homemaker program and The Displaced Homemakers Network, Inc., an umbrella organization, was formed from approximately 300 existing local programs. See Marano, "Displaced Homemakers."

64. However, the government's rapid acceptance of these programs, along with their use of the socio-emotional term homemaker, reflects their essentially palliative nature. The programs typically define areas of need to emphasize personal psychological counselling (dealing with feelings of anger, failure, etc.; building self-esteem) and help in developing life skills (e.g. balancing a checkbook) while job development and specific vocational education have a lower priority. Such psychologically oriented intervention would seem to be more helpful to women of middle class background as the programs assume, would then be able to "market" skills "acquired in homemaking." See Marano, op. cit., for an example of this emphasis.

9

Carole Joffe

Why the United States Has No Child-Care Policy

One seeming puzzle of American society is the inadequacy of its child-care facilities. In view of the steadily increasing participation of women in the labor force, it appears surprising, first, that there does not seem to be enough child care to meet demand.[1] Second, when comparing the United States with other industrialized countries,[2] it is striking that there is nothing resembling a "national policy"[3]—there is no attempt at the federal level to meet, or even define, the needs of the some 8 million children under the age of six whose mothers work. The U.S. government is only minimally involved in the direct provision of child-care services; similarly, there are only minimal attempts at forcefully regulating the child care provided by the private sector.

The child-care system in the United States is essentially a "nonsystem"; it is a mixture of public and private programs of tremendously varying quality that serve different constituencies for different purposes. Although we have no conclusive hard data on how many potential working mothers are kept from the labor market because they have literally no child-care arrangements, or how many women are forced to leave jobs because of the inadequacy of their arrangements, or, probably most commonly, how many families experience considerable strain because of the lack of fit between work and family, we have ample "soft" data to suggest that all three factors are prevalent in American life. Why, then, has there been no effective governmental action to deal with this obvious problem? This essay discusses some factors that have inhibited the development of a child-care policy in the United States.

To be sure, neither of the accusations made above, that the government in the United States does not provide sufficient child care nor adequately regulate the private supply, seem very startling in the present Reagan era. *All* social services are being massively cut back; virtually all past governmental attempts at regulation—of social services and otherwise—are similarly being curtailed. But though the current weak state of child care is consistent with the demoralized state of social services in general, I argue in this paper that the difficulties of achieving a child-care policy long predate the Reagan era. Even in periods of greater overall support for service spending, child-care programs have always been underfunded. And while admittedly one can argue that in this society there has always been considerable difficulty in reaching consensus on any aspect of "family policy,"[4] articulating goals for "normal" children and their families (e.g., nonhandicapped, nonneglected) has proved most difficult of all. The stalemate over child care must be attributed not only to fiscal considerations but also to a complex of cultural and political forces that arise from the deep contradictions in this society about the meanings of children, women, and families.

This chapter first gives a brief overview of the history of child-care programs in the United States. I describe the major forms of current governmental involvement, as well as privately provided child care, and discuss the relationship between the two. I then place the discussion of child care in the larger context of current discourse on "the politics of the family," focusing in particular on the roles of the New Right and the feminist movement. I discuss each group's historical and current relationship to the issue of child-care policy. The chapter concludes with some general remarks on factors accounting for the failure of a strong child-care system in the United States.

THE HISTORY OF CHILD CARE IN THE UNITED STATES

"Day nurseries," established in the middle and late nineteenth century, represented the first formalized efforts in the United States at the out-of-home care of young children.[5] The initial nurseries were the philanthropic efforts of wealthy women in the larger northeastern cities; these women had become concerned over the growing problem of immigrant children left unsupervised as their mothers took jobs in factories. Some of these early day nurseries were independent entities; others became absorbed into the settlement houses of the period.

In today's terminology, the content of these early day nurseries was "custodial" rather than "developmental." That is, the major purpose was to provide a safe, healthy environment for the children. Hygiene, in particular, seems to have been a central concern; one observer of the period reports seeing a toothbrush for each child displayed in one of the nurseries.[6] But the format of these early nurseries was also very "experimental" when compared to much of contemporary child-care efforts. Infants were routinely accepted into programs, centers operated very flexible hours—including evenings and weekends—and the nurseries often served as an informal employment bureau for neighborhood mothers.

The earliest nurseries were essentially "nonprofessional" efforts, staffed only by a matron and an occasional assistant. Gradually, however, professionals began to enter the centers. The newly developed specialties of kindergarten and nursery teachers were hired to give an educational component to the program; similarly, the new profession of social work became represented at the administrative level (replacing the charity women) and as deliverers of "casework" services to participating families.

The entrance of these new "helping professions" into the day nurseries brought mixed benefits. On the one hand, again using contemporary terminology, the professionals certainly "upgraded" the programs. Yet each of these professional groups sought to reshape the character of day care according to the logic of their professional training—in ways not always compatible with the needs of the client families. Early childhood educators, for example, refused to work the long hours (corresponding to the workday) that had been the norm in the nurseries and balked at working with children under the age of three; the social workers claimed their casework skills were most appropriate for "problem" families, not simply families that happened to have a working mother.

Around World War I, a variety of forces—the passage of a Mother's Pension Act,[7] the further development of social work and early childhood education—combined to alter significantly the character of day care. The availability of mothers' pensions meant that some women no longer needed the services of day nurseries. The educators became more strongly identified with "nursery schools," institutions that served a largely middle-class population, and whose half-day format precluded their usefulness for working women. Social workers, finally, became more firmly entrenched in "day care centers"; but, unlike the earlier day nurseries, these centers were oriented to families defined as "pathological" and hence in need of casework.

On two occasions after World War I, there were brief periods of a "national child care policy"—that is, widely available child care, coordinated and funded by the government. During the Great Depression, the WPA sponsored a network of nursery schools;[8] during World War II, the Lanham Act authorized the opening of child-care centers.[9] In each instance, the federal support of child care was in response to a national crisis, with support being withdrawn once the crisis passed. More significantly, neither effort was primarily concerned with the needs of children: The major purpose of the WPA program was to provide jobs for unemployed adults; the purpose of World War II child care was to enable women to work in war-related industry.

The two most consequential child-care events since World War II were the development of the Head Start program in 1965 and the congressional passage (and subsequent presidential veto) of the Child Development Act in 1971. Head Start, established as part of the "War on Poverty," has proved to be one of the most enduring of the Johnson-era social programs; it survived the dismantling of the Office of Economic Opportunity, and as of this writing it appears that the program will similarly survive Budget Director David Stockman's call for its demise.

Head Start, though it originated specifically as part of a program of social reform, and though its population continues to be limited to low-income children, did much to change the image of early childhood programs generally. The program, especially in its early days, inspired a great deal of research on the cognitive possibilities of early childhood; it facilitated the introduction of "early learning" into preschool programs (a still controversial point in preschool circles).[10] Furthermore, Head Start enhanced the concept of "comprehensive" (as opposed to merely "custodial") preschool services; that is, "quality" child care should provide a combination of medical, psychological, nutritional, social, and educational services.

Thus Head Start, for a time at least, moved the focus of child-care debates away from the centrality of the employment of the parent (as in the early day nurseries and in World War II centers) or from the job needs of adults (as in the WPA-sponsored day care during the depression) and made the needs and possibilities of young children the core issue. To be sure, Head Start serviced only a very specialized, not very large clientele. But the project's political popularity and cultural visibility did have considerable impact in the late 1960s and early '70s. The Head Start phenomenon might be viewed as an important contributory source to an emergent "children's lobby" that was seeking to make available to a more universal audience some of the perceived benefits of quality child care that Head Start, at its best, represented.[11]

The children's lobby, made up of traditional children's advocates—both within government and without—such as educators, psychologists, minority-group specialists—reached its peak in the early 1970s. Joining forces with a newly reemerged feminist movement, this lobby was able to achieve, in late 1971, passage in both houses of Congress of a Child Development Bill that would have authorized some $2 billion for the establishment of new child-care facilities. This measure was shortly vetoed by then President Nixon, who earlier in his administration had expressed interest in broader government involvement in day care. The veto was accompanied by a message that has since come to be regarded as one of the more memorable documents of American social policy. The message read, in part:

> . . . our response to this challenge [child development] must . . . be consciously designed to cement the family in its rightful position as the keystone of our civilization. . . . Good public policy requires that we enhance rather than diminish both parental authority and parental involvement with children. . . .
>
> . . . for the Federal government to plunge headlong financially into supporting child development would commit the vast moral authority of the National Government to the side of communal approaches to childrearing over against the family-centered approach.[12]

Several explanations have subsequently been offered for the Nixon veto.[13] One focuses on the objections Nixon had to the "community control" aspects of the bill, which made the legislation look too much like "1960s" programs. Another explanation links the veto to Nixon's diplomatic overtures to China, which had enraged the right wing in the United States. The veto, and the strong language used in the message, were thus to be seen as an appeasement gesture to the Right, which had lobbied strongly against the bill. Whatever the precise reason, the veto made eminently clear the potentially explosive character of attempts at national child-care programs, and in particular, the enormous interest of the Right in stopping such attempts.

After the near-victory in 1971, the children's lobby, with the aid of sympathizers in Congress, made two more attempts at child-care legislation, in 1975 and

1978–79. Each was unsuccessful, though each bill was far more modest than the 1971 effort. The right wing again proved to be a potent force, engaging in intensive lobbying and launching unusually vitriolic smear campaigns against individual supporters of the bills in Congress. Furthermore, the mid and late 1970s' efforts were complicated, and weakened, by infighting among child-care forces. The major issue was that of control over any new child-care programs that might be authorized. Education forces, led by the American Federation of Teachers, argued that the schools should be presumed "prime sponsors" of all such child care; other members of the coalition held out for a broader base of support. By the time of the 1978–79 effort, the collapse of the child-care lobby became evident. Not only was the right wing engaged in its usual oppositional activities, but support had evaporated from the key day-care personnel within the Carter administration. The hearings on the 1979 bill, S.4, were abruptly canceled by its chief sponsor, Alan Cranston of California.

Several points can be drawn from the failures of child-care legislative attempts in the 1970s. Perhaps the most obvious ones, as already suggested, are the enormous political difficulties in effecting social programs designed for "normal" families, and in particular, the strength of the "profamily" wing of the New Right in the 1970s that could be readily mobilized against any child-care initiative.

But the failed attempts of the 1970s—especially the two latter efforts—also revealed the fragility of the pro-child-care forces. Not only were some key children's advocates inept political operatives, as Steiner argues,[14] but more fundamentally, the child-care forces, in fact, contained quite different notions of the purposes and shape of the new programs they were seeking. One strand of the coalition put children's needs as paramount and saw quality child care as a "social utility" that would benefit all children; feminists, as we will shortly discuss at greater length, used as a starting point the needs of women, especially working women (as did labor unions); for other members of the coalition, for example those representing some minority groups, the promise of massive child-care funding was the empowerment that would come through community controlled child care. Finally, both Nixon's and Carter's interest in child care—such as it was—seemed largely confined to the possibilities of getting welfare recipients back to work or into job-training programs. Faced with a very active right wing and a growing antipathy toward the funding of social programs in Congress, the child-care lobby was met with the unmanageable task of promoting a program on whose target population, actual content, administrative control, and even ultimate purpose there was not internal agreement. In sum, even before the Reagan cutbacks of the 1980s, child care as an object of public policy had fizzled out.

CURRENT GOVERNMENT PROGRAMS

Title XX

Though there is currently no national "policy" on child care, the federal government is involved in a number of child-care programs, the most important being

Title XX of the Social Security Act. Under the Title XX program, states receive 75 percent matching funds for various social services, including child care, which they provide to families that meet income eligibility criteria. Federal matching is available only for services to families with incomes that do not exceed 115 percent of the state's median family income, adjusted for family size. Federal funding for child care and all other social services provided through Title XX have been subject to an annual limit of about $3 billion; the Reagan administration has called for a 25 percent reduction in Title XX funding. For the past few years, day-care programs have received about one-quarter of all Title XX funds spent, with approximately three-quarter million children receiving services. In the vast majority of cases, these must be children of parents who work or who are students. That day care will continue to receive such a hefty proportion of Title XX funds in the Reagan years is unlikely.

Head Start

As mentioned, this is one of the few survivors of the War on Poverty. It is now located within the Administration for Children, Families and Youth, within the Department of Health and Human Services. Head Start continues to be a program for poor children; 90 percent of its enrollees must be from poor families. Approximately 375,000 children are currently enrolled in Head Start programs.

AFDC–Related Day Care

The federal government is involved in two day-care programs specifically targeted to AFDC families. One is the "Child care as a work expense" provision under Title IV, Part A, of the Social Security Act, under which states must deduct the cost of child care in order to determine the welfare eligibility of a working parent. The Work Incentive Program (Title IV, Part C, of the Social Security Act) provides 90 percent matching federal funds to states to purchase child care for AFDC mothers in job training or in actual employment, up to a period of ninety days.

Tax Provisions Relating to Child Care

The 1976 amendments to the Internal Revenue Code provided for a tax credit for child-care expenses incurred by working parents. As of 1982, a credit may be claimed for 20 percent of child-care expenses, up to a maximum of $2400 for one dependent and $4800 for two or more (resulting in a maximum tax credit of $480 for one dependent and $960 for two or more). This provision covers both in-home and out-of-home child care. It is estimated that nearly 4 million tax returns claimed a slightly lower credit in 1977, amounting to a reduction in tax liability of about $756 million.[15] Congress continues to work on various tax reductions relating to child care; one of the most recent developments is a provision that makes employer-provided child care a nontaxable benefit for employees.[16] One significance of these tax-related programs is that, of all current federal involvement in day care, these are the programs that are most directly beneficial to the middle class.

Other Programs

Among the other federal child-care programs are preschool services to the handicapped, child nutrition programs (providing free breakfasts and lunches to licensed day-care centers), special programs for Native American and migrant children, and loans by the Small Business Administration to owners of proprietary child-care centers. All of the above can be expected to be cut back (or eliminated) in the future, but the precise nature of these cutbacks is not evident as of this writing.

NONGOVERNMENTAL PROGRAMS

The majority of day-care programs in the United States are not government provided but are purchased directly by consumers. (For example, in 1976, in contrast to a total of $2.5 billion spent by the government on all child-care programs, an estimated $6.3 billion was spent by consumers.[17] This gap can be expected to increase sharply as federal expenditures contract.) These programs include private proprietary centers as well as nonprofit ones, family day-care homes, employer-provided child care, nursery schools and other educationally defined programs (some half-day, some full-day), and of course, a vast informal network of care offered by relatives and babysitters.

A major point to be made about this private child-care system is that, like virtually all other social services in the "private" sector, there is considerable overlap with the public service system. This is because of the widespread system of the federal government "purchasing" services from approved private providers instead of directly supplying services itself. Hence all the "private" child-care systems mentioned above have a clientele of "publicly funded children"—that is, children whose family income or welfare status makes them eligible for subsidized care.

This widespread interlocking of the public and private child-care systems leads to considerable complexities and in itself must be understood as a factor inhibiting progress toward a federal "policy." The major stumbling point in the public-private relationship has centered on the issue of regulation—in particular the "FIDCR" (Federal Interagency Day Care Requirements), the body of regulations that hypothetically governs all centers, including private ones, that have publicly funded children among their clientele. The FIDCR controversy reached its height in the mid-1970s when a newly revised set of regulations, issued by the day-care bureau within HEW (now HHS), was vehemently opposed by a coalition of private providers and some state social welfare departments. This coalition argued that the cost of implementing the new regulations would put them out of business. The main point of contention in the FIDCR controversy concerned mandated staff-child ratios, but also involved such issues as staff education, health referral services, and mechanisms to ensure parental involvement in the centers. The new FIDCR were suspended while Congress authorized HEW to undertake several massive day-care studies to assess to the desirability of the new regulations. Such studies were completed by the late 1970s,[18] but with the advent of the Reagan administration, the issue seemed to become moot. As of this writing, the new FIDCR have been indefinitely suspended.

In addition to lessened regulation, two particularly noteworthy developments in the private child-care market during the Reagan era will be the growth of industry-provided care and the renaissance of the so-called child-care franchisers (in many instances, the latter providing the former). The amount of company-provided child care—which usually implies on-site care, but can also mean supplying employees with vouchers to purchase their own services—has been rather negligible in the past but recently has shown signs of significant growth.[19] This is, of course, due to the decrease in the amount of publicly provided child care, as well as the various tax initiatives now underway to make it more beneficial for employers to provide this benefit. Inevitably, this new commitment on the part of companies to provide child care is leading to a rejuvenation of child-care franchises—companies that market packaged day-care programs on a national basis. When such franchises made their initial appearance in the 1960s, they had relatively little success and were the targets of much criticism by children's advocates who questioned the quality of the operations[20] and posed the still relevant question whether it was possible to offer quality child care on such a basis and still turn a profit.

CONTEMPORARY CHILD-CARE POLITICS

The New Right

Throughout the 1970s, right-wing groups were vigorous and effective foes of child-care policy initiatives at the federal level. Such anti-child-care activities can be understood as among the early forays of a broad "profamily" campaign, allied with the New Right, that was to gather full momentum around the time of the 1980 election. Currently, however, there are intriguing signs of a tactical, if not ideological, turnaround in the New Right's position on child care. The most prominent of these is the endorsement given to child care in the Family Protection Act,[21] perhaps the major manifesto of the New Right's social agenda. To be sure, this support for child care is very much in keeping with New Right approaches to social policy generally. The FPA day-care provisions do not call for any government spending on new programs, nor for any form of regulation; they do call for tax incentives for employers to provide on-site day care for employees. Nevertheless, in view of earlier virulent right-wing attacks on day care—*any* form of care by other than relatives—it seems ironic indeed that the major congressional initiative on child care at the moment emanates from the New Right.

The New Right's softening on the child-care issue was perhaps first evident at the U.S. meeting of the International Women's Year in Houston in 1977. (This meeting is especially noteworthy because it marked the first confrontation, at a national level, of feminism and the rapidly mobilizing "profamily" coalition.) While there was enormous conflict at the meeting over other traditionally contested items—the ERA and abortion in particular—child care did not seem to be a burning issue for either side. A resolution supporting child care, in general terms, was passed with minimal discussion.

Similarly, at the three regional meetings that composed the White House Conference on the Family in 1980, child care was not a major preoccupation of the now even more prominent profamily group. While the latter did go on record as disapproving of government-provided child care, a more general resolution supporting the importance of child care as an aid to working parents was allowed to pass without opposition. Again, this essentially low-keyed approach to child care on the part of both feminists and profamily forces contrasted sharply to the emotions (and walkouts) generated by the issues of reproductive rights, the ERA, and homosexual rights.

As the above incidents suggest, the right-wing retreat from its historic anti-child-care positions at both Houston and the White House Conference could possibly be explained as much by the collapse of the pro-child-care forces as by changing right-wing ideology. It is certainly true that starting in the mid-1970s, and continuing through to the present, a disproportionate share of the resources of organized feminism has been allocated to reproductive rights' issues and ERA. Correspondingly, therefore, other aspects of the feminist agenda, such as child care, have continued to receive rhetorical support but little concrete attention. (Furthermore, as I will shortly argue, one can raise certain questions as to how profound feminism's support for day care ever was.)

Yet the present weakness of conventional pro-child-care forces does not in itself adequately explain the striking New Right shift on this issue. Rather, the qualified approval now given to child care in right-wing publications[22] and, above all, in the Family Protection Act, suggests a more fundamental change. The change has come about, I submit, because of recognition that a considerable portion of the New Right's constituency are, in fact, actual or potential users of child care. Given the massive entry of women with young children into the labor force—a long-term trend that is being intensified by inflationary pressures, as well as the equally dramatic rise of single-parent families—it stands to reason that among New Right adherents are many working couples and single working parents.

Feminism

Where does feminism stand in relation to child care at the present moment? The immense tasks of promoting the ERA and defending earlier abortion victories, which started to monopolize feminist energies in the mid-1970s, are even more urgent today. Child care, as a specific object of feminist concern, now seems rather peripheral. Whether such preoccupation with the two "big issues," to the near exclusion of all others, is inevitable or even tactically correct, is beyond the scope of this paper.[23]

The more relevant inquiry here is the quality of support given by the feminist movement to child-care issues *before* the ERA and reproductive rights became so all-consuming. On one level, it could be argued that child care has been a key concern of contemporary feminism. Unlike the first phase of American feminism, which was almost exclusively concerned with the issue of suffrage, the "second wave," which started in the late 1960s, was greatly concerned with the "family."[24] Feminist theoretical writings of that period saw the place of women in the family as critical to an understanding of the larger political situation of women. Until women were relieved from exclusive responsibilities for child care, they would never be "equal" participants in society. An additional concern of feminists writing in this period was the injurious effects of the nuclear family on children: Children in the conventional middle-class home had too intense a relationship with their mother (and virtually no relationship at all with their father); being exposed to the sexist division of labor in their families would replicate the pattern in the next generation.[25] Not surprisingly, therefore, the feminist platform soon came to include "universally available child care."

The problem, in retrospect, is that the support given to child care by the feminist movement had trouble moving beyond the rhetorical. To be sure, at the local level, many centers and parent cooperatives were doubtlessly initiated by women influenced by the women's movement. But in terms of sustained involvement in child care as in issue of national policy and, in particular, of joining meaningfully with children's advocates to articulate appropriate principles for the out-of-home care of children, the contemporary women's movement has a rather limited record. This is not to argue that feminist groups and individuals did not lobby for child-care bills. They did, to a considerable degree. Rather, it is to suggest that except for an insistence on "nonsexist environments," feminists have not had much to say about child care as a *children's* issue. Gilbert Steiner's comments are most perceptive on the gap between feminists and children's advocates on child care:

> Important differences in style and technique exist between those groups taking children as the principal point of departure and those groups taking women as the principal point of departure . . . neither the literature of women's equality movement nor its spokeswomen deal with operational questions bearing on workable plans for policy development—locations, earliest entering age, adult child ratios, length of time a child should stay. It is the general principles about women that come through. Women should be free to develop their capacities to the fullest. . . . Childcare centers should ease the burden for women so they can develop freely.[26]

The above comments are not intended to suggest that it is inappropriate for a feminist movement to focus on the present situation of, and needed changes for, women. Nor would it be correct to argue that if only the feminist movement had more deeply concerned itself with detailed matters of child-care policy, then the legislative battles of the 1970s would have turned out differently. My point, rather, is that a fully mature feminism must move beyond rhetorical support for child care and begin to consider the complexities of a child-care "policy" from the child's standpoint as well as the adult's.

This implies not only rethinking political strategies to regain support for children in the present climate. More fundamentally, it means a willingness to move beyond the by now automatic refrain—"child care is good for women and for kids too"—and to consider the ways in which a child-care policy may promote the needs of one party at the expense of the other. A child-care system that makes no provision for sick children is protecting the other children in its care but puts immense pressures on a working parent, particularly if she is in a work situation that is not sympathetic to child-related absences; a mother of an infant may need nine hours or more of child care a day in order to adequately support her family, but this length of time in an institutional setting may not be maximally beneficial to the infant, and so on.

Acknowledging such incompatibilities between the needs that adults and children each bring to child care does not mean these problems are ultimately manageable. Confronting these issues, in fact, would seem a first step toward the recognition that the best-intentioned child care—in itself—can never solve the problems faced by working women, the inequities within family systems, and the developmental needs of children. All these problems call for new understandings about workplace-family relationships, about the division of labor between men and women within the home, and about the allocation of social resources (i.e., for health and nutrition) to children.[27] And that is why feminism—the most articulate and visible social force calling for changes at both the personal and political level—must begin to engage in a more profound consideration of what a humanistic child-care policy would entail.

CONCLUSION

To return to the question which began this essay—why is there no child-care policy in the United States?—we can now pull together some answers from the preceding discussion. First and foremost, child care serves as a prime example of the enormous difficulty—the "futility," as Steiner puts it[28]—of attempts at family policy in this society. Any system of massive government involvement in programs involving young children inevitably raises images of "state-controlled childrearing." Though most of the events spoken of in this paper involved right-wing opposition to child care, we should recognize that government-provided child care raises concern on the left as well.[29] In particular, the coercive aspects of AFDC-related child care has received much criticism.

Attempts at a national child-care policy become further complicated as the solutions offered to offset the "family intervention" objections themselves become repudiated for political reasons. For example, the strong "community control" aspect of the 1971 Child Development Bill, which arguably might have ensured substantial parent involvement in the new centers, was offensive to Nixon and other conservatives because it conveyed too much of a "1960ish" social reform flavor. Similarly, later in the 1970s, during the FIDCR debates, we saw that parent involvement aspects of the requirements were strongly resisted by private providers; in short, there was the rather paradoxical situation of a government agency attempting to strengthen family participation in a social program but being resisted by the private sector on antiregulatory grounds.

A second impediment to a meaningful child-care policy has been the racial and class stratification that has characterized all publicly provided programs to date (with the brief exceptions of depression and World War II programs). Whether such programs were targeted toward children of low-income wage earners (the earliest day nurseries and the present Title XX programs), children of "problem" families (day nurseries during the 1920s and some specialized programs now for abusive families), or children from "culturally deprived" backgrounds (Head Start and its many imitators), public day care has never succeeded in presenting itself as a universally desirable program. Title XX, which had the potential to reach a broader audience through its sliding scale provisions, for various reasons never lived up to this promise.[30] Thus, like many similar social programs that serve only the poor and otherwise devalued, public day care is caught in a cycle of social stigma and underfunding—something to be avoided if one possibly can. This stigma, it must be emphasized, extends only to *public* programs, not to child care per se; if one counts all out-of-home care for children, including nursery schools, as child care, then there are more middle-class children in child care than lower-class ones.[31]

Finally, there is the considerable frailty of the child-care coalition itself. As we have discussed, this coalition is weakened by lack of political expertise, by professional self-interests and corresponding infighting, and by a quite understandable demoralization at the present moment. The greatest problem, however, seems to be the unclarified nature of what the child-care lobby actually stands for. As in other coalition situations, "child care" has come to mean too many different things to too many actors. To the extent that this coalition will be able, in the near future, to articulate a priority, my assumption is that it will claim child care for working women as its first allegiance. But even if this is achieved, it still leaves a number of pertinent questions never adequately answered in all the years of child-care politicking—questions pertaining to program eligibility, actual content, staffing, and so forth.

To summarize then, the near future will bring a decrease in all forms of child-care regulation generally, but we can expect an increase in the actual amount of child-care places. The seemingly unstopping increase of labor force participation of women with young children has already shown signs of stimulating the private child-care supply, in particular, employer-provided care.

While the understandable tendency of child-care advocates might be to take at least some comfort from these developments—in the 1970s after all, the very notion of out-of-home care was under attack—I suggest we must view these trends with great caution. We must recall that the debates over the desirability of child care in the 1970s, including all the conservative rhetoric about family sanctity, coexisted with a well-established (still functioning) child-care system for welfare recipients—a system that was, and continues to be, minimally responsive to parental input. Similarly, we might ask if the highly visible move toward employer-provided child care is a way of ensuring the participation of women in low-paying jobs.[32] As with AFDC recipients, the child care provided in many of these cases will be of minimum quality and will allow no significant parental choices.

Thus, the admittedly considerable task for a reconstituted child-care lobby is to articulate a child-care platform that acknowledges the economic and political realities of the 1980s but is not paralyzed by them; that, more particularly, can offer a reasonable program of regulation that is not overly stifling or too costly to implement, but yet which keeps alive the principle of quality. One hopes that the feminist movement, which has a record of achievements concerning the working woman and an as yet undeveloped potential for formulating a conception of a decent life for all members of society—including children—will take the lead in a reconstituted child-care movement.

NOTES

1. Because of the predominance of informal and unlicensed facilities (as much as 90 percent of family day-care homes are estimated to be unlicensed), it is virtually impossible to know exactly how many children are in day care or what the actual day-care "supply" is. A 1975 HEW estimate put the number of licensed places at 1.5 million—in a period in which some 6.6 million children under the age of six had parents who worked.

Opponents of the expansion of day care argue that the above figures merely reflect parental preferences for informal arrangements. See, especially, B. Bruce-Biggs, "Child Care: The Fiscal Bomb," *Public Interest* 49 (Fall 1977): 87–102; and Suzanne H. Woolsey, "Pied Piper Politics and the Child Care Debate," *Daedalus* 106 (Spring 1977): 127–46. Proponents of expanded child care argue that the present supply—both informal and licensed—is simply inadequate. One of the most recent statements of this inadequacy is found in U.S. Commission on Civil Rights, *Child Care and Equal Opportunities for Women* Pub. No. 67, (Washington, D.C.: Government Printing Office, June 1981). The report quotes estimates of some 32,000 preschoolers and 2 million school-age children (7–13) caring for themselves in the absence of child care (p. 9). The report also emphasizes how the perceived lack of child care prevents many women (16 percent of unemployed women with children under twelve, according to one study) from even attempting to enter the labor force (p. 10).

Janet Boles, in "The Politics of Childcare," *Social Service Review* (September 1980), pp. 344–62, makes the useful observation that this lack of a commonly agreed upon data base must be understood as a key contributing factor to the lack of a child-care policy. This uncertain data base concerns not only the alleged insufficiency of the child-care supply but also the costs and claimed benefits of child-care programs.

2. For a recent comparative statement, see Sheila Kamerman and Alfred Kahn, *Child Care, Family Benefits, and Working Parents: A Study in Comparative Policy* (New York: Columbia University Press, 1981).

3. There are many, both within government and without, who question whether a "policy" is, in fact, required in the area of child care. Such opponents of policy (here referring to governmental regulation as well as funding of services) argue that the private market is adequate to meet child-care needs; if parents are dissatisfied with a program, they can

simply switch their child to another. Governmental regulations in this field, as in others, it is argued, keeps the supply down and the costs up.

In response, the proponents of policy, from a child advocacy standpoint, show the extremely uneven quality of care that exists, particularly in unlicensed facilities (and in situations where existing regulations are not adequately monitored). One of the best-known exposés of poor-quality child care is Mary Dublin Keyserling, *Windows on Day Care* (New York: National Council of Jewish Women, 1972). This study—frequently cited as a justification for regulation—lists a number of "horror stories"—children tied to beds, mentally incompetent caretakers, and so on—that abound in the child-care world, especially unlicensed facilities.

Furthermore, while opponents of regulation argue that federal involvement is unnecessary in view of state licensing mechanisms, in fact there have long existed enormous variations among the states with respect to the licensing and monitoring of child care. Most recently, there have been reports of some states simply abandoning existing licensing enforcement because of the fiscal crisis. See *The Advocate for Human Services, National Association of Social Workers*, (Washington, November. 1981), p. 2; and Gwen Morgan, "The Politics of Day Care," *Day Care and Early Education*, Fall 1981, pp. 27–29.

4. See Sheila Kamerman and Alfred Kahn, *Family Policy* (New york: Columbia University Press, 1978); and Gilbert Steiner, *The Futility of Family Policy* (Washington, D.C.: Brookings Institution, 1981).

5. The most useful secondary source on the early day nurseries is Margaret Steinfels, *Who's Minding the Children? The History and Politics of Day Care in American* (New York: Simon & Schuster, 1973). See also Sheila Rothman, "Other People's Children: The Day Care Experience in America," *Public Interest*, Winter 1973, pp. 11–27; and Virginia Kerr, "One Step Forward—Two Steps Back: Child Care's Long American History," in *Child-Care—Who Cares? Foreign and Domestic Infant and Early Childhood Development Policies*, ed. Pamela Roby (New York: Basic Books, 1973).

6. Rothman, "Other People's Children."

7. On Mothers' Pensions—sometimes called "widows' pensions"—see Mark Leff, "Consensus for Change: The Mothers' Pension Movement in the Progressive Era," *Social Service Review*, September 1973, pp. 397–417.

8. On WPA child care, see *Emergency Nursery Schools During the First Year (1933–34). Report of the National Advisory Committee on Emergency Nursery Schools* (Washington, D.C.: Government Printing Office, 1935); Kerr, "One Step Forward"; and Samuel Braun and Esther P. Edwards, *History and Theory of Early Childhood Education* (Worthington, Ohio: Charles P. Jones, 1973).

9. On World War II day care, see Howard Dratch, "The Politics of Child Care in the 1940's" *Science and Society*, Summer 1974, pp. 167–204; Kerr, "One Step Forward"; and Braun and Edwards, *Early Childhood Education*.

10. On this, see Carole Joffe, *Friendly Intruders: Childcare Professionals and Family Life* (Berkeley: University of California Press, 1977).

11. On the development of this children's lobby, see Gilbert Steiner, *The Children's Cause* (Washington, D.C.: Brookings Institution, 1976); for a recent appraisal of Headstart, see Edward Ziegler and Jeannette Valentine, eds. *Project Headstart: A Legacy of the War on Poverty* (New York: Free Press, 1980).

12. *Congressional Record*, 10 December 1971, pp. S21129–30.

13. The most useful analyses of the veto can be found in Steiner, *The Children's Cause*, Chap. 5.

14. Ibid., Chap. 10.

15. Committee on Finance, U.S. Senate, *Child Care: Data and Materials* (Washington, D.C.: Government Printing Office, 1977), pp. 25–26. For a critique of these tax cuts, see Jill Norgren and Sheila Cole, "Child Care Tax Credit: Heaven Help the Working Mother," *Nation*, 23 January 1982, pp. 77–79.

16. "Child Care Grows as a Benefit," *Business Week*, 21 December 1981, p. 60.

17. *Statistical Highlights from the National Child Care Consumer Study* (Washington, D.C.: U.S. Department of Health, Education, and Welfare, 1976), p. 15.

18. The most important of these is Richard Ruopp et al., *Children at the Center: Final Report of the National Day Care Study*, vol. 1 (Cambridge, Mass.: Abt Associates, 1979).

19. "Child Care Grows as a Benefit," pp. 60–63.

20. See, for example, Joseph Featherstone, "Kentucky Fried Children," *New Republic*, 12 September 1970, pp. 12–16. On the lukewarm success of the franchises initially, see "Growing Pains: Day Care Franchises Beset with Problems, Find Allure Is Fading," *Wall Street Journal*, 27 November 1972, p. 1. On their current rejuvenation, see the *Business Week* article cited directly above.

21. Family Protection Act, introduced 17 June 1981, by Senators Jepsen and Laxalt, S.1378.

22. See, for example, the column by Paul Weyrich, a leading New Right ideologue, in the May 1981, issue of *Conservative Digest*: "We have to have a vision of what, given the current state of things, society should look like in the next twenty years. It isn't enough to simply oppose federalized day-care centers ... we must look at creative solutions to real problems. Taking government out of these problems is only a partial solution" (p. 14. Such a statement contrasts sharply with earlier conservative writing on daycare. See, for example, George Gilder, "The Child Care State," in *Sexual Suicide* (New York: Quadrangle Books, 1973)

23. I have elsewhere argued for the necessity of linking the defense of abortion to a larger campaign of reproductive freedom. Carole Joffe, "The Abortion Struggle in American Politics," *Dissent*, Summer 1981, pp. 268–71.

24. This point is especially well argued by Barbara Easton, "Feminism and the Contemporary Family," *Socialist Review*, May 1978, pp. 11–36.

25. For an example of early feminist writing on day care, see Louise Gross and Phyllis MacEwan, "On Day Care," in *Voices from Women's Liberation*, ed. Leslie B. Tanner (New York: New American Library, 1970), pp. 199–207.

26. Steiner, *Children's Cause*, pp. 153, 156.

27. On the alleged hostility of the United States to children's needs, see Alvin Schorr, *Children and Decent People* (New York: Basic Books, 1974).

28. Steiner, *Futility of Family Policy*.

29. One of the best-known such statements is Katharine Ellis and Rosalind Petchesky, "Children of the Corporate Dream: An Analysis of Day Care as a Political Issue under Capitalism," *Socialist Revolution*, November-December 1972,: pp. 9–28.

30. See Gwen Morgan, *The Trouble with Title XX: A Review of Child Daycare Policy* (Washington, D.C.: Day Care and Child Development Council of America, 1977).

31. Joffe, *Friendly Intruders*, p. 3.

32. It is beyond the scope of this paper to discuss the concept of women as a secondary labor force. The reader is referred to the special issue of *Signs* on "Women and Work" (Winter 1976), particularly the article by Heidi Hartmann.

10

Nancy D. Polikoff

Gender and Child-Custody Determinations: Exploding the Myths

The belief that women have an unfair advantage over men in divorce courts circulates widely through media, culture, and popular consciousness. Specifically with respect to child-custody determinations, the myth that women are virtually guaranteed custody of the children has gone unchallenged and has spawned groups of angry fathers demanding "equal rights" to custody, insisting that they are the victims of sex discrimination as pernicious as that affecting women in the workplace. The rhetoric of the fathers' rights movement has been couched in the language of destruction of sex-role stereotyping, increased options for men and women as both parents and workers, and sexual equality. It has been difficult for feminists to respond to the fathers' rights movement effectively because such rhetoric seems to mirror feminist goals of equality and increased participation by fathers in childrearing. Critical analysis is necessary, however, both because the claimed factual basis of discrimination against fathers is questionable and because the underlying model of equality reveals the inadequacies of current legal strategies.

A basic premise of the fathers' rights movement is that men are routinely denied custody of their children upon divorce and are required to make unfair financial payments to their former wives. *Weekend Fathers*, a recent book by the president of Fathers' Rights of America and his second wife, paints the picture, entirely unsupported by statistical evidence, of conscientious fathers paying child support while being denied all access to their children, of men living at the poverty level because they pay exorbitant alimony and child support, of women's power in divorce court bolstered by lawyers and judges, all to the disadvantage of men.[1] In June 1981, 125 delegates from 200 local organizations in 21 states met as the National Congress for Men to fight to extend sexual equality to men and women. It claimed as the greatest single inequality against men the loss of child custody, loss of home, and loss of assets upon divorce.[2] Perhaps most significant is the 1979 Academy Award winning film, *Kramer vs. Kramer*, which led millions of viewers to believe that a woman who abandons her seven-year-old child, barely sees him for eighteen months, and has a time-consuming career can prevail in court over a father who has provided excellent, stable care for the child for eighteen months. The movie successfully garnered enormous sympathy for the father and brought the ire of the viewing public on the judge and the legal system that would deny him his son.[3]

In fact, during the past few years there is evidence that mothers are losing custody cases for inappropriate reasons. Legislation, judicial decisions, and public support that focus on fathers being denied custody reflect a misperception of which parent suffers the greater share of sex discrimination. The discussion of custody disputes must be refocused to examine the criteria currently in use and to answer the question of how mothers, who still are the primary caretakers of children within marriage, can lose custody on divorce.

This article initally examines some of the premises of the fathers' rights movement. It then evaluates the factors courts have used in recent custody decisions in order to show both how these factors inappropriately disadvantage women and how the equality model fails in the family law context. Finally, the article analyzes why this phenomenon is occurring and its implications for women's lives.

The claim that fathers are discriminated against in custody decisions tends to center on the statistic that about 90 percent of the children of divorce are in the custody of their mothers, and the "tender years" presumption, a doctrine of historically short duration that made it extremely difficult for fathers to gain custody of children of tender years unless the mother was proven unfit.

WHAT THE "90 PERCENT" DOESN'T SAY

There is no doubt that in the vast majority of divorces, the children remain with their mother. This is no proof of unfairness to fathers, however, unless the fathers in all instances *want* the custody of their children. In fact, most children remain with their mothers by consent of both parents or because the father leaves. The final court award, rubber stamping the arrangement of the parties themselves, does not reflect a bias on the part of the court system toward mothers because the court system plays an entirely passive role.

To prove that courts are biased toward mothers, the fathers' rights movement would need to show that mothers have a statistically significant advantage over fathers in *contested* custody cases, those conflicts that produce a head-on battle between the parents. If a father wants custody of his children and fights for them, the picture is very different from that which both popular belief and fathers' rights movement ideology would suggest. Little systematic statistical data exists, and more will need to be gathered in order to fully understand contemporary changes, but what does exist is startling.

In a California study of divorce, sociologists Lenore J. Weitzman and Ruth B. Dixon found that in 1977, 63 percent of all fathers who requested custody in court papers were successful.[4] This figure compared to 35 percent in 1968 and 37 percent in 1972. The authors focus, as does the fathers' rights movement, on ultimate percentages and determine that in both 1972 and 1977 women received 88–90 percent of all custody awards. They therefore conclude that the maternal preference is still strong. Within these data, however, is the deeper and more significant truth: The power to decide child custody often lies with the father, not the mother. If he wishes to exercise that power, he is likely to win. In the Weitzman-Dixon study, only fifteen contested cases were settled by trial in 1977, resulting in ten awards to mothers and five to fathers. This one-third success figure, five years ago, is a far cry from the gross unfairness still claimed by the fathers' rights movement.

The Legal Aid Society of Alameda County, California, reports that of thirteen actually contested custody trials in 1979, there were eight awards (62 percent) to mothers and five (38 percent) to fathers.[5] A study of 196 Minneapolis cases showed a paternal success rate of 45 percent. One New York family court judge who decided sixty to seventy custody cases over five years during the 1970s awarded custody to men as often as to women.[6] Authors of a single-father study reported in 1979 that, in their survey of North Carolina judges, men who fight for custody of their children prevail in nearly one-half of the cases.[7] In interpreting the significance of these data, it is necessary to bear in mind that there has not been a revolution in childrearing, and mothers still bear most of the responsibility. Therefore, data showing a success rate for fathers in courtroom battles of one-third to one-half during the 1970s suggest the possibility that men who have not been the primary child-care providers are prevailing over women who have been.

Thus, while the 90 percent figure on custody awards to mothers is certainly indicative of who performs childrearing in our society, it is not indicative of the *power* to determine who rears children upon divorce. By not wanting custody, men and not judges are responsible for the 90 percent figure. Continued failure to acknowledge the reality of the situation permits judges, in the name of righting a nonexistent social wrong, to bend over backward to award custody to fathers.

Some fathers' rights advocates would no doubt argue that men are not freely choosing to leave their children with mothers but are socially conditioned to do so and frequently so encouraged by teachers, counselors, clergy, and lawyers. This is without question true. We would argue that an educational and political movement geared toward changing social attitudes about parenting is vitally important. Its contribution would be especially welcome if its primary aim were a restructuring of work to permit and encourage co-parenting. Men will not expect their wives to retain custody if they have been equal participants in childrearing; and teachers, counselors, clergy, and lawyers will not encourage men to relinquish custody if this co-parenting is obvious. We thus question the fathers' rights movement's focus on male parenting at the time of divorce rather than on social change facilitating co-parenting during marriage.

HISTORICAL BACKGROUND OF CUSTODY DISPUTES

Until the mid-nineteenth century, fathers retained custody of their children upon separation or divorce.[8] This was an unequivocal paternal right. Among many examples of the application of this right in England was a case in which a mother was denied custody of a child although the father was in prison and his mistress, who provided child care, brought the child to him for visits.[9] In the United States, in spite of some early cases that indicated judicial discretion to remove custody from fathers,[10] the presumption in favor of fathers flourished. *Commonwealth* v. *Briggs*, an 1834 Massachusetts case, affirmed the principle that absent a "clear and strong case of unfitness," the father was entitled to custody.[11]

In 1839, an English statute directed that children under the age of seven could be awarded to their mothers, although initial interpretations of the law returned children to the custody of the father when they were older.[12] In the United States, occasional early nineteenth-century case law shows awards to mothers, but these instances were still clearly a minority, producing the demand in the 1848 Seneca Falls Convention Declaration that a mother be permitted to retain custody of her children. By and large, American judges of the period adhered to the concept of paternal right, sometimes citing the importance of the father-child relationship in promoting education, advancement, status, and inheritance.[13] During most of this period, children were an economic benefit to their families, and fathers, in retaining custody of the children, retained a valuable economic asset.

Later in the nineteenth century, a shift toward maternal preference for custody of young children, which was by no means an absolute practice, reflected a changing picture of the society's view of mothers and children.[14] This change corresponded in time to the industrial revolution and to a shifting role for children, such as compulsory public education, which reduced their economic value to their families.

Most accounts of the "tender years doctrine" fail to note that in its early years it did not require that the mother be awarded child support to assist in the care of the children in her custody. In fact, for many years the father was entitled to any economic fruits of his child's labor even if the mother had custody. Subsequently, women with custody obtained the right to their children's economic value, but the father's support obligation ceased if he did not have custody because he had no more right to his children's services.[15] Because those services were worth less and less, only those women able to provide support through their own means or, more likely, that of their families, were even in a position to request custody of their children. Although some judges late in the nineteenth century did require fathers to pay child support, this did not become the widespread accepted practice until the 1920s. Only then did the developed tender years doctrine gain its true significance. One commentator does not consider the tender years doctrine to have been firmly established until the 1940s.[16]

According to this legal principle, unless the mother is unfit, custody of children of "tender years" goes to the mother.[17] "Tender years" has never been uniformly defined, although the age of seven, derived possibly from the 1839 English statute, is frequently cited, and one historian has placed the age at eleven or twelve.[18] Unfitness was customarily equated with the mother's adultery.[19] Thus, even during the most extreme period of maternal preference, custody law was used to regulate women's behavior.

Today, two-thirds of the states have entirely rejected the tender years doctrine,[20] so that it is no longer found in judicial discussions. Of the one-third that retain reference to it, the doctrine is subordinated to the more recent "best interest of the child" standard.[21]

Although a minority of states still refer to a tender years presumption, it is not the doctrine of decades ago, which required maternal unfitness in order to award young children to their father. In 1979, for example, a Kansas court awarded one-year-old twins to a working father rather than to a mother who could stay home with them, even though it considered the tender years presumption as one factor, because the father was found to be able to provide the better home environment.[22] The higher court, in upholding the decision, made it clear that the mother could lose even if she was fit, under the best interests of the child standard. That the tender years doctrine is dying a circuitous rather than a direct death in a few American jurisdictions should not be permitted to fuel the fires of the father's rights movement. No recent appeals court decision has been found overturning a custody award to a father, or upholding one to the mother, on the basis of the tender years doctrine;[23] several have been found that have upheld awards to fathers in spite of the supposed continued existence of the tender years doctrine.[24]

CASE ANALYSIS[25]

The theme that runs throughout current case law is the failure of judges to give major consideration to the role of the mother as primary caretaker, as Goldstein, Freud, and Solnit in their landmark work, *Beyond the Best Interests of the Child*, define the psychological parent: one "who, on a continuing, day to day basis, through interaction, companionship, interplay, and mutuality, fulfills the child's psychological need . . . as well as the child's physical needs."[26]

In the 1981 West Virginia Supreme Court case of *Garska* v. *McCoy*, which squarely required a preference for the primary caretaker, the following factors were enumerated as comprising, at least in part, primary parenting:

> (1) preparing and planning of meals; (2) bathing, grooming and dressing; (3) purchasing, cleaning, and care of clothes; (4) medical care, including nursing and trips to physicians; (5) arranging for social interaction among peers after school, i.e., transporting to friends' houses or, for example, to girl or boy scout meetings; (6) arranging alternative care, i.e., babysitting, day care, etc.; (7) putting child to bed at night, attending to child in the middle of the night, waking child in the morning; (8) disciplining, i.e., teaching general manners and toilet training; (9) educating, i.e., religious, cultural, social, etc.; and (10) teaching elementary skills, i.e., reading, writing and arithmetic.[27]

Inattention to the question of primary caretaking tends to devalue and in fact negate the traditional maternal role. It may be that this inattention is the result of elimination of the "tender years" maternal preference. Judges may believe, as one

Oregon case reflected,[28] that weighing nurturance, which is associated with mothering, would be the equivalent of applying a maternal preference and would therefore violate sex-neutral custody standards. But the only appropriate purpose of a sex-neutral standard is to require evaluation of who is providing primary nurturance without automatically assuming it to be the mother;[29] its purpose should not be to eliminate the importance of nurturance from the custody determination and equate the provision of financial support with the provision of psychological and physical needs. A North Dakota appellate court made just such an equation, declaring "both care and support are important," and denying a woman who had been a full-time mother and homemaker custody of her three children.[30]

This interpretation of sex neutrality equates elimination of maternal preference with elimination of preference for the primary nurturer because mothers have traditionally performed that role. Rather than extend equal rights to nurturing fathers, the only legitimate purpose of sex-neutral statutes, this analysis instead elevates in the judge's mind significance to the child of the traditional paternal role of financial support and permits judges to make their custody determinations without evaluating parent-child bonds.

Employed mothers are victims of a corollary misconception—that if both parents work outside the home, then the care of the children is evenly divided. With this assumption, the mother is performing more than her traditional parental role, making the father seem more attractive as a custodian. In reality, employed mothers overwhelmingly continue to be primarily responsible for childrearing, and the refusal of judges to recognize and acknowlege this is punitive toward women who have lives outside as well as within the home. In a 1979 case, a Missouri appellate court analyzed the tender years presumption as based upon the mother being home to care for the child and develop his or her moral, spiritual, civic, social, and religious responsibility. The court then stated, relying on 1968 case law, that "if the mother goes and returns as a wage earner like the father, she has no more part in the responsibility than he. . . ."[31] This assumption has almost uniformly replaced any maternal preference the law once provided; one judge carried this fallacious reasoning so far that, faced with two employed parents, he chose to hear testimony in the custody dispute only on the subject of the provision of child care while the parents worked.[32]

While some cases reveal judicial assumptions that an employed mother and an employed father have been equally involved in childrearing, others show a strong tendency to judge women's employment more harshly that that of men. In one case, an "energetic and ambitious career woman" was found to have a diminished ability to care for her child, while the child's father's employment was not even evaluated for its impact on his childrearing ability. The appellate judge who dissented from the affirmance of the award of custody to the father noted that there had been "undue emphasis on [the mother's] career" and that the trial judge had been "especially preoccupied with [the mother's] job status."[33] In another case, the judge referred to the father's ability to "spend a normal working father's time with the children," although the father's work was by no means normal because he was an oil company president.[34] The same judge noted that the mother's work gave her little time with the children, but there was no reference to a normal working *mother*'s time, because "normal" and "working" mother are still considered inconsistent.

The failure of courts to value primary nurturing is starkly apparent when women who have been full-time homemakers but must seek employment upon divorce are denied custody. A woman entering or reentering the work force will have less control over her hours and other workplace requirements and may need to devote some time to training or education as well as paid work in order to improve financial security for herself and her children. If a judge does not consider the mother-child bond that has resulted from years of primary parenting, then the mother may lose because she appears less settled and often has fewer hours to spend with the children during the adjustment period.[35] In fact, the substantial employment and education decisions that women face upon separation and divorce often result in more changes than for men who continue in their current employment. This transition period can penalize women, as judges view the mother as less stable and do not credit the strength of her bond with her children.[36]

There is an undercurrent of punitiveness throughout custody decisions involving employed women, who, after all, comprise the majority of divorced and separated mothers. Although the best interests of the child standard is not a fault-based standard, the woman who chooses to leave a marriage and expects to keep her children and a job is likely to find her behavior punished by judges who disapprove of her independence, even if under an honest "best interests" test she would be better able to provide nurturance to the children. Since wives are traditionally saddled with the responsibility of keeping the marriage together, even when the divorce is not the woman's choice she may find herself blamed for not having done enough to "keep her man." Under either scenario, the mother's employment, even if a matter of absolute financial necessity, is the easiest excuse a judge has to find her the less adequate parent.

Although the above analysis might lead to the conclusion that mothers who are available to provide full-time care of their children are guaranteed custody, such is not the case. Although a mother's absence for work reasons counts heavily against her as an indication that she has not performed or will not perform the principal parenting role, her constant presence as a traditional good mother is not often preferred, under the interpretation of sex neutrality we believe to be in operation, to that of a traditional good father. If continuity of primary caretaking is not equated with the best interests of the child, then judges can make decisions based on the currently popular notion that female-headed households create problem children[37] and that the father is the more appropriate authority figure in a patriarchal world.

When financial ability is used as criterion in awarding custody, either explicitly[38] or implicitly, it will almost always work to the father's advantage. One trial court judge awarded custody to a father because he worked full-time and earned $14,000 to $15,000 a year, while the mother earned $1000 to $3000 working part-time. The facts in that case showed without doubt that the mother had been the primary caretaker of the children. The appeals court noted that the trial judge's evaluation of the economic circumstances of the parties would preclude virtually all mothers from obtaining custody.[39]

At a time when the myth that men are unfairly denied custody has pervaded public consciousness, judges can latch on to the father's economic superiority as a reason to support paternal custody. Legal aid lawyers report that their clients on welfare lose custody to husbands or ex-husbands who are employed even when the necessity for welfare has stemmed from undependable, insufficient, or nonexistent child-support payments.[40] Some judges may view paternal custody as a means of reducing welfare rolls.

The catch-22 for a divorcing woman is now apparent. If she does not work outside the home or works part-time hours to spend more time with her children, she will be less able to provide material benefits. If she does hold a full-time job, she will be considered to have abandoned the maternal role. What gets lost in this construct is the value to the child of the bond created by primary parenting and the identity of the woman as mother resulting from such primary parenting.

A custodial father who turns a significant amount of child care over to another woman, often a live-in housekeeper or his mother,[41] is not hurt in judicial evaluation because judges do not really expect men to perform "mothering," and this delegation of responsibility is considered normal. Nowhere is this more apparent than in the case of paternal remarriage. An increasingly common scenario is the father agreeing to maternal custody at the time of the divorce and then filing for a change upon his remarriage. Judicial consideration of remarriage disadvantages mothers both because divorced women remarry significantly less than divorced men[42] and because a woman's remarriage does not ever provide a new stay-at-home wife. Even if the stepmother is employed, her female presence is assumed to be advantageous to the children; whereas a stepfather would not be expected to be a primary, or even assistant, child care provider.

Case review supports this analysis. One court removing children from an employed mother with a live-in housekeeper and giving them to an employed father with a stay-at-home wife made frequent reference to "[more defined] parental authority in the [father's] home" and a "more stable home environment" with the remarried father. The appeals court sanctioned this reasoning, noting that the trial court's choice was between placing the children "in the custody of a series of housekeepers or in the custody of the children's stepmother."[43] No employed mother could ever prevail under such a test. The emphasis on the father's remarriage in this case is in stark contrast to another in which the remarriage of an employed mother was not even discussed in ruling granting custody to her ex-husband, who was not remarried but lived with his mother.[44] When a court focuses its inquiry properly on the performance of primary parenting, remarriage of either party will be irrevelant.[45] Mothers are not fungible, and one woman will not do as well as another in rearing children. Judicial preference for two-parent families is also inappropriate, as it focuses the inquiry away from the parent-child bond and onto broader social prejudices.

Loss of custody has long been one punitive measure used against mothers who engaged in nonmarital sexual behavior. Although most judges view the sexual activity of either parent as a negative factor in determining custody, there is some recent indication that women are penalized for behavior that a judge is willing to overlook in men. In Illinois, three appeals court decisions upholding custody awards to the father on the basis of the mother's sexual behavior, including the publicly discussed case of *Jarrett* v. *Jarrett*, were distinguished from a later case in which a father was awarded custody although he sometimes slept with his woman friend while his son was present and had been doing so for three years.[46] Lesbian mothers have been and continue to be especially vulnerable to loss of custody, as they are perceived to embody both an extreme of unacceptable sexual behavior and an independence from men that removes them from the traditional female role.[47] That loss of custody has traditionally resulted from the mother's sexual activity is good evidence that the best interests of the child standard has been interpreted more according to judicial prejudice concerning proper female behavior in general than according to a rigorous analysis of the needs of the children involved. Thus it is not surprising that punitiveness, coerciveness, and the advancement of judicially determined social policy all play a greater part, consciously or unconsciously, in custody decisions than an evaluation of the child's need for continuity of primary care.

There is a caveat to the suggestion that a preference for the primary parent be incorporated into the best interests of the child standard: The evaluation of behavior to determine primary parenting is still a subjective exercise. Case analysis reveals a tendency to overrate small paternal contributions to parenting because they are still so noticeable, and to concomitantly overemphasize lack of total maternal parenting. In other words, the emphasis in evaluating mothers is on what they do not do, because they are expected to do everything. By this standard, men will always look good for doing more than nothing, and women will always look bad for doing less than everything.

This analysis is particularly troubling in its application to the period just preceding the separation or divorce. If the mother goes into the work force to prepare for financial independence or if she goes to school to facilitate her entry into the work force or if she makes demands for adjustment of child-care responsibilities as part of an unsuccessful attempt to make the marriage work, it will appear superficially that the father's parenting has become more significant. Thus in *Dempsey* v. *Dempsey*, in which the husband's low level of participation in family life was the reason Mrs. Dempsey wanted a divorce, the judge was very impressed with the father's increased participation with the children pending the divorce, consisting of making breakfast and school lunches for the children and buying groceries. In granting custody to the father, the judge also noted that the mother, who had been a full-time homemaker, had developed personal interests outside the home.[48]

The ease with which judges find fault with maternal care is especially evident in those cases in which the mother actually leaves the children in the care of their father or someone else for a short period of time. This behavior, which is especially common in women who go from daughter to wife to mother with no time on their own, is considered tantamount to abandonment and is seen as negating the preceding years of primary parenting. Contrary to the outcome of *Kramer vs. Kramer*, an eighteen-month absence is almost a guarantee of loss of custody.

THE EQUALITY PRINCIPLE

Sex-neutral custody laws imply that a father and a mother come before the court on an equal footing. Men and women are not equal in this society, however, and legislating equal treatment does not correct the underlying inequalities. Legislating equality, by itself, can be a superficial act, obscuring the issue of whether genuine equality has been achieved and avoiding a rigorous analysis of the needs of children.

Sex-neutral laws are appealing because they decategorize men and women, treating each person as an individual. They accommodate the fact that not all women are more suited than all men to rear children. But when the stereotypes reflect a concrete, material reality, law and public policy must decide whether to acknowledge that reality or ignore it. Our suggestion that the primary caretaker be preferred as custodian is a sex-neutral standard, which attempts to take account of reality without undermining the possibilities for change. Such a proposal is bound to be criticized for the very reason that it will encourage custody awards to mothers. We are prepared to defend it on those grounds because it is inappropriate for men to complain about maternal care of children after marriage but to expect it or even insist on it during marriage.

The overwhelming trend toward mandating joint custody is an outgrowth of sex neutrality in custody determinations and has been a major demand of the fathers' rights movement.[49] Joint custody is a complicated concept with different meanings in different states. Often, statutes differentiate joint "legal" custody from joint "physical" custody.[50] Thus, while the children may physically live with one parent, both parents have equal legal control over the children's lives. Overwhelmingly, children live with their mothers when there is joint legal custody, with the result that fathers get equal rights without incurring equal responsibility.[51] An analysis of joint custody by the National Center on Women and Family Law points out that

> the majority of fathers still prefer women to remain the physical custodians of their children, although with decreased financial support and increased limitations on her [*sic*] lifestyle and freedom of choice, vis-a-vis employment, sexual mores, travel and place of residence, and decision-making authority.[52]

A complete analysis of joint-custody legislation and litigation has been provided elsewhere,[53] but the accumulating evidence suggests that this trend is part of the sex-neutrality model that ignores years of primary parenting by mothers and provides fathers with an inappropriate bargaining tool in the name of equality.

In the employment and education fields, it has been understood that equality is a meaningless concept without certain material prerequisites. Thus we have seen the development of affirmative action job-training programs. More analysis needs to be done regarding sexual equality in family law. Currently it is often used to divert attention from the serious inequities that befall women upon divorce. The perfect example of this was the 1979 Supreme Court case of *Orr* v. *Orr*, which eliminated as unconstitutional statutes permitting alimony awards to women but not men.[54] Although now the handful of men who deserve alimony will be eligible to receive it, the real problem with alimony is its inadequacy and unreliability for thousands of women who need it.[55] Attention to the sexual equality aspect of alimony, therefore, displaces what should be the appropriate focus.[56] It is not necessary to oppose sexual equality, but only to gear public debate properly.

So with child-custody cases, sexual equality is not the issue, and can become a trap. While we advocate that criteria in custody cases be applied equally, without conscious or unconscious double standards for men and women, it is also necessary that the application of criteria recognize the underlying inequalities between men and women. An equal evaluation of financial ability or workplace stability, for example, will disproportionately disadvantage women without furthering the legitimate interests of the children. While equal evaluation of nurturing disadvantages men, the focus on nurturing is most closely related to the best interests of the child and is therefore appropriate. If in the short run this standard produces many more awards of custody to women than to men, it is not because of unfairness; it is an appropriate result of the different parent-child experience of mothers and fathers.

There are, to be sure, some fathers who have been primary nurturers. There are also some families for whom joint custody works well. These minority instances are not our concern. The concern lies with mothers who lose custody although they have performed the primary nurturing role throughout the marriage. A system that produces such a result is one that penalizes women and children, denigrates the mothering role, and shifts yet another form of social control to men.

THE IMPLICATIONS

Although each custody case is an individual matter, the cumulative result of custody dispositions is a significant social phenomenon. The banner of "father's rights" addressing this phenomenon is not necessarily motivated by caring for children, as often the issue is control of children and women.

In a 1968 book entitled *Divorce and Custody for Men*, Charles Metz offered the following viewpoint:

> Our children must be taught values that are essential to the development of moral citizenship. They must be taught a code by which they can determine what is right and what is wrong. . . . The training of children demands respect for family law. . . . The father who is the head of a household is best able to demand the respect that makes teaching

> possible. He is the traditional symbol of authority. His traditional authority was not given to him by women. It has been earned in political corridors, on battlefields, through the profits of industry and the intricacies of the arts. As the chief provider and defender of homes, he is rightly the symbol of authority.[57]

Metz suggests the following three questions in determining custody: Who can best teach the children to be moral and responsible citizens? Who can best care for them? Who can best support them? His answer to questions one and three is obvious. With respect to question two, the answer may be in how "care" is defined. Another passage provides a clue.

> . . . [E]ven absent from the home, [the father] can supply love and guidance through a good housekeeper. When he does come home, his competent presence is all the more valuable. No child needs to be in contact with a parent twenty-four hours a day.[58]

Of course not. But when it is the mother who is not present twenty-four hours a day, the level of her concern and care for the children is instantly suspect. A 1975 publication favoring custody for men put it this way:

> How is teaching love, respect and discipline possible in the broken home? The traditional . . . authority by the Father is involved. . . . Any judge should agree it is far better to have a situation where the child is in the custody of a full time, loving, warm, conscientious father, than a piece of a mother, who finds her role in childrearing unrewarding.[59]

A hard-working father with normal outside interests is still a full-time father; a hard-working mother with normal outside interests is "a piece of mother."

The most antiwoman implications of custody for fathers are laid out, without mincing words, by Daniel Amneus in his 1979 book, *Back to Patriarchy.*[60] It is most instructive reading for its ability to tie together antifeminism with the currently fashionable antigovernment position. Amneus is blunt: Fathers should get custody of their children; all alimony and child support should be eliminated; women who want to compete in the work world should do so unencumbered by children, and should leave those children to fathers who will remarry women who want to stay home and take proper care of them.

According to his theory, men are motivated to productive work by the need to provide economic security for their wives and children, a theory articulated earlier by George Gilder, a current guru of the Reagan administration, in his book *Sexual Suicide.* The similarities in the writings of the two men make it difficult to write off Amneus as an extremist with no following.

We do not suggest that all proponents of so-called equal rights for fathers adhere to these positions.[61] Many believe that fathers should play a more nurturing role in their children's lives and should give up power in the public sphere if necessary to accomplish this. Many also contend that women no longer feel the sense of responsibility in childrearing that they once felt and that they want men's fuller participation. Repeatedly, women's employment is used to justify custody awards to fathers.

Yet neither the increase in male participation in the home nor mothers' time away at work necessarily diminishes who has ultimate psychic and nurturant responsibility for children. Fathers, who typically do not bear this ultimate responsibility, often have a disproportionate opinion of the importance of small undertakings. A telling study revealed that when middle- and upper-income fathers of under-one-year-old children were asked how much time they spent in the presence of their children each day, the average response was 15 to 20 minutes. Clinical observation revealed the actual amount of time per day to be 38 seconds![62]

Judges, who are mostly men, often have little understanding of what is involved in taking daily primary responsibility for a child. They are therefore very impressed with the changing of a fraction of the number of diapers, preparing a fraction of the number of meals, presiding over a fraction of the number of baths, providing solace for a fraction of scraped knees and hurt feelings. Similarly, mothers know that equating employment with an abdication of nurturing is an oversimplification of parenting functions and not a true reflection of contemporary family life. In spite of its seductive rhetoric, therefore, the fathers' rights movement, with its battle cry of equal custody rights, is perhaps best understood as part of the current wave of antifeminist backlash.

Not only are women with determined husbands likely to lose their children in court for the wrong reasons, but all women can be intimidated by the threat of losing their children into accepting disadvantageous financial settlements upon divorce. Women faced with a contested custody hearing are unlikely to turn down a proposed settlement which removes that threat, no matter how low the child support or how disproportionate the property settlement. The West Virginia Supreme Court explicitly recognized this dilemma and attempted to avoid it by enacting a primary caretaker presumption so that custody would not be a bargaining tool.[63] Lawyers who are honest with themselves know that this form of bargaining is commonplace. One fathers' rights advocate who claims that the economic motivation is minimal because it costs more to maintain a home for children than to pay child support[64] misses the point; it is least expensive of all to threaten to fight for custody and then back off in return for the lowest possible financial terms. And of course the high costs of contested litigation are typically more accessible to men than to women.[65] When husbands hire "bomber" lawyers, some women give up custody to avoid a fight that would damage the children, or a fight that they cannot afford, or both.[66] The system needs to be altered to prevent such scenarios.

Since fathers' rights have become fashionable, legal commentators have rarely challenged sex neutrality in custody determinations.[67] When they have, the maternal preference is supported based on the valid presumption that the mother has been the primary caretaker; only if the father has in fact assumed that role during the marriage should the presumption in favor of the mother yield. Lucy Katz perceptively noted that when the mother has been the primary caretaker, every ambivalence or difficulty she has had weighs against her. The father, who has not had the responsibility and is not judged by the same standard, may deceptively appear to be the better parent.[68] Commentators also note that a maternal preference would decrease contested custody litigation and that this by itself is a benefit to children. While those who advocate fathers' right to custody rarely discuss the impact of the litigation itself, the West Virginia court specifically attacked custody battles as injurious to children and offered the primary caretaker presumption as a legitimate means of avoiding such litigation.[69]

Katz also warned that mothers whose custody is threatened may fear any increased paternal involvement with the children.[70] Case law and court experience support this as a legitimate fear, as judges frequently justify custody to fathers by noting their increased, albeit recent, attention to their children, or that they have been solely responsible for their children for a short period of time after years of maternal care. Since strong father-children ties are generally healthy, these should be promoted by everyone, including the mother, who should not need to fear losing custody and cannot be expected to be supportive if she is under such a threat.

The presumption that children remain with their primary caretaker would be more reflective of reality if it encompassed a presumption that this person was the mother unless the father could prove otherwise. This would be advantageous to women because it would obviate minute scrutiny of paternal behavior, which is certain to be colored by the undue importance fathers often place on their small increases in parenting. It would not unduly burden the father who was in fact the primary parent because it would simply require that he sustain the burden of proof. This suggestion is of course unlikely to be met with approval within the context of prevailing conceptions of equality. Thus the approach of the West Virginia court comes closest to recognizing the reality of contemporary parenting while not violating the cardinal principle of gender neutrality.

Some feminists may feel that our emphasis binds women who have been mothers first to remain in that role even if they do not so choose. That is not our intention. If a woman with legal custodial priority agrees that her husband should have permanent custody, or agrees to joint custody, that is her legitimate decision. It should be the mother's choice, however, because she has earned it by providing years of primary child care. To look toward sexual neutrality in custody awards for reinforcement of such choices is misplaced and, without truly encouraging options for women, only penalizes women who have been primary parents and want to continue in that role.

In consciously egalitarian marriages with truly shared childrearing, we suggest that joint custody will be and is now the norm by choice and that legislation is necessary only in those states that have refused to accept joint custody if both parents want it. Mandatory joint-custody legislation should be opposed because joint custody, with its concept of equal decision-making authority and therefore continued intimate contact between parents, must be earned by the father through joint parenting during marriage. Additionally, older children should, as they often do now, have control over their placement.[71]

Sex neutrality should never be interpreted to mean that the traditional father role, even modified by small amounts of assistance to the mother, is as valuable to the child's development as the traditional mother role of primary nurturance, care, and responsibility. Such an interpretation, which is already infiltrating custody decisions and is found in the extreme profather literature, comes frighteningly close to an elevation of men as valuable transmitters of "male" social values and devaluation of women to fungible caretakers with only derivative authority. The implication of such reasoning would be a rigidification of traditional sex roles through paternal custody rather than a destruction of those roles. Similarly, the mandate of sex equality in child-custody determinations should be interpreted to encourage male nurturance while the family is intact, in order to move society closer to genuine equality in childrearing.

NOTES

1. Gerald A. and Myrna Silver, *Weekend Fathers* (Los Angeles: Stratford Press, 1981).

2. *New York Times*, 15 June 1981, p. B–9. In the economic arena, all evidence establishes that divorced men fare substantially better than divorced women. For a thorough analysis of the misplaced belief that ex-wives are supported in style by struggling ex-husbands, see Lenore J. Weitzman and Ruth B. Dixon, "The Alimony Myth: Does No-Fault Divorce Make a Difference?" *Family Law Quarterly* 140 (Fall 1980): 141.

3. Legal experts agreed that the result of the custody dispute in *Kramer vs. Kramer* was inconceivable. See, for example, *New York Times*, 21 December 1979, p. B-6.

4. Lenore J. Weitzman and Ruth B. Dixon, "Child Custody Awards: Legal Standards and Empirical Patterns for Child Custody, Support and Visitation After Divorce," *University of California Davis Law Review* (1979): 471.

5. Data gathered by Adele Hendrickson, Attorney in Charge, Family Law Unit, Oakland, California.

6. Michael Wheeler: *Divided Children: A Legal Guide for Divorcing Parents* (New York: Norton, 1980), p. 40. Although Wheeler suggests that the high success rate for fathers may be the result of self-selection of only men with strong cases contesting custody, case analysis reveals nothing unusual, and certainly nothing compelling, about those fathers who pursue custody.

7. Dennis K. Orthner and Ken Lewis, "Evidence of Single Father Competence in Child Rearing," *Family Law Quarterly* 8 (1979): 27, 28.

8. Review of the early history of child-custody determinations may be found in Allen Roth, "The Tender Years Presumption in Child Custody Disputes," *Journal of Family Law* 15 (1977): 423, 425–32; and Henry H. Foster and Doris Jonas Freed, "Life with Father: 1978," *Family Law Quarterly* 9 (1978): 321, 325–29.

9. *Ex Parte Skinner*, 9 Moore 278 (1824). In *King* v. *Demanneville*, 3 East 221, 102 Eng. Rep. 1054 (1800), a nursing infant was awarded to a French enemy alien father, even though the mother and child had left the home because of the father's cruelty.

10. See Jamil S. Zainaldin, "The Emergence of a Modern American Family Law: Child Custody, Adoption and the Court, 1796–1851," *Northwestern University Law Review* 73 (1979): 1038, 1052–59.

11. 33 Mass. (16 Pick.) 203 (1834). Unfitness for a father was not the same as the later test of unfitness for a mother under the tender years doctrine. For example, in *Rex* v. *Greenhill*, 4 Ad. & E. 624, 111 Eng. Rep. 922 (K.B. 1836), a father living in open adultery was nonetheless granted custody of his three daughters.

12. 2 & 3 Vict. C. 54 (1839).

13. Zainaldin, "Modern American Family Law," p. 1067.

14. In terms of statutory law, however, only fourteen states had altered the common law rule of paternal preference by 1900. Roth, "Tender Years Presumption," p. 429.

15. A discussion of the authorities is found in Carol Brown, "Mother, Fathers and Children: From Private to Public Patriarchy," in *Women and Revolution*, ed. Lydia Sargent (Boston: South End Press, 1981), pp. 253–56.

16. Orthner and Lewis, "Single Father Competence."

17. This was viewed as the natural extension of the role of mothers. An example of the reasoning is found in *Bruce* v. *Bruce*, 14 Okla. 160, 168, 285 p. 30, 37 (1930): "Courts know that mother love is a dominant trait in the heart of the mother, even in the weakest of women. It is of divine origin and in nearly all cases far exceeds and surpasses the parental affection of the father. Every just man recognizes the fact that minor children need the constant bestowal of the mother's care and love."

18. Zainaldin, "Modern American Family Law," p. 1072 n. 151. Some state statutes reflected an explicit preference that custody of older children be awarded to their fathers. *See* Oklahoma Stat. 30–11, stating that "... other things being equal, if the child be of tender years, it should be given to the mother; if it be of an age to require education and preparation for labor or business, then to the father."

19. E.g., *Wolpa* v. *Wolpa*, 182 Neb. 268, 153 N.W. 2d 746 (1967); *Parker* v. *Parker*, 222 Md. 69, 158 A. 2d 609 (1960).

20. Henry H. Foster and Doris Jones Freed, "Divorce in the Fifty States: An Overview," *Family Law Quarterly* 14 (1981): 229.

21. In 1970, the National Conference of Commissioners on Uniform State Laws, in its Uniform Marriage and Divorce Act, recommended a best interests test but noted that the preference for the mother of young children when all things are equal was a shorthand means of expressing what was in the child's best interests. U.L.A. 9 (1970): 455.

22. *Neis* v. *Neis*, 599 P. 2d 305 (Kan. App. 1979).

23. In *Casale* v. *Casale*, 549 S.W. 2d 805 (Ky. 1977), an award of custody to a political science assistant professor father was overturned and custody awarded to an English instructor mother on the basis that all things were equal and that therefore custody of a young child should go to the mother. In response, the legislature enacted a sex-neutral custody statute in 1978. A 1979 decision appearing to continue the maternal preference tie-breaker approach, *Moore* v. *Moore*, 577 S.W. 2d 613 (Ky. 1979), was actually tried before the effective date of the new statute and is not therefore an indication of current preference for mothers in Kentucky.

24. E.g., *Boyle* v. *Boyle*, 615 P.2d 301 (Okla. 1980); *In re Marriage of Shepherd*, 588 S.W.2d 174 (Mo. App. 1979).

25. The only way to understand the factors that govern decisions in custody disputes is to analyze each case in an attempt to understand judicial reasoning. Most trial court decisions are not reported in legal texts and are therefore not easily accessible for review. If a trial court decision is appealed to a higher court, the opinion of the appeals court is normally reported, and it is these opinions from which this review of current case law is constructed.

The advantage of analyzing appellate decisions lies in the fact that such analysis enlightens the reader on the reasons for the opinions of both the trial court and the reviewing court. In addition, appeals court decisions are viewed as providing guidance to all trial judges within the state who hear similar cases. The disadvantage of analyzing appellate rather than trial court opinions lies in the fact that most states give great discretion to trial court judges, whose decisions are not likely to be overturned. The largest concentration of power to determine the course of custody litigation, therefore, lies with trial court judges. Although some states provide explicit statutory guidance to judges in the form of enumerated factors to consider in determining the best interests of the child and other states provide no such definition, the trial court judge still has great latitude because she or he is the only judge who observes the parties and their witnesses directly and is considered to be in the best position to evaluate their demeanor and credibility.

26. Joseph Goldstein, Anna Freud, and Albert J. Solnit, *Beyond the Best Interests of the Child* (New York: Free Press, 1979), p. 98.

27. 278 S.E.2d 357, 363 (W. Va. 1981).

28. In *Van Dyke* v. *Van Dyke*, 48 Ore. App. 965, 618 P.2d 465 (1980), the trial court judge awarded custody of a two-year-old son to his father on the basis that, as both parents were fit, an award to the mother because she was the mother and, as such, the primary caretaker, would violate the requirement of sex neutrality. The appellate court has the sense to see through the faulty logic and reversed, holding that which parent was the primary caretaker was a relevant consideration. In this case the appellate court awarded custody to the mother, who had stayed at home with the child and been a traditional homemaker.

29. This was exactly the position of the West Virginia Supreme Court in *Garska* v. *McCoy*, 278 S.E.2d 357, 361 (W. Va. 1981), which modified its earlier maternal presumption into a primary caretaker presumption.

30. *Porter* v. *Porter*, 274 N.W.2d 235 (N.D. 1979). See note 36, *infra*.

31. *In re Marriage of Shepherd*, 588 S.W.2d 174 (Mo. App. 1979), quoting *Stanfield* v. *Stanfield*, 435 S.W.2d 690, 692 (Mo. Ap.. 1968).

32. *Avella* v. *Avella*, 74 App. Div. 2d 592, 424 N.Y.S.2d 526 (1980). The trial court judge awarded custody to the father solely because his mother would care for the child in his absence. The appellate court ordered the trial court to hear broader testimony before making a custody determination.

33. *Gulyas* v. *Gulyas*, 75 Mich. App. 138, 254 N.W.2d 818 (1977). The case is an especially good example of judicial consideration of the mother's employment. A law review article analyzing the case and discussing the trial court record and findings reveals that the six-year-old girl had been in a two-month day-care progam at her kindergarten and first grade and that she spent no more than eight hours a week at a neighbor's until her mother came home from work. Nonetheless, the trial court judge stated that "the wife's career and need for obtaining a livelihood heretofore has diminished her manifested ability to care for the child other than in day care. . . ." The law review article also noted that in a five-page opinion the trial judge mentioned the mother's working eleven times and began the opinion by saying that the case had a background of complaints by the husband regarding the wife's work. In a revealing comment, the trial judge noted that the "marriage was normal until the wife felt compelled to go to work to help support the family." The commentator, after thorough analysis, concluded that ". . . courts may lose sight of the best interests of the child in an effort to accord fathers equal treatment in custody determinations," and "theoretically, the parties now come before the court on an initially equal footing to better assure determination of the child's best interest. When judicial biases are allowed to control, however, we run the risk of merely shifting a presumption for one parent to the other. . . ." Marilyn

Hall Mitchell, "Family Law—Child Custody—Mother's Career May Determine Custody Award to Father," *Wayne Law Review* 24 (1978): 1159, 1161, 1171.

34. *Simmons* v. *Simmons*, 223 Kan. 639, 576. P.2d 589 (1978).

35. In *Porter* v. *Porter*, 274 N.W.2d 235 (N.D. 1979), for example, a mother who had been a full-time homemaker for her three children prior to the separation and who had temporary custody during the separation, lost custody because the job she was able to get upon separation was as a waitress/hostess working four to five hours a night. During this time she left the children with a babysitter. The mother testified that she did not work a day shift because if she did, no one would be home when the children returned from school. She also said that she had found a part-time job cleaning apartments in the afternoon on a trial basis and that she would quit her evening job and return to it only if necessary. Without analyzing the nature or quality of past parenting, the judge awarded custody to the father, who was an air force captain, because he would be able to spend evenings with the children and because he was better able to support them. The case was affirmed by the appellate court, although the mother specifically argued that she had lost because of the consequences of staying home with the children during the marriage and thereby foregoing career opportunities.

36. In *In re Marriage of Little*, 26 Wash. App. 814, 614 P.2d 240 (1980), a Washington State trial court judge believed at the time of divorce that it would be detrimental to the children to give custody to the mother because she was planning to move to the District of Columbia, remarry, and enter an educational program. The judge specifically identified his concern as the fact that the mother was in transition. He gave temporary custody to the father and, nine months later, when he no longer thought the mother to be in transition, he awarded custody to her of the two younger children. The appellate court reversed, awarding custody to the father, claiming that the children were integrated in his home. Therefore, the trial judge's misplaced focus on the mother's transition, rather than on primary parenting during the marriage, cost the mother custody of her children.

37. See, for example, Silver, *Weekend Fathers*, p. 26; and George Gilder, *Sexual Suicide* (New York: Qundrangle, 1973), pp. 106–7, 114–115. There is no data to support the contention that custody to fathers produces healthier children. There is also no data on the effects on children of mandatory joint custody. It should also be noted that the parent without custody has visitation rights and does not disappear, except by choice, from the life of the children. These visitation rights are minimally every other weekend and a portion of school and summer holidays, and are often more. Thus it is inappropriate for judges to assume both that the absence of a father is unhealthy and that such absence will necessarily occur if the mother has custody. It is also inappropriate to draw any conclusions from children whose fathers virtually abandon them about children whose fathers will have continued contact through visitation. Although "fathers' rights" advocates pretend that men are routinely frustrated by the ex-wives in their attempts to exercise visitation (see Silver, *Weekend Father*, pp. 55–59), this is another distortion. The current trend is to emphasize the importance of the child's relationship to the noncustodial parent and to require the custodial parent to encourage such a relationship under the threat of losing custody. Adele Hendrickson and Joanne Schulman, "Trends in Child Custody Law: What It Means for Women" (paper presented at the National Family Law Seminar, 13–15 September 1981, available from the National Center on Women and Family Law, 799 Broadway, New York, 10003). As Hendrickson and Schulman point out, courts do not value the child's need for a male influence enough to *require* a father to visit his children. See *Louden* v. *Olpin*, 118 Cal. App. 3d 565, 173 Cal. Rptr. 447 (1981). Visitation is the right of the father, not the child. If

public policy were truly concerned with a continued male presence, it would penalize fathers who failed to exercise visitation rights.

38. See, for example, Michigan Compiled Laws Annotated 722.23 (c), which requires the court to consider, as one of the factors in evaluating potential custodians, "the capacity and disposition of the parties involved to provide the child with food, clothing, medical care, and other material needs."

39. *Dempsey* v. *Dempsey*, 95 Mich. App. 285, 292 N.W.2d 549 (1980), *aff'd in part and rev'd in part*, 409 Mich. 495, 296 N.W.2d 813 (1980). In the *Porter* case, discussed earlier (note 36), the father's ability to support was also given as an explicit reason for granting him custody, although the mother's lesser ability to provide financial support was obviously a result of her years of providing primary parenting in the home.

40. Information gathered informally at the National Family Law Seminar, co-sponsored by the Legal Services Corporation Research Institute and the National Center on Women and Family Law, September 1981. Most divorced mothers on welfare receiving little or no child support have former husbands earning comfortable salaries. Marian P. Winston and Trude Fosher, "Nonsupport of Legitimate Children as a Cause of Poverty and Welfare Dependence" (Rand Corporation Study, 1974). The average amount of child-support payments in 1974 for a national sample of families headed by women and containing children younger than 18 was "far less than half of the poverty level that year for those families, even though 93 percent of the absent fathers has incomes that were twice (or greater than twice) the poverty level for their current families." Judith Cassetty, *Child Support and Public Policy: Securing Support from Absent Fathers* (Lexington, Mass.: Lexington Books, 1978), p. 103.

41. See, for example, *Neis* v. *Neis* 599 P.2d 305 (Kan. App. 1979); *Gulyas* v. *Gulyas*, 75 Mich. App. 138, 254, N.W.2d 818 (1977); *Avella* v. *Avella* 74 App. Div. 2d 592, 424 N.Y.S.2d 526 (1980) (trial court decision).

42. In the 25–44 age range, the remarriage rate of divorced men is almost double that of divorced women. See U.S. Department of Health and Human Services, National Center for Health Statistics, *Vital Statistics Reports, Final Marriage Statistics* 6, 12 September 1980.

43. *Simmons* v. *Simmons*, 223 Kan. 639, 576 P.2d 589 (1978).

44. *Gulyas* v. *Gulyas*, 75 Mich. App. 138, 254 N.W.2d 818 (1977).

45. In *Handy* v. *Handy*, 44 Ore. App. 225, 605 P.2d 738 (1980), the trial court judge awarded custody of two children to their father based on his plan to remarry and the judge's high opinion of the father's future wife. The appellate court, which in an earlier case had mandated consideration of primary parenting, reversed the trial court on the basis that the mother had had temporary custody and performed the primary parenting role.

46. *Blonsky* v. *Blonsky*, 84 Ill. App. 3d 810, 405 N.E.2d 112 (1980).

47. See, generally, Nan D. Hunter and Nancy D. Polikoff, "Custody Rights of Lesbian Mothers: Legal Theory and Litigation Strategy," *Buffalo Law Review* 25 (1976): 691.

48. 96 Mich. App. 285, 292 N.W.2d 549 (1980).

49. Silver, *Weekend Father*.

50. For example, California Civil Code 4600.5 (c) permits the court to award joint legal custody without awarding joint physical custody.

51. Hendrickson and Schulman, "Trends in Child Custody," p. 20, citing a *New York Times* article that 95 percent of the joint custody awards made by a Los Angeles Superior Court judge specified joint legal and not joint physical custody. G. Dullea, "Weighing the Importance of a Joint Custody Law," *New York Times*, 27 April 1981, p. C-19.

52. Hendrickson and Schulman, "Trends in Child Custody."

53. "Second Thoughts on Joint Child Custody: Analysis of Legislation and Its Implications for Women and Children," National Center on Women and Family Law (publication in process).

54. 440 U.S. 268 (1979).

55. Alimony is awarded in only approximately 14 percent to 17 percent of all divorces. When awarded, the amounts result in divorced husbands at every income level having about twice as much disposable income as their former wives. For a thorough analysis, see Wietzman and Dixon, "Alimony Myth."

56. It is telling to note that the sexual equality issue in *Orr* was raised not by a man who thought he was entitled to receive alimony but by a man who wanted to avoid paying it.

57. Charles V. Metz, *Divorce and Custody for Men* (Garden City, N.Y.: Doubleday, 1968), pp. 103–4.

58. Ibid., p. 103.

59. Edward J. Winter, Jr. *Fathers Winning Custody Cases* (Miami: River Trails Publishing, 1975), p. 68.

60. Daniel Amneus *Back to Patriarchy* (Arlington House, 1979).

61. The more moderate "fathers' rights" literature includes Ira Victor and Win Ann Winkler, *Fathers and Custody* (New York: Hawthorn 1977); and Stuart Kahan, *For Divorced Fathers Only* (New York: Monarch, 1978).

62. P. Ban and M. Lewis, "Mothers and Fathers, Girls and Boys: Attachment Behavior in the One Year Old" (paper presented at the Eastern Psychological Association, New York, April 1971), reported in Rena K. Uviller, "Father's Rights and Feminism: The Maternal Presumption Revisited," *Harvard Women's Law Journal* 1 (1978): 107, 121.

63. *Garska* v. *McCoy*, 278 S.E.2d 357, 360, 361, 362 (W. Va. 1981).

64. Victor and Winkler, *Fathers and Custody*, p. 151.

65. This was specifically recognized by the West Virginia Supreme Court in *Garska* v. *McCoy*, 278 S.E.2d 357, 362, (W. Va. 1981).

66. Some fathers' rights advocates acknowledge this and suggest that such maternal behavior is appropriate and that women who do make such decisions should be given proper credit by society. Victor and Winkler, *Fathers and Custody*, p. 63.

67. Two such challenges are Uviller, "Fathers' Rights"; and Lucy Katz, "The Maternal Preference and the Psychological Parent: Suggestions for Allocating the Burden of Proof in Custody Litigation," *Connecticut Bar Journal* 53 (1979): 343.

68. Ibid., p. 347.

69. *Garska* v. *McCoy*, 278 S.E.2d 357, 361 (W. Va. 1981).

70. Katz "Maternal Preference."

71. *Garska* v. *McCoy* recognized this principle by applying its primary caretaker presumption only to children of tender years. A fourteen-year-old was considered conclusively entitled to choose his or her custodian, and for children under fourteen the court held: "Where a child is old enough to formulate an opinion about his or her own custody the trial court is entitled to receive such opinion and accord it such weight as he feels appropriate. When, in the opinion of the trial court, a child old enough to formulate an opinion but under the age of 14 has indicated a justified desire to live with the parent who is not the primary caretaker, the court may award the child to such parent" (278 S.E.2d 357, 363 [W. Va. 1981]).

11

Nan D. Hunter

Women and Child Support

From 1970 to 1980 the number of divorces in the United States doubled, and the number of children living with one parent increased by 50 percent to a total of 12.2 million children, or one child in five.[1] The great majority of those children have a living noncustodial parent from whom they are entitled to receive support payments. Thus, approximately 20 percent of the nation's children are involved, at least potentially, in the child-support system. Despite the widening impact of the system, it remains in many ways primitive; it is characterized by inadequate awards, irrational disparities in standards, and patterns of enforcement that range from weak to nonexistent.

Scholars and policymakers who have examined the child-support system agree that its overall effectiveness is virtually nil. Although the criticism is widespread the recognition that the policy issues involved are different for women than for men is minimal. The effect of such a grossly flawed child-support system is more than a lowered standard of living for millions of children, for it also forces women to bear the costs of raising children. In 1978 there were 7.1 million single mothers with custody of their children in the United States.[2] Of all children who live with only one parent, more than 90 percent live with the mother.[3] Mothers with custody pay far more than half of the costs of childrearing, both because the support amounts ordered from the fathers are low to begin with and because payments are usually irregular, if made at all.[4] Perhaps the most dramatic single statistic is that 41 percent of all custodial mothers are not awarded any child support.[5]

At the turn of the century, whether a divorced father had any legal duty to provide support for his children was debated in the courts. The traditional rule was that the father had the right to the child's labor and services and the reciprocal duty to support the child during the marriage; some jurists believed that he should be relieved of both if the mother gained custody upon divorce.[6] By the 1920's, courts had ceased to treat the child as an item of property, and the father's obligation to continue providing support after divorce was established as a matter a law.[7] In practice, however, then as now, much of the support was not paid.[8] A 1948 survey of families in Detroit found that the divorced wife "receives relatively little property from the split of joint possession, is given very little child support, and in two-fifths of the cases does not receive this support regularly."[9]

By continuing policies that purport to establish and enforce child support but succeed only in hiding the reality of paternal nonsupport, the courts function in an unarticulated but systematic way to force the costs of divorce upon women. Though child-support law is neutral on its face, its economic effects, which are profound, are directly tied to gender.

POLITICAL AND POLICY ISSUES FOR WOMEN

Underlying all family law principles in the American legal system is the concept of the privatized, closed family system, the belief that intrafamily duties such as support should be left to the private parties for resolution, however they see fit, unless the family unit breaks down. In this model, courts are and should be used only as a last resort. This noninterference principle has always been selectively applied, as illustrated by laws that do not permit husbands to be prosecuted for the forcible rape of their wives but do criminalize certain consensual sexual acts between spouses. Even if it were uniformly applied, however, the privatized model of family law is not neutral. The "hands off" principle functions to increase the control of the more powerful party in an institution such as marriage in which one party has the benefit of various forms of social control over the other. For example, the rule that neither spouse has an enforceable right to a definite amount of support from the other during the ongoing marriage[10] may be neutral on its face, but, given the likelihood of who will have uninterrupted, full-time employment and the higher earned income, it has a very different impact on women than on men. It is only when the marriage ends that spousal support, if any is ordered, is set at a specific amount and is enforceable by legal action. The same approach is true for child support. The care and support of children is treated as an entirely private concern, exclusively within the realm of the nuclear family unless the situation degenerates into one of neglect. Only when one parent leaves or never joins the household unit can an amount of support, and thus a standard of care, be determined for a given child. Even then, the standard set is a private one.

Although child support is established through the public mechanism of the court, the amount is determined on a family-by-family basis as each situation is interpreted by the judge hearing the case. There is no benchmark figure for what is an adequate amount to raise a child, and typically there are no standardized tables of suggested amounts for parents in various income categories. Once the amount is set, the legal system does virtually nothing to see that it is collected, other than to provide a forum in which the payee parent can seek a remedy if she can afford the costs of the lawsuit necessary to enforce the support amount. This approach is justified by the desire to keep the law out of personal affairs, and again, it operates to the detriment of women as a group. Women are the custodians of children in the great majority of divorced families, and it is women who are made to cushion the impact of divorce on society by paying the costs of divided households.

There is one partial exception to the rule of privatization. The aid to Families with Dependent Children (AFDC) is the social backup system for single parents who are unable to provide even subsistence-level support for their children. Almost all the recipients are women—mothers who are divorced, separated, or were never married to the fathers of their children. AFDC sets a benefit level in the public sector that, despite having become the primary source of support for several generations of poor children, is still so low that the incentives for privatized responsibility are not seriously threatened.

Because, on the whole, the social costs of divorce are kept private and are routinely imposed on women, the dependence of women on men is reinforced. This process operates in tandem with the generally lower economic status of women. Single women raise children on earnings that average 59 percent of male earnings,[11] a gap that reflects a highly sex-segregated labor market. Among the effects of this income differential is the pressure it creates for women to marry and remain married in order to raise their standard of living.[12] Once a married couple has children, the pressures caused by the income difference increase, all the more so if the woman ceases to work full-time. The threat of divorce is far more dangerous financially to her than to the father because she may be forced to assume the sole support of herself and her children. Even when child support is received, it will almost certainly not be in an amount proportionate to the incomes of the two parents.

Women perceive the existence of this threat. One recent study found that of Michigan women with children about to receive a divorce, 29 percent of the women who were either unemployed or on welfare indicated that they wanted to reconsider or to attempt reconciliation, compared with only 8 percent of the full-time working women.[13] The possession of a full-time job, even with a women's wage, may well be the threshold point at which many married women can carry through with a divorce. Research has demonstrated a negative relationship between a wife's income and the stability of the marriage, for on the average, each thousand-dollar increase in a wife's earnings produces a 1 percent increase in the rate of separation.[14] This linkage appears to be less significant for black women than for white women, probably because black women historically have been forced by economic need into higher rates of labor force participation at lower wages than white women. Thus their earnings are less likely to produce either the perception or the reality of greater independence.[15]

The impact of women's economic dependency as a form of social control does not terminate with the decision to end a marriage. For the divorced woman with children, there is a strong economic incentive to remarry. Remarriage is the surest method for the custodial mother to increase her standard of living. A survey of women from one county in Michigan in the mid-1970s and a survey of Detroit women in the 1940s both found that remarriage had a significant impact on income. The Detroit study found that the average weekly dollar amount available to the woman for expenses almost doubled if she remarried. The contemporary study found that the percentage of employed-mother-with-children units living at the level of an intermediate budget or higher (assuming full compliance by the father with the child-support award) increased from 62 percent to 80 percent upon remarriage, and the proportion at below the lower budget level dropped from 15 percent to 4 percent.[16] Thus policies that minimize the child support to be provided by the divorced father strengthen the bonds that tie women to men and marriage as an institution.

No doubt a major reason for the snail's pace of reform in the child-support system is that, just as it penalizes women, it directly benefits men. Custodial mothers experience a sharp drop in their living standard and their disposable incomes after divorce, but divorced fathers realize a financial gain.[17] A father ordered to pay one-third of his income for child support, for example, has 67 percent of his net earnings left for discretionary expenses and is financially better off than when he was married.[18] An examination of child-support orders in Cleveland from 1965 to 1978 found that divorced fathers actually retained about 80 percent of their predivorce income, and the higher the man's earnings, the greater the proportion of income he retained.[19] In fact, the proportion of the average father's income ordered for child support declined between 1965 and 1978, again especially so for more affluent men.[20] Data from the University of Michigan's nationwide sample indicated that 86 percent of divorced fathers were economically better off than their former wives and children, and more than 64 percent had income-poverty ratios[21] that were two or more times greater than those of their former wives and children.[22] In the Cleveland study, divorced fathers alone were found to have from 10 to 20 percent more after-transfer income than the mother-children unit; and if the two parents were compared with each other, fathers had three times as much after-transfer income.[23] Thus men, as a group, are the winners in almost any child-support award.

The economic penalty for women of the present child-support system is severe. Some right-wing "pro-family" forces, however, believe that it is not severe enough. Their goals, exemplified by the writings of George Gilder[24] and the tax provisions of the proposed Family Protection Act,[25] are built on attempts to supplement the "family [male] wage" and provide tax incentives for the maintenance of a nonworking spouse. Gilder advocates deliberately lower salaries for women together with the payment of a family allowance, similar to that in several European countries, to "intact" two-parent families irrespective of income. Gilder's method is designed to keep mothers in the home and to foster the economic viability of one-wage-earner families. Gilder's support of a policy often thought to be a progressive income redistribution mechanism is a signal, once again, that family policy considerations for women and men differ greatly. One major issue for women is the elimination of a system that hides the social costs of child care in the private sector by imposing them on women. Equally important, any policy that attempts to allocate these costs on a society-wide basis must do so in a way which does not undermine the independence of women from men.

Having identified some of the more theoretical issues involved for women, we next discuss how and why the present child-support system functions as it does and what options exist for the future. Because they are administered autonomously, the private family system and the AFDC system are described separately. Both, however, are characterized by a pervasive disregard for the rights and economic security of custodial mothers.

THE PRIVATE FAMILY SYSTEM

It is hard to overstate the extent of the postdivorce child-support crisis in the United States. Judith Cassetty reported that the average amount of child-support payments in 1974 for a national sample of families headed by women and containing children younger than 18 was "far less than half of the poverty level that year for those families, even though 93 per cent of the absent fathers had incomes that were twice (or greater than twice) the poverty level for their current families."[26] Lenore Weitzman and Ruth Dixon found that the amount of child support awarded in Los Angeles in 1972 was only half the amount needed to raise children in low-income families at 1960–61 prices and that it amounted to no more than 25 percent of the father's net income.[27] A study of child-support practice in Denver found that two-thirds of the fathers were ordered to pay less for child support than they reported spending on monthly car payments.[28]

How the amount of support should be determined is a question that domestic relations courts have wrestled with for years. The statutes that govern child support tend to provide for the award of an amount that is "reasonable and just" or is based on a list of vague criteria such as the financial resources of each parent, the needs of the child, and the child's previous standard of living.[29] A few courts have adopted uniform tables of suggested amounts or formulas for setting amounts, but most women going through a divorce do not know how much child support to expect until they hear the judge's order.[30] The case-by-case method leads to enormous disparities in the amounts ordered for families in similar financial situations.

The adoption of tables, however, does not necessarily yield equitable results. For example, one can hypothesize a middle-class family in which the father earns an annual gross salary of $29,000 and a monthly net of $1400; the mother earns an annual gross of $13,000 and a monthly net of $815. They have two children, ages five and ten; the mother has custody of both. The chart that follow displays the results of applying seven methods of setting child support to the same set of facts. The highest amount in the chart is 65 percent more than the smallest.

Source of Method Used to Calculate Amount	*Monthly Support Amount*
Delaware state guidelines[31]	$399.10
Oregon formula[32]	585.83
Pennsylvania guidelines[33]	466.00
Los Angeles guidelines[34]	575.00
American Bar Association Family Law Section[35]	408.60
Eden system[36]	602.95
Franks system[37]	364.53

The methods that lead to the most divergent results deserve special note. Maurice Franks, whose calculations yield the lowest support amount, is also the author of *How to Avoid Alimony.*[38] Franks' method begins with a computation of child support divided proportionately between the parents according to income. He then subtracts from that an amount calculated to represent what the noncustodial parent spends on the child during visitation, based on the number of days per year he sees the child. The subtraction is made regardless of the mother's income. Most courts have rejected attempts by fathers to cut their support obligations by claiming a credit for any money spent on the child during visitation. Yet in 1981, the Oregon Supreme Court, although it did not accept Franks' visitation credits, did favorably cite his article as a critique of current methods of determining support.[39] With the trend to joint and shared custody one can expect more men to press for reduced support payments on the ground that they spend more money directly for the child. On the other hand, custodial mothers may see support amounts, which are already low, shrink even further while their household expenses decrease very little.

The method in the chart that led to the highest support amount is that of Phillip Eden, a forensic economist who bases his figures on government data on the average cost of raising a child. The final support amount is based on a formula that reduces by the same percentage the amount each new household would need to maintain the family's prior standard of living. In other words, the method is set up to produce an equally shared burden between the two households, on the assumption that neither can afford its previous life style.

Eden's system is one of only a few proposals that seek explicitly to equalize the burden of dividing one household into two so that each adult and child suffers roughly the same level of downward readjustment.[40] One of the major debates now raging among economists and social workers active in the issue of child support is whether the central principle used to set amounts should be based on cost sharing or income sharing. Critics of income sharing argue that those formulas provide an incentive for custodial mothers to avoid paid employment and amount to an extension of financial commitments based on marriage past the point of divorce. Income-sharing advocates respond by pointing out that there is no universal standard for the "cost" of a child. Cost cannot be determined except by reference to the economic status of the parents, which is likely to be different, at least insofar as it is based on earnings, for the mother than for the father. There is also the question whether a cost figure should be based on the expenses actually incurred for the child or on the amount that would have been spent if the marriage had not dissolved.[41] The income-sharing model is a method of equalizing the relative well-being of each household.

Many court systems now use the simplest of cost-sharing approaches, which is to ask the custodial parent to complete a financial statement itemizing all the children's expenses. Based on that and on the net earnings of each spouse, the court apportions costs between the parents more or less relative to their incomes. Such a method meets the reasonableness standard under which most courts operate. But it is quite possible for a child support award to be "reasonable," an amount that the father can afford and the mother and children can get by on, and also inequitable as a skewed reallocation of limited resources. A division of costs almost always results in the mother-children household unit living on a lower posttransfer income than the single-father household. Most child-support awards produce a minimal amount to defray expenses for the mother and children and a relative increase in disposable income for the father.

Much of the literature on child support has focused on the issue of how the absence of uniform tables or formulas leads to gross disparities in the awards.[42] A study of actual awards in the Denver court, for example, found that a father with a net monthly income of $450 was ordered to pay $120 for the support of two children; another father with two children earned $900 net and was ordered to pay $50 a month; and a father who made $1342 net was ordered to pay $100 a month for one child's support.[43] In Denver the court had tables as guidelines, but the judges ignored them.

The removal of such disparities is important, but the trend to uniformity of amounts is an example of procedural fairness that is not necessarily related to substantive fairness. The implementation of universal formulas will not ensure an equitable result unless they are designed to produce amounts that equalize the financial burden between mothers and fathers. Within the private family model, the central issue for women is the dollars-and-cents size of the award and the principle on which it is based. Unless the goal of equalization is accepted, however, the adoption of standardized tables will result in predictability but will also freeze women in their role of absorbing a disproportionate share of the costs of child care.

When one turns from the issue of amounts to that of enforcement, the second aspect of the child-support crisis becomes apparent. The Census Bureau found that of all women who had court orders entitling them to receive child support in 1978, only 49 percent received the full amount. On the average, thirty-five cents out of every dollar owed for child support was never paid.[44] An examination of the standard procedures for payment reveals why noncompliance is so widespread.

When the typical father is ordered to pay child support, he is usually told to send the mother a check every pay period. Keeping track of the payments or lack of them is up to her. Most courts have a system for keeping the record on computer, but judges frequently do not order that this be done, especially for middle- and upper-middle-class fathers, for whom it is considered embarrassing.[45] Even when the bookkeeping is maintained on a computer, if the father does not pay, often nothing happens. It is up to the mother to institute enforcement proceedings. Many months will pass before the amount owed to her equals or exceeds the retainer she will have to pay a lawyer to bring suit. By the time it becomes worth it to sue, her financial plans and budgeting may be in turmoil. If the amount due builds up and the case does get to court, judges in some states are permitted to decrease the amount of arrearage retroactively if they believe it is too large for the father to afford (the children, after all, have managed to survive).[46] The system, then, provides virtually every incentive for fathers not to pay.

The literature on child support is replete with ideas for improving enforcement mechanisms. Many courts have acquired automated recordkeeping systems, and some have developed automatic notice procedures so that a father is at least contacted and perhaps summoned when a payment becomes delinquent. A number of states have substituted administrative procedures for full-scale court hearings in their processes for both establishing and enforcing support.[47] The effectiveness of using imprisonment for nonsupport as a deterrent has also been studied.[48] The greatest attention has been paid to developing procedures for garnishments and automatic wage withholding systems that would have the employer deduct support payments from fathers' wages like a tax deduction and then send the support amount to the court. One proposal suggests that a federal income withholding system be instituted that would allow support orders to follow the parent from job to job until the obligation is ended.[49] Another author has suggested a "federal floating wage assignment," which would in essence be a nationwide garnishment system so that there would be a uniformly national remedy for violation of a support order.[50]

Any proposal that succeeded in increasing child-support enforcement would benefit most women enormously. All of these ideas are refinements of judicial procedures, however, and none goes beyond the legal system in the search for a better model. Each is geared to the improvement of the private family support system rather than the development of a single society-wide child-care policy. Proposals for equalizing the costs of raising children between women and men in each given family, do not address the issue of parents who lack enough resources to divide.

THE AFDC SYSTEM

The program of Aid to Families with Dependent Children is the second component of the American child-support system. Begun during the 1930s as a way to provide for widows, AFDC became the only alternative to the purely private family support system. Since that time, the number of recipients has mushroomed, increasing by 225 percent during the 1960s and peaking in 1976.[51] AFDC now operates as a major subsystem of support. However narrow were the original goals of the program, its current function is the maintenance of some 10.5 million children and their mothers. [52] The role of AFDC and the issue of a government-funded backup system has thus become an inextricable part of any discussion of child-support reform.

Indeed, it was a reaction to the increasing costs of AFDC and the desire to cut back expenses, not social alarm over the plight of mothers raising children with insufficient support amounts, that led to most of the current attention on child-support enforcement. The drive to decrease welfare expenses by collecting support from the absent parent was the basis of Governor Ronald Reagan's welfare reform legislation in California in the early 1970s.[53] A 1974 study by the Rand Corporation on nonsupport by affluent fathers as a cause of welfare dependency was a starting point for much of the later research on the issue of child support.[54] The relationship between paternal nonsupport and the poverty of many unmarried mothers and their children has been well established.[55]

Congress responded by amending the AFDC entitlement provisions to require cooperation with the state in establishing paternity and obtaining support payments from the fathers as a condition of eligibility.[56] Concern over the dangers to women from filing suits against physically abusive fathers resulted in a compromise "good cause" exception that waives the requirement to cooperate when the recipient can prove that there is a reasonable likelihood of physical or emotional harm to her or the child. To qualify, emotional harm must be serious, demonstrable, and of such impact that the individual's functioning will be substantially impaired.[57] The "good cause" exception is rarely invoked.[58] The great majority of women who receive AFDC are given no choice but to name the fathers and "cooperate" in locating and suing them. The loss of privacy is made the price of the benefits they receive. If they lie about the father's identity or whereabouts, they run the risk of prosecution for fraud.

From the viewpoint of the best interests of the child, it has been suggested that some AFDC mothers may be the worst group to coerce into pursuing child support because of the possible resultant loss of a kinship and secondary support system that exists in many low-income communities. Studies have found that poor black families rely on tight kinship bonds and unstructured mutual aid systems to cope with the conditions of poverty. Some poor children receive material, psychological, and social support from their father or, most likely, from their father's kinship network, despite his absence from the home. If the father refuses to acknowledge the child for fear of incurring legal obligations, the child may lose a form of support that is arguably more significant than the amount of public funds saved by decreasing the welfare budget.[59] In any case, the decision to seek monetary support should be made by the mother.

Thus, in contrast to the women not on AFDC, who often are precluded from enforcing orders for child support by the difficulty and expense involved in initiating collection suits, women who receive AFDC are forced into prosecutions over which they have no choice or control.

After women establish AFDC eligibility, a variety of incentives built into the law function to lock them into the system.[60] Because of the requirement that the family grant be reduced dollar for dollar based on the private support award and totally eliminated once the private support award equals the family's need level, it is often to the advantage of both recipients and program administrators to collect only enough child support from absent fathers to reduce, rather than eliminate, the family's AFDC payment. The final dollar that leads to termination of AFDC also results in ineligibility for other programs, most significantly Medicaid, which require AFDC enrollment to qualify for benefits. Thus the recipient who succeeds in completely going off AFDC suffers a financial loss of in-kind benefits. In addition, the unreliability of private child support merely results in the revolving-door phenomenon of recipients being terminated and then later having to reapply, leading to financial chaos for the families and higher administrative costs for the program.

Finally, the agency has a better statistical record if it can show each month all the dollars being saved by decreased grants than if the grants are entirely eliminated and the agency reports only total dollars spent. For all these reasons, the incentives are to remain on AFDC once a family is enrolled.

OPTIONS FOR THE FUTURE

Probably the most achieveable option in the United States would be reform of the private family system by increasing the amount of support ordered and adopting effective enforcement procedures. Whether to choose income sharing, cost sharing, or some other model as the basis for determining amount would be an initial question for law-makers. If equalization of the support burden between the two parents were adopted as the new policy, the economic penalties of divorce imposed on women with children by the present system would be eliminated. In turn there would be major consequences for men, who would then have an economic incentive to remain married or to fight more frequently and more vigorously for custody. Because changes in the standards for setting support amounts would have to be enacted on a state-by-state basis, comprehensive reform would be very difficult. Even if accomplished, it would still leave the AFDC system untouched and would do little to break down the underlying privatization of family law.

Another option would be to adopt a unitary child-support system to encompass both the private family system and what is now AFDC. One such mixed public-private model, which combines a credit income tax with a public child-support payment program, has been proposed by Irwin Garfinkel of the Institute for Research on Poverty at the University of Wisconsin.[61] Its child-support component would be financed by a tax imposed on the absent parent, in an amount determined by that parent's income and the number of children for whom support was owed. It would be collected by the same withholding method used for other taxes. For children whose fathers were poor, there would be a statutory minimum amount, which would be financed by general revenues but distributed in the same manner, probably by a social services agency, as the support amounts collected from individual fathers. If adopted at the federal level, this method would nationalize the privatized system by bringing child-support payments under central control. Combining the private system with AFDC would at least make invisible the "welfare" status of many indigent families. Such a change could remove the stigma without necessarily altering the stinginess of the minimum amount or the coercive methods used to ensure the "cooperation" of mothers in tracking down potential payor fathers.

Its impact on women would depend largely on whether the formula for setting the support amount accurately gauged the proportion of the father's income to be used for child care at the same level as the mother's. Because the noncustodial parent's income and the number of children would be the only variables considered in Garfinkel's plan, there would be no consideration given to the mother's earnings level, and thus it would be impossible to equalize the standard of living in the two households. The only advantage of this model for women lies in the absolute guarantee that support would be paid. This factor alone could be used as a tremendous incentive to gain the endorsement of women who now see support awards of any size as useless pieces of paper. Such a guarantee would make married mothers who desire divorce feel more confident in carrying out that decision, thus perhaps reducing at least a psychological component of economic dependency. Financial viability after marriage would become more reliable even if the actual dependency continued, buffered by the government as an intermediary. But the inequity of how the burden is divided would continue. Men, on the other hand, would face for the first time a disincentive against remarriage because their support amounts would not be reduced on the basis of obligations incurred by starting new families.

Yet another set of options is illustrated by the family allowance programs operating in various European countries. The Swedish and French governments pay a fixed allowance to all parents with children. In Sweden, the government also advances payments of private child support that are due. The family allowance was begun in each country as a pronatalist measure; the French payment originally was received only after the birth of a second child. In France, eligibility is conditioned on the family's income level, and only relatively low-income families benefit significantly. Single-parent families, however, receive a supplement of 50 percent of the basic allowance.[62] In Sweden, all families with children receive the allowance, regardless of income.[63] In both countries, the allowance is paid upon divorce to whichever parent has custody.

The amount of child support owed is determined in Sweden, as in the United States, in a judicial procedure. Once it is set, the state pays that sum each month to the mother and assumes responsibility for collecting from the father. The mother continues to be paid regardless of whether the state succeeds in obtaining reimbursement. Further, there is a minimum statutory child-support amount. When the amount owed by the father is set by a court or by private agreement at less than the statutory entitlement, the government makes up the difference from its general revenue funds.[64]

In both countries, there has been at least some awareness of the impact of these programs on the lives of women. A family allowance alone could easily function as a strong incentive to remain at home for the woman in an ongoing marriage, leading, upon divorce, to an abrupt need to enter the work force despite a lack of job skills and experience. The French have attempted to lessen this effect by developing the most extensive system of public child-care services in any western European country. More than 95 percent of children aged three to six, and 27 percent of the two-year-olds, are enrolled in free day-care facilities.[65] Thus the availability of out-of-home child-care militates against the tendency to use a family allowance as a substitute for income that could be earned by the wife.

In Sweden, although the public child-care system is less extensive, the conscious shaping of family policy to help achieve sex equality is more accepted. An example, often cited, is the parent insurance program that allows either or both parents to take a fully paid employment leave after the birth of a child, up to a certain maximum number of days. In the 1976 parliamentary elections, the issue of this childbirth leave payment split the socialist and nonsocialist parties. The latter grouping advocated various designs for such a program, which the socialist parties opposed on the grounds that the provisions would preserve the traditional breadwinner-homemaker families and slow the expansion of needed day nurseries. Although nonsocialists won the election, the flexible design developed later by the Social Democrats eventually was enacted.[66] Perhaps the single most significant factor in the social context in which Swedish family policy operates is that median female wages are 85 percent of median male wages. [67]

The Swedish and French systems reflect a substantially greater commitment to a deprivatization of child-care responsibility than is usually proposed by mainstream policy makers for the United States. In addition to the cash allowances, what is probably at least equally important to women is that both governments have undertaken to provide widespread public child-care services. For women who are divorced, the burdens of childrearing are shared with the state. Although the principle of equalizing the financial burden with the father does not appear to be accepted the state, rather than women, absorbs much of the impact of divorce.

A final possible choice would be the open acknowledgment that most noncustodial fathers do not pay adequate, if any, child support and a decision to eliminate or decrease the legal obligation for them to do so. The loss of emotional bonds and psychological parenthood that occurs as the divorced father and his children lead increasingly separate lives could be the rationale for such a course.[68] The feelings of a father for his children, and theirs for him, will inevitably undergo change if a stepfather becomes the daily, at-home father figure or the divorced parents find themselves living a great distance apart. Divorced men then would have an even greater freedom to remarry and begin new families than they do now. If mothers received a full range of financial benefits and child-care services from the state in exchange for this loss of paternal support, the economic impact on women would not be so devastating as it might first appear. Many men, of course, would not want to abdicate their father role, especially insofar as that would mean an acceptance of the loss of important emotional relationships. If support payments were expected from fathers who were more involved in parenting, however, there would be an economic penalty on fathering. Moreover, women themselves might oppose this policy choice because it runs directly counter to their long-standing goal of increasing both the involvement and the responsibility of fathers in the childrearing process. Although an elimination of the duty of support by the absent parent may sound like the most radical of the options we have analyzed, in many ways it is merely a reflection of how the child-support system actually operates now.

Ultimately, the extent to which fathers assume a greater role in child care in or outside marriage and demonstrate a stronger commitment to continued financial support of their children will not be determined by the child-support system. It will be produced by changes in the relationships between men and women and by improvements in the social condition of women that give them the power necessary to pressure men and institutions into new arrangements. In the meantime, child-support programs must not be premised on the assumption of an economic equality between men and women or an idealized degree of paternal involvement that does not now exist. Rather, child-support reform should be designed to guarantee sufficient economic resources for women with children so that they can achieve the level of autonomy that is a prerequisite for the social change to occur.

CONCLUSION

In contrast to most other industrialized nations, the United States is regarded as having no explicit "family policy." The absence of officially articulated goals or a specific statutory scheme, however, is not the same as a policy void. American family policy exists; it is one of completely privatized responsibility, alleviated only by a backup welfare program to prevent destitution, and it assumes not only that women will provide child care but that they will marry in order to do so properly. The rapid increase in the rate of divorce and consequently in the number of women who have been forced to take on greater financial responsibility for childrearing have placed this policy under strain. Political forces are competing to resolve the tension, either by establishing the husband-worker, wife-homemaker family as the only sanctioned form or by initiating programs to aid a wider range of options.

The current child-support system is a specific example of general family policy in the United States. Beneath the surface chaos of support amounts that are widely discrepant and enforcement practices that range from effective to nonexistent, there is a thread of consistency in the selective imposition of the economic and social costs on women rather than men. Although the American political and legal system publicly expresses a belief that individual parents should bear financial responsibility for their children, in reality this obligation operates only for the mother and is allowed to lapse as to the father. This practice, in turn, reflects the patriarchal and capitalist forms that permeate the society. The changes that women must advocate for the child-support system, therefore, go beyond the limited boundaries of the court system itself. The burden of child-support needs to be both equalized between the two parents and deprivatized by the addition of state-subsidized child-care facilities. For so long as divorced mothers continue to win or be left with custody of their children, the provision of public child-care services will be necessary to prevent further pressure on women to remain in the home. Women must fight for a new public policy on child-support that results not only in greater financial security for themselves and their children but also fosters their independence from male control.

NOTES

1. "U. S. Census Bureau Says Divorces and Unmarried Couples Increased in 70s," *New York Times*, 19 October 1981.

2. U. S. Department of Commerce, Bureau of the Census, *Child Support and Alimony: 1978*, Series P-23 (Washington, D.C.: Government Printing Office, September 1981).

3. See *New York Times*, note 1. Throughout this chapter, "mother" is used to denote the custodial parent and "father" to denote the absent parent. This choice of words is meant to reflect the current social reality underlying the statistics. No implication that these role divisions should continue is intended.

4. In 1978 the mean annual child-support amount for those women who actually received support was $1800, or $150 per month. Child support represented about 20 percent of their mean total income of $8944. The annual figure broke down by number of children to mean amounts per month of $100 for one child, $164 for two children, $210 for three children, and $230 for four or more children. These monetary computations exclude the 3 out of 10 women who, after having gotten an award of child support, were receiving nothing. *Child Support and Alimony: 1978*, pp. 1, 5. In a much smaller sample drawn from other nationwide data, Judith Cassetty found that the average annual child-support payment actually made in 1974 was $539. Judith Cassetty, *Child Support and Public Policy: Securing Support from Absent Fathers* (Lexington, Mass.: Lexington Books, 1978), p. 72. See also David L. Chambers, *Making Fathers Pay: The Enforcement of Child Support* (Chicago: University of Chicago Press, 1979), pp. 42–50.

5. *Child Support and Alimony: 1978*, p. 1.

6. *State v. Langford*, 90 Or. 251, 176 P. 197 (1918). In *Baldwin v. Foster*, 138 Mass. 449 (1885), Justice Oliver Wendell Holmes, then of the Supreme Judicial Court of Massachusetts, wrote that the duty of the father to support a child living apart from him and with the mother was dependent on whether the mother's separation from her husband was justified. A legal contemporaneous treatise concluded that fathers were liable only for the "bare maintenance" of children in their mother's custody. G. W. Fields, *The Legal Relations of Infants* (Rochester: Williamson & Higbie, 1888).

7. James Schouler, *A Treatise on the Law of Marriage, Divorce, Separation and Domestic Relations* 6th ed. (Albany: Matthew Bender, 1921); Carol Brown, "Mothers, Fathers and Children: From Private to Public Patriarchy," in *Women and Revolution*, ed. Lydia Sargent (Boston: South End Press, 1981).

8. Schouler, *Treatise on Marriage.*

9. William J. Goode, *After Divorce* (New York: Free Press, 1956), p. 222.

10. Barbara Babcock, Ann Freedman, Eleanor Holmes Norton and Susan Ross, *Sex Discrimination and the Law: Causes and Remedies* (Boston: Little, Brown, 1975), p. 623; *McGuire v. McGuire*, 157 Neb. 226, 59 N.W. 2d 336 (1953); Blanche Crozier, "Marital Support," *Boston University Law Review* 15 (1935): 28, 33.

11. U.S. Department of Labor, Bureau of Labor Statistics, *Perspectives on Working Women: A Databook*, Bulletin 2080 (Washington, D.C.: Government Printing Office, October 1980, Table 52, p. 52.

12. See Heidi I. Hartmann, "Capitalism, Patriarchy, and Job Segregation by Sex," *Signs: Journal of Women in Culture and Society* 1, no. 3, pt. 2 (Spring 1979).

13. Chambers, *Making Fathers Pay*, p. 52.

14. Heather L. Ross and Isabel V. Sawhill, *Time of Transition: The Growth of Families Headed by Women* (Washington, D.C.: Urban Institute, 1975), p. 57.

15. Frank L. Mott and Sylvia F. Moore, "The Causes and Consequences of Marital Breakdown," in Mott, ed., *Women, Work and Family* (Lexington, Mass.: Lexington Books, 1978).

16. Chambers, *Making Fathers Pay* pp. 56, 63–66; Goode, *After Divorce*, 230–31, 236.

17. In addition to the studies cited in the text, see Lenore J. Weitzman, "The Economics of Divorce: Social and Economic Consequences of Property, Alimony, and Child Support Awards," University of California Los Angeles Law Review 28 (1981); Karen Seal, "A Decade of No-Fault Divorce," *Family Advocate*, Spring 1979; and Sandra Stencel, *Single-Parent Families, Editorial Reports on the Women's Movement: Achievements and Effects* (Washington, D.C.: Congressional Quarterly, 1977).

18. Chambers, *Making Fathers Pay*, p. 48.

19. Gloria Sterin and Joseph M. Davis, *Divorce Awards and Outcomes: A Study of Pattern and Change in Cuyahoga County, Ohio* (Cleveland: Federation for Community Planning, 1981), p.158.

20. Ibid., pp. 94–97. In 1965 fathers were ordered to pay an average of 15 percent of their monthly gross income for child support. By 1978 that figure dropped to 11.6 percent. Lenore Wietzman found the same inverse relationship between the amount of the father's income and the proportion paid for child support in her study of California divorces. In Weitzman, "The Economics of Divorce."

21. The ratio of individual or family income to the poverty level developed by the Social Security Administration for the appropriate number of persons. For example, a four-person family with a 1974 income of $7000 per year would have an income-poverty ratio of 1.5 because the 1974 S.S.A. poverty level for that size family was $4680.

22. Cassetty, *Child Support*, pp. 70–71. Using a sample base of almost 2.3 million households, Cassetty found that absent fathers had income-poverty ratios twice as large as those of the mother-children unit in 1,476,000 families. By contrast, the same difference in favor of the mother-children unit was found in only 159,500 families, or approximately 7 percent of the total sample. Cassetty noted that separated families, which measured about the same in "well-offness," numbered approximately 195,000, or 8.5 percent of the sample.

23. Sterin and Davis, *Divorce Awards*, p. 160. This comparison included only those mothers who had full-time jobs.

24. George Gilder, *Sexual Suicide* (New York: Quadrangle 1973).

25. S.1358, 97th Cong., 1st sess. *Congressional Record* 127, no. 92 (17 June 1981).

26. Cassetty, *Child Support*, p. 103.

27. Lenore J. Weitzman and Ruth B. Dixon, "Child Custody Awards: Legal Standards and Empirical Patterns for Child Custody, Support and Visitation After Divorce," *University of California Davis Law Review* (1979): 473, 497.

28. The average father for whom data was available paid $136.97 per month for his car and $113.59 per month for his 1.6 children. Lucy Marsh Yee, "What Really Happens in Child Support Cases: An Empirical Study of the Establishment and Enforcement of Child Support Orders in the Denver District Court," *Law Journal Denver* 57 (1980): 21, 36.

29. Judith Areen, *Family Law: Cases and Materials* (Mineola, N.Y.: Foundation Press, 1978), pp. 630–36; Doris Jonas Freed and Henry H. Foster, "Divorce in the Fifty States: An Overview," *Family Law Quarterly* (Winter 1981): 229, 258; Kenneth R. White and R. Thomas Stone, "A Study of Alimony and Support Rulings with Some Recommendations," *Family Law Quarterly* (1976): 75, 83.

30. We refer to court cases, rather than to the also common situation of an amount being negotiated between the parties and included in a settlement agreement, because negoti-

ated amounts are no more predictable than adjudicated amounts; they often depend in large part on how much each party's attorney believes would be awarded if the dispute were settled by a judge.

31. "Delaware Child Support Formula (Melson Formula)," Family Court of the State of Delaware, June 1980.

32. *Smith* v. *Smith*, 626 p. 2d 342 (Ore. 1981). Decision of the Oregon Supreme Court to adopt a formula.

33. "Scale of Suggested Minimum Contributions For Support by Absent Parents," Interim Statement of Pennsylvania Child Support Enforcement Program, *Family Law Reporter 3* (10 May 1977): 3101. Table of specific amounts.

34. Los Angeles County Superior Court, Family Law Department, "Guidelines for Initial Order to Show Cause," 1 July 1977. Table of specific amounts.

35. "Family Law Section's Recommendations," *Family Advocate*, Spring 1979. Formula.

36. Philip Eden, "Forensic Economics—Use of Economists in Cases of Dissolution of Marriage," *American Jurisprudence* 17, *Proof of Facts* 2d 345 (1978); Philip Eden, *Estimating Child and Spousal Support* (Berkeley: Techpress International, 1977). Formula.

37. Maurice R. Franks, "How to Calculate Child Support," *Case and Comment*, January–February 1981, Formula. To arrive at the amount in the table, we assumed that the father had visitation for 87 days per year: roughly 30 days in the summer plus alternate weekends and holidays.

38. New York: Signet Books, 1975.

39. *Smith* v. *Smith.*

40. The first methods proposed for allocating the costs of childrearing between divorced parents on an equalization principle were in Isabel V. Sawhill, "Developing Normative Standards for Child Support and Alimony Payments" (Urban Institute Washington, D.C. Paper, February 1977), which is described in Areen, *Family Law* pp. 653–54; and Cassetty, *Child Support*. Eden's system is used in the chart because its calculations are more easily applied to the hypothetical data.

41. The policy arguments about income-sharing versus cost-sharing are explored in Judith Cassetty, ed., *The Parental Child Support Obligation: Research, Practice and Policy* (Lexington, Mass: Lexington Books, 1982).

42. In addition to the Denver study discussed in the text, see White and Stone, "Alimony and Support Rulings." A related issue, which explains why disparities are accommodated so easily by the courts, is the absolute class basis of child support. Judges are used to setting a support award for one ten-year-old at $200 per month and another at $1000 per month. That a janitor's child will have "needs" that are assessed as a fraction of those of a lawyer's child is just one of the givens in the system. Compared to disparities such as those, the difference between ordering one father to pay $200 more per month than another father with the same income and number of children does not seem so strange or urgent.

43. Lucy Marsh Yee, "Child Support Cases."

44. *Child Support and Alimony: 1978*, pp. 1, See also Sterin and Davis, *Divorce Awards* p. 188.

45. Arkansas, for example, did not adopt a procedure for making payments through the clerk of court until 1981. *Family Law Reporter 7* (9 June, 1981): 2509. The resistance of judges to ordering payment through a court registry was acknowledged in Note, "Enforcement of Maintenance and Support Under the Missouri Dissolution Act," U.M.K.C. Law. Review 44 (Spring 1976): 416, 432.

46. See Annotation by John J. Michalik, "Divorce: Power of Court to Modify Decree for Support of Child Which Was Based on Agreement of Parties," (1975): 61 657.

47. U.S. Department of Health and Human Services, Office of Child Support Enforcement, "Comparative Analysis of Court Systems Procedures and Administrative Procedures to Establish and Enforce Child Support Obligations" (Paper, December 1980).

48. Chambers, *Making Fathers Pay*; Chambers, "Men Who Know They Are Watched: Some Benefits and Costs of Jailing for Nonpayment of Support," *Michigan Law Review* 75.

49. Chambers, *Making Fathers Pay.*

50. David Clayton Carrad, "A Modest Proposal to End Our National Disgrace," *Family Advocate*, Fall 1979.

51. Frances Fox Piven and Richard A. Cloward, *Regulating the Poor: The Functions of Public Welfare* (New York: Vintage Books, 1971), pp. 341, 350; Gilbert Y. Steiner, *The Futility of Family Policy* (Washington D.C.: Brookings Institution, 1981), p. 113.

52. Steiner, *Futility of Family Policy*, p. 113.

53. Ronald A. Zumbrun and Richard N. Parslow. "Absent Parent Child Support: The California Experience," *Family Law Quarterly 8* (1974): 329.

54. Marian P. Winston and Trude Forsher, *Nonsupport of Legitimate Children by Affluent Fathers as a Cause of Poverty and Welfare Dependence* (Santa Monica: Rand Corporation, 1974).

55. Cassetty, *Child Support.*

56. 42 U.S. Code Section 602(a) (26) (B).

57. *Federal Register* 43 (3 October. 1978) 45742.

58. The 1980 Annual Report of the Office of Child Support Enforcement of the U.S. Department of Health and Human Services reported 31,522 refusals to cooperate, in which good cause was found in 2830 cases. *Annual Reports* 5, Table 27.

59. Carol B. Stack, *All Our Kin: Strategies for Survival in a Black Community* (New York: Harper & Row, 1974); Carol B. Stack, "Extended Familial Networks: An Emerging Model for the 21st Century Family," in *The Family in Post-Industrial America*, ed. David P. Snyder (Boulder, Colo.: Westview Press, 1979); Colin C. Blaydon and Carol B. Stack, "Income Support Policies and the Family," *Daedalus*, Spring 1977.

60. The analysis in the text is a summarization of Judith Cassetty, "Program Conflicts and Human Considerations," *Public Welfare Journal* 37, no. 4 (Fall 1979).

61. Irwin Garfinkel, *Child Support: Weaknesses of the Old and Features of Proposed New System* (Madison: Institute for Research on Poverty, University of Wisconsin, February, 1982).

62. Nicole Questiaux and Jacques Fournier, "France," in Kamerman and Alfred J. Kahn *Family Policy: Government and Families in Fourteen Countries*, ed. Sheila B. (New York: Columbia University Press, 1978).

63. Irwin Garfinkel and Annemette Sørensen, "The Swedish Child Support System: Lessons for the U.S.," *Social Work*, forthcoming.

64. Ibid.

65. Sheila B. Kamerman, "Work and Family in Industrialized Societies," *Signs: Journal of Women in Culture and Society* 4, no. 4 (Summer 1979).

66. Rita Liljeström, "Sweden," in Kamerman and Kaln, ed., *Family Policy.*

67. Kamerman, "Work and Family," p. 644.

68. Chambers, *Making Fathers Pay*, pp. 277–80.

12

Anne L. Harper

Teenage Sexuality and Public Policy: An Agenda for Gender Education

Public preoccupation with teenage sexuality has intensified enormously in the past decade. Teenage sex used to be less visible. Not only was there less of it, but girls who got pregnant dropped out of school and usually either married or moved away from home for nine months and then gave up their babies for adoption. All that has changed. Pregnant girls are more likely to choose to have abortions or to bear and raise their children themselves than to marry or to give up their children. In a way, these teenagers have moved from the private domain to the public, from the concern of families and charities to the concern of public health professionals, social workers, and public policy makers.

This essay examines the politics of teenage sexuality: its emergence as a significant public issue, the policy responses of the Carter and Reagan administrations, and some alternative responses that feminists might offer. Teenage girls are now caught in the crossfire between those who want to keep abortion legal and to provide contraceptive advice and prescriptions to as many teenagers as possible and those who want to make abortion illegal and to require parental consent for pregnancy counseling and birth control prescriptions. Liberals complain that it is inconsistent to oppose abortion *and* contraception *and* sex education. Conservatives complain that the availability of all three encourages precocious sexual intercourse.

For some time now, many feminists have been saying that "the sexual revolution is not our revolution." Although feminists have advocated an end to the double standard for male and female sexual conduct, they generally have been well aware that so-called sexual liberation under present social conditions may actually reinforce inequality between women and men and preclude the possibility of genuine liberation and equality. While feminists must continue to support the availability of contraception and abortion, we need to develop a new model of sex education that links sexual relations to the relations of women and men in society at large.

I wish to thank Irene Diamond, Gregory Nobles, and Gary Meyers for their comments on the drafts of this paper.

First, we must examine the key factors that have brought teenage sexuality to a prominent position on the public policy agenda: morality, cost, federal intervention, and race. The data on teenage sexuality, pregnancy, and childbearing are often confusing at first glance, and certainly are subject to diverse interpretations. Contrary to popular opinion, teenage childbearing in the United States has actually been declining during the past two decades (see Figure 12.1). Despite a 58.1 percent increase in the number of girls aged 15–19 in the population between 1960 and 1977, the actual number of births to them has decreased slightly, from 586,966 in 1960 to 559,154 in 1977. Their overall birthrate has declined substantially; from a peak of 97.3 births per 1000 women aged 15–19 in 1957, the teenage birthrate fell to 53.7 births per 1000 teenagers in 1977. Nevertheless, births to teenage women now comprise a higher proportion of the total births to women because the birthrate for older women has declined even more than that for teenagers.[1]

Perhaps the most important change is in the marital status of teens who give birth. From 1960–64 to 1970–74 the proportion of births *conceived* out of wedlock remained steady at about 50 percent. However, the proportion *born* out of wedlock increased substantially because the number of births legitimated by marriage declined from about 65 percent to 35 percent. Although out-of-wedlock births have increased, their rate of increase is still slower than it was in the 1960s (13 percent compared with 34 percent; see Table 12.1).[2]

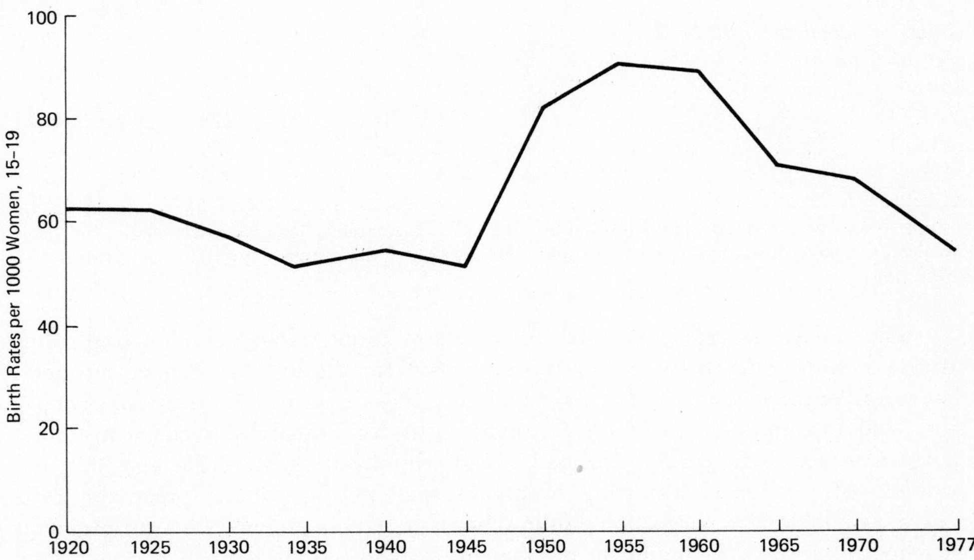

FIGURE 12.1 Birthrates of U.S. Women Ages 15–19, 1920–1977. Reprinted by permission from Maris A. Vinovskis, "An Epidemic of Adolescent Pregnancy? Some Historical Considerations," *Journal of Family History* 6, no. 2.

TABLE 12.1
Selected Natality Indicators for Women under Twenty Years of Age, United States, 1950–1977

	Year						
Age	*1950*	*1955*	*1960*	*1965*	*1970*	*1975*	*1977*
No. of births (in 000s)							
15–19	—	484	587	591	645	582	559
18–19	—	334	405	402	421	355	345
15–17	—	150	182	189	224	227	214
<15	—	5	7	8	12	13	11
Birthrates (per 1000 women)							
15–19	81.6	90.3	89.1	70.4	68.3	56.3	53.7
18–19	—	—	—	—	114.7	85.7	81.9
15–17	—	—	—	—	38.8	36.6	34.5
<15	1.0	0.9	0.8	0.8	1.2	1.3	1.2
Birthrates by marital status							
Marital (per 1000 married)							
15–19	410.4	460.2	530.6	462.3	443.7	315.8	—
Out-of-wedlock (per 1000 unmarried)							
15–19	12.6	15.1	15.3	16.7	22.4	24.2	25.5
18–19					32.9	32.8	35.0
15–17					17.1	19.5	20.7
Ratios of out-of-wedlock births (per 1000 births)							
15–19	—	142	148	208	295	382	429
18–19	—	102	107	152	224	298	344
15–17	—	232	240	327	430	514	566
<15	—	663	679	785	808	870	882

SOURCE: Reprinted by permission from Frank F. Furstenburg, Jr., Richard Lincoln, and Jane Menken, *Teenage Sexuality, Pregnancy, and Childbearing* (Philadelphia: University of Pennsylvania Press, 1981).

Some analysts argue that much of the alarm about teenage childbearing stems from a greater concern for public morality than for the lives of teenage mothers. The negative consequences of teenage childbearing—in terms of education, occupation, and income—are as severe for married as for unmarried teenage mothers. When teenagers married and dropped out of school during the 1950s and '60s, the problem of teenage childbearing simply escaped public notice.[3] Since the 1972 federal law making it illegal for public schools to expel students who are pregnant or who are mothers, a significant number of pregnant young women are remaining single and staying in school. Moreover, they are keeping and raising their babies either in separate households or in their original households with the help of parents and other relatives. Today, about 90 percent of all children born out of wedlock are kept by their mothers, whereas ten years ago about 90 percent of them were given up for adoption.[4] The phenomenon of single teenage mothers, especially as heads of households, is perhaps what is most striking to the news media, the public, and policy makers.

These newly formed households not only violate the traditional sense of a family but are often in need of public assistance in the form of Aid to Families with Dependent Children (AFDC), Medicaid, and food stamps. Kristin Moore of the Urban Institute estimates that women who were teenagers when their first child was born account for more than half of the total AFDC budget and 71 percent of all recipient mothers under age thirty.[5] Thus, in addition to moral concerns about childbearing outside marriage, the public has also been concerned with the reduction of related public-sector expenditures.

The single motherhood boom is only one aspect of the moral concerns. Although we have no accurate information about the sexual behavior of previous generations of Americans, we do know that in the past decade there has been an increase in the proportion of young women who have had heterosexual intercourse at each age. In 1978 it was estimated that slightly over four million unmarried teenage girls had had heterosexual intercourse: about half of these (1,958,000) were 18-to-19-year-olds, 1,522,000 were aged 16–17, and 646,000 were 13–15 years old.[6] Equally alarming to many people has been the increasing use of contraception and abortion by unmarried teenagers. While 362,000 unmarried teenagers had babies in 1978, another 434,000 teenagers had abortions. Approximately one-third of the abortions performed each year are for teenagers.[7] Although abortion has been an important factor in bringing down the adolescent birthrate, the controversy over the legal status of abortion has drawn increased attention to teenage sexuality.

The adolescent birthrate has also declined because more teenagers are attempting contraception. Only five out of ten unmarried teenage women surveyed in 1971 said they had used a birth control method at their last intercourse; by 1979, seven in ten had. Between 1976 and 1979 there was a substantial increase in the use of some method of birth control at first intercourse and in the consistent use of a method, as well as a marked decline in those who never used a method. By 1979, 27 percent of sexually active teenage girls surveyed had never used any method of protection, while 34 percent always did and 39 percent sometimes did.[8]

Despite studies like Moore and Caldwell's that show no relationship between the availability of abortion and contraception and teenagers' decisions to initiate heterosexual intercourse, a vocal and well-organized minority of citizens continues to hold the federal government responsible for facilitating premarital sex.[9] Although the federal government has cut off Medicaid funding for abortion, the government is deeply involved in the funding of family planning clinics, authorized by the 1970 Family Planning Services and Population Act (Title X of the Public Health Service Act). There has been a rapid expansion of the number of teenage clients seen in those clinics—from about 214,000 in 1969 to about 1.5 million in 1979. As with abortion, critics often charge that federally funded clinics encourage teenagers to have heterosexual intercourse by providing them with contraceptives, usually without requiring parental consent. But studies have shown that most teenagers who come to clinics have been sexually active for six months to a year before visiting a clinic. First visits are often initiated only when a girl believes that she may be pregnant and goes for a pregnancy test.[10] The claim that the federal government has encouraged premarital sex is further weakened by the fact that the number of teenage clients obtaining contraceptives from private physicians is almost as high as the number getting services from public clinics.[11] Moreover, the number of abortions was rising even before the 1973 Supreme Court decision that legalized the procedure.[12]

Significant racial differences in teenage sexual behavior are another reason why the public is concerned about premarital sex. While more unmarried black young women have intercourse than do whites, the rate of increase for whites is faster. The rate of sexual activity for white girls aged 15–17 doubled in the 1970s, thus closing the gap between whites and blacks considerably. Furthermore, the recent increase in out-of-wedlock births has been confined to whites (a 27 percent from 1970 to 1978), particularly younger girls aged 15–17 (a 40 percent increase). Although the birthrate among unmarried black teenagers is still much higher than among their white counterparts, it actually declined by 7 percent in the 1970s; among younger black girls the decline was even greater. Furstenberg, Lincoln, and Menken have noted that "as early childbearing is seen more clearly as a problem affecting the white middle class, more vocal demands for attention and solutions are being heard."[13]

While this brief account of trends in adolescent sexual behavior gives some indication of why teenage sexuality has surfaced as a public concern and a potential object of public policy, it by no means completely explains how teenage sexuality got on the public agenda. In 1976, Planned Parenthood's research arm, the Alan Guttmacher Institute, published *Eleven Million Teenagers: What Can Be Done About the Epidemic of Adolescent Pregnancies in the United States*. This publication assembled and interpreted much of the available data, labeling teenage pregnancy an epidemic and creating a sense of urgency. Given the growing reaction against the burgeoning women's movement and the organized opposition to abortion, it is not surprising that the Guttmacher report sparked a public controversy.

The Carter administration, setting up operations in 1977 after a campaign that included plenty of profamily rhetoric, could hardly ignore the question of teenage pregnancy. The difficulty was in deciding what kind of government intervention would be appropriate. President Carter's Secretary of Health, Education and Welfare, Joseph Califano, assembled a large interagency "team" that recommended in August 1977 a program to prevent unwanted pregnancies. Their recommendations were to include a call for better adolescent family planning clinics, greater incentives to states to encourage sex education in the classroom, incentives to encourage schools to allow teenage mothers to enroll, more abortion information, counseling and referral services, and encouragement to states to permit adolescents to receive contraceptives without requiring parental consent. The last two recommendations in particular appealed to neither Califano nor Carter, both in terms of their personal convictions and the political pressures from Catholics and Protestant fundamentalists to provide some government policies that would appear to strengthen family life and specifically to counteract legalized abortion.[14]

Califano returned to a policy option suggested earlier by an HEW Special Task Force. This group had recommended a Family Development Program that would "provide practical, ethical and politically viable alternatives to abortion" and would result in "verifiable improvements in family life."[15] The suggested program was modeled on one begun by the Department of Obstetrics at the Johns Hopkins Medical School, designed to improve services to adolescent obstetrical patients. These young women needed training and support to cope with labor, as well as guidance in prenatal health and nutrition, infant care, and birth control—services not usually readily accessible to single teenage mothers. The Hopkins program also added vocational and educational counseling and other postnatal services for young mothers and their infants. The program has been successful in improving the young women's health—smoother deliveries and lowered rates of prematurity, toxemia, and anemia—as well as in preventing repeat pregnancies within eighteen months.[16] Most Hopkins clients return to school or find employment.

This Hopkins "life support" model, rather than the interagency program, became the prototype for a national program of comprehensive services to pregnant teenagers that was embodied in the Carter administration's bill, the Adolescent Health, Services and Pregnancy Prevention and Care Act, adopted in October 1978, just before the mid-term elections. Although the bill authorized some services to sexually active nonpregnant teenagers, its primary emphasis was on comprehensive services to teenage girls who were already pregnant or were mothers. Maris Vinovskis, deputy staff director of the U.S. House Select Committee on Population in 1978, emphasizes the key role played by Senator Ted Kennedy (D-Mass.) and by Eunice Shriver and the staff of the Joseph P. Kennedy, Jr., Foundation in the passage of a bill that focused on already pregnant teenagers and neglected nonpregnant teenagers in need of preventive services like sex education and contraception.[17] Califano's decision to locate the newly created Office of Adolescent Pregnancy Programs under the Assistant Secretary for Health, rather than the Deputy Assistant Secretary for Population Affairs, who handles Title X funding of birth control clinics, further signaled that the emphasis of the program was to be on the health of pregnant young women rather than the prevention of pregnancy among nonpregnant, sexually active teenagers. The scope of the program was inevitably limited further by the high cost of such comprehensive services, estimated to be about $2000 a year for each client.

Implementation of the Adolescent Pregnancy Act (P.L. 95-626) was hampered by a delay in appropriations of funds by Congress. While the initial year's authorization was for $50 million, the program actually only got $18.5 million in appropriations over two years. It funded twenty-seven programs, many in the "linkage" category specified by the legislation for the development of networks of various services already available in communities but not previously connected or oriented toward the pregnant teenage population.

While the programs under Carter's Adolescent Pregnancy Act were underfunded, they were potentially useful for dealing with teenage mothers and their infants because they addressed the unmet health, educational, and job counseling needs of these young women. But they were not programs to prevent teenage pregnancy in the first place. One of the major critics of the administration's approach was Planned Parenthood, the largest and most influential family planning organization in the United States. Planned Parenthood objected to treating teenage sexuality as a health problem requiring expensive comprehensive services to teenage women. Its own approach regards teenage heterosexual behavior as a normal part of growing up and emphasizes the need to provide young women with readily available birth control information and methods. The number of teenagers served by family planning clinics increased 600 percent between 1969 and 1976, and Planned Parenthood advocates the expansion of the clinics so that more teenage women can have access to contraceptive services, services that cost only about $70 a year per client.[18]

When the Reagan administration and the Republican Senate came to power in January 1981, some senators set about the task of augmenting the Carter legislation by focusing on nonpregnant teenage women. But the vision these men had was far from that of Planned Parenthood or feminists. Rather than accept teenage heterosexual intercourse as a normal part of adolescent behavior, Senator Jeremiah Denton (R-Ala.) drafted a bill calling for the promotion of teenage "chastity" as a solution to "the problem of adolescent promiscuity."[19] The final version of Denton's Adolescent Family Life Bill (S. 1090), cosponsored by Senator Orrin Hatch (R-Utah), left out that particular language, but did authorize one-third of its funding (up to $6.6 million) to be used for outreach prevention services whose orientation would be to tell teenagers "it's okay to say 'no.'"[20]

After passage in the Senate, the bill became part of the Reagan administration's Omnibus Budget Reconciliation Bill and came up for discussion in conference. At that point, Representative Toby Moffett (D-Conn.) labeled Denton's approach "store-front chastity centers" and warned his colleagues that they would be "laughed out of every junior high school in America for being irrelevant."[21] While Moffett's label may have been unfair, he asked why conservatives would want the federal government to go into the business of counseling on sexual mores. In a letter to the *New York Times*, 15 June 1981, Denton and Hatch made it clear that they believe that current government-sponsored family planning programs are already in the sexual counseling business, encouraging unmarried teenagers to have heterosexual intercourse:

> We do not wish to create and promote a Government ideology about sex. We wish to change the ideology that the Government is promoting. . . . In the past decade, we have spent $1.5 billion of the taxpayer's money on "family planning." . . . The goals of some "family planners" spread far beyond providing contraceptives. They frequently promote their own version of morality, which implicitly, if not explicitly, includes the following tenets:
>
> Teenagers' sexual activity is inevitable and acceptable so long as no pregnancy results; contraceptives should be made available to teenagers

> at Government expense; if unwanted pregnancy does occur (and, according to this mentality, virtually all pregnancies are unwanted), abortion is the only logical alternative.[22]

Other members of Congress such as Representative Henry Waxman (D-Calif.), were willing to keep the Denton bill in exchange for retaining separate federal funding of family planning programs. Waxman successfully prevented a Senate plan to give the states control of federal family planning funds and expressed the hope that the Adolescent Family Life Bill would simply provide another alternative and not be politicized by the administration. Many others in the field believe the overall program will be useful. Up to one-third of the money can be spent on "scientific research on the causes and consequences of premarital adolescent sexual relations and pregnancy."[23] One-third could be spent on prevention services, and the rest would be spent to continue the Carter administration program (P.L. 95-626) that provides prenatal care, nutrition counseling, and other "life support" services to pregnant teenagers. The program was authorized at $30 million for each of the next three years, although as of this writing the funds have not actually been appropriated.

Liberals and feminists opposing the bill are most upset by two key provisions. First is the restriction that none of the demonstration projects will be allowed to make any reference to abortion during counseling sessions unless a girl or her parents request such information. The major emphasis of the pregnancy counseling is supposed to be on adoption as an alternative for girls who do not want to raise a child. Currently only about 4 percent of unmarried pregnant teenage girls choose adoption, and it is difficult to imagine that counseling will have much impact unless some much needed research (which the bill may very well fund) comes up with some suggestions as to what might lead young women to change their attitudes toward adoption.

Of even greater concern to liberals and feminists is the provision that a teenager must have parental consent in order to receive any counseling under the program. Parental consent is not required, however, merely to obtain a pregnancy test or treatment for venereal disease. Also, if the teen is the victim of incest involving a parent or if a close adult blood relative is notified, the requirement can be waived. Clearly the parental notification will discourage some teens from using the services, although studies show that most pregnant teens consult their parents, even if they plan to obtain abortions.[24] Furthermore, clinics with mandatory notification procedures are less likely to offer parental counseling and other family services than are clinics that encourage teenagers to voluntarily inform their parents of their participation in clinic services. The mandatory notification apparently serves as a substitute for the more active parental involvement that takes place in voluntary clinics.[25] Mandatory parental notification or consent for counseling, contraceptive, or abortion services not only violates the right of teenage girls to privacy, but fosters authoritarian familial relationships with no sense of trust among family members.[26] Furthermore, the burden of the requirement, like many other consequences of teenage heterosexual activity, falls on girls rather than boys, since there is no requirement that the parents of the sexual partner of a girl who needs help be informed of the request for services.

Although Senator Denton has earned a reputation as a near-fanatic on this issue, the provisions of the bill do not depart substantially from the Carter program for pregnant teens. In addition, the bill authorizes more much needed research on the causes and consequences of premarital heterosexual relations and provides for some demonstration projects in the area of prevention. Given our sex-saturated society, the potential $6.6 million that may be spent trying to discourage teenagers from engaging in premarital heterosexual intercourse may be a waste of money. However, a recent educational film called *Saying No*, produced in anticipation of this legislation, relayed a very subtle feminist message: It portrayed a girl resisting pressures for sexual intercourse from a boy by asserting her independence from him rather than only a fear of pregnancy or a desire to save intercourse for marriage.[27] Such efforts should be welcomed by feminists who have recognized that "the sexual revolution" has turned sour for many women, especially teenage girls, who often lack the self-confidence and self-respect to resist male sexual demands and peer pressure for heterosexual intercourse.

The language of the bill allows that "federal policy . . . should encourage the development of appropriate health, educational, and social services where such services are now lacking" in the area of prevention. Although the bill emphasizes that the "prevention of adolescent sexual activity and adolescent pregnancy depends primarily upon developing strong family values and close family ties," it does not rule out educational projects so long as they "promote the involvement of parents with their adolescent children" and "emphasize the provision of support by other family members, religious and charitable organizations, voluntary associations, and other groups in the private sector."[28] This provision may open the door to some federal demonstration projects in the area of sex education, despite its heavy "pro-family" rhetoric.

Unfortunately, research on sex education programs and their effects is very limited. This is so primarily because such programs have always been a matter of state or local initiative and administration and no federal program has ever been directly initiated and thus no national data have been gathered. Several studies have tried to determine how many of the 15,000 school systems in the United States offer sex education; their estimates range from 10 percent to 55 percent. Differing definitions of sex education on questionnaires undoubtedly account for much of the variation in these estimates. There is even discrepancy in the studies on state requirements in sex education; but the most recent study found that only the District of Columbia, Maryland, and New Jersey require local districts to provide sex or family life education. A majority of states leave the decision to local school officials. Six out of thirty-one states have explicit sex or family life education policy statements that "encourage but do not require" local districts to offer such courses. Twenty states have extremely limited or no policies regarding sex education, thus allowing local communities complete discretion. Differences within particular states are often greater than differences between states.[29]

Survey data indicate that although schools may offer sex education, a majority of students do not receive any sex education at school. A Gallup poll in 1980 showed that only 43 percent of youth aged 13–18 had received some form of sex education at school, with regional variations from 30 percent (in the South) to 55 percent (in the West). Several studies have shown that female students are somewhat more likely than males to have received some sex education.[30]

There is little systematic information about sex education programs offered by religious organizations, local social service agencies, youth organizations, and other community groups. But such programs do exist, and particular ones are described in the literature for sex education professionals. Nonschool programs appear to involve teens, parents, and community members in both planning and participation more often than is the case with school programs.[31]

Nevertheless, state-level policies usually strongly support parental responsibility and participation in planning for school-based programs. Eight of thirty-one states with policies require parental involvement, and eight states suggest that schools should provide sex education for parents and other adults in the community. Most states also require or recommend that parents may request their children to be excused from sex education courses, although very few parents actually do.[32] While there is little data about parental involvement in locally developed school sex education programs, most of the professional literature in the field emphasizes it as a "must" for a successful program. Thus Senator Denton's bill stressing parental involvement in this area is nothing new. Government policy at all levels seems to have included this concept for some time.

Most studies show that where parents are the main source of sex education and where children identify positively with their parents, first intercourse of the children occurs at later ages, contraceptives are used more effectively, and fewer sexual partners are likely. In particular, good-quality mother-daughter relationships are correlated with delay of daughter's first intercourse.[33] Unfortunately, a 1980 study shows that parents are more likely to teach their sons premarital sexual permissiveness, thus conveying a double standard to their sons and daughters.[34] Although parents seem to be the best source of sex education, many are apparently unwilling or unable to give it. A 1978 study discovered that 98 percent of parents surveyed said they needed help in discussing sex with their teenage children. Several other studies show the difficulty most parents and children have in discussing sexual matters, particularly sexual intercourse and birth control.[35]

Traditionally, the goal of sex education was the prevention of venereal disease and premarital pregnancy. But the sex educators of the late 1960s were uncertain that sex education could accomplish this goal unless they went beyond biological facts to the development of a new set of attitudes toward human sexuality that emphasized "sexual health"—a concept incorporating "positive sexual attitudes and self-understanding."[36] Rather than emphasize guilt over sexuality and perpetuate fear of the consequences of premarital sex, these sex educators reasoned that the goal of reducing unintended pregnancies and venereal disease could be better achieved by a frank admission rather than denial of one's sexual desires and activities and a responsible attitude toward protection against undesirable outcomes. Integral to this approach, in their view, would be the creation of "healthy and loving sexual relationships."[37] Some sex educators not only advocated responsible sex but wanted to impart sexual competence by stressing the joy of sex if performed with skill, enlightenment, and the appropriate emotional balance.

The "prosex" orientation of this "new sex education" is inherently unsatisfactory from a feminist perspective and requires us to examine more seriously the right-wing critiques of this approach. Onalee McGraw, writing for the Heritage Foundation, summarizes what she calls "the new orthodoxy" as a "humanistic 'pro-choice' message" that conveys to teenagers the idea that heterosexual intercourse is normal behavior that can be engaged in responsibly with the use of contraceptives and abortions when contraception fails.[38] The predominant perspective of textbooks and other materials produced in the past decade is indeed a supposedly value-free behaviorism that provides information about sexual anatomy, reproductive physiology, contraception, and a variety of sexual practices, sometimes including homosexuality and masturbation. The materials assume that scientific knowledge about human sexuality is nonjudgmental and can be used by students in making their own choices about sexual behavior.

But whether the goal of sex education has been constraint and contraception or competence and performance, the more serious problem with this kind of sex education is that it isolates human sexuality from the rest of human relations. Too often it focuses on sexual organs as though they are only tenuously connected to bodies and those bodies are only tenuously related to one another as human beings. The lack of any social and historical context for the study of sex means that a crucial aspect of human sexuality is ignored—the societal relations of men and women. Too few people think of sexuality as a socially created phenomenon because most of us experience our own sexuality as completely "natural" and immutable. In a common-sense way, sexuality seems to be primarily an aspect of nature rather than culture. But human sexuality has a history that is beginning to be rediscovered by contemporary social historians who have been studying the social organization of daily life for ordinary people. Their research has uncovered new insight into women's and men's work and family lives, emphasizing the dynamic nature of the relations between men, women, and children.

French social historian Michel Foucault postulates that the historical emergence of the very concept of sexuality was an aspect of new ways of organizing knowledge, which in turn affected the organization of social and sexual relations. He argues that there has been a growing, explicit commentary on sexuality, beginning in the seventeenth century: "What is peculiar to modern societies, in fact, is not that they consigned sex to a shadowy existence, but that they dedicated themselves to speaking of it *ad infinitum*, while exploiting it as *the* secret."[39] Originating in the Christian confession, the will to knowledge about sex came to be administered in the nineteenth century by the medical profession, which scrutinized and codified sexual behavior, producing a *scientia sexualis*. Despite "the guise of its decent positivism," the science of sexuality has functioned as a kind of erotic art by inventing a different kind of pleasure, "the pleasure of analysis."[40]

Thus Foucault rejects the hypothesis that Western societies have repressed human sexuality as a result of "Victorian" mentalities in favor of the hypothesis that they have used sexuality as a mechanism of social control. He views sexuality as instrumental and amenable to the most varied strategies, rather than as an autonomous agency that produces effects in the nonsexual realm. The very malleability of sexuality allows it to serve nonsexual ends, from selling cars and toothpaste to preserving family inheritances. While the particulars of Foucault's theory remain to be substantiated with more empirical data, there does seem to be enough evidence to show that sexuality was not always understood as an intrinsic personal characteristic. It came to be so understood in the late nineteenth century as changes in the mode of production created the notions of work and family as separate spheres of human relations within the bourgeoisie. "The very creation of work as 'work'—that is, the transformation of role-defined useful work into value-producing wage labor"—is central to the creation of sexuality as "sexuality"—that is, the transformation of disparate sexual acts and relations into personality-defining instincts or drives.[41] By the twentieth century, sexuality appears both "as narrow and limited and as universal and ubiquitous. Its role is both overestimated as the very core of being and underestimated as a merely private reality."[42]

Individuals today are encouraged to think of their identity as most authentic in their private lives, apart from work and politics. The "real me" is detached from socioeconomic characteristics, which appear, by contrast, as external and imposed. Sexuality thus seems to be located in some inner space, experienced as an "expressive state" rather than an "expressive act." It is something we are, not something we do.

> It appears as a *thing*, a fixed essence, which we possess as part of our very being; it simply *is*. And because sexuality is itself seen as a thing, it can be identified, for certain purposes at least, as inherent in particular objects, such as the sex organs, which are then seen as, in some sense, sexuality itself.[43]

Because sexuality is identified as a fixed essence located within the individual, contemporary sexual categories—such as the male, the female, the bisexual, the lesbian—are often assumed to be universal divisions equally useful in the analysis of any society and its members. But this is where a historical and cross-cultural perspective is vital, to show that while sexual acts may be universal, the meaning and validity of those acts depends on the relationships of members of entire groups of people. The sexual relations that are possible for individuals at any point in time are conditioned and limited to a large extent by the existent social relations.

In 1978 Linda Gordon and Allen Hunter recommended that a "good sex education" program "cannot be merely physiology; it must be a political women's liberation education as well as one based on pro-sex attitudes."[44] But if sexual relations are only as good as the social relations of which they are a part, there can be no "prosex" attitudes apart from the social relations of the day. In fact it was the mistake of sex educators in the 1960s and '70s to believe that "positive attitudes" toward sex could develop without addressing the fundamental relationships among people in society.

The first premise of a feminist sex education must be the recognition that human sexual relations, although grounded in physiology, are primarily an aspect of human social relations. Like social relations, sexual relations change, and therefore they have a history that contributes to what they are at present. Each person has a personal history of sexual relations, which is influenced by the more general history of sexual relations in a particular society. It is important for young people to recognize that sexual relations involve public issues for societies as well as personal issues for individuals. The personal experience of sexuality both molds and is molded by the social institutions of sexuality in a dialectical process over time. Thus institutions like marriage must be studied as part of the sex education curriculum, along with public policy issues like contraception, population control, occupational health and safety, abortion, treatment of homosexuality, child care, rape, prostitution, pornography, and sex education itself.

Feminists must be the first to admit that while effective contraception and legal abortion have made women less vulnerable to unintended pregnancies, they have made women more vulnerable to male sexual demands. Thus we must struggle to attain the social prerequisites that would enable women to use contraception for their freedom rather than their exploitation. Part of achieving those social conditions must be offering a kind of sex education that helps young women and men to recognize that contraception is merely a technology that, like all technologies, can be used to liberate or to oppress human beings. The fundamental prerequisite to its use for human liberation is the genuine social equality of women and men, which is a complex requirement involving life opportunities for women that provide sources of respect, love, and pride for women, not only from raising children, but from making other contributions to society. We must have opportunities for employment, political participation, artistic achievement, and so on, that provide women with aspirations in addition to motherhood.

One of the ways in which to teach men and women about the purpose of birth control is to make sure that we teach them about the history of birth control. This would include information about various methods used from ancient times to the present, to make clear the fact that women (and men) have always tried to control their fertility. Most important, the history of birth control as a political movement should be taught because it demonstrates the actions of women to secure legal and safe methods of contraception. Ideally every woman who uses a diaphragm or the pill should know about Margaret Sanger and the many other women and men who struggled politically to make these contraceptives available to the public. Knowing that history might make women and men of this generation more conscious of the political significance of birth control and of the dangers of the technology being used for purposes other than to free women from excessive childbearing.

But a feminist sex education should attempt to teach more than the history of birth control. It must address the question of the history of the social relations between the sexes generally. Reproductive control must be linked to a knowledge of women's lives in the past and of their status today. Such a history must deal with women's oppression and with their (often successful) strategies to oppose their oppression. Knowledge of the history of women has the potential to increase the understanding that both women and men have of the relationships between them in the economic, social, and political realms, as well as in their sexual encounters. The inequality between men and women in many of these areas should highlight the difficulty for women of resisting unwanted sexual intercourse and of using birth control for more rather than less control over their lives.

To this end we must try to move sex education away from the health and biology curricula and toward the humanities and social studies curricula. John Passmore has suggested that sex education ought to encompass some understanding of love, through consideration of history, art, and philosophy.[45] To that I would add the importance of politics and economics. Perhaps we should call it "gender education" to signal a break with the overly simplistic "prosex" attitudes of the 1960s and '70s and a new era of attention to the social factors that affect our motivations in sexual encounters. Above all, we must begin to think of sex education not only as education about the sex organs and intercourse but as education about the social relations between women and men.

Although a feminist sex education is a long-range goal rather than an immediate mass strategy to cope with teenage sexuality, its values must inform the short-range policies that we pursue. We must not promote either mindless chastity or mindless contraception, but freedom to say yes or no.

NOTES

1. Maris A. Vinovskis, "An 'Epidemic' of Adolescent Pregnancy? Some Historical Considerations," *Journal of Family History* 6, no. 2 (Summer 1981): 208.

2. Ibid., pp. 211–12. The Alan Guttmacher Institute, *Teenage Pregnancy: The Problem That Hasn't Gone Away* (New York: The Institute, 1981), p. 25.

3. Frank F. Furstenberg, Jr., Richard Lincoln, and Jane Menken, *Teenage Sexuality, Pregnancy, and Childbearing* (Philadelphia: University of Pennsylvania Press, 1981), p. 2. Kathleen Rudd Scharf, "Teenage Pregnancy: Why the Epidemic?" *Working Papers for a New Society* 6, no. 6 (March/April 1979): 64.

4. Vinovskis, "'Epidemic' of Adolescent Pregnancy," p. 212.

5. Kristin A. Moore and Martha R. Burt, *Teenage Childbearing and Welfare: Policy Perspectives on Sexual Activity, Pregnancy, and Public Dependency* (Washington, D.C.: Urban Institute, 1981), pp. 28–30.

6. Alan Guttmacher Institute, *Teenage Pregnancy*, pp. 7–9.

7. Alan Guttmacher Institute, *Teenage Pregnancy*, pp. 16–21.

8. Ibid., pp. 43, 11.

9. Kristin A. Moore and S. B. Caldwell, *Out-of-Wedlock Pregnancy and Childbearing* (Washington, D.C.: Urban Institute, 1976).

10. Alan Guttmacher Institute, *Teenage Pregnancy*, p. 44.

11. Ibid., p. 41.

12. Susan B. Hansen, "State Implementation of Supreme Court Decisions: Abortion Rates Since *Roe* v. *Wade*," *Journal of Politics* 42, no. 22 (May 1980): 375.

13. Furstenberg et al., *Teenage Sexuality*, p. 2. Alan Guttmacher Institute, *Teenage Pregnancy*, p. 25.

14. Gilbert Y. Steiner, *The Futility of Family Policy* (Washington, D.C.: Brookings Institution, 1981), pp. 80–81.

15. "Family Development Program," submitted to the Secretary of HEW by a Special Task Force, 17 March 1977, *Fertility and Contraception in America, Hearings*, 2: 656, as quoted in Steiner, *Futility of Family Policy*, p. 82.

16. Ibid.

17. Vinovskis, "'Epidemic' of Adolescent Pregnancy," pp. 215–22.

18. Steiner, *Futility of Family Policy*, pp. 83, 88.

19. Harrison Donnelly, "Teen-age Pregnancy Bill Approved by Senate Panel," *Congressional Quarterly Weekly Report*, 29, no. 26 (27 June 1981): 1153.

20. Ann Pelham, "Conferees Vote Teen-age Chastity Program," *Congressional Quarterly Weekly Report*, 39, no. 31 (1 August 1981): 1388.

21. Ibid.

22. *New York Times*, 15 June 1981.

23. Summary of S. 1090, Senate Report No. 97–151. See Theodora Ooms, *Comments on Adolescent Family Life Demonstration Projects* (Washington, D.C.: Institute for Educational Leadership, 9 September 1981), p. 3.

24. Mary Chamie, Susan Eisman, Jacqueline D. Forrest, Margaret Terry Orr, and Aida Torres, "Factors Affecting Adolescents' Use of Family Planning Clinics," *Family Planning Perspectives* 14, no. 3 (May/June 1982): 135. Judy Mann, "Teen-Age Sex," *Washington Post*, 22 January 1982.

25. Frank F. Furstenberg, Jr., Roberta Herceg-Baron, Dorothy Mann, and Judy Shea, "Parental Involvement: Selling Family Planning Clinics Short," *Family Planning Perspectives* 14, no. 3 (May/June 1982): 142. The Department of Health and Human Services has proposed that all family planning projects receiving federal funds under Title X of the Public Health Service Act notify both parents or the legal guardian of unemancipated minors within 10 days after providing them with prescription drugs and devices for the first time. With the close of the 60-day public-comment period on 23 April 1982, the department could issue the final, legally binding regulation, but as of September 1982, it had not done so due to public outcry.

26. I am indebted to Philip Green (Smith College Department of Government) for pointing out how few people on either side of the so-called squeal rule controversy have raised the issue of the need for trust among family members and the deleterious effect that mandatory notification will have on this dimension of family life.

27. *Saying No*, Perennial Education, Inc., 477 Roger Williams, P.O. Box 855, Highland Park, IL 60035.

28. Senate Bill 1090.

29. Moore and Burt, *Teenage Childbearing and Welfare*, pp. 70–71. This report contains a good overview and bibliography of much of the research in this field.

30. Ibid., p. 72.

31. Peter Scales, "Sex Education and the Prevention of Teenage Pregnancy: An Overview of Policies and Programs in the United States," in *Teenage Pregnancy in a Family Context: Implications for Policy*, ed. Theodora Ooms (Philadelphia: Temple University

Press, 1981), pp. 229–35. This is a very helpful anthology deriving from the Family Impact Seminar.

32. Moore and Burt, *Teenage Childbearing and Welfare*, pp. 76–77.

33. Greer Litton Fox and Judith K. Inazu, "Patterns and Outcomes of Mother-Daughter Communication About Sexuality," *Journal of Social Issues* 36, no. 1 (1980): 7–29. This issue of *JSI* is entitled "Teenage Parenting: Social Determinants and Consequences." This point should be further explored by feminists and "profamily" advocates alike.

34. Constance Hoenk Shapiro, "Sexual Learning: The Short-changed Adolescent Male," *Social Work* 25, no. 6 (November 1980): 489–93.

35. Moore and Burt, *Teenage Childbearing and Welfare*, p. 75. See also Elizabeth Roberts and John Gagnon, *Family and Sexual Learning: A Study of the Role of Parents in the Sexual Learning of Children* (Cambridge, Mass.: Population Education, 1978), pp. 55–60.

36. *The National PTA Comprehensive School/Community Health Education Project Report* (Chicago: National PTA, n.d.). See also James Hottois and Neal A. Milner, *The Sex Education Controversy: A Study of Politics, Education and Morality* (Lexington, Mass.: Heath, 1975); and Mary Breasted, *Oh! Sex Education*! (New York: Praeger, 1970).

37. Peter Scales and Sol Gordon, "Preparing Today's Youth for Tomorrow's Family" (recommendations of the Wingspread Conference on Early Adolescent Sexuality and Health Care, 3–5 June 1979), *Journal of the Institute for Family Research and Education*, October 1979. Cited by Onalee McGraw, *The Family, Feminism, and the Therapeutic State* (Washington, D.C.: Heritage Foundation, 1980).

38. Ibid., p. 61.

39. Michel Foucault, *The History of Sexuality*, vol. 1, *An Introduction*, trans. Robert Hurley (New York: Random House, 1978), p. 35.

40. Ibid., p. 71.

41. Joseph Interrante and Carol Lasser, "Victims of the Very Songs They Sing: A Critique of Recent Work on Patriarchal Culture and the Social Construction of Gender," *Radical History Review* 20 (Spring–Summer 1979): 34.

42. Robert A. Padgug, "Sexual Matters: On Conceptualizing Sexuality in History," *Radical History Review* 20 (Spring–Summer 1979): 7.

43. Ibid., pp. 7–8.

44. Linda Gordon and Allen Hunter, "Sex, Family and the New Right," *Radical America* 11/12, no. 6/1 (November 1977–February 1978): 9–25. See Ruth Bell et al., *Changing Bodies, Changing Lives: A Book for Teens on Sex and Relationships*, (New York: Random House, 1980) for a feminist sex education that is still ahistorical.

45. John Passmore, "Sex Education: A Philosophical Essay," *New Republic*, 183, no. 14 (4 October 1980): 27–32.

13

Sarah Begus
Pamela Armstrong

Daddy's Right: Incestuous Assault

The sexual molestation of children is often referred to as the last frontier of child abuse. Silence about the issue on the part of society, the family, and the victim makes it nearly impossible to know the extent of its incidence. But incest is a prevalent part of the reality and experience of female sexuality. An analysis of incest uncovers the oppressive power relations of patriarchal—that is, male-dominated, authoritarian—family structures. Because of this, although incest is prevalent, the topic is forbidden since it touches on a basic power relation in our society: the sanctity of father-right and the patriarchal family structure.

Generally, the term incest is used to refer to a variety of different sexual relations between blood relatives, consensual and forced. It is most often associated with societal regulation through taboo. Anthropologists state that the origins of civilization lie in the incest taboo with its resultant drive toward exogamous family formations.[1] Historically, legal sanctions against incest have been promulgated to ensure the maintenance of exogamous marriage and sexual relations. However, it is a mistake to confound differences in the forms of incest. It exists as consensual relations between siblings, but most often, incest occurs as abusive sexual relations that involve power and not consent. This essay focuses on the sexual assault on female children by their fathers. In our society, the overwhelming majority of incest occurs between fathers and daughters or female children and the father figures in their lives: stepfathers, uncles, grandfathers, mother's lovers.

Incest is prevalent in our society because patriarchal family structures are unable to fill the emotional and sexual needs of parents and children, because power relations within families and in society are unequal, and because male sexuality in our society is very often socialized into forms of violent domination of women and children. The sexual assault on female children is part of the pervasive sexual abuse of women in patriarchy. Incest is a process wherein a father teaches his daughter the social relations of heterosexual sex: male aggression and power. Judith Herman, a psychiatrist at the Somerville, Massachusetts, Women's Mental Health Center,

An earlier version of this paper was read at the 1979 National Women's Studies Meeting at Lawrence, Kansas. That version was co-authored by Chris Novak. The authors would like to acknowledge her contributions of insight and effort.

notes that the abuse of paternal authority occurs most often in families with strict authoritarian structures and values, where the power of the father is absolute and girls in the family are socialized into traditional female roles of victimization and passivity. In such families, parental abuse often takes the form of sexual abuse by the men of the female children in the family.[2]

The most-quoted studies on incest victims are those of the American Humane Association. Their figures point to sexual abuse being "more prevalent than the reported incidences of physical abuse."[3] The Maryland Department of Human Resources states that "some authorities believe that sexual attacks on children may be the single most common type of abuse."[4] The *New York Times* reports estimates that in the United States, 700,000 children yearly are physically abused, and 1 in 4 kindergarten-age children are sexually molested.[5]

According to the American Humane Association (1969), more than 90 percent of incest offenders are men, and over 80 percent of the victims are girls.[6] Like virtually all forms of sexual assault in our society, men are the assailants and women are the victims. Incestuous abuse ranges from indecent exposure and fondling to masturbation, cunnilingus, fellatio, and penetration. Penetration occurs most often when the girl is near the age of puberty and is often the culmination of years of sexual abuse. Incest is not usually an isolated assault; incidents of incest are often repeated attacks occurring over a period of weeks or years.[7] And while there is not always physical violence involved in child sexual molestation, there is always emotional violation, an effect that is not visible.

Statistical data taken from past studies on the incidence and nature of incest are inaccurate because of cultural biases and unrepresented populations. The studies are based on reports from city and state agencies, courts, hospitals, and clinics that service family members who, because of "social disorganization" (poverty, for example), have already been thrown into the labyrinth of social service institutions. This bias incorrectly implies that sexual abuse occurs mostly in poor families. For affluent families, treated by private practitioners, incest can be hidden forever. Although health practitioners, social service agencies, law enforcement officers, and teachers are now required by law to report suspected cases of sexual abuse, incestuous abuse by upper-class males is rarely recognized. Parents from middle- and upper-class families can afford to buy silence and protection. Thus, documented cases of incest in these families rarely appear in the literature. But incestuous abuse is rampant in all social classes. In fact, "victims are white, black, Latin and Asian. They are male and female. They are 5, 7, and 12 years old. They are fat, skinny, ugly, beautiful, poor, wealthy, and middle class. Incest is relentlessly democratic."[8]

Recent studies seek to correct the class and race stereotypes about incest, and newer data document its pervasive character. Sandra Butler reports that as a result of strengthened reporting statutes in Connecticut, from 1973 to 1974 the number of reported cases rose from 19 to 47; the number of suspected cases jumped from 669 to nearly 2000. The jump in statistics is confirmed by reports from the Child Sexual Abuse Treatment Program in San Jose, California. During the first year of its existence, this program treated 30 predominantly white, middle-class incestuous families from Santa Clara County. In 1977, 600 families were treated.[9] Thus, with stronger reporting laws and more public discussion of the issue, the true incidence of incest is slowly being discovered. But, it is currently believed that as many as 50 to 90 percent of sexual assaults on children remain unreported.[10]

In the past, the topic of incest was the exclusive territory of psychoanalytic theory, juvenile court systems, social workers, and psychologists who "generally view incest as psychopathology." But it is misleading to label all male assailants as aberrant psychopaths. Because of the astounding prevalence of incest, it is necessary to acknowledge that all fathers are capable of sexually abusing their daughters and, in fact, many ostensibly "normal" fathers do. "At least one girl in 100 is sexually abused by her father."[11]

> Incestuous fathers are not a readily identifiable deviant population; they are often "good providers" and well respected in their communities. Within their families, however, they are tyrants who seek to impose their will on all family members and to isolate the family from society . . . The dynamics of the incestuous family represent a pathological exaggeration of the societal norms of male dominance.[12]

The sexual abuse of women cannot be dismissed as aberrant, whether that abuse is manifest as rape by a stranger or rape by a father. Unfortunately, traditional social science fails to grasp this, and the phenomenon of incest is addressed only on the individual level in terms of the perpetrator. Because most social and legal responses to incest focus on changing individual behavior, they do not address the larger social dynamics that have an impact on the family—for instance, economic inequality that makes it difficult for single women to provide adequate support for their families. Nor are they likely to provide remedies that will significantly decrease the incidence of child sexual abuse. Successful intervention and prevention of incest must be based in analyses of the social conditions that foster it. The fact that incest cuts across classes, races, and ethnic groups and is so commonplace suggests that it is the family dynamic that contributes to or causes the sexual abuse of children. It also indicates that our society implicitly condones the act, shrouding it in secrecy with a loudly proclaimed but virtually unenforced taboo. Prevailing ignorance and current psychology concerning child molestation distort the nature, causes, and extent of the problem, thereby making successful treatment or prevention unlikely.

POWER, SEXUALITY, AND PRIVATE PROPERTY IN PATRIARCHAL FAMILY STRUCTURES

In order to find the causes of sexual assault, there must be an understanding of the nature of power relations within the family that lead to, encourage, and protect with secrecy the sexual abuse of children. Moreover, there must be an understanding of how power dynamics within individual families are related to external social institutions and values. External social relations of power and domination are reproduced within the family, and it is in the family that children are socialized into accepting and maintaining these relations.

Patriarchal family configurations guarantee power and property rights to male members. Historically, in Western industrial societies, women and children have been legally considered the private property of the father. Moreover, the property rights of the father extend to the sexual use of women in the family and in family structures that are nonnuclear, property rights of the father may be exercised by all the males in the family constellation: stepfather, uncle, older brother, mother's lover, and so on. For example, in most states the sexual violation of a wife by her husband is not considered rape; rather, "sexual satisfaction," or the demand for sex, is considered the marital right of the husband. Often male assailants, when discussing their feelings concerning their sexual assault on their daughters, will claim that because their wives did not "fulfill" them sexually, they turned to their daughters, whom they believed were obligated to provide them with their sexual "due."[13] The sexual, physical, and emotional abuse of children and wives is a common constituent of family life.

The sexual abuse of children is sometimes defined as "exposure of a child to sexual stimulation inappropriate for the child's age and level of development."[14] But this definition ignores power in sexual relations. The "inappropriateness" of sexual contact between parents and children does not consist in children being "too immature" for sexual experiences. Children are sexual beings, and there is nothing inherently "evil" or psychologically destructive in children having sexual experiences. What is inappropriate is power inequity that inevitably inhibits choice, trust, and consent, thereby creating oppression and exploitation. Inequality and oppression are deleterious in sexual relations whenever and among whomever they occur. In patriarchal society, fathers and daughters are not peers. This imbalanced power relationship precludes nonexploitative sexual relations between fathers and daughters. As long as children remain powerless in the family and father-right prevails as a practice and institution in society, sexual relations between men and girls will be abusive.

The power structure of the patriarchal family socializes and reinforces male sexuality as exclusively genital and aggressive.[15] In the family, boys and girls learn the realities of father-right, and in the family human sexuality is socialized by gender into male aggression and female passivity and masochism. Men's emotional needs for intimacy tend to be manifested in sexual feelings that are directed toward genital contact and penetration. Further, since it is through aggression and its threat that domination is achieved and maintained, male sexuality is inexorably tied to violence in our culture. If we understand these dynamics as a cause of the violent domination of women, we can understand how natural, harmless, sexual feelings of a man toward children, especially young girls, can turn into genital molestation and sexual abuse. Moreover, it seems clear that as long as patriarchal power relations exist in any society, every child is a potential incest victim, and every father a potential rapist.

But domination and control occur not only in the private world of interpersonal relations, where individual men physically and sexually dominate their wives, daughters, and neighbors, but also in the public sphere. In patriarchal society, female sexuality is construed to be for male use. In our society, female sexuality is used as a commodity to be bought and sold or to sell other commodities. Within the relations of production, sex-role stereotyping confines women into traditional female jobs and sexual harassment in the workplace further controls the tenure and position of women in the labor force. Throughout society, rape functions to keep women vulnerable to and dependent on the "good intentions" and protection of men. It is within this larger framework of the sexual relations of domination that the sexual molestation of children must be analyzed.

MOTHERS AND DAUGHTERS

Patriarchal ideology continually blames women for the abuses heaped on us. We are seen as the child victim who seduces her father or as the wife who pushes him on his daughter or as the cold and unloving mother. These beliefs are prevalent, not just in offenders' minds, but in the incest literature, where the victim's mother is often presented as the "true" abuser in the family, engineering the entire incestuous relationship or perpetuating it through her unconscious consent.[16]

In cases of incestuous abuse, the mother may be aware of it, but is often powerless to stop it. Her emotional and economic dependence on her husband may prevent her from confronting the situation, and she becomes a silent bystander in the abusive family dynamic. The dependence may be reinforced by the threat of male aggression and social pressure to accept a passive female role. In the words of one battered mother of a sexually abused fifteen-year-old runaway daughter, "I tried to give her the only things I had to offer: some money and the strength to get the hell out of there."[17]

In families where "the mothers are rendered unusually powerless, whether through battering, physical disability, mental illness, or the burden of repeated childbearing," there is high risk for sexual abuse of a child, especially if a daughter has taken on major household responsibilities.[18] In those families, fathers typically do not assume a nurturing parental role, and the daughter is led to believe that she must comply with her father's sexual demands in order to keep the family together. Although most incest involves the oldest daughter, once the sexual relationship has been established, the behavior is often repeated with younger daughters.

FATHER-RIGHT IN INSTITUTIONS

The powerlessness and victimization of children are not limited to the family but extend into social institutions: the law, policy-making agencies, social services, and treatment programs. Father-right and the corresponding powerlessness of children is re-created in the institutions designed to mitigate children's victimization. Legal, economic, and social welfare agencies are restricted from intervention in families, even on behalf of children, unless there is a "reasonable cause to suspect" child abuse.[19] Post facto protection of children is a meager, reactive measure. Even so, it can be taken only if there is a complaint and some reasonable evidence. But "most services are targeted to identify children experiencing the most continuing serious abuse or neglect," visible and repeated evidence of serious bodily assault or neglect.[20] They are not targeted toward invisible, internal, sexual assault and injury. Consequently, sexual abuse is not likely to be identified by the usual sources: teachers and nurses. It is likely to be identified only during a physician's internal examination of a child. Yet, less than one-third of child abuse cases seen by physicians are reported.[21] Since most physicians fail to consider or report physical abuse of children, it is not likely that they would consider or report sexual abuse. In fact, Susan Sgroi, a pediatrician who has worked extensively with incest victims, states that "willingness to consider the diagnosis of suspected child sexual molestation frequently seems to vary in inverse proportion to the individual's level of training. That is, the more advanced the training of some, the less willing they are to suspect molestation."[22] Less than half of suspected cases are reported by social authorities. It is usually left to the victim to report her abuse. One study found that 60 percent of reports of child sexual abuse to protective services were victim initiated; the median age of those girls was 12.6 years.[23]

The avenues of action open to incest victims often reenact and compound the damage. A child being assaulted by her father has few places of refuge. If she runs away from home to a life on the streets, it is likely that economic necessity and emotional trauma will involve her with drugs and prostitution. Often a dependent relationship with a pimp will recapitulate a victim's earlier abusive relationship with her father. In studies of female prostitutes and drug users, it was found that as many as 44 percent of them had been sexually abused as children. James found that approximately 30 percent of the prostitutes she interviewed had been sexually exploited in their childhood.[24] Often, the only means of survival for a sexually abused child is silent acceptance.

Even if she is brave enough to report her abuse, when social service systems enter into the dynamic of incest, a new level of trauma is usually experienced by the participants. "Many authorities agree that the emotional damage resulting from the intervention of the 'helping agents' in our society may equal or far exceed the harm caused by the abusive incident itself."[25] Often, the female victim of incest is subjected to a traumatic gynecological examination in a hospital emergency room by a male physician, possibly her first pelvic examination. Then she is forced to relate her story repeatedly, in lurid detail, to convince a succession of clinicians that the incest occurred. Thus, even with the intervention of protective services, the dynamics of father-right continue, and the child is further victimized.

LAW, CRIMINAL JUSTICE, AND THE PROSECUTION CONTROVERSY

In all states, incest is a criminal offense. Every state has jurisdiction over child protection and statutes defining child abuse. These laws are enforced through civil procedures. Statutes defining child abuse empower states to protect children from abuse by transferring custody of the victims. An incest case can be prosecuted under the criminal laws covering incest and child molestation or under civil laws covering child abuse. Criminal statutes on incest are strictly defined to prohibit marriage and inbreeding between kin and to protect exogamous marriage, not children.[26] Only five states include sexual conduct other than intercourse in their incest statutes.[27] Other forms of sexual abuse of children generally fall under criminal statutes of forced sexual relations (e.g., statutory rape, molestation, offensive touching) and civil statutes of child protection.[28] For example, sexual intercourse between stepfathers and stepdaughters is covered under statutory rape laws. Sexual abuse other than penetration by any adult of any child is covered under forced sexual relations laws.

The primary concern of the criminal justice system is the punishment and deterrence of offenders. The treatment of perpetrators and the safety of victims is secondary. However, child protection laws regard incest as a form of child abuse that threatens the welfare of the child, rather than an issue of forced sexual relations. Thus, children's protective services are concerned primarily with the safety of victims of abuse through intervention and treatment of offenders, rather than prosecution. As a result, legislation regarding incestuous abuse varies in definition, scope, violation, and penalties, and it varies in treatment across states and within them.

Because state criminal justice and child protection services have contradictory goals and approaches, debate has arisen as to the utility of prosecution. Some, like Giaretto[29] and Herman,[30] believe that prosecution aids treatment because it provides relief and support for the victim by showing social condemnation of her abuser, it has a generally salutory effect on family members, and the threat of incarceration is useful in keeping offenders in treatment as a term of their probation. Others, such as Halperin,[31] argue that prosecution inhibits treatment because prosecution and incarceration do not deter or rehabilitate *offenders*; rather, the threat of harsh penalties, loss of economic support, and family dissolution deters *victims*, family members, and even professionals from reporting incestuous abuse. Moreover, reporting and identification are crucial first steps in the prevention and treatment of incest offenders and their families. The controversy over prosecution of offenders affects the direction of policy concerning incest and the design of treatment programs for aiding victims.

Incest offenders almost never seek treatment. In a study of forty incestuous families, Herman found that in no case did the father himself stop the abuse.[32] Fathers' rights to privacy and parental control over children, as well as the threat of severe criminal penalties to the security of other family members, combine to protect incestuous abusers from exposure. Even with prosecution, the accused offender has greater legal protection than his victim. The right to be held innocent until proven guilty and the possibility of release while awaiting trial allow the abuser continued access to his family and home. During this period the victim has usually been removed from her home and family and placed in protective custody. The abuser may pressure and rally other family members to his support, turning them away from the victim, while she is living with strangers, lonely, afraid, feeling guilty, and powerless.

In court, the accused father has the right to confront and cross-examine her, and the victim is subject to interrogation and challenge from an unfamiliar, antagonistic defense attorney. Thus it is not uncommon for victims to refuse to testify against their fathers in court. In some states, corroboration of the victim's story by other witnesses is required to obtain conviction.[33] Because of the clandestine nature of incest, this corroboration is virtually impossible to obtain.

The following study illustrates numerically the inability of current judicial proceedings to redress incestuous abuse and protect child victims:

> In a study of 256 known cases of sexual abuse of children involving 250 offenders conducted by the Brooklyn Society for the Prevention of Cruelty to Children, parents and family found the police process so trying and frightening to the children that 76 cases were dropped, leaving 174 cases eligible for prosecution. Once charges were officially made, the number of interrogations and court appearances resulted in such trauma to the children and their families that another 77 were so discouraged that they too dropped the charges. This left 97 cases. Of this number 39 offenders either absconded, were acquitted, or were left pending, leaving 58 to be tried. Of this number, 49 pleaded guilty in order to take a lesser charge such as assault rather than rape or incest; 4 were found guilty as charged, and 5 were committed to mental institutions. Of the 53 found guilty, (excluding the 5 sent to mental institutions), 30 escaped jail sentence by suspension or fine, 18 were sentenced to jail from 6 months to a year, and 5 received indeterminate sentences.[34]

In view of these difficulties, state attorneys are generally unwilling to prosecute, rarely obtain convictions, and even less often incarcerate offenders. Moreover, as with all criminal activity in this country, the race and class of the offender are the primary indicators of whether he will be processed through the criminal justice system. Thus the traditional approach of the criminal justice system is a failure, and the power of fathers to sexually abuse their daughters with impunity remains secure for most abusers.

But, the debate over prosecution is not the salient issue. Rather, it is that legislation and enforcement within the criminal justice system uphold and protect father-right because the legal balance of power is vested in the parental and due process rights of fathers, not in children's rights. This fosters immunity from exposure and punishment for offenders rather than the protection of children's safety and welfare. To redress this imbalance, reform of legislative and judicial responses to incest is needed so that public policy is directed toward the protection of children, *not* the protection of father-right.

FEDERAL POLICY, CHILDREN'S SERVICES, AND "MAINTAINING THE FAMILY"

In 1974 Congress created the National Center on Child Abuse and Neglect. The Center was an attempt to create a national, coordinated effort to prevent and treat child abuse. Its specific purpose was to encourage uniformity in legislation, produce and coordinate research and information, and create and assist successful treatment programs by providing funding assistance to the states according to substantive eligibility criteria. These criteria require states to have mandatory reporting and investigation laws of all suspected child abuse cases and statutes providing for transference of custody of endangered children.[35]

In 1976 Dr. Douglas Besharov, director of the Center, mandated a new treatment approach in the funding guidelines. Programs would be funded that use the multidisciplinary treatment model originated in 1974 by Kempe and DeFrancis.[36] This model includes group, individual, and family therapy; family and parenting training; and cooperation between community social service agencies. This assistance-oriented, nonpunitive approach attempts to treat the causes of abuse and to create a healthy environment for the family by healing the damage to the child and retraining the parents. It is believed that strengthening the family will prevent repeated abuse, and the ultimate goal is "to reunite the family as quickly as practicable."[37]

At this time, incest and sexual abuse of children in families was considered a type of child abuse. But in 1978 the Child Abuse Act was amended in response to research showing higher than suspected rates of incest, an increasing awareness of special treatment problems in incest cases, and the fact that most child abuse programs did not provide treatment for incestuous families. Since sexual abuse was henceforth to be considered a special type of child abuse, requiring its own research and treatment programs, the law was amended to specify funding for no less than three national programs treating sexual abuse.[38] By 1981, forty-six states were eligible under the federal guidelines.[39] This legislative effort resulted in a national, coordinated policy on child physical and sexual abuse. The stated goals of this policy are to protect the best interests of the child, to preserve the family whenever possible, and to establish curative rather than punitive approaches.[40] This policy effectively resulted in a national and state-by-state commitment to the establishment of family-oriented child protective services as the primary approach to the intervention, treatment, and prevention of child abuse.

The policy of "maintaining the family" whenever possible is a controversial issue, particularly in the case of incestuous abuse. The current implementation of this policy is to provide for the child's protection by removing her from the home, while the incestuous father is allowed to remain at home for the family's protection. Proponents of this approach claim that evicting fathers destroys otherwise viable families because it removes economic and emotional support from other family members and it disrupts socialization and the healthy development of other children in the family.[41] Moreover, it is argued that strengthening the family aids in treatment. Advocates of incest victims (Herman, Rush, Armstrong et al.) criticize this policy of "maintaining the family" as a male-headed unit because it assumes that the measure of an "intact" family is the presence of a male head, rather than a household of children and their caretakers; it punishes the daughter-victim rather than the father-perpetrator. It further assumes the universality and superiority of the nuclear family as the optimal medium for child development, even though a majority of children live in nonnuclear families and the majority of incest occurs in male-headed families. These advocates claim that the easiest and surest way to protect daughters and stop incest is to remove the perpetrator and prevent his access to his victim. That is, to "un-nuke" the family by removing the male head-of-household perpetrator, thus disarming him of his power to dominate the family.

The issue of "maintaining the family" centers on the definition of family and on which configuration of family members is most conducive to the treatment and prevention of future abuse. Most experts agree on two points about successful treatment of incestuous families: the need to restrict and control the excessive power of incestuous fathers and the need to restore and reinforce the mother-daughter relationship as the nucleus of the rehabilitated family.[42] The controversy arises not simply out of conflicting definitions of family but also out of the actual relationship between individual rights, children's rights, and child protective services.

The actual authority of children's services to intervene in abusive families is limited to the immediate removal of the child if she is in danger. Other intervention to protect the victims, such as temporary or permanent custody and restrictions on parental visitation, require juvenile court orders since they restrict individual rights to property, privacy, and free movement. Court orders almost invariably require charges to be filed prior to issuance. Child protective services have no authority to restrict or control a father's power in the family. They also have no authority to compel compliance to a voluntary arbitration agreement if fathers choose to withdraw their consent. Thus, under current policy, child protective services' sole power of intervention is removal of the daughter-victim from her family. A change in this situation would require a shift in policy and legislation to promote, protect, and advocate children's rights to health, safety, and welfare within their own families over the father's rights to privacy and property, which protect his sovereignty within the home and family.

TREATMENT PROGRAMS AND MODELS

The issues and controversies raised above are reflected in new treatment programs designed to implement national policy on sexual abuse of children. An analysis of two treatment programs that differ in their approaches exemplifies the ideological and policy debates on what constitutes effective treatment and prevention.

The best known of the new programs is the Child Sexual Abuse Treatment Program (CSATP) in Santa Clara, California, directed by Henry Giaretto. Originated in 1971, it is a nonvoluntary, family-oriented, psychosocial treatment program whose goal is "to hasten the process of reconstruction of the family and of the marriage, if possible, since children prosper best in normally functioning families headed by the biological parents.[43] To be accepted into the CSATP, all offenders must go through the criminal justice system. Acceptance for treatment results in suspended sentences or parole for most offenders.[44] The treatment process consists in individual counseling of the victim, the mother, and the perpetrator, followed by marital and family therapy in which the father acknowledges to his daughter his full responsibility for his abuse. The final stage of treatment is the reunion of family members in their home supplemented by continued family therapy and self-help peer groups.

Giaretto claims a 90 percent success rate of reconstitution of families with no recurrence of incest. He credits the success of his program to the combined use of prosecution and family treatment. "The reward for cooperation . . . is the return of the victim or the father to the home."[45] Criticism of CSATP has been raised, although Giaretto's program is held, throughout the literature, to be the most successful program as well as the best model for treatment of incest, and it has received heavy federal funding. It is generally agreed that reincidence is an inadequate measure of the success of treatment.[46] Reincidence may not be detected, may not occur until treatment is over, or may reoccur with a younger daughter without detection by the program.[47] In addition, since CSATP is targeted toward white, middle-class, nuclear families its applicability to varying racial, socioeconomic family formations is limited. Moreover, as shown earlier, tying treatment to mandatory prosecution limits a program's clients to those who are willing and able to be convicted. Also, even though therapy requires the father to take full responsibility, intervention and treatment in fact punish the daughter because she is removed from her home and placed in foster care. Her return depends, not on *her* treatment, but on her father's rehabilitation or her mother's willingness to separate from him.

In programs like the CSATP, the underlying dynamic of father-right is not recognized; rather, incest offenders are treated as "sick" individuals to be cured and sent home to their wives and daughters. Because programs like CSATP focus solely on changing individual behavior, they do not address the larger social dynamics that impact on the family, nor are they likely to provide treatment models that will significantly decrease the incidence of sexual abuse of children.

The Christopher Street Program in Minneapolis, Minnesota, is an elaborately structured victim-advocacy, self-help program organized for and staffed by incest survivors. Its goal is to encourage victims to become survivors by overcoming their incestuous experience through self-knowledge and self-confrontation.[48] Treatment begins in a "holding group" where new clients acknowledge their incest and self-destructive behavior. Next, in "learning lab"—small, highly structured, intensive-support groups—lectures, therapy exercises, and strict rules enable victims to relive and work through their experience. Finally, in "aftercare," they reexamine their lives and identify self-destructive patterns so that they can heal and remake themselves.[49] This enables victims to put their past experiences behind them and become survivors. A survivor successfully completes the program when she no longer allows herself to be subjected to any sort of abuse.

The strength of this program lies in its advocacy for victims through well-organized peer groups where victims find comfort, understanding, and validation. They are provided with a social analysis of personal problems and with the opportunity for collective action reforming public institutions and increasing public awareness by working with the program.[50] Because of its advocacy stance, the Christopher Street Program does not treat offenders. In the words of one counselor, "I am here to help *her*—he's been helped all his life."[51] The staff excludes men from participation in the program, arguing that men cannot work with incest victims because victims feel unsafe with and untrusting of them. This treatment model does not blame or punish victims. It provides successful therapy and strong support networks to incest survivors. Its major shortcoming is that while it empowers victims to escape from their current and/or future abusive situations, because the program does not treat offenders, it cannot prevent fathers' future sexual abuse of other children.

A salient issue for any successful treatment program is the empowerment of mothers in their families since "incestuous abuse occurs in families where the mothers have been subjugated and rendered powerless."[52] Legal, policy, and treatment reforms must limit the power of fathers in families, strengthen mother-daughter bonds, and establish priority for children's rights and safety. For example, the perpetrator could be held in a halfway house where he maintains his job and the economic support of his family, proceeds with therapy, and is prevented from continuing his abuse, while the victim and her siblings remain with their mother. If incestuous abuse, along with all other forms of child abuse, is to be treated effectively in the present and prevented in the future, family relations must be created that empower mothers and children economically and psychologically.

CONCLUSION

It should be reiterated that rape by fathers is only one of the many forms of the sexual violation of females. The dynamic of incestuous abuse is a training ground for female passivity and victimization in adult sexual relations. If we are to stop the incestuous abuse of the children, heal ourselves of its destruction, and stop patriarchal oppression of women's sexuality, our analyses, laws, policy, and treatment programs must be child loving and woman-identified. They must redress the economic inequality between men and women so that mothers can support their children if they so need or desire. A successful strategy for the elimination of incest must acknowledge and change the following realities: the inequality of family structures under patriarchy; the powerlessness of children in society and in their families; the economic and emotional dependence of mothers and children; and the refusal of individual men, in families and collectively throughout society, to accept responsibility for the violent misuse of their sexuality.

NOTES

1. See, for example, Claude Levi-Strauss, *The Elementary Structures of Kinship* (Boston: Beacon Press, 1969). And Gayle Rubin, "The Traffic in Women: Notes on the 'Political Economy' of Sex," in *Toward an Anthropology of Women*, ed. Rayna Reiter (New York: Monthly Review Press, 1975).

2. Judith Herman, "Father-Daughter Incest," *Professional Psychology* 12, no. 1 (February 1981): 76.

3. Vincent DeFrancis, "Protecting the Child Victim of Sex Crimes Committed by Adults" (American Humane Association, Children's Division, Denver, 1969), p. 68.

4. H.E.L.P. Resource Project, *Child Abuse: Facts and Fiction* (Baltimore: Maryland Department of Human Resources, n.d.), p. 4.

5. *New York Times*, 21 July 1981, p. 18.

6. DeFrancis, "Child Victim," p. 68.

7. Ibid.

8. Sandra Butler, *Conspiracy of Silence: The Trauma of Incest* (New York: New Glide Press, 1978), p. 28.

9. Ibid., p. 14.

10. Ibid., p. 12.

11. Kate Rist, "Incest: Theoretical and Clinical Views," *American Journal of Orthopsychiatry* 49, no. 4 (October 1979): 680.

12. Herman, "Father-Daughter Incest," p. 77.

13. Florence Rush, "The Sexual Abuse of Children: A Feminist Point of View," in *Rape: The First Sourcebook for Women*, ed. Noreen Connell and Cassandra Wilson (New York: Plume Books, 1974), p. 15.

14. A. Rosenfeld et al. "Incest and the Sexual Abuse of Children," *Journal of the American Academy of Child Psychiatry* 16 (Spring 1977): 331.

15. For a discussion of the dynamics of gender differentiated personality development, see Nancy Chodorow, *The Reproduction of Mothering* (Berkeley: University of Calif. Press, 1980). As this theory applies to male proclivities toward incestuous relations with female children, see Judith Herman, *Father-Daughter Incest* (Boston: Pergamon Press, 1981).

16. Christine A. Dietz and John L. Craft, "Family Dynamics of Incest: A New Perspective," *Social Casework: The Journal of Contemporary Social Work* 61 (December 1980): 602.

17. Kee MacFarlane, "Sexual Abuse of Children," in *The Victimization of Women*, ed. Jane Roberts Chapman and Margaret Gates (Beverly Hills: Sage, 1978), p. 91.

18. Judith Herman and Lisa Hirschman, "Families at Risk for Father-Daughter Incest," *American Journal of Psychiatry* 138 (July 1981): 969.

19. Vincent J. Fontana and Douglas J. Besharov, *The Maltreated Child*, 3rd ed. (Springfield, Ill.: Charles C. Thomas, 1977), p. 37.

20. Michael Halperin, *Helping Maltreated Children* (St. Louis: C. V. Mosby, 1979), p. 79.

21. Fontana, *Maltreated Child*, p. 31.

22. Susan Sgroi, "Sexual Molestation of Children: The Last Frontier in Child Abuse," *Children Today*, May–June 1975, p. 70.

23. Lorna M. Anderson and Gretchen Shafer, "The Character-Disordered Family: A Community Treatment Model for Family Sexual Abuse," *American Journal of Orthopsychiatry* 49 (July 1979): 437.

24. MacFarlane, "Sexual Abuse of Children," p. 91.

25. Ibid., p. 97.

26. Leigh B. Bienum, "The Incest Statutes," in Herman, ed., *Father-Daughter Incest*, p. 221.

27. Herman, *Father-Daughter Incest*, p. 162.

28. Ibid.

29. Henry Giaretto, "The Treatment of Father/Daughter Incest: A Psycho-Social Approach," in *Traumatic Abuse and Neglect of Children at Home*, ed. Gertrude J. Williams and John Money (Baltimore: Johns Hopkins Press, 1980), p. 474.

30. Herman, *Father-Daughter Incest*, p. 169.

31. Halperin, *Maltreated Children*, p. 85.

32. Herman, *Father-Daughter Incest*, p. 151.

33. Ibid., p. 165.

34. Rush, "Sexual Abuse of Children," p. 157.

35. Child Abuse Treatment and Prevention Act of 1974, P.L. 93–247, sec. 4 (2).

36. Fontana, *Maltreated Child*, p. 45.

37. Halperin, *Maltreated Children*, p. 80.

38. Child Abuse Treatment and Prevention Act of 1978, P.L. 95–266, sec. 104.

39. Brian G. Fraser, "Sexual Child Abuse: The Legislation and the Law in the United States," in *Sexually Abused Children and Their Families*, ed. Patricia Beezley Mrazek and C. Henry Kempe (New York: Pergamon Press, 1981), p. 57.

40. Model Act of 1978, sec. 1.

41. Herman, *Father-Daughter Incest*, p. 159.

42. Ibid., p. 131.

43. Giaretto, "Father-Daughter Incest," p. 470.

44. Anderson, Character-Disordered Family," p. 443.

45. Ibid., p. 440.

46. A. Harris Cohn and M. K. Miller, "Evaluating New Modes of Treatment for Child Abusers and Neglectors: The Experience of Federally Funded Demonstration Projects in the U.S.A.," *Child Abuse—The International Journal* 1 (1977): 453.

47. Herman, *Father-Daughter Incest*, p. 158.

48. Ibid., p. 199.

49. Ibid.

50. Ibid., p. 198.

51. Ibid., p. 200.

52. Herman and Hirschman, p. 969.

14

Joyce Gelb

The Politics of Wife Abuse

In the last decade, the pervasiveness of violence in the American family has been brought into the public arena. Although a precise determination of the extent of wife battering is impossible to ascertain because reporting and recordkeeping are incomplete and reporting rates are a function of public consciousness of the issue, available evidence suggests that abuse is common.

Studies of homicide victims have found that one-third were killed by husbands and/or lovers.[1] Many divorce complaints cite wife abuse as a major reason for seeking separation. Surveys have revealed that as many as one-sixth of married couples experience one or more violent episodes annually and that as many as 60 percent of all women are subject to abuse at some time during marriage. Estimates of men who engage in "regular" beatings of their wives range from 10 to 20 percent of the population.[2] A 1979 Louis Harris poll found that 10 percent of the women interviewed had experienced domestic violence within the last year.[3] Evidence suggests that abuse occurs across class and racial lines, not just among the lower and working classes, as many believe.[4]

Wife abuse thus seems to be widespread and, some would argue, on the increase. Colleen McGrath has suggested that what appears to be an increase in male-perpetuated violence against their wives may be a result of women's increased labor force participation. Although male authority in the larger society may be threatened, the quest for individual power in the family and over wives persists and resulting tensions are expressed through violence.[5]

THE EMERGENCE OF WIFE ABUSE AS A PUBLIC ISSUE

Wife battering came to contemporary public attention in London, England, where in 1971 Erin Pizzey founded Chiswick Women's Aid, an advice center to which women and children could come and discuss their mutual concerns. The overwhelming majority who came were battered women. In 1974 Pizzey published *Scream Quietly or the Neighbors Will Hear*, the first contemporary book about wife abuse. Her movement spearheaded the subsequent mobilization of the British

Women's Aid Federation. In the United States the first shelter was established in 1974 in St. Paul, Minnesota; rapid development of additional shelters resulted in a total of about 250 by 1979.[6] There is widespread agreement among activists in the domestic violence movement that the existence of the rape crisis movement provided a base for the emergence of wife abuse as an issue at the grass-roots level. Local rape hotlines responded to problems of countless battered women, and gradually many rape task forces developed "safe homes" and shelters to which women in need could turn.[7] By the late 1970s domestic violence had emerged from behind "closed doors" and was viewed by many concerned with the isolation of women as a legitimate issue for state and potential federal legislative intervention.

The remainder of this chapter examines policy issues raised by advocates of new approaches to wife abuse, the response of state and federal governments, and the outlook for continued reform.

APPROACHES TO REFORM—THE STATES

Recent efforts at changing the treatment of battered women have centered on three basic reforms: seeking improvements in the responsiveness of the legal system to complaints of wife battering, the creation of shelters and auxiliary supportive services for battered women, and legislation to operationalize the first two reforms through public funding and commitment.[8]

Because wife abuse is an issue that emerged at the grass-roots level, it is not surprising that major activity to deal with the problem has occurred at state and local levels. During the last five years, most states have passed some form of reform legislation to combat domestic violence. By 1981, 49 states and the District of Columbia had done so—the only state not to take action on the issue in recent years was South Dakota.[9] Most statutes create new civil and criminal remedies for abused persons. They specify in detail the duties of the police who answer domestic violence calls. Better recordkeeping and reports have been mandated, and finally and possibly most important, at least from a short-term perspective, funds have been appropriated for shelters and other services (including job training, child care, and legal and psychological counseling) for abused women.[10]

THE ISSUES

Although according to Blackstone's Commentaries the common law right of husbands to discipline their wives persisted until the mid-seventeenth century, even during this time it was to be constrained within "reasonable bounds."[11] Elizabeth Pleck has contended that wife beating was actually illegal in most American states by the 1870s. "The difference between the past and the present is not a modern intention to prohibit wife beating but a change in the manner of regulation . . . The bureaucratic control of the family . . . has resulted in the growth of modern police forces, social agencies and family courts and an increase in the power of the state(s) as against the power of the individual family."[12] Nonetheless, the tradition that a man striking his wife is a legitimate exercise of spousal authority has limited and contradicted efforts at effective intervention by the criminal justice system. "The key problem with criminal remedies for domestic violence is that police will not arrest, prosecutors will not prosecute, juries will not convict, and judges will not sentence."[13]

In the past, because of the pervasiveness of the ideology of women as men's private property, police were typically content to seek to end the immediate conflict and avoid arrest, by stressing mediation and minimizing the event's seriousness. Intervention of this sort tended to permit later violence to continue, often with dire consequences for the victim.[14] Increasingly, efforts by activists have centered on improvement in police intervention in domestic violence disputes. A 1976 case, *Bruno* v. *Maguire*, in New York City, provided a model for subsequent efforts in this area. This class action suit, which alleged that the police had not provided adequate services to the abused by arresting wife beaters, ended in a consent decree agreed to in 1978. The decree provided for substantial changes in police practices including arrest without a warrant if there is "reasonable cause" to believe that spousal violence has been perpetrated and aid in the process of criminal prosecution.[15] Demonstration projects funded by state and federal government agencies have established "crisis intervention" and "conflict management" training programs for police to aid them in responding more effectively to cases of domestic violence. But while training police in such techniques may sensitize them to the victim's needs and thus lessen the degree of police abuse, reforms of this sort tend to reinforce the belief that wife abuse is not a criminal matter.

Prosecutors and judges have tended to perceive wife assault as a domestic problem, social rather than criminal in nature, and not suitable for resolution in the criminal process. In addition to holding traditional views about the privacy of family life, prosecutors are often concerned about the viability of spouse abuse cases, due to the frequent unavailability of witnesses, the complainant, or tangible evidence. Many prosecutors fear that assaulted wives will eventually drop charges against their husbands and often will insist on the victim's filing divorce charges in order to demonstrate her sincerity. (In fact, abuse victims frequently drop charges against their abusers, largely out of fear of retaliation or a lack of understanding of the criminal justice system).[16]

As a result of these attitudes, many domestic violence cases have been "diverted" from the criminal process, with a resulting, and usually ineffective, focus on "rehabilitation" and counseling. Domestic violence cases have been given lower priority than cases involving crimes between strangers. Domestic or family relations courts have frequently been given jurisdiction over wife abuse cases and seek to resolve or conciliate rather than punish the offender with criminal sanctions.

For these reasons, reformers have turned toward strengthening criminal prosecution of spouse abuse. Criminal penalties may be more effective than civil penalties in changing abusive behavior because they provide for a greater perceived or actual threat of punishment.[17] Nonetheless, as in rape cases, the burden of proof in criminal proceedings is on the victim, and stiffer sentences may in fact have a negative effect (because they may ensure fewer convictions).[18] Hence, advocates of reform have sought to provide a blend of civil and criminal remedies designed to meet the individual victim's needs. Protection orders (restraining orders or temporary injunctions) are now legal in thirty-six states; these generally provide broader, more flexible, and more immediate relief than criminal charges and may be preferred by victims depending on circumstances.[19] Under protection orders abusers may be evicted from residences shared with victims and may be ordered to refrain from abuse or contact with the victim, to attend a counseling program, or to pay support, restitution, or attorney's fees. Most states make the issuance of a protection order contingent on present or former cohabitation, typically providing for sanctions against violators that may include imprisonment and/or a fine.[20] Injunctions pending divorce are also available to abuse victims in many states. In addition, twenty-eight states have improved data collection procedures and thirty-seven states have approved funding for services to violent families including shelters, counseling, and employment training for victims.[21]

REFORM EFFORTS—THE FEDERAL GOVERNMENT

The history of federal efforts to deal with domestic violence also needs to be understood. The major thrust for federal intervention was domestic violence legislation, twice considered in the Congress, which failed narrowly to gain passage in 1980 after a three-year campaign.

Federal lobbying efforts were built on the consciousness raised by state, national, and even international forums and meetings. Following the 1975 creation by the National Organization for Women (NOW) of a Task Force on Battered Women/Domestic Violence, a 1976 meeting in Milwaukee, Wisconsin, intended for state-based activists in the shelter movement, attracted interested representatives from all over the country. This meeting led to the creation of a new group, the National Coalition Against Domestic Violence, which began to mobilize on a national basis and became a force for pressure on national decision makers. As a result of the impetus provided by the International Women's Year (IWY) Convention in 1977 (which highlighted wife abuse as a major problem for collective action) and the U.S. Commission on Civil Rights Hearings on Battered Women in 1978, the issue of domestic violence gained national attention. In response to pressure from women within the executive process and from those outside it who were interested in the issue of battered women, the Carter administration in 1979 appointed an International Committee on Domestic Violence to formulate a plan for future action. In addition, in that year an Office on Domestic Violence (ODV) was established to coordinate information regarding domestic violence, to fund technical assistance programs in the area, to disseminate educational material to the public, and to fund demonstration projects. No direct service grants were permitted.[22] The agency staff viewed its mission as that of "gadfly"—inducing other agencies to adopt measures to combat wife abuse. During the late 1970s, several administrative agencies did adopt and develop such programs, or, with the aid of ODV, expanded existing projects to improve the responsiveness of the criminal justice system to domestic violence. LEAA (Law Enforcement Assistance Administration) had been supporting direct service and court mediation programs for battered women since 1974.[23] The Department of Housing and Urban Development's (HUD) guidelines permitted purchase of emergency shelters and limited provision of social services under the Community Development Block Grant program.[24] The Department of Defense sponsored local family violence programs on military installations and service-wide efforts to provide and coordinate services for violent families.[25] In 1979, the Department of Defense issued a directive requiring the services to establish family violence programs on installations. The ODV, together with the Department of Defense and the National Institute for Mental Health (NIMH), sponsored a national survey on domestic violence to determine its incidence and seriousness and to aid in revealing gaps in service and means to improve options. Because the Office of Management and Budget (OMB) refused to approve the survey forms, the study was never completed.

In Congress, efforts to provide federal funding and support for shelters began in 1977, when what Smelser has called "structural conduciveness for change" seemed to have occurred.[26] Sensitized to the issue by the IWY and later Civil Rights Commission hearings, bills dealing with domestic violence were introduced in both the House and Senate. Two different approaches to the legislation were apparent at this time: one, which followed a "grass roots" approach—the "direct service" model, possibly to be located in ACTION (umbrella agency for volunteer programs); the other, a research and demonstration project approach—the "academic" model, which might be housed at NIMH. Community activists in the shelter movement in particular rejected the approach offered by the "academic" model, based on experience with rape crisis legislation, which had ultimately provided limited direct service but numerous grants for researchers. As the "direct service" approach gained adherents, however, it became evident that another political "home" in administrative structure would have to be found for it because the ACTION agency was under political attack. HEW (Department of Health, Education and Welfare) was agreed upon.[27]

A 1978 bill sponsored by Mikulski, Boggs, Steers, and Miller (D-Calif.)—the Domestic Violence Assistance Act—to fund shelters and other community activities was passed by voice vote in the Senate but was defeated in the House by a 201–205 vote. (Contributing to the defeat of the legislation was the fact that it had been presented on a suspension of the rules.[28])

Its sponsors were unprepared for the bill's defeat, largely because no opposition had emerged in hearings and because the modest sum of money involved in this version of the bill ($15 million in FY 1979) seemed unlikely to cause anxiety.[29] The upset seems to be attributable to several causes, only some of which are directly related to the substantive issues raised by the bill. House members resented the "suspension of the rules" procedure utilized, which they felt had been abused in an effort to push through legislation hurriedly at the end of the legislative session. Further objections were raised, as they would continue to be with increasing frequency, to federal intervention into family life and to the appropriation of still more money for federal social programs. Fleming points to objections raised to the designation of HEW as the administering agency, as opposed to LEAA; Steiner suggests that a limited administrative commitment to the legislation weakened its impact.[30] In addition, the issue was seen as one of primarily state and local significance, not an area for federal intrusion.

The bill was reintroduced in the 96th Congress, and hearings were held in the House and Senate. An extremely broad range of groups testified on behalf of the bill: representatives of feminist and traditional women's groups, service providers, the police, prosecutors, religious groups, the National Football Players League, the Junior League and even Representation Henry Hyde (D-Ill.), a leading opponent of federally funded abortions.

Opposition to the bill was muted, and by this time a new organization had emerged to assume a leadership role in the struggle for domestic violence legislation, the National Coalition Against Domestic Violence (NCADV), which had received its organizational impetus from the state and local shelter movement. By 1979, the NCADV held its first national conference in Washington, D.C., and established headquarters in the capital. The coalition comprised 350 groups and 25 state coalitions, and provided a network through which member organizations could share information and provide mutual support. Committed to preventing cooptation by traditional service-provider agencies, the NCADV believes in permitting battered women to control their lives and assume power. The group's emphasis is on community education to change the system, advocacy of political change at state and local levels, and provision of shelter and other services to battered women.[31] Under the aegis of NCADV, a broad-based coalition comprising more than 50 groups lobbied government officials continually throughout the period during which the bill was under consideration.

A scaled-down version of the bill rejected in 1978 was passed overwhelmingly by the House on 12 December 1979 by a vote of 292–106.[32] Several amendments that would have crippled the bill were voted down, including one giving state legislatures the right to terminate federal funds for domestic violence at any time.[33] As approved, the three-year program was to provide federal "seed money" for local shelters.[34]

The measure's passage may be attributed to several causes. First, in contrast to 1978, the bill was brought up under normal procedures. Second, the activists who worked hard to lobby for the bill felt that in the interim period, prior to the election, numerous congressmen had visited local shelters and spoken with local law enforcement officials, and in this manner grass-roots constituent pressure both regarding the need for and effectiveness of shelter programs became manifest. Robert Bauman (R-Md.) was quoted as saying: "It is very difficult . . . for a politician to vote against this bill and open oneself to be charged with voting for domestic violence."[35] Although some opposition did emerge in the House, other issues eclipsed its impact, and the opposition proved to be neither well coordinated nor effective.

A similar bill was approved by the Senate Labor and Human Resources Committee in April 1980, but in the Senate, unlike the House, the domestic violence bill became the target of a concerted attack by right-wing groups. Conservative Republicans led the fight against the bill, and intense lobbying by conservative Christian groups including the Moral Majority, "The Right Woman," and Family America became evident. The Moral Majority, working in conjunction with the Pro-Family Coalition, led a "lobby blitz" to prevent passage of the bill.[36] Karl Moor, the organization's head, organized the group's fifty state chapters against what he termed "radical feminists . . . coming to the federal trough for a $65 million feed."[37] Conservative groups used phone calls from constituents to put pressure on senators perceived as wavering on the bill, while the NCADV spearheaded a counterdrive for the bill's passage via mail and phone lobbying and also invited senators to visit shelters for victims of domestic violence, a tactic used successfully in the House. The bill passed the Senate narrowly, by a vote of 46–41, as some senators, concerned about antagonizing conservative groups, switched their votes at the last minute to oppose the legislation.[38] The final conference bill provided for progressively increased funding from 1981 to 1983 ($15–$20–$30 million respectively) for a total of $65 million prior to the programs termination in 1984. Local funds were to match the federal resources, with individual grants limited to $50,000 annually or $150,000 for the three-year period. All grants were to be funneled through the states, with the bulk of the money allocated for emergency shelters.[39]

The House approved the bill by a 276–117 vote on 1 October 1980. The Senate put off the vote until after the election, a delay that did not enhance possibilities for its approval, given the large conservative electoral gains on 4 November. Conservative senators threatened to filibuster when senator Alan Cranston tried to slip the conference bill through on 17 November. The 46 votes by which the bill has originally passed (*before* the election) fell far short of the 60 needed for cloture of debate. The conference report was withdrawn, the bill never brought to the floor again, and federal domestic violence legislation died.

ANALYSIS

Opponents of domestic violence legislation sought to argue that the federal government should not be involved in private family matters and contended that the matter should be dealt with on a local basis. To the extent that opponents perceived the existence of a problem, it was seen as a relatively limited one; the major concern of opponents of legislation was an "intact family rather than an intact wife."[40] The bill and its supporters were portrayed as "antifamily."[41] And with the ascendancy of Reaganomics, issues of federal spending and antipathy to categorical grants provided the final death knell. Although the coalition supporting the bill was broadly based and highly "respectable," opponents exploited allegations of radical feminist dominance within shelters. Occasional tensions did arise on stategy between shelter activists (NCADV) and the more traditional service providers, perhaps because NCADV feared a "takeover" of the issue to the potential exclusion of the grass-roots advocates who had founded the shelter movement. However, such differences did not appear to affect the overall lobbying effort.[42] Perhaps more important was the fact that with the exception of the NCADV, whose staff and resources are limited, few groups viewed domestic violence as their major priority. Only the NCADV lobbied continuously and vigorously.

Proponents of domestic violence legislation felt that in the House in 1979 a strong network was established that included the Congresswoman's Caucus, particularly Representatives Boggs and Mikulski, and strong supporters such as Representatives George Miller. Information was shared, a strategy developed in coordination with the NCADV and the coalition members and sponsors remained strongly committed to the legislation throughout. In the Senate, in contrast, criticism of Senator Cranston's leadership on the issue was frequent. Activists felt that the senator's office had maintained less contact and obtained less input from the coalition for a domestic violence bill than his counterparts in the House. The delay in consideration of the bill during the first stage of Senate passage in the 96th Congress—a delay that extended well into 1980, as other domestic matters were given priority—helped ensure the legislation's defeat. In addition, in contrast to representatives, senators proved less responsive to constituent pressure from shelter advocates in local communities. Finally, a *Washington Star* editorial critical of the legislation, published on 30 June 1980 (before the first Senate vote), may have served to weaken support.[43]

The domestic violence legislation defeated by the Senate was far less costly than the bill approved two years earlier. As a footnote to the act, which is now considered a "dead letter" by its supporters, the "Family Protection Act" of 1981 (pending in Congress) contains a provision prohibiting general funding for domestic violence programs.

Thus, unlike child abuse, another policy issue involving legislative intervention in the family and one that was the subject of favorable federal legislation in 1974 and again in 1977, the issue of wife abuse was unable to move beyond the agenda-setting stage of public policy in federal politics. The contrast in legislative acceptance may relate, as Steiner suggests, to the long history of private intervention and concern, high quality of research, and support from the medical profession with regard to the issue of child abuse.[44] Perhaps even more convincing as an explanation of differential treatment of two seemingly related policy issues is the suggestion that while efforts to end child abuse may achieve a broad public consensus, the idea of government intervention in marriage, even at the risk of permitting violence to continue, is "too great a taboo to be challenged."[45]

THE FUTURE

The failure of domestic violence legislation brought an end to the Office of Domestic Violence, whose continued existence depended on the bill's funding. Some of the ODV staff were transferred to the National Center on Child Abuse and Neglect (NCCAN) where projects funding aid for victims of violence may still be available, but only if these address the needs of children (e.g., for care of children of battered women residing at shelters).[46] The ODV-sponsored Clearinghouse on Domestic Violence has been closed down. The LEAA's Family Violence Program began to be phased out in fall 1980, and LEAA itself is virtually defunct. In addition, numerous other sources of federal aid that provided assistance to battered women in shelters have been cut back or eliminated totally.[47]

The consolidation of federal categorical grants into state block grants has resulted in cutbacks of 25 percent in federal spending, a shift in responsibility for service provision to the state level, and increased competition in the states for those resources that remain, particularly for such relatively recent claimants as battered women.

An issue that emerged from the grass roots seems destined for the time being to return there if support is to be mobilized and sustained. The prospects for federal legislation are nonexistent in the present political climate, and the Reagan administration has fought to return responsibility for social programs to the states. As suggested at the outset of this chapter, prospects at the state level are brighter than one might anticipate. Three-quarters of the states have changed their laws regarding battered women in recent years, and most provide some, if limited, funding for shelters and improved access to the criminal justice system. Some states are beginning to obtain financing for battered women's programs by adding a surcharge to marriage licenses.[48] This novel innovation involves forwarding marriage license fees to a special fund within the state treasury. Three states, Florida, Montana, and Ohio, were the first to use this surcharge, which is particularly useful in states facing budget cuts. In Wisconsin, there is a 10 percent surcharge on all court fines in criminal cases in which the defendant is convicted of criminal conduct involving domestic abuse.[49]

Recent efforts in Illinois seem illustrative of the significance of state lobbying coalitions, usually centered on the state's coalition against domestic violence (CADV). In Illinois, following the model of coalition inclusivity adopted in the second round of congressional lobbying efforts, a wide spectrum of groups was involved in pressuring for new legislation.[50] These included police chiefs, state's attorneys, hospital administrators, judges, the private bar, and others. The groundwork for the campaign was laid one year prior to legislative consideration; twelve mailings were sent to potential supporters. Two lobbying clinics were held for activists, as well as a "Lobby Day" to explain strategy and tactics. Legislative sponsorship was carefully selected with a view to bipartisanship. The five chief sponsors in the General Assembly comprised four Republicans and one Democrat; in the Senate, the president and fourteen co-sponsors led the effort. An effort was made to present the effort as "profamily" (i.e., public oriented and nondefensive) to counter right-wing opposition. The "family" issue was confronted by statements that asserted: "HB 366 offers new remedies for victims of domestic violence who are not necessarily ready to seek a dissolution of marriage and need to consider their options in the safety and calm of a violence free home . . . But the bill is born of a recognition that domestic violence has reached epidemic proportions in our society. HB 366 is born of a recognition that victims of violence in their own homes—often women, children and elderly parents—not only receive protection from further harm but are permitted to break the cycle of violence that is being transmitted from generation to generation." Victims of domestic violence were called upon to testify in each chamber. The bill readily passed both houses and received gubernatorial support. The final legislation provides new tools for police enforcement. Marriage licenses and divorce filing papers are subject to fees to provide services to battered women.[51]

The passage of this legislation at the same time that the Illinois legislature refused to ratify the Equal Rights Amendment is worthy of comment. No doubt pressure to "do something" for women in the face of opposition to the ERA contributed to the easy passage of the Illinois Domestic Violence Act of 1981. Partisanship played virtually no role, even after the Illinois House came under a Republican majority in January 1981. A "thank you" letter was sent out to all supporters and under the aegis of the Illinois CADV, implementation of the new legislation will be carefully monitored.

This highly successful effort (from September 1980 to July 1981) may serve as a model for others. Success appears to be based on: (1) a broad-based coalition providing legitimacy and access; (2) use of nonthreatening symbols (e.g., stress on ending *violence* and desire to preserve the *family* if possible, thus blunting right-wing attacks and effectively neutralizing their efforts in the political process); (3) political sophistication including development of effective lobbying strategies, coordination, feedback, use of media, continuing analysis of strengths and weaknesses; (4) strong legislative and executive support and leadership, bipartisan if possible.

CONCLUSION

The last several years have demonstrated the politicizaton of feminists and the public with regard to the pervasiveness of wife abuse. The issue has become permanently entrenched as a legitimate one for public discussion, as symbolized by the near victory in Congress and by continuing success at the state level. In addition, the importance of government intervention to correct abuses in the once sacrosanct private family has been recognized by activists, many politicians, and large segments of the public.

This chapter has suggested that efforts to reform the policy process with regard to battered women have had several goals. One has been to reform the response of the police and the judicial system by providing numerous, enforceable legal remedies. Another has been to gain access to funding for shelters and other social services; the use of new funding mechanisms at the state level has been particularly noteworthy in this regard. Documentation and media coverage have helped heighten public awareness and sensitivity to the issue and have demonstrated the continuing need for continued and expanded services. The creation of a network of public activists has served as a basis for continued pressure as well, providing a mechanism for sharing information, performing advocacy functions within the criminal justice system, and raising public consciousness on the issue. Anti-domestic violence activities such as these have met with considerable success in the decade since the issue emerged on the political scene. Nonetheless, it should be noted that these goals are largely *reactive*—they deal with abuse after it has already occurred and treat its consequence, not its causes. Ultimately, preventive efforts may well prove more useful in ending the centuries-old tradition of sexual violence by altering the subordinate role of women in society and the family.[52] Continuing efforts to sustain existing gains and achieve new, long-range goals will be met with opposition from right-wing forces that seek to "reprivatize" the family and ignore its problems.

NOTES

1. Colleen McGrath, "The Crisis of Domestic Violence," *Socialist Review* 43 (January/February 1979): 12.

2. Janet Baker Fleming, *Stopping Wife Abuse* (New York: Doubleday Anchor, 1979), pp. 154–55.

3. *Response* (Center for Women Policy Studies) 4, no. 3 (January/February 1981): 2.

4. McGrath, "Crisis of Domestic Violence," p. 12; Fleming, *Stopping Wife Abuse*, pp. 330–32. See also R. Emerson Dobash and Russell Dobash, *Violence Against Wives* (New York: Free Press, 1979), p. 7.

5. McGrath, "Crisis of Domestic Violence," pp. 22–23.

6. Sandra Wexler, "Battered Women and Public Policy" in Ellen Boneparthe, ed. *Women, Power and Policy* (New York: Pergamon Press, 1982), p. 188.

7. See Jo Freeman, *The Politics of Women's Liberation* (New York: Longman, 1975), p. 70. See also Ann B. Costain, "Representing Women: The Transition from Social Movement to Interest Group," in Boneparth, *Women, Power and Policy*, pp. 19–37. This is an instance, common in the annals of reform group emergence, of new groups building on the resources and infrastructure created by those previously organized.

8. Improved data collection is a secondary albeit key goal; it could document the incidence of wife abuse, enabling activists to educate police and other policy makers about domestic violence and to press for increased systemic responsiveness.

9. *Response* 4, no. 7 (September/October 1981): 2.

10. Ibid., p. 3.

11. Sue Eisenberg and Patricia Micklow, "The Assaulted Wife: 'Catch 22' Revisited" *Women's Rights Law Reporter* 3 (1977): 138.

12. Elizabeth Pleck, "Wife Beating in Nineteenth-Century America," *Victimology* 4, no. 1 (1979): 71. She argues that informal systems of regulation common before the twentieth century often contained powerful deterrents against wife beating that have gone unrecognized.

13. Julie Hamos, *State Domestic Violence Laws and How to Pass Them*, Monograph Series, No. 2 (National Clearinghouse on Domestic Violence, June 1980), p. 43.

14. As reports were rarely filed in the absence of arrest, patterns of abuse often went undetected.

15. Fleming, *Stopping Wife Abuse*, pp. 224–5.

16. Eisenberg and Micklow, "Assaulted Wife," p. 151; *Response* 4, no. 3 (January/February 1981): 2–3.

17. *Response* 4, no. 7 (September/October 1981): 3.

18. Ibid.

19. Ibid., pp. 1–2. Most states provide full protection orders if abuse is threatened and temporary or emergency orders to increase access to protection.

20. Ibid.

21. Interviews with June Zeitlin, former director, ODV, and with Ann Langley, former deputy director, ODV, October 1981. See also Gilbert Steiner, *The Futility of Family Policy* (Washington, D.C.: Brookings, 1980), p. 173.

22. *Response*, March/April 1981, p. 2.

23. Fleming, *Stopping Wife Abuse*, p. 422.

24. *Response*, March/April 1981, p. 2.

25. *Response* 4, no. 1 (October 1980): 5. Among the other accomplishments of the ODV (together with LEAA) were funding to aid the continued publication of *Response*, a Center for Women Policy Studies newsletter disseminating information relating to all aspects of policy and research concerning to battered women; assistance to establish a National Clearinghouse on Domestic Violence; and demonstration programs in several states to aid victims of wife abuse.

26. Neal Smelser, *The Theory of Collective Behavior* (Glencoe, Ill.: Free Press, 1962).

27. See Steiner, *Futility of Family Policy*, p. 160, for a detailed account of this issue and Fleming, p. 265.

28. Under suspension of the rules, only 40 minutes are allowed for floor debate and floor amendments are not permitted. A 2/3 vote—a majority of 271 votes would have been required for passage.

29. This account is primarily from *Congressional Quarterly Almanac* 34 (1978): 580.

30. Fleming, *Stopping Wife Abuse*, p. 265; Steiner, *Futility of Family Policy*, p. 172.

31. *Response*, March/April 1981, p. 5.

32. *Congressional Quarterly Almanac* 34 (1978): 580.

33. *Congressional Quarterly Almanac* 35 (1979): 508.

34. Ibid.

35. Ibid.

36. *Congressional Quarterly Weekly Report*, 38, no. 42 (13 September 1980): 2718.

37. Ibid.

38. *Congressional Quarterly Weekly Report* 38, no. 52 (27 December 1980): 3662; idem, vol. 38, no. 37 (13 September 1980): 2719. The primary defeat of Senator John Buchanan (D-Ala.) two days earlier, whose successful opponent had, with strong Moral Majority support, campaigned against the incumbent's "liberal" record, may have contributed to last-minute switching.

39. *Congressional Quarterly Almanac* 36 (1980): 444; *Congressional Quarterly Weekly Report* 38, no. 42 (October 1980): 3116.

40. Interview with Mary Morrison, National Coalition Against Domestic Violence, October 1981.

41. *Congressional Quarterly Almanac* 36 (1980): 445.

42. Several observers felt that, especially at the outset of the legislative effort, NCADV was too little concerned with developing inclusive coalitions reflecting compromise and differing perspectives.

43. Because executive leadership is often a crucial variable in the passage of controver-

sial legislation, the role of President Carter may have been a key factor. Some suggest that the President and his staff entered the fray too late to be effective. However, President Carter did support the bill with a letter to every member of the 96th Session of Congress (December 1979 for the House, August 1980 for the Senate). Members of his staff, including aides Sarah Weddington and Stuart Eisenstat, worked to gain support for the measure on the floor. The President requested $10 million funding in his proposed FY 1981 budget, largely in anticipation of the pending domestic violence legislation. Prolegislation groups maintained an activist, compromise-oriented position throughout the three-year lobbying period. It is difficult to see how they could have altered their strategy to combat the unforeseen conservative sweep of 1980 or anticipated the fear aroused by counterlobbying from right-wing groups, who made the bill a major target.

44. Steiner, *Futility of Family Policy*, pp. 171–72.

45. See Barbara Nelson, "Reviewing Child Abuse Policy in America: A Social Science Approach," *Policy Studies Journal* 9, no. 3 (Winter 1980): 459.

46. Interview with June Zeitlin and Jeannie Santos, October 1981.

47. *Response* 4, no. 4 (March/April 1981): 3, 6. These programs include the Comprehensive Employment and Training Program (CETA), Community Development Block Grants (CDBG), Community Service Administration (CSA, which funded local Community Action programs), Title XX of the Social Security Act, food stamps, Medicaid, Medicare, child nutrition, and AFDC (Aid to Families with Dependent Children). Legal aid from the Legal Services Corporation (and National Center on Women and Family Law) is threatened as well.

48. *Response* 4, no. 6 (July/August 1981): 10.

49. Hamos, *State Domestic Violence Laws*, pp. 61–62.

50. This section is drawn from an interview with Julie Hamos, chair, Illinois CADV and assistant state's attorney, Illinois, and from written material documenting the entire legislative campaign (19 September 1980–23 July 1981) that she kindly supplied.

51. Fees of $10 and $5 under the new legislation would raise approximately $1.3 million annually.

52. Hamos, *State Domestic Violence Laws*, pp. 1–2, 79–80, suggests a similar approach.

Part III

Visions and Strategies

15

Ellen Boneparth
Emily Stoper

Work, Gender, and Technological Innovation

Women's present disadvantage in the labor market stems in part from the fact that, unlike men, most women in the work force are also doing a second major job during many of their prime working years, namely, raising children and maintaining a home for their families. The demands of family work and paid work—as currently organized—are in competition with each other. While the twentieth-century trend is toward fewer children and more paid work for women, we would argue that the majority of women will not give up either family or paid work. Yet since women combine both kinds of work and men do not, and since paid work is organized on the assumption that all workers are men or can adapt to male work patterns, most women are at a perpetual of disadvantage in both the labor market and the home.

The government policies initiated in the 1960s and '70s relating to women's employment do not address this conflict between family roles and work roles. They focus, rather, on providing equity for women in work roles by eliminating sex discrimination and expanding employment opportunity. The Equal Pay Act of 1963, Title VII of the 1964 Civil Rights Act, and Executive Order 11246 on affirmative action, amended to include sex discrimination by Executive Order 11375 in 1967, seek to eliminate discriminatory employment practices in hiring, training, and promotion and open up more jobs to women.[1] These policies suffer from poor enforcement by government and often provide only limited coverage of female workers. Moreover, they often engender either direct opposition or indirect sabotage by employers in their implementation.

Efforts to reduce occupational segregation based on sex through nontraditional job training, education, and counseling often founder owing to limited funding and resistance from male-dominated management and unions. Today women are found in greater concentrations in clerical and sales and service occupations than when these policies were initiated.[2]

The failure of these policies to reduce the income gap between male and female workers or reverse the continuing trend of increasing occupational segregation based on sex have given rise to new policy demands in recent years such as equal pay for work of comparable worth and flexible work patterns.[3] While raising salaries in traditionally female occupations and providing workers with more flexible work hours are important goals, the position of women workers as a secondary labor force will not be changed without a major restructuring of work.

Several aspects of work must be restructured. First, the deep split between home and work must be healed. That split is not only spatial but is also one of values (home focuses on personal relationships, work on the expansion of wealth) and structure (home is a small group, work is likely to be a giant bureaucracy).

Second, the rigidity of work-time requirements—over a day, a year, a lifetime—must be eased, not only to accommodate family responsibilities but also to make room for flexible patterns of education and leisure and to facilitate work itself.

Third, work needs to be organized less hierarchically so that it is possible for people to have some autonomy and influence in the work setting without making the major commitments of time and education currently necessary for the assumption of management positions.

It is crucial that these changes occur not only in the work of women but in men's work as well, for a transformation that is limited to women's work would merely reinforce the sex segregation of the work force. And it is sex segregation rather than direct discrimination on an individual basis that has been the chief factor in keeping most women in the lowest-paid, least interesting, least influential jobs.

There is reason to believe that the kinds of changes necessary for the transformation of gender stratification could occur. Alvin Toffler, a noted futurist, predicts imminent changes in work because of the needs of a transformed Third Wave economy.[4] The "Third Wave," according to Toffler, is the new kind of economy that is emerging as the "Second Wave" (mass-production industry) recedes. (The "First Wave," which was preindustrial agriculture, receded earlier when the Second Wave emerged.) Whereas the Second Wave was characterized by mass production and rigid work discipline necessitated by the rhythm of the machine, the Third Wave is typified by computerized production tailored to individual preferences. Handling the Third Wave's vast flow of information requires a more flexible style of work and involves more creative problem solving and less repetitive drudgery.

E. F. Schumacher, a less optimistic futurist, has warned that if we fail to alter radically the scale of our organizations and technology, as well as the values underlying them, we risk ecological and spiritual disaster.[5] Yet the changes he calls for, involving decentralization and a renewed emphasis on the quality of human relationships rather than merely the standard of living, share certain consistencies with the needs of the Third Wave economy as described by Toffler.

In this chapter, four possible transformations of the organization of work are discussed: the content, styles, and values of work; the organization of work time; the split between home and work; and the exercise of power in the economy.

FOUR INTERLOCKING TRANSFORMATIONS

New Content, New Work Styles, New Values

During the industrial Second Wave, men typically worked in manufacturing and women performed support services for them in the home while raising future workers. There was a vast difference in the personal qualities considered desirable for each sphere. For the manufacturing sphere, emphasis was placed on the "masculine" qualities of physical strength and stamina, emotional self-control, logical and objective thought, initiative and aggressiveness (for bosses), practical problem-solving ability, technological ability, and a willingness to focus on efficiency of physical production for a profit, if necessary at the expense of the quality of human relationships (which could be called "ruthlessness").

For the home sphere, emphasis was placed on the "feminine" qualities or patience, nurturance, skill in smoothing interpersonal relations, aesthetic appreciation, attention to detail, concern about health and cleanliness, ability to do several things at once and willingness to subordinate one's own interests to those of the family group.

These character differences fit the needs of Second Wave work. The manufacture and marketing of "long runs" of identical products can be performed adequately with mostly masculine qualities. But as the economy shifts toward customized services and the manufacture of individualized items,[6] work consists increasingly of dealing with other people and of the coordination of vast amounts of data about individual needs and preferences. Some traditional "masculine" qualities, such as technological ability, are more important than ever; others, like physical strength, are becoming increasingly irrelevant. At the same time, many of the qualities needed to work effectively during the Third Wave are those traditionally considered feminine, most notably the ability to identify and respond to the needs of other persons.

We are not suggesting here that only women, or even mainly women, should be the ones who bring these "feminine" qualities into the work force, except possibly during a transition period. What we are saying is that because the qualities traditionally called "feminine" are central to Third Wave work, some of the rationale for discriminating against women (they are "emotional," parochial, and so on) may disappear.

The need for feminine qualities is already felt in services traditionally staffed by men. The masculine-dominated medical profession, for example, is notorious for its impersonality and its consequent inability to utilize the connection between the body and the mind, in understanding patients' emotional motives to be ill, in communicating with patients about the reasons for the treatment and the need to alter their personal habits, and in preventing illnesses resulting from emotional factors like stress. The rapid growth of a counterculture of medical care that includes the feminist self-help movement as well as acupressure, osteopathy, homeopathy, and many other approaches falling under the rubric of "holistic medicine" is testimony to the inadequacies of masculine medicine. Significantly, women have been particularly active in alternative health movements both past and present.[7]

The delivery of services, as well as the management of personnel, has been affected by a shortage of feminine values in the workplace. Workers increasingly are unwilling to accept a lack of autonomy and variety on the job. Prime Minister Pierre Mauroy of France has said, "There will be no industrial development in this country if working conditions and factory life continue to repel wage-earners."[8] The continuing use of Second Wave masculine structures—jobs set up for technical efficiency at the expense of the quality of work experiences—is less and less tolerable to workers whose values and expectations have been influenced by the Third Wave. People increasingly expect their work to be grounded in other values besides profit and growth.[9]

Management is beginning to respond to those expectations. Some business schools, for example, now focus on inculcating "people-oriented" even more than "task-oriented" management skills. Today, for many workers, "human factors" means not merely one of the determinants of the amount of profit but one of the central purposes of work: to nurture the human being who does it. As workers increasingly demand that work be fulfilling in and of itself, "feminine" values and experience will be seen not only as helpful in achieving the goals but also as a major source of the goals themselves.

Time Flexibility: Breaking Out of Lockstep

Many feminine values derive from women's work in the home, namely, sustaining the quality of human relationships and maintaining pleasant physical surroundings. Because most women need more flexibility in order to meet the needs of their families, they are often unable to take full-time jobs with rigid hours. An increase in time flexibility in every kind of work could make an enormous difference in diminishing the disadvantage in paid work of women (or men) who have major home responsibilities. If time flexibility at work were the norm for all workers, much of women's disadvantage in the job market could be altered.

In the 1970s a great deal of attention was given to two innovations in work-time schedules, flexitime and job sharing. Under flexitime, each employee has the right to choose, on a day-to-day basis, when his or her hours of work will begin and end, within certain limits. While the total number of hours worked are not necessarily reduced, an employee can choose at what time to start and end work within a band of two or three hours in the morning and afternoon; everyone has to work certain core hours in the middle of the day. In an advanced form of flexitime, employees can work extra hours on one day and then take time off on another day of their choice. The movement toward flexitime was encouraged when Congress passed Public Law 95–390, which suspended obstacles in labor legislation to such "banking" of hours. Some 12 percent of all U.S. employees were on flexitime in 1981, up from 6 percent in 1977.[10]

Flexitime is enormously popular with both employers and employees[11] since it increases productivity and at the same time makes it somewhat easier for employees to adjust their work schedules to their personal needs—including being somewhat more available when their children need them.[12] Studies of the impact of flexitime on family life, however, have yielded mixed results.[13] In its most limited form, flexitime does not always increase the amount of time parents spend with children.[14] However, more advanced forms of flexitime, accompanied by changing values, have the potential to do so.

In job sharing, the newest version of part-time work, two people hold a job that was formerly a single full-time job. True job sharing must be voluntary and must involve fringe benefits for both workers. Two workers sharing a job may "split" it—by hours or days, by task, by area of responsibility—or "share" it, working collaboratively but for fewer hours each.

Job sharing has the great virtue of opening up managerial and professional jobs that would otherwise be closed to people who only want to work part-time, such as many mothers of young children. It is, however, often difficult to obtain promotions from shared jobs because of the inability to claim full credit for one's work, the slower accrual of seniority, and the fact that higher-level jobs are rarely available on a job-sharing basis.[15]

Although both flexitime and job sharing are desirable innovations, neither will make much real impact in lessening the disadvantage of women in the job market. Flexitime, because it is limited and does not reduce the number of hours worked, does not go far enough in easing the burden of dual roles; job sharing, because it is done almost entirely by women, could even reinforce the sex segregation of the work force.

There are, however, several emerging trends in work-time flexibility that could make an enormous difference to women. Flexitime may someday be expanded around the clock, throughout the year, and even over the life span. The expansion of flexitime around the clock will become possible when many more people can work independently in their homes at computer terminals, as Alvin Toffler[16] predicts, or in neighborhood-based firms, as E. F. Schumacher[17] would like to see. If flexitime were expanded around the clock, one could clock in on one's computer and work could be done whenever the baby was sleeping or playing quietly, the spouse was available for child care, or the supermarkets were crowded. If the job involved teamwork with other people, core hours would still be necessary, but the timing of the flexible hours could vary: They might be late at night or very early in the morning, during off-peak hours for computer and power lines, the quietest time of the daily cycle, and the highest-energy time for "night people" or "early birds."

Existing trends, such as the move toward more night work[18] and the practice of an estimated one-quarter of all employed parents of arranging their work shifts so that one or the other parent can be at home with the children all or most of the time, are often unappealing to workers.[19] The expansion of flexitime around the clock would create the possibility for such patterns more often to be a matter of choice rather than uncomfortable adaptation.

An even more meaningful increase in work-time flexibility would come from the introduction of "flexiyear," which is now being tried in a few West German firms. Under flexiyear, every employee contracts annually with management for a certain amount of work time (hours per day, days per week, months per year, or however they want to break it down). Management can then plan to have a work force of appropriate size for slack and busy times, while workers can strike a continually changing balance between work time on the one hand, and time for family, education, travel, leisure, or starting small businesses on the other. The distinction between part-time and full-time workers, which has been so damaging to women, then breaks down into a series of gradations. Workers need no longer forfeit any claim to "seriousness" if they want to work less than every day or even every month.[20]

An even more radical idea along these lines, the "full cyclic plan," has been developed by Fred Best.[21] Under this plan, education, work, and leisure would be much more evenly distributed over the life span, instead of being concentrated in youth, the middle years, and old age respectively. Best's survey of workers' preferences found that 46 percent of workers preferred the full cyclic plan, while only 20 percent preferred the traditional breakdown. The third choice was a "moderate cyclic plan," concentrating education in the younger years but redistributing leisure and work over the middle and later years. One device for doing this would be sabbaticals (an option of every seventh year off, usually at reduced pay), a benefit now available to few workers other than teachers.

Work flexibility over the life cycle, if widely adopted, could make taking off a few years for childrearing a routine and easily accommodated work pattern, rather than the troublesome violation of work norms it is today. There is no solid reason to have the prime career-building years and the prime childrearing years (the twenties and thirties) coincide, as they usually do today. Individuals could be freer to set their own timetables for childbearing, education, and intensive work. Women could set timetables that eliminated much of their disadvantage as childbearers. And men could arrange to take time out for participation in childrearing with much less damage to their education and work.

The introduction of a plan such as Best's would also facilitate current trends toward lifelong education, early retirement, and childbearing over an increasingly wide age span, from fifteen to forty-five. Many people are already beginning to break out of the lockstep, in which education was completed by age twenty-four at the latest,[22] childbearing was over by the late twenties, and extended periods of leisure had to be postponed until at least sixty-two.

In the more highly technological economy of the future, possibilities may increase enormously for changes in both when we work and where we work.

The Home-Work Split

In the traditional view, women's work occurs in the home and men's work in the factory, fields, or office, a split brought about by the industrial revolution and the resulting trends toward urbanization, suburbanization, and consumerism. Yet, as we have seen throughout, the contemporary realities of work and family in the United States clearly belie the traditional view. Over half of the women in the United States are working outside the home, and the enormous expansion of the female work force in recent years has been due to the increasing employment of married women and mothers. The nuclear family ideal of breadwinner husband, homemaker wife, and children living at home is met by a very small percentage of the population.

Unfortunately, the new realities of work and family have had only a small impact on American institutions; as a consequence, there is a growing conflict in women's lives between home and work.[23] In an ideal world of the future, work and family roles would be integrated for both sexes. This integration could be accomplished by bringing either home closer to work or work into the home or neighborhood. In our society where the home is regarded as the nest, both the emotional womb and the heart of individuality, arrangements that remove activities associated with the home into the workplace are not likely to have wide appeal.

A more promising approach involves bringing paid work into the home. Such an arrangement already exists for a small number of professionals—writers, academics, and therapists, for example—and a small number of sales workers who conduct their business by telephone. Couples who are able to take advantage of such arrangements find that working at home allows them to share child care and housework more equitably.[24] They have more time for domestic responsibilities and leisure when freed from the demands of travel to and from work and from the time constraints of a nine-to-five job. Single heads of households are in even greater need of time away from the job to manage a home and family.

The technological revolution we have been discussing may stimulate the expansion of work at home as more and more workers—managers, professionals, white-collar workers, and technicians—utilize computer systems to perform their daily tasks. Home terminals, telephone hookups, teleconferencing, and many other imminent technological innovations provide opportunities for instant communications among workers and at the same time allow work to be done at decentralized locations.

A modification of the work-at-home approach might involve the creation of work in the neighborhood. The same technology that would enable workers to work at home could, in principle permit work at small neighborhood centers within walking distance from home, instead of commuting the U.S. average of 19 miles a day.[25]

Besides allowing women and men to better integrate their work and family roles, work at home or in the neighborhood could help break down the sexual division of labor. If men's work were located in women's traditional sphere, the home, the psychological distinction between women's work and men's work could be lessened. Men and women who performed paid work in the home might be more likely to share unpaid work there as well. It should not be expected, however, that child care and housework will become shared responsibilities overnight or automatically.

A new paradigm integrating home and work need not follow any single model. Bringing home to work through workplace child-care centers may be the only way to alleviate the home-work split for workers engaged in Second Wave production. Bringing work into the home or neighborhood may be appropriate only for those jobs that lend themselves to high technology. Whatever the approach, it is clear that women are becoming less willing or able to perform dual roles without assistance and that the traditional sexual division of labor no longer meets either individual or social needs. If the technology of tomorrow changes the way we work, that change can be used not only to increase productivity and efficiency but also to create better integrated human beings.

Control in the Organization: Democratic Structuring

The rebirth of feminism in the 1960s brought with it an interest in the restructuring of power relations to expand responsibility, participation, and accountability. In the early movement years, most of this discussion focused on feminist organizations rather than government bureaucracies, factories, and corporations.[26]

Yet the workplace may now be a possible locus for transformation. With more women working and moving into responsible positions in the public and private sectors, the womanpower exists to begin the process of change. Moreover, without changes in the control of work, women workers, despite their increasing numbers, will continue to constitute a secondary labor force.

How can workers exercise more power over their work lives? One approach followed in numerous enterprises in European countries has been to bring workers into management, either by having workers' representatives on boards of directors or by creating workers' councils to participate at the level of a particular firm and/or shop floor. The degree of worker participation in management varies considerably from country to country depending on the relative political power of the unions and the commitment of ruling parties to industrial democracy. It seems clear, however, that successful experiments with worker participation have resulted in greater identification of workers with their enterprises, as in Yugoslavia, and in high productivity, as in West Germany and Sweden.[27]

The American labor movement, because of its primary emphasis on economic rather than political issues, has shown little interest in worker participation in management. The growing alienation of American workers, however, suggests that worker control over jobs may soon become a more important issue. While male-dominated unions have paid little attention to alleviating the home-work split, women workers, who carry dual burdens of family and work roles, have begun to press demands for benefits such as child care, flexible work schedules, and more work autonomy.[28] As women workers organize around these issues, they may see worker control as a more efficacious route to achieving their demands than trying to pressure unions to respond to their needs. But worker control need not develop at the expense of unions; unions could take the lead in achieving greater economic democracy. They will need, however, a push from somewhere, and feminist pressure may be just the catalyst needed to move unions in this direction.

Other approaches to democratic structuring of organizations involve ownership and corporate social responsibility. While some businesses have tried to increase the workers' stake in the enterprise through profit sharing, these schemes have not addressed the fundamental division between owners and workers. Yet in the rare case where ownership has been restructured to include workers in a meaningful way, businesses have flourished.[29]

Even without any kind of real movement for worker control, greater work-time flexibility could have an impact on worker autonomy. To the degree that workers decide when to work they may have more freedom to decide how to organize the work, in what order to do different tasks, and what aspects of the work to devote more time to. Petty supervision is far more difficult if the supervisor simply cannot be there during all of the workers' hours.

Insofar as work is done by groups or teams, members will have to learn each other's jobs so that they can stand in for those not there. They may often be expected to take some responsibility for finding a replacement when they "flex out" for an hour, a day, a month, or a year. This expansion of job autonomy and responsibility for ordinary workers is especially significant for women because under present conditions they are often unwilling or unable to make the commitment in education or time to become management or participate in management as worker representatives.

INTERCONNECTIONS

These aspects of work—content, work styles, values, time flexibility, location, and control—are clearly interconnected, for a change in one will affect the others. Changes in the content of work, for example, could lead to a demand for changes in the schedule and location of work, each of these changes both reflecting and stimulating the desire of workers to have more control over their work lives. Likewise, new management styles and increasing worker participation in management could lead to new ways of structuring the times and places that work is performed—and the other way around.

These possibilities are suggested by changes in the underlying economy. Toffler and Schumacher, the two futurists on whose work this study is largely based, have contrasting views of the relationship between the underlying economy and the changes in work we have been discussing. Toffler sees them as the nearly inevitable result of the new possibilities created by the explosion in high technology; Schumacher, in contrast, sees them as the probable, but by no means inevitable, outcome of the moral confusion that has led to inappropriate technology, excessively large-scale institutions, and environmental destruction. Perhaps there are elements of truth in both; changes may occur because of past failures and/or future possibilities. Neither theorist, however, pays much attention to the barriers impeding these changes—except insofar as Schumacher implies that the moral blindness that led us into our present predicament will keep us from making the changes necessary to extricate ourselves. The next two sections examine the barriers to change and suggest ways to overcome them.

BARRIERS TO CHANGE

In order to travel from here to there, we must realistically examine the barriers on the road. A major barrier is that many persons do not subscribe to the values expressed or implied in the future world described above. We need to recognize that social arrangements have shaped, and continue to shape, our values. For those who lack the desire to organize their own time, major increases in time flexibility will be unwelcome. Both for people who like to be supervised and for those who like to supervise others, more work autonomy would be difficult to accept.

For others, the advantages of eliminating rush hour or the weekend rush to the beach will be offset by the lack of a sense of social rhythms and by the fact that family and friends may not be free from work at the same time they are. Moreover, more workers may experience anxiety over the allocation of their time or may find work worries seeping into leisure time, problems now experienced mainly by managers and professionals.

Some people might respond to the new time flexibility by working longer and harder, thus putting at a disadvantage those who seek a balance between education, work, leisure, and childrearing. On the other hand, in a period of change the absence of fixed norms may encourage the tendency in others to postpone work and thus get very little done. And given the present construction of work and family life, some people appear to like having work that involves little thinking or responsibility.

Similarly, for many workers, the home-work split may be valued. Going to work may be an opportunity to escape for many hours every day from the demands of family life and perhaps even from interpersonal relations as such (though this may simply postpone dealing with problems in these areas). Conversely, for many people, the idea of applying what seem to be work norms to housework and child care may arouse fears of loss of an emotional center for their lives and an emotional grounding for their children's personalities.

Schumacher may have the key to all these locked doors, though, in his emphasis on something like the golden mean. Just as there is a technology appropriate to each economic task, there may be a work style appropriate to each person. People whose values or character structures make them feel uncomfortable with the more modern organization of work need not be forced into the mold. For many years there will continue to be numerous tasks for which the older style of work organization is appropriate, just as small farms left over from the First (agricultural) Wave have continued to survive throughout the Second Wave in many places where they are most appropriate both socially and ecologically. Even Toffler points out that only a minority of workers in the next twenty or thirty years will have distinctively Third Wave work patterns.[30]

It is important to emphasize that efforts to change society's values regarding work must be accompanied by efforts to upgrade women's roles in the work force. After all, none of the transformations discussed in this study will necessarily alter the sexual division of labor. While the future may bring more work to the home and neighborhood, there is no guarantee that such work will involve both men and women. In fact, the arrival of "homework," if only performed by women, could further isolate women and intensify distinctions between men's and women's work.

Likewise, while the content of work may change through computerization, there is no assurance that the cybernation field will not become as sex segregated as most other occupations, with women working at low-level, low-paid jobs and men dominating the high-paid professional positions. Similarly, flexible work patterns, if adopted only by women, may make it more difficult to compete with men for top-level posts. If the location, content, and scheduling of work do not change the position of women in the work force, there is no reason to believe the efforts to achieve greater worker control and corporate responsibility will do anything to meet women's special needs as workers.

POLICIES TO START US ON THE ROAD

What is needed, then, is public policy that addresses the sexual division of labor as a future transformation of work that cuts across all other changes discussed above. Women workers must participate as equals in the technological revolution. Women must be reeducated on an equal basis with men in the new technologies.

We are already seeing women workers take on new responsibilities in word processing, computerized accounting, and a wide range of information-management tasks[31] that have been revolutionized by the new technology. Some women, formerly chained to the typewriter, have been freed to perform management tasks. But far more effort is needed to recognize and compensate women workers for their new skills and expertise. Women's work must be upgraded through comparable worth policies that remunerate office workers fairly for the increasingly complex tasks they perform.

A second need is for policies that assist organizations in adapting to new modes of work that benefit both male and female workers. Incentives must be provided to organizations to develop alternative work patterns. For example, Congresswoman Patricia Schroeder is sponsoring legislation, the Short Time Compensation Act of 1981, which encourages the states to make partial payments of unemployment compensation benefits to employees working under an employer-designed, union-approved, work-sharing plan. To reduce the home-work split the federal government could provide subsidies and tax benefits for introducing flexible work schedules over the week, year, and life span and for relocating workers in the home and neighborhood. "Sabbaticals" could be extended by allowing workers time off with government benefits in exchange for later retirements.

Finally, a new set of professionals is needed to organize and lobby for transformations in the world of work. Labor organizers are needed whose perspectives extend beyond those of contemporary union leaders. The push for higher wages and more fringe benefits, while important, does not meet all the needs of workers carrying a dual burden of work and family roles, nor does it speak to the need for organizations to become more democratic and socially responsible. The organizational development experts of the future must understand how the new technology can be used to heal the home-work split caused by the present organization of work.

These new professionals, many of them women, have already made an appearance in the environmental, women's and alternative work patterns movements, as well as in some of the more progressive labor unions. The socialization of women as nurturers, their experience with the dual burden of work and family roles, their subordinate positions in the work force, all make them especially suited to roles as advocates for humane changes in the world of work.

Perhaps most important, women must persuade policy makers and business leaders that the elimination of the sexual division of labor will foster rather than hinder economic well-being. Appropriate control of the new technology helps make that promise possible. A new political coalition built around the issue of work must be organized in order that women, men, and children may successfully navigate rather than drift on the waves of change.

NOTES

1. For a full discussion of the policies of the 1960s and '70s, see Jo Freeman, "Women and Public Policy: An Overview," in *Women, Power and Policy*, ed. Ellen Boneparth (Elmsford, N.Y.: Pergamon Press, 1982), pp. 48–67.

2. In 1961 women constituted 76 percent of clerical workers and 43 percent of sales workers, according to Francine D. Blau, "Women in the Labor Force: An Overview," in *Women: A Feminist Perspective*, ed. Jo Freeman (Palo Alto: Mayfield, 1979), p. 285. By 1975, these figures had risen to 80 percent of clerical and 45 percent of sales workers ("Women in the Labor Force: Some New Data Series," Bureau of Labor Statistics, October 1979). p. 3. See also Boneparth, *Women, Power and Policy*, p. 72.

3. Wendy Kahn and Joy Ann Grune, "Pay Equity: Beyond Equal Pay for Equal Work," and Emily Stoper, "Alternative Work Patterns and the Double Life," in Boneparth, ed., *Women, Power and Policy*, pp. 75–108.

4. Alvin Toffler, *The Third Wave* (New York: Bantam, 1981). Other works worth consulting on the future of work and family are Daniel Bell, *The Coming of Post-Industrial Society: A Venture in Social Forecasting* (New York: Basic Books, 1973); Jessie Bernard, *The Future of Motherhood* (New York: Penguin Books, 1974); Edward Cornish, ed., *1999 The World of Tomorrow: Selections from the Futurist* (Washington, D.C.: World Future Society, 1978); Robert T. Francoeur and Anna K. Francoeur, eds., *The Future of Sexual Relations* (Englewood Cliffs. N.J.: Prentice-Hall, 1974); Betty Friedan, *The Second Stage* (New York: Summit Books, 1981); Rhona Rapoport and Robert N. Rapoport, *Dual-Career Families Reexamined: New Integrations of Work and Family* (New York: Harper & Row, 1977), pp. 111–25.

5. E. F. Schumacher, *Small Is Beautiful* (New York: Harper & Row, 1973). Many feminist writers have expressed similar values. See Susan Griffin, *Woman and Nature: The Roaring Inside Her* (New York: Harper & Row, 1979); and Marge Piercy, *Woman on the Edge of Time* (New York: Knopf, 1976).

6. Toffler, *Third Wave*, pp. 179–93.

7. Barbara Ehrenreich and Deidre English, *For Her Own Good: 150 Years of the Experts' Advice to Women* (Garden City, N.Y.: Anchor Books, 1975).

8. *In These Times*, 30 September–6 October 1981, p. 9.

9. Daniel Yankelovich, *New Rules: Searching for Self-Fulfillment in a World Turned Upside Down* (New York: Random House, 1981).

10. Stanley D. Nollen and Virginia H. Martin, *Alternative Work Schedules, Part 1* (New York: AMACOM, 1978), p. 6; and Friedan, *The Second Stage*, pp. 271–72.

11. Some unions have opposed flexitime out of fear either that management will pressure workers to adapt their schedules to management's needs, thus reducing overtime income, or that management will fail to pass on to workers the rewards of increased productivity. These objections can be met by requiring that unions participate in the development and implementation of flexitime programs. For a more complete discussion of union resistance to alternative work patterns, see Stoper, "Alternative Work Patterns," pp. 100–104.

12. Pam Silverstein and Jozetta H. Srb, *Flexitime: Where, When and How*? (Ithaca, N.Y.: Cornell University Press, 1979).

13. Halcyone H. Bohen and Anamaria Viveros-Long, *Balancing Jobs and Family Life: Do Flexible Work Schedules Help*? (Philadelphia: Temple University Press, 1981); and unpublished study by Dr. Richard A. Winett, Institute for Behavioral Research, Silver Spring, Maryland. Bohen found that the main beneficiaries of flexitime were not mothers (who experienced equal amounts of stress on flexitime and on a standard schedule) but employed women without children, fathers with nonemployed wives, and single people. Winnett found that workers who had young children were somewhat more likely to use flexitimes and also that workers who changed their hours under flexitime increased their time with their children more than did workers who chose not to change their schedules.

14. Stoper, "Alternative Work Patterns," pp. 75–108.

15. Gretl S. Meier, *Job Sharing: A New Pattern for Quality of Work and Life* (Kalamazoo: W. E. Upjohn Institute for Employment Research, 1979) p. 84.

16. Toffler, *Third Wave*, p. 198.

17. Schumacher, *Small Is Beautiful*, p. 289.

18. Toffler, *Third Wave*, pp. 248–50. Between 15 percent and 25 percent of all employees in all technological nations are on night work.

19. Pamela Roby, *Child Care: Who Cares*? (New York: Basic Books, 1973), p. 115.

20. Willi Haller, *Flexyear: The Ultimate Work Hour Concept* (New York: Interflex, 1977); Bernhard Teriet, "Flexiyear Schedules—Only a Matter of Time?" *Monthly Labor Review*, December 1977, pp. 62–65.

21. Silverstein and Srb, *Flexitime*, p. 43.

22. *Statistical Abstract of the U.S. 1980* (Washington, D.C.: Bureau of the Census, 1980), p. 145. Only 8.1 percent of the population aged 25–34 were in school in 1979.

23. Constantina Safilios-Rothschild, *Women and Social Policy* (Englewood Cliffs, N.J.: Prentice-Hall, 1974), pp. 18–73; and Dolores Hayden, *The Grand Domestic Revolution: A History of Feminist Designs for American Homes, Neighborhoods and Cities* (Cambridge: MIT Press, 1981). The former gives a general discussion of social policies about home and workplace and the latter describes the history of efforts to rationalize and communalize housekeeping in order to free women for work and other pursuits.

24. Rapaport and Rapaport, *Dual-Career Families Reexamined*.

25. Toffler, *Third Wave*, p. 200.

26. Jo Freeman, "The Tyranny of Structurelessness," in *Women in Politics*, ed. Jane Jaquette (New York: Wiley, 1974), pp. 202–14; Nancy MacDonald, "The Feminist Workplace," and Alexa Freeman and Jackie MacMillan, "Building Feminist Organizations," in *Building Feminist Theory: Essays from Quest* (New York: Longman, 1981), pp. 251–67.

27. Paul Blumberg, *Industrial Democracy: The Sociology of Participation* (London: Constable, 1968), pp. 168–234; and G. David Garson, ed., *Worker Self-Management in Industry: The West European Experience* (New York: Praeger, 1977), pp. 25–96.

28. Stoper "Alternative Work Patterns," pp. 104–6.

29. Schumacher, *Small Is Beautiful*, p. 289. See also Martin Carnoy and Derek Shearer, *Economic Democracy* (White Plains, N.Y.: M. E. Sharpe, 1980).

30. Toffler, *Third Wave*, pp. 248–50.

31. Sharon Johnson, "Word-Processors Spell Out a New Role for Clerical Staff," *New York Times*, 11 October 1981, Sec. 12, p. 30. In 1980 there was one word processor for every ten clerical workers; the figure projected for mid-decade is one for every three.

16

Jean C. Robinson

Women in a Revolutionary Society: The State and Family Policy in China

The oppression of women and the transformation of the family have posed a policy dilemma for revolutionary states. In socialist societies this dilemma derives from a belief that the twin goals of socialist transformation—rapid economic development to establish the material base for a distribution of goods "according to need" and equality and the destruction of all society based oppressions including the liberation of women from domestic labor and the restructuring of the family[1]—cannot be achieved simultaneously.

These goals of socialism need not be in conflict, but the emphasis on economic transformation has meant that the goal of equality, especially with reference to women and the family, has been subordinated to economic change. While Marxism postulates that changes in material relations must occur before the superstructure is completely transformed, this does not mean that changes in the family or in sex relations cannot be pursued concurrently. Indeed, in the same way that women's emancipation for Marxists is tied to female participation in productive labor, the reform of the family is tied to its incorporation into progressive economic relations. Such a connection cannot occur until two conditions have been met: the economic relations of society and women's domestic labor must be socialized. With the inclusion of the family in the socialized, and thus public, realm of society, the family and women's place within it are *ipso facto* transformed.

Family policy making in socialist societies proceeds on the assumption that oppression exists within the family because it is privatized and isolated from society. The dawning of private property, according to Marx and Engels, created two societal spheres where women were confined to the private sphere, most notably represented by the family and its patriarchal authority and a sexual division of labor. The privatization of the family can be overcome, theorists have argued, by enabling women's full participation in public labor. The public-private split, by implication, is a major source of inequality and oppression in society.[2]

An earlier version of this paper was presented at the American Political Science Association annual meeting, 28 August–1 September 1980. I would like to thank Irene Diamond, Mary Lyndon Shanley, Berenice Carrol, Philip West, and Jack Bielasiak for their comments.

The seeming contradiction between goals of economic development and equality and the public-private distinction is clarified when socialist policies of family transformation and women's emancipation are examined. The relationship can be visualized in terms of Figure 16.1. Economic goals necessitate state intervention into the public sphere. Goals of equality, on the other hand, require state intervention in both public and private realms. Since women are by definition subsumed primarily within the private sphere, and since economic development is not predicated upon equality, a primary emphasis on economic goals does not lead to either family transformation or the emancipation of women from the isolated, privatized family. Socialist understandings of economic development do not typically include intervention in the private sphere.

FIGURE 16.1 State Intervention Policies with Regard to Women and Family

	Economic Goals	*Equality Goals*
Public Sphere	factory organization agricultural organization investment technological innovation education	equal-pay legislation equal rights act child care
Private Sphere	family planning	marriage reform equal rights act family planning child care

There is one exception to the apparent division between public and private spheres and economic and equality goals. Intrinsic to the question of family transformation and women's liberation is the deployment of sexuality to bolster state and/or societal goals. The connection of sexuality to public policies is most manifest in contraceptive and family planning programs, and in these areas the state has felt it proper to involve itself in the private realm. The one area in which socialist societies have *legitimized* intervention in the private sphere for purposes of economic development has been in efforts to increase or limit population growth. In those instances when the population is to be *limited* to overcome unemployment and imbalanced population-production ratios, the population policy has also been justified as leading to greater equality for women. In this case, incorporating the private sphere into the economic development schema necessitates reference to goals of equality so as to confer legitimacy on intervention into personal areas. Despite this one exception, examined later, it is apparent that until state intervention in favor of equality is as prominent as state control over economic development, the inclusion of the family—and thus women—in the public sphere is problematic.

Family policy in the People's Republic of China (PRC), as in other socialist societies, has tended to follow orthodox interpretations of Marxism-Leninism. Essentially the Marxist argument proposes that women's oppression can be erased only by the socialization of domestic labor and child care, which in turn is contingent on a strong economic base. The economic liberation of women occurs through their participation in public productive work. (Household labor, child care, nurturing, and fulfilling emotional needs are not considered to be socially productive by orthodox Marxists.) Once the economy reaches a certain (unspecified) level of advancement, a revolutionary family will be created based on equal and free relations where the familial unit is no longer isolated from society and where the drudgery associated with domestic work and childrearing is no longer a personal responsibility of individual wives and mothers.[3]

In practice, Marxist-Leninist systems have usually encouraged women's productive labor, but the remainder of the deterministic chain has not developed. Thus, while women may be liberated in terms of greater access to the economic sector, their roles within the family remain privatized and a source of oppression. The continuing emphasis on women as *primarily* wives and mothers ensures that their full participation in the public sector cannot be realized. The sexual division of labor continues unabated as long as economic determinism defines the development of family policy. While Marxist theoreticians have, of course, urged that forces other than economic be brought to bear on family transformation,[4] the basic model that connects family transformation to women's liberation through economic development continues to be followed in policy formulations in socialist societies.

Family policy in the PRC provides us with an example of policy making within these traditional parameters. While Chinese policy has been seen as a prototype for participatory, inexpensive, and transformative state intervention in family life, the Chinese family has retained intact much of patriarchal authority, as well as the sexual division of labor. Some of this traditionalism can be explained by the conservatism of rural China, but inconsistencies in implementing family policy and a reluctance on the part of the state to address the privatized existence of women must share the blame. Chinese family policies remain subject to the exigencies of economic development. Chinese women are urged to assist in economic development in the public sphere, often without the support of effective policies in the private sphere. The uniqueness of population policy in terms of addressing both economic and equality issue in China provides a compelling example of the force of economic imperatives.

WOMEN AND FAMILY POLICY IN CHINA, 1949–78

One of the first acts of the new state of the People's Republic of China was to promulgate the 1950 Marriage Law, which asserted that unions should be based on the free choice of both partners, on monogamy, and on equal rights for both sexes.[5] Minimum ages were established for marriage; and bigamy, child betrothal, concubinage, bride price, and hindering the marriage of widows were outlawed. Marriage was placed in the public sphere by stipulating explicit guidelines requiring registration of the marriage with local officials and by making the implementation of the law a responsibility of the population.[6] The Chinese Communist party (CCP) responded to the beliefs that traditional marriage customs had oppressed women by keeping them out of social production and by subjecting young women to the total dominance of men and mothers-in-law by calling for sweeping changes in marital relationships, kinship ties, and sex inequality.

The intended effect of the Marriage Law of 1950 was to still the use of women as items of exchange (as in child brides or bride price), to break down traditional parental authority by giving state sanction to free-choice marriages, and to encourage women's work outside the home and equal status inside the home. Between 1949 and 1953, the CCP launched large-scale campaigns to publicize and enforce the law, but by the end of this period it had become apparent that traditional values continued to dominate. In 1953 a new campaign was begun to educate both officials and the population with the intent to strengthen the law.

The Marriage Law did not stand alone in the revolutionary regime's effort to change traditional family structures. Through the Land Reform campaign (begun in 1950 and lasting thirty months) and land collectivization women were given their own shares of land, and thus some economic independence.[7] In addition, measures were taken to provide urban women with employment opportunities in industry; contributing to the household income gave these women an economic status comparable to that which peasant women gained through land reform.

The keystone of family policy in the PRC until 1955 lay in the combination of the Marriage Law, agrarian reform, industrialization, and collectivization of agriculture. Official statements in the media and party documents implied that the new family would be created through enlarging women's roles in production and ensuring women's equality in marriage. An effort was made to establish equality between husband and wife and to restructure the relationship between mother-in-law and daughter-in-law, a relationship that in the past had been characterized by unequal authority and tension.[8]

The ideal "new democratic family" was one in which husband and wife together raised children to become good citizens, while both participated in society as much as possible. In practice, men and women were evaluated on the basis of their contribution to the public sphere,[9] freer marriage and easier divorce were introduced, and reduction and the redistribution of domestic tasks within the family were encouraged.

Beginning in 1955, broad participation in all spheres of Chinese life were denigrated as inhibiting the development of production and rapid industrialization. The First Five-Year Plan (1953–57, but not instituted until 1955) emphasized the creation of a strong industrial base to be built upon the fruits of the now collectivized agriculture. Peasants' migration to the cities added to an already significant unemployment in urban areas.[10] Women's employment was thus seen as adding strains to the social and economic fabric. The state therefore encouraged women to become "new socialist housewives" by returning home to be full-time wives and mothers. The state began to impute social value to domestic labor. The media noted that women should be patient in expecting employment since it would be a long time before all women could be given jobs.[11] Nevertheless, housewives were told they were fulfilling an important, and economic, function:

> The family is a microcosm of society . . . . If the family is well run, those of its members who are taking part in socialist construction won't "look back over their shoulders" but devote themselves whole-heartedly to raising production . . . thrifty household management can greatly promote an increase in national production and can further the national, collective and family interests . . . .[12]

Giving social value to housework rationalized the regime's failure to employ women by implying that domestic labor was productive labor and thus advantageous to women's emancipation. Articles such as "Doesn't doing the housework and caring for the children count as work?" gave superficial value to domestic work but did not signal a rethinking of the sexual division of labor. The CCP stated:

> By suggesting that a husband should take the revolutionary attitude of equality toward his wife, do we mean that both husband and wife should divide housework equally, or that the husband should devote more of his time and effort to housekeeping and attend to his wife's other needs? No, this is not so. If housework is divided in this way, it cannot be considered as true equality for the key to the question does not lie in the form of household chores but rather in the attitude of the husband toward the wife after he is back home.[13]

Clearly, domestic work remained women's work. During this period the ideal of the new family had not changed, but the effect of the policies hindered transformation of the family by seeing women primarily as reproducers in privatized structures.

In this period a new line *was* proposed in support of population control. Until 1956, the PRC leadership had held that overpopulation was a Malthusian myth perpetuated by capitalists who used it as a justification for labor exploitation. The CCP argued that large populations were beneficial to economic development. This perspective was reassessed when China began suffering under the double brunt of food shortages and high unemployment. Birth control education and devices were disseminated on an uneven basis in 1956, but a major family planning campaign was aborted when the Great Leap Forward was initiated.

The Great Leap Forward, from 1958 to 1960, represented yet another swing in family policy. The economic and social programs of the Great Leap emphasized the participation of all members of society in the effort to modernize the economy. Rural people's communes were praised not only as a major step toward communism in the realm of economics but also as the road to women's complete emancipation. By providing collectivized services that replaced privatized domestic labor, the new communes freed women to engage in all forms of agricultural and primitive industrial activity. In the cities, factories, enterprises, and residential communities established maternity and child health centers and child-care facilities. In both urban and industrial areas women were identified primarily as participants in public life; their domestic roles were secondary, and indeed their future was to lie in equal participation with men in production. These Great Leap policies provide a rare example of PRC extension of economic development into the private sphere, and indeed the justifications for the radical policies emphasized the necessity of raising consciousness as a prerequisite to social modernization.[14]

The socialization of housework in this period was short-lived. By 1959, economic problems had begun to develop and criticism of communal kitchens specifically had surfaced. The state, through the All-China Women's Federation (ACWF), warned that "the socialization of housework does not mean there will be no housework at all. At present, women still have to do some; they will be required to do so in the future."[15] By 1961, participation in communal mess halls and service stations had declined, and women reassumed the responsibility for household chores. This reprivatization resulted from the general economic failures of the period, which the leadership took as a sign that China did not yet have the technological ability to free women from domestic labor. The Great Leap's contention that lack of expertise could be overcome by the enthusiastic participation of men and women had encouraged women to participate in production, but the level of collective welfare proved inadequate to meet the needs of replacing women's labor in the family. Further transformation of the family had to wait.

As communal service facilities were dismantled and technical expertise in employment was emphasized, the number of jobs available to women decreased. Women once more were told that their duties as wives and mothers were glorious and patriotic; efficiently performed domestic labor contributed to overall productivity by the nurturing of workers. The ACWF publication, *Zhongguo Funu* (*Women of China*), praised the model wife who "never bothers her husband with domestic affairs, for she feels he has enough responsibilities outside the home."[16] Publishing articles such as "How to Choose a Husband" and "What Do Women Live for?" the magazine promoted the family as a relationship where women serve husbands and children, and by keeping them happy, promote socialism.

While women were encouraged to find social fulfillment within the family, the state also delineated the need for limiting family size. Contraceptive devices were widely distributed, abortion (legalized in 1958) became easily obtainable, and propaganda focused on the dangers inherent in early marriage and excess childbirth for both men and women. Public discussions about sexuality, which had been rare in post-1949 China, addressed the benefits accruing both to the state and to individuals if marriage, and thus sexual intercourse, was delayed. The assumption was that the repression of sexual intercourse meant that more energy was available for work and study. Men, it was said, could suffer from "overindulgence of the sexual impulse"; early pregnancy was said to lead to calcium deficiencies, cancer, and other health risks to women.[17] In an era of unemployment and recovery from economic disasters, the PRC removed childbirth from the private arena because family size was viewed as integral to the development of the national economy.[18]

During the Cultural Revolution (1966–76), the special needs of women were ignored in favor of viewing women as potential revolutionary successors. "Destroy the old and establish the new" was the basis for attacking male authority in the family, traditional wedding customs, and homemaking as women's primary task. Women were expected both to work for socialism and to manage their family chores, but the emphasis was on the former. More stress was put on the training and appointment of women leaders, but little attention was given to "personal" interests such as childbearing, childrearing, and domestic roles.[19] Nevertheless, efforts were made to reestablish canteens, creches, and other services so that the family would be served without taking all of women's labor.[20] A campaign was launched in the name of equal pay for equal work.[21]

During the Cultural Revolution, the ACWF was dissolved as an active women's organization. Their mistakes included

> displaying the signboard of solving so-called personal problems of women, *Zhongguo Funu* publicized revisionism and tried to make the women's class viewpoint blurred and lead women to show no concern over major state affairs but merely to show concern over the life of their individual families. . . . It tried to dissolve the women's revolutionary spirit and make a breach in China for the comeback of capitalism, the individual and the private.[22]

The attack on women's domestic concerns did not result in the transformation of the family but rather ensured the continuation of the status quo.

WOMEN AND FAMILY POLICY: THE FOUR MODERNIZATIONS

With the death of Mao Zedong in 1976 and the arrest and criticism of the "Gang of Four" in the following years, the stage was set for intraparty struggles over the direction of social and economic policy in China. Beginning in 1978 with the institutional transition to the Four Modernizations, China's leaders have placed foremost emphasis on modernization of the economic structure, technology, science, education, and national defence as a means of reaching communism.[23] This has meant a new stress on education, on population control, and on the production of consumer goods. As part of its effort to increase productivity and raise living standards, the state has reexamined its family policies. A new marriage law, planned parenthood policies, and increased efforts to involve women in production have been implemented. There has been renewed discussion on family reform, especially in terms of the continued existence of bride price, traditional (and expensive) wedding ceremonies, patrilocality, the desire for sons, and domestic labor.

Alongside the new effort to win women's hearts (and reproductive organs!) has come a resurgence of the effort to redefine the relationship of the family to the economy and society. In the spirit of "walking on two legs," the state is making some effort to provide support services for families where both husband and wife work, but at the same time, women are expected to be self-reliant in solving problems of child care, cooking, cleaning, and other aspects of domestic labor.

The new constitution of the PRC, passed in 1978 by the Fifth National People's Congress, stipulated:

> Women enjoy equal rights with men in all spheres of political, economic, cultural, social and family life. Men and women enjoy equal pay for equal work. Men and women shall marry of their own free will. The State protects the marriage, the family, and the mother and child. The State advocates and encourages family planning.[24]

The constitution inaugurated a new phase of state intervention: reproduction, family size, and even the spacing of children are now within the domain of the public sphere.

In mid-1979 the decision was made to proceed with a revised population policy that called on couples to marry later and have fewer children. Both urban and rural couples were encouraged to take pledges to have no more than one child. Because the state expected resistance to the one-child policy, it suggested that all provinces provide a system of benefits for couples who pledged to restrict the number of their children. The benefit system was crucial in rural areas where family income was dependent on the number of workers in the household and suffered when daughters left home upon marriage. In such households the number of children could determine the prosperity of the family. The proposed system consisted of two parts. In the countryside rural couples who pledged to have only one child and took contraceptive measures were to be awarded additional monthly work points, given the same grain ration as two-child families, and given the same size plot and housing as two-child families. Urban areas provided a fixed stipend to each couple using birth control methods, allocating living space to one-child families as if it were a two-child family, giving the single child special consideration for admission to schools and application for jobs, and providing parents with a higher than normal retirement pension.[25]

The party and state have developed complex incentive systems for controlling marriage and childbearing decisions including denying university, college, or technical school admission to married individuals and expelling students who give birth to or father a child.[26] Rewards for having one child and penalties for having more than one child have been increased: a one-child mother is given extended postnatal leaves, full payment of pregnancy expenses, free schooling, and medical care for the child, in addition to the rewards listed above. If a couple has more than one child, the mother forfeits not only pregnancy and postnatal leaves but in some cases must pay all medical charges for prenatal and delivery services. The family may be charged a 15 percent excess child fee until the child reaches the age of fourteen.[27]

Despite the fact that both men and women are legally responsible for population control, evidence suggests that it is women who bear the final responsibility. In most instances, women are responsible for contraception, as evidenced by the use of IUDs, oral contraceptives, and spermicides. While both tubal ligation and vasectomy are provided free of charge by the state, the majority of contraceptive operations are for tubal ligations. Finally, while both husbands and wives have been punished for having excess children, women seem to be punished more severely. In one case, where both husband and wife were CCP members and yet had a fourth child, the husband received a penalty of not receiving bonuses for one year; the wife was denied bonuses for three years.[28]

The question of equality between men and women has been part of the population policy effort. The Chinese state has criticized the preference for sons that leads to multiple pregnancies until a male child is born. Such thinking is deemed "old" and "feudalist,"[29] and combating these ideas appears to have led to an increase in the number of abortions undergone by women, with a significant rise in abortions for unmarried women. This increase can be attributed to the more strictly enforced legal ages for marriage and to the overzealousness of government officials to fulfull targets for population decrease.[30] While abortion is not viewed by the state as a contraceptive device, recent reports from provincial newspapers suggest that some women are coerced into having abortions. This state control over abortion has led to conflicts among men; government cadres have been attacked by irate peasant husbands after the wives were "encouraged" to have abortions.[31] The effect of the family planning policies has been to undermine the autonomy of women while relegating the conflict to one between husbands and the state. Simultaneously, the consequences of women's practical responsibility for contraception has absolved men of most accountability in sexual matters. While this has not been the intent of the family planning policies (and indeed research on male contraceptive is continuing in the PRC), in reality women's control over their sexuality has been limited by the effects of the policies. Thus, despite an attempt to incorporate women's equality within the family planning program, the evidence suggests that the *implementation* of policies has sustained inequalities, at least in terms of sexual relationships.

Sexual autonomy, however, has not been an issue that the state or media has addressed in the context of contraception. The deployment of sexuality in China, in contrast to the West, contains fewer objects of discourse; thus limiting the number of births is linked, as it was in the 1960s, only to increased health benefits for women and children. Even more obvious has been the connection drawn between family planning and increased prosperity of the household. The interventions of the state into the personal lives of men and women have been based primarily on the need to secure control over those areas (e.g., population) determined to affect significantly material forces and production in the nation.[32]

In sharp contrast to state intervention for population control, there has been little resolution of problems associated with domestic labor and child care. Instead, women are held responsible for creating the domestic arrangements that will permit their participation in "socially productive labor." This has led to problems for younger women workers, who are considered to be less productive, and thus earn less, because of their family responsibilities. The situation has exacerbated the continuing inequality in the workplace, where equal pay for equal work is still a *goal*, not a reality. Formal response to this problem has been to educate young married women to pay more attention to work and arrange their family responsibilities so that they will not intrude in labor. A woman official in a Beijing iron and steel plant has given this analysis of the problem and its resolution:

> Our department has generally found that unmarried women workers and middle-aged ones whose children are grown work with greater enthusiasm than the young married women. This is because the latter are weighed down by the responsibilities of taking care of their children and by household chores, their attendance and studies are affected. Many factories have conducted education drives to help them correctly handle problems of love, marriage and family planning and to encourage them to properly deal with their household affairs so that their work and studies will not be hurt.[33]

There is a tension between women's resolution of their "household affairs" and state assistance to families. For instance, disagreements between mother-in-law and daughter-in-law are resolved through the employment of the young wife,[34] but the needs of working mothers are not met with adequate child-care facilities.[35] In the province of Jiangsu, for instance, a *goal* had been set that by the end of 1981, nurseries would care for 70 percent of the children of urban workers and 60 percent of peasant children. The goal was not realized; in the meantime, mothers arranged with retired workers living in their apartment building, grandparents, or older children to take care of infants and babies. As Parish and Whyte noted in their discussion of village child care,

> collective nurseries are seen as freeing more women for outside work and providing collective political and moral training not available in the home. However the superiority of this kind of care is not seen as sufficient to warrant a major campaign to universalize collective pre-school care.[36]

The state has acknowledged that women are saddled with dual responsibilities and has responded with two types of policies: One encourages factories, enterprises, and residential committees to establish support services for working couples within the context of self-reliance; the other encourages men to help with domestic tasks. Both policies have been much more effective in urban areas, where community resources and attitudes are more advanced.

Residential and neighborhood committees have established service groups that clean, sew, cook, wash and iron, shop, babysit, and do household repairs for set fees. These service units, staffed by retired workers, unemployed housewives, and youth, are supported by neighborhood factories as well as by user fees. Local governments have encouraged the establishment of such units, but the problem remains that such services help only those couples who can afford to pay for the assistance.[37] The net effect is a reduction of the double burden for only small segments of the urban population.

In the countryside, household tasks and child care remain the responsibility of individual women. Because fieldwork is flexible, infant care and feeding is somewhat easier to manage, but because of the greater poverty in the countryside, few communes provide extensive support services.[38]

An alternative to neighborhood support services is to redistribute work within the family. Here there has been even less effort to challenge the sexual division of labor. Although official policy promotes the ideal that men should share in housework, this is not a major concern of current policy. Several urban factories have held forums to encourage male workers to share in household duties.[39] In communes, husbands have been reported to share the housework when wives earned as many work points as they did.[40] Women's Federation officials have begun a new campaign "to stress that husbands and wives should share housework,"[41] but only articles in honor of International Women's Day and in *Zhongguo Funu*[42] have pursued the topic.

There is a long tradition of a sexual division of labor in domestic tasks in China. Care of children, cleaning, cooking, fetching water, and similar tasks have been considered beneath the dignity of men. Parish and Whyte have reported that in villages of southern China, where both men and women work in the production brigades, at night the husbands sit and talk while the wives cook, clean, fetch water, and work on the family plot. Although customs are more advanced in cities, only recently have husbands begun to help (not necessarily share) in the housework. Reports suggest that younger couples in urban areas are forging new patterns.

Editorials in honor of International Women's Day noted that household duties and manual labor mean that women's lives are more restricted than the lives of men. Both men and women are urged to work harder to develop technology because only advances in science and technology can socialize housework.[43] Yet women are told that

> it is their unshirkable responsibility to train and educate the children and youngsters so that they might become healthy both physically and mentally. There is a saying 'the hand that rocks the cradle governs the nation.' Let us women set a good example for our children and shoulder the sacred duty of bringing them up in the proper way to become reliable successors to our cause of national construction.[44]

In policies affecting child care and domestic labor, just as in family planning policies, the rationale given by officials is that the policies must be effective, must complement the achievement of the Four Modernizations, and must help maintain social order. The state has enunciated a policy that theoretically supports family transformation and women's emancipation but that fails to accomplish its goals because of a deferral of issues of equality in favor of economic growth.

The new family policies of the PRC are contained in the state's call to have people establish "revolutionary, democratic and harmonious new families." Helpfulness, thrift, industry, equal respect, and an effort between husbands and wives to share the housework and the raising of children are the key words in the policy.

Unlike the family planning policies, however, there is no legal benefit or penalty attached to the management of child care and domestic labor. In pragmatic terms, pursuit of equality has been a fiction. Transformation of the family is held to be impossible until science and technology create the conditions for the socialization of housework.

CONCLUSION

It has been noted that the goal of Chinese family policy is not the destruction of the family but rather the elimination within it of "feudal" elements.[45] It should be apparent that much of the "feudal" tradition remains intact. Women's responsibility for child care and household labor suggests that the traditional division of labor continues within the family. The propaganda efforts to convince and reward parents to have just one or two children (even if both are girls) make it clear that sons are more valued than daughters.

The glaring disparity between the major efforts put into birth control and the rather minor attempts to redistribute the sexual division of labor within the family suggest that only when practices directly affect the achievement of economic goals will the Chinese leadership dare to act in ways that might upset the balance between traditional and revolutionary forms of family life. Family planning is perceived to be of crucial importance for the achievement of the Four Modernizations, so the party and state have pursued a transformative birth control policy. In contrast, the PRC has defined household work and domestic divisions of labor as only indirectly affecting economic growth. Childbearing is considered to be within both the domain of public policy *qua* economic development *and* political intervention; housework is within the domain of public policy *qua* equality *but* outside the domain of political intervention. In effect, the domestic division of labor is reduced to the nonpolitical and personal. The state has defined it away until such time as attitudes and the economic base change.

Earlier I suggested that the implementation of family policies in socialist societies has been dependent on a view of development that calls for economic development before issues of equality can be fully addressed. This perspective has led to an unwillingness on the part of the state to confront the privatization of women and the family unless such action is seen as directly beneficial for economic development. The case of family planning in particular demonstrates the willingness of the Chinese state to intervene in the private sphere when such intervention can be justified in terms of economic growth. Indeed, family planning may lead to greater equality within the household because women are freed from years of childbearing and rearing. However, such intervention in China has also meant greater state control over childbearing and abortion, which itself limits women's sexual autonomy. An important issue that remains to be addressed by feminists and social planners alike is the relationship between sexual autonomy and other forms of liberation. Intrinsic to this question are the interconnections of genuine sexual freedom and scientific or commercial discourses on sexuality that may impose new constraints on women's lives. Thus it would appear that Chinese women are free from the commercialization, but not the economization, of their sexuality.

If data from the American experience are correct, then having smaller families is no guarantee of equality. Similarly, the American experience suggests that, despite Chinese claims, technology does not effectively reduce household labor,[46] nor does it break down the distinctions between the public and private spheres. Instead, the Chinese experience during the Great Leap Forward and some of the current efforts in the PRC suggest that technology and population control are necessary but not sufficient conditions for removing inequalities. The acknowledgment that attitudes must be changed and domestic labor be socialized complete the conditions necessary to transform the family and ensure that women become full participants in the society. Given the economic imperatives of revolutionary societies, these conditions must be linked to economic development as well. In other words, what will change inequality is a perception that the existing division of labor has a negative effect on production relations and forces.

It is at this point that the seeming contradiction between goals of economic development and equality is shown to be vacuous. Experiences in China prove that women contribute to production in a wide variety of ways, but women's participation in production can help create a stronger economic base only when the familial issues have also been addressed. A revision of the inequality in the sexual division of labor in the family can directly contribute to both economic development and the equality.

There are several ways in which this assertion can be established. Currently in the PRC there is an awareness of the negative impact of the sexual division of labor on women's productivity. Women in China have also acknowledged the utility of putting women's demands for equality in terms of economic development issues; since the promulgation of the 1980 Marriage Law, ACWF cadres have been discussing the ways in which women's organization can mobilize to protect women's interests while enhancing productivity.[47] The importance of mobilizing and organizing women has long been recognized as a tactic by revolutionary socialist parties; the same tactic can be used to resolve the continuing problems women face in postrevolutionary societies. Mobilizing women may help to make a discourse on the sexual division of labor possible. At the same time, an analysis of the costs to the state of failing to socialize domestic labor will make the issue an economic rather than an ideological one. In China, as in most developing and Third World countries, it is the economic imperatives of development which must be addressed. When the state begins to tackle the economics of the public-private split, then the pursuit of economic development will not be at the cost of women's equality.

NOTES

1. See, for instance, Mao Zedong, "Report of an Investigation into the Peasant Movement in Hunan," in *Selected Works of Mao Tse-tung*, vol. 1 (Peking: Foreign Languages Press, 1972); and V. I. Lenin, "From a Great Beginning," in Lenin, *The Emancipation of Women* (New York: International Publishers, 1966).

2. Friedrich Engels, *The Origins of the Family, Private Property and the State* (New York: International Publishers, 1973), pp. 137–39, 221.

3. See Aleksandra Kollontai, *Communism and the Family* (Highland Park, Mich.: Sun Press, 1976), p. 14.

4. See, for instance, Leon Trotsky, *Women and the Family* (New York: Pathfinder Press, 1970), pp. 20–26. Kollontai, *Communism*, pp. 8–10; and Lenin, "Great Beginning," pp. 63–64.

5. See *The Marriage Law of the People's Republic of China* (Peking: Foreign Language Press, 1950).

6. Delia Davin, *Woman-Work: Women and the Party in Revolutionary China* (Oxford: Clarendon Press, 1976), pp. 84–86; and William Parish and Martin K. Whyte, *Village and Family in Contemporary China* (Chicago: University of Chicago Press, 1978), passim.

7. See Charles Cell, *Revolution at Work: Mobilization Campaigns in China* (New York: Academic Press, 1977), passim; Davin, *Woman-Work*, pp. 115–116; and Elisabeth Croll, *Feminism and Socialism in China* (London: Routledge and Kegan Paul, 1978), pp. 239–42.

8. For the classic discussions of traditional family and kinship in China, see Marion Levy, Jr., *The Family Revolutionary China* (New York, Octagon Books, 1971), esp. pp. 147–51; and Maurice Freedman, *Family and Kinship in Chinese Society* (Stanford: Stanford University Press, 1970). Also see Croll, *Feminism and Socialism.*

9. Davin, *Woman-Work*, p. 108. Also Deng Yingzhao, "The Women's Movement in China," *People's China*, 1 March 1982.

10. See Christopher Howe, *Employment and Economic Growth in China* (Cambridge: Cambridge University Press, 1971), p. 149.

11. "The Problem of Female Employment Can Only Be Met Gradually," *Jiefang Ribao* (*Liberation Daily*), 13 December 1956.

12. Zhang Yun, "Build Up the Country Economically, Manage the Household Thriftily and Struggle for Socialist Construction," in *Documents of Third National Congress of Chinese Women* (*Zhongguo funu disanci quanguo daibiao dahui zhongguo wenxian*) (Peking: 1957). Also cited in Davin, *Woman-Work*, p. 66.

13. *Renmin Ribao* (*People's Daily*), 8 January 1956.

14. "People's Communes—the Way to Women's Complete Emancipation," in *Women of China* (December 1958. n.p.); "Peking Housewives Plunge Into Production," in *Chinese Women in the Great Leap Forward.* (Peking: Foreign Languages Press, 1960); and Mao Zedong, *A Critique of Soviet Economics*, trans. Moss Roberts (New York: Monthly Review Press, 1978).

15. *Zhongguo Funu*, 16 May 1959.

16. "Team Leader Yin has a Good Wife," *Women of China*, March 1962, pp. 1–2.

17. See John Aird, *Population Policy and Demographic Prospects in the PRC* (Washington, D.C.: Department of Health, Education, and Welfare, n.d.), pp. 289–91, for a startling collection of Chinese media presentations on the negative effects of early marriage and childbirth.

18. Fu Lienchang, "The Positive Significance of Planned Families," *Zhongguo Funu* 4 (1 April 1963), in *Selections from Chinese Mainland Magazines* (*SCMM*) 364 (13 May 1963): 38; and Chung Cho-huan, "This Is Not an Embarrassing Thing or an Unimportant Matter," *Nanfang Ribao* (1 December 1963), in *Selections from China Mainland Press* (*SCMP*) 3128 (30 December 1963).

19. "Treat the Relationship between Work, Children and Household Chores in a Re-

volutionary Spirit," *Zhongguo Funu*, no. 1 (1963); also see Croll, *Feminism and Socialism*, pp. 311–16; and "Socialism Brings Women Genuine Emancipation," *Women of China*, no. 2 (1966).

20. "Welfare Services for Peking Textile Workers," *Xinhua News Agency*, 9 March 1973; "A Saleswoman's Home Life," *China Reconstructs*, January 1973.

21. "Seriously Carry Out the 'Equal Work, Equal Pay' Policy between Men and Women," *Xian Lian*, 25 May 1964; "How Our Village Got Equal Pay for Work," *China Reconstructs*, March 1975.

22. Editorial, *Zhongguo Funu*, 10 July 1966.

23. Deng Xiaoping, "On Science and Modernization," *Beijing Review*, 24 March 1978. Also "Carrying Out the Four Modernizations Is the Biggest Politics," *Renmin Ribao*, editorial, 11 April 1979.

24. "The Constitution of the People's Republic of China," *Chinese Law and Government* 11, nos. 2–3, p. 171.

25. "Nu kexue jiamen de xinyuan," (The Wishes of Our Women Scientists), *Guangming Ribao*, 7 March 1980, p. 1.

26. "Birth Rate Reduced in Two Shanghai Wards," *Wenttui Bao* (18 January 1980), p. 1.

27. "*Nanfang Ribao* Details Guangdong Planned Parenthood Rules," *Nanfang Ribao* (13 February 1980) in *Joint Publication Research Services (JPRS)* 75291 (12 March 1980): 50.

28. "Bejing Couple Suffers Economic Sanctions for Fourth Child," *FBIS-Daily Report: China*, 21 April 1980.

29. *FBIS-Daily Report: China*, 25 March 1980; also "Use Progressive Scientific and Cultural Knowledge to Equip the Broad Masses of Women" (*Yong Xianjinde Kexue wen hua zhishi de wuzhang guangda funu*), *Guangming Ribao*, 8 March 1980, p. 1.

30. Katherine Chiu Lyle, "Planned Birth in Tianjin," *China Quarterly* 83 (September 1980): 559–61.

31. See, for instance, "Guizhou Officials Punished for Birth Control Failures," *Guizhou Bibao* (22 June 1980), translated in *FBIS* (27 June 1980): Q–1.

32. Xinhua News Service, 2 February 1980. While sexuality is still not a topic for discourse in China, it should be noted that the lack of commercialization of sex there has the effect of allowing sexuality, in some ways, to be a very personal and individual mode of human expression. This contrasts strongly with the Western experience where sexuality has become a marketplace commodity. For further discussion of these issues, see Michel Foucault, *The History of Sexuality*, vol. 1 (New York: Vintage, 1980); and Siecus Report, "The Walls of China," vol. 10, no. 2 (November 1981).

33. "Chinese Women Discuss Life and Work," *Beijing Review* 10 (9 March 1980): 20.

34. "Jobs Found for Unemployed Youth in Beijing," *Beijing Ribao*, 18 November 1979, p. 1.

35. "Yunnan Nursery Work Conference," *JPRS* 75255 (5 March 1980): 76; "Jiangsu Childcare Work," *JPRS* 75023 (29 January 1980): 99; "Guangdong Vice-Governor Calls for Improving Children's Nurseries," *FBIS-Daily Report: China*, 23 April 1980.

36. Parish and Whyte, *Village and Family*, p. 392.

37. Tan Manni, "Lightening the Load for Working Mothers," *China Reconstructs*, March 1980, p. 22.

38. See Parish and Whyte, *Village and Family*; also author's research in China, May–July 1982.

39. "Employment Opportunity," *Beijing Review* 10 (9 March 1979): 20.

40. "Equal Pay for Equal Work," *Beijing Review* 10 (9 March 1979): 21.

41. "Love and Marriage," *Beijing Review* 10 (9 March 1979): 22.

42. The significance of publishing articles in *Zhongguo Funu* or in honor of International Women's Day is limited. *Zhongguo Funu* reaches an audience of women who may need to be persuaded that husbands should share domestic labor. On International Women's Day in China, every newspaper is replete with articles on women's liberation, the Women's Federation, prominent female scientists and leaders. During the other 364 days of the year, reportage on the women's question is slim. For policies redistributing domestic labor to be fully implemented, there needs to be much wider dissemination and discussion among men as well as women.

43. "Use Progressive Scientific and Cultural Knowledge"; "Glorious Fighting Day for Women Throughout the World," editorial, *Renmin Ribao*, 8 March 1980, p. 1.

44. "Glorious Fighting Day."

45. Parish and Whyte, *Village and Family*, p. 155; Judith Stacey, "Toward a Theory of Family and Revolution: Reflections on the Chinese Case," *Social Problems* 26 (5 June 1979): 500.

46. See Heidi Hartmann, "The Family as the Locus of Gender, Class and Political Struggle: The Example of Housework," *Signs—Journal of Women in Culture and Society* 6, no. 3 (Spring 1981): 382–85.

47. See "Zhejiang Women's Group Urges Protection of Rights," *Hangzhou-Zhejiang Provincial Service*, in *FBIS-China* (12 December 1980), pp. 0–4; "Gansu's Song Ping Addresses Women's Federation," *Gansu Provincial Service* (4 December 1980) in *FBIS-China* (5 December 1980), p. T–1; and "Kang Keqing Addresses Women's Federation Executive Committee," *Xinhua*, in *FBIS-China* (24 October 1980), p. L–2.

17

Ruth Nielsen

Family Responsibilities as a Labor Market Issue: A Scandinavian Perspective

The labor market constitutes the main focus of most public policy concerned with women in the Scandinavian countries. This is increasingly true also in respect to women's role in the family. Measures are taken to help integrate women's family role with their role in paid employment and to promote a more equal sharing of family responsibilities between the sexes. But only on rare occasions does the state address family problems for their own sake, with no view to their labor market implications.

Two major strategies for handling family responsibilities in a labor market perspective can be discerned in the policies pursued in the Scandinavian countries. The first consists of enabling women to fulfill a double role as housewife and paid employee. This can be furthered by increasing sexual segregation both in the family and in the labor force. Women can more easily function as double workers if part of the labor market is specifically designed for them with "soft" working conditions that are reconcilable with the work load in the family. This can be achieved by allowing part-time work in this special part of the labor market and by giving wide access to leaves for family responsibilities, such as leaves during pregnancy and in the first period after confinement, as well as leaves to take care of sick children and for other family purposes. The "soft," female part of the labor market typically carries low wages and low status.

The other strategy consists in breaking down sexual segregation in the labor force, that is, the division between "male jobs" and "female jobs." This can be furthered by equalizing working conditions and promoting an equal distribution of family tasks between the spouses. If put into practice, it will entail equal pay and equal treatment in the labor market.

The distinction between these two strategies is an analytical one. In real life they are mixed together, resulting in an incoherent labor market policy where measures are taken both to reinforce sexual segregation and to reduce its importance. In the rest of this essay I specify the more decisive elements of these measures.

MAKING FAMILY AND PAID EMPLOYMENT COMPATIBLE

The percentage of women in paid employment is relatively high in Scandinavia, but this reflects a very wide spread use of part-time work. More than 40 percent of female employees work part-time, and for married women the proportion is even higher. Not all jobs are open to part-timers, whose job opportunities therefore are more restricted than those of full-time workers. Part-time jobs differ from full-time jobs with regard to terms and conditions of employment. Occupations that can be done on a part-time basis fall into two main categories: (1) Most are low-paid occupations that demand no special skills (e.g., cleaning, retail trade, and work in hotels and restaurants); (2) a second group consists of professional occupations such as nursing and teaching. Thus, in Scandinavia the part-time market is divided into jobs that require higher education and jobs characterized by low educational requirements. Terms and conditions of employment also fall into two groups with the professional part-time jobs carrying better rates and more secure working conditions than the unskilled part-time jobs.

No conscious and consistent public policy on part-time work is pursued. The emergence of a dual part-time market occupying about half the married women in the labor force is the result of a number of counteracting factors, among which the employers' demand for employees to fill part-time occupations probably is more important than the need on the part of women to restrict their work for family reasons.[1]

In all the Scandinavian countries—Norway, Sweden, and Denmark—women are entitled to maternity leave during the last period of pregnancy and the first period after confinement.[2] In addition, Norwegian and Swedish laws permit fathers to take paternity leave. Norway and Sweden also provide for leave to take care of sick children, whereas in Denmark, this leave exists only for groups of workers who have acquired it by collective agreements. Finally, in Sweden, parents are entitled to reduce their work time to six hours a day (with a loss of pay).

The length of leaves differs from country to country; it is longest in Sweden and shortest in Norway. Indeed, Swedish periods of leave are so long that some people ask if they are not likely to affect women adversely rather than work to their benefit. Swedish sociologist Karin Widerberg is currently working on a project[3] investigating the leave to take care of sick children, which provides a leave of 60 days per year per child, thus enabling a woman with three children to be away from her job on family responsibility leave (with pay) for more than half her working time. Widerberg is exploring the working of the act at workplace level and will eventually assess its consequence for women's employment opportunities; the results may well be more negative than positive. The leave provisions in question are framed in sex-neutral terms, but in their practical implementation they are obviously related to women, who are the main users of family responsibility leave.

By and large, the objective of enabling women to combine family responsibilities and some kind of paid employment has been achieved in Scandinavia. The vast majority of women with children are employed or seeking employment. The fact that about half the married women are working part-time suggests that the availability of part-time jobs is essential in this context, whereas the relevance of the provisions on family responsibility leave is difficult to assess.

COMBATING THE SEGREGATION BETWEEN MEN'S JOBS AND WOMEN'S JOBS

In contradistinction to the aim of making family work and wage work compatible, the goal of desegregating the labor force has definitely not been achieved in Scandinavia, which probably has one of the most sexually segregated labor markets in the world. Nevertheless, some measures have been taken to change this. The two most important are the pursuance of an active public labor market policy in favor of women, and the adoption of equality legislation.

The active labor market policy includes special courses and training programs for women in order to support their entrance into what typically are men's jobs. In Sweden state subsidies are given to employers who train and/or hire women for traditional male jobs and men for traditional female jobs, and regional development aid to employers is given on the condition that either sex constitutes at least 40 percent of the work force. Special "break" projects have also been initiated to help promote the breakdown of sexual barriers in the labor market, and again especially in Sweden, the public sector in its capacity as employer has been trying to lead the way by demonstrating good equal employment opportunity practices. So far, the effect of these measures appears to be marginal.

Equality legislation was adopted in the Scandinavian countries in the late 1970s. In Denmark, which is a member of the European Community (EC), an equal pay act was enacted in 1976 and an equal treatment act in 1978 in order to comply with the EC-Directives on equal pay and equal treatment. In Norway and Sweden, which are not members of the EC, such legislation was adopted a little later; in Norway the Equal Status Act came into force in 1979, and the Swedish Act on Equality in Working life became effective in 1980.

All the laws ban direct and indirect sex discrimination. There are differing opinions as to how to interpret the concept "indirect discrimination," but it is beyond dispute that it covers discrimination based on marriage or family situation. The new laws thus render it unlawful for an employer to take an employee's family situation into consideration when making employment decisions, for example, in hiring, promotion, transfer, working conditions, and dismissal.

The Norwegian act applies to all areas of society, whereas the Danish and Swedish laws are confined to the labor market. This means that in Norway the ban on sex discrimination applies to internal relations in the family; it is, for example, a violation of the act if parents commit sex discrimination against their children. In normal cases, the Norwegian Equal Status Act is enforced by legal machinery (Equality Ombud and Board) set up by the act, although in matters concerning the family these bodies cannot enforce the law. But a case can be taken to the ordinary courts and a claim for damages made. This would be possible, for example, if a daughter considered her parents to have discriminated against her on grounds of sex.

All Scandinavian laws on equality provide for an exception from the ban on sex discrimination in cases of positive action, for example, to help eliminate the effects of past discrimination.

In addition to the ban on sex discrimination, the Swedish Act on Equality in Working Life (but not the Danish and Norwegian acts) imposes a duty on the employer to work actively for equality. The employer is required to endeavor to promote an even balance between the sexes in his workforce.

The new laws on equality aim at combating sexual segregation in the labor market. They have been in operation for so short a time that their effect cannot yet be assessed. But it is recognized, for example, at EC-level[5] that a ban on sex discrimination and discrimination due to family status is not enough to bring about any substantial change in the pattern of work, including its distribution between the sexes.

WHAT OUGHT TO BE DONE?

There are differing views not only among policy makers but also in the women's movement about whether women's position ought to be improved by raising the standard in typical women's jobs (and preserving those jobs *as* women's jobs) or by breaking down the sexual segregation of the labor market and promoting an even distribution of women and men in all jobs, under equal terms and conditions. In my opinion, the higher priority should be given to the desegregation of the labor market; making family work and wage work compatible should be subordinated to this. An active labor market policy and effective equality legislation are more important than access to part-time jobs and family responsibility leave, which might even damage women's opportunities in the labor market.

NOTES

1. For a more detailed analysis, see Gunvor Strømsheim: "Part-Time Work as a Labour Market Phenomenon," in ed. Kirsten Jørgensen, Kirsten Hvidtfeldt, and Ruth Nielsen, *Strategies for Integrating Women into the Labour Market* (Copenhagen: Women's Research Centre in Social Science, 1982).

2. In Norway, provisions concerning parental leave are contained in the work environment and the general social security legislation. The present provisions date back to 1978. Women are entitled to 18 weeks paid maternity leave, of which 6 weeks must be taken by the mother after confinement. The remaining 12 weeks can be shared between the mother and the father or be used by the mother alone. In addition, both mother and father are entitled to unpaid leave during the child's first year but not more than a year's leave total. If the father uses this right, it reduces the mother's access to leave. The father or another person who takes care of mother and child in connection with the childbirth is entitled to 2

weeks' "care-leave" without payment. A mother who breast-feeds her baby is entitled to a half hour break twice a day for this purpose without pay. Any employee (male or female) with children under 10 years of age is entitled to 10 days a year paid leave per child to take care of a sick child.

The Swedish act on parental leave dates back to 1974, but has been amended several times since. The parents are entitled to 6 months parental leave with parental benefit and 6 months leave with special parental benefit. They can share this leave between them or it can be used solely by one of the parents. Parents of either sex are entitled to 60 days off per year per child to take care of sick children, and they have a right to reduced working hours (6 hours per day instead of 8) until the child reaches the age of 8. There is no direct economic compensation for reduced working hours but the special parental benefit can be taken out in full, in half, or in a quarter so that the loss of earnings resulting from reduced working hours may be covered.

A more detailed description of the Swedish system is given by Lotta Westerhäll-Gisselson in "Pregnancy Benefit in Sweden," *European Women's Law* no. 2 (Kvindevidenskabeligt Forlag, Copenhagen 1982), which also contains statistical information on the use of the various schemes.

The Danish provisions on maternity leave are less generous. They are contained in a special act on pregnancy and childbirth leave and in the act on sickness and maternity benefits. Only women are entitled to leave under these provisions; there is thus no statutory parental leave system in Denmark. The mother is entitled to 18 weeks' maternity leave with economic compensation. Some collective agreements provide for parental leave and/or more extended maternity leave. There are no statutory provisions on other kinds of family responsibility leave, for example, to take care of sick children, but provisions to this effect are included in a number of collective agreements.

3. The project is briefly presented (in Swedish) in *Årbog for Kvinderet 1982* (*Yearbook of Women's Law 1982*) (Copenhagen, 1982).

4. There is a considerable literature in the Scandinavian languages on this subject; see, for example, *Årbog for Kvinderet 1982* (*Yearbook of Women's Law 1982*), which, in addition to articles, contains overviews of literature, projects, and so forth. Swedish public reports very often contain English summaries, and some of them are translated into English, for example, *Step by Step. National Plan of Action for Equality* (SOU, 1979).

5. In December 1981 the EC Commission drafted a proposal for a Community Action Program to promote equal opportunities based on this assumption.

18

Jean Bethke Elshtain

Antigone's Daughters: Reflections on Female Identity and the State

This essay advances a note of caution. It argues that feminists should approach the modern bureaucratic state from a standpoint of skepticism that keeps alive a critical distance between feminism and statism, between female self-identity and a social identity thoroughly tied to the ongoing public-political world revolving around the structures, institutions, values, and ends of the state. The basis for my caution and skepticism is neither strategic nor utilitarian. Instead, it is a sober recognition that any political order in our time that culminates in a state is an edifice that monopolizes and centralizes power and eliminates older, less universal forms of authority; that structures its activities and implements its policies through unaccountable hierarchies; that erodes local and particular patterns of ethnic, religious, and regional ties and identities; that standardizes culture, ideas, and ideals; that links portions of the population to it through a variety of dependency relationships, often undertaken at popular urging and for humane reasons that nevertheless allow for widespread manipulation and coercion; that may find it necessary or convenient to override civil liberties and standards of decency for *raison d'état* or executive privilege; and that, from time to time, commits its people to wars they have had neither the opportunity to debate fully nor the right, in advance, to challenge openly.

For feminists to discover in the state the new "Mr. Right," to wed themselves, for better or for worse, to a public identity inseparable from the exigencies of state power and policy would be a serious mistake. This is a serious charge. I defend and develop my argument by considering, first, the ways in which certain important feminist thinkers, at times somewhat casually and carelessly, have presumed the superiority of a particular sort of public identity over a private one. I trace out the logic of these arguments, indicating what a fully public identity for women would require, including the final suppression of traditional female social worlds. Finally, I reclaim for women a social identity that locates them very much *in* and *of* the wider world but that positions them against overweening state power and an overarching public identity under its terms. My aim is to define and defend a female identity and a feminist perspective that enables contemporary women to see themselves as the daughters of Antigone. To recognize that women as a group experience their social worlds differently from men as a group complicates feminist thinking, deepens female self-awareness, and calls attention to the complexity and richness of our social experiences and relations.

The feminist protest of the past several decades has largely concentrated on the ways, official and unofficial, ideological and practical, by which women have been excluded from equal participation in public life and coequal share in official power in government and business life. Responding to constraints that curbed their participation as citizens and constrained expression of their individual autonomy, the end of feminist protest was conceived as the full incorporation of women into the power, privileges, and responsibilities of the public arena, political and corporate. The stated aim of the largest feminist political organization, the National Organization for Women (NOW), founded in October 1966, is to gain "truly equal partnership with men." To this end, NOW's Bill of Rights contained a list of proposals and demands required to attain such "equal partnership." These demands included the establishment of government-sponsored child-care centers open around the clock, abortion on demand, equal pay for equal work, aggressive recruitment of women for top positions in all political and business hierarchies, and so on. The presumption behind these demands, as stated by Betty Friedan's "first stage" *The Feminine Mystique*, was that the contemporary woman suffered a particular assault against her identity by being housebound; the man, with other "able, ambitious" fellows, entered the success-driven ethos of the American public world and kept "on growing."[1] Friedan contrasted, and devalued, the activities and identities of women in their "comfortable concentration camps" with the exciting, fulfilling, and presumably worthwhile world of the successful professional male.[2] In her more recent "second stage," Friedan remains cultivatedly innocent of any tensions between simultaneous commitments to full intimacy and mobile success on market terms. She evades any serious questioning of her feminist project by transcending (her favorite word) *every* conflict that poses a clash of interests, values, or purposes or that presents obstacles to her version of feminism's "second stage."[3]

Liberal feminists have not been alone in urging that private woman join public man. Susan Brownmiller, a radical feminist, presumes that all the central features of the *current* male-dominated power structure will remain intact indefinitely; therefore, women must come to control these structures fifty-fifty. Armies, she indicates casually, will probably be around for a while, and so they "must be fully integrated, as well as our national guard, our state troopers, our local sheriffs' offices, our district attorneys' offices, our state prosecuting attorneys' offices—in short the nation's entire lawful power structure (and I mean power in the physical sense) must be stripped of male dominance and control—if women are to cease being a colonized protectorate of men."[4] Women should prepare themselves for combat and guard duty, for militarized "citizenship" with a feminist face.

Similarly, one fundamental presumption underlying more deterministic modes of Marxist feminism is the insistence that women will never be "liberated" to join hands with those men whose identities bear the teleologic seed of the future revolutionary order—the proletariat—until they are sprung from the ghetto of the home and wholly absorbed in the labor force, there to acquire an overriding public identity as members of the class of exploited workers. The realm of intimacy is recast, crudely, as the world of reproduction, an analogue of the productive process.

These moves to transform women into public persons with a public identity that either primarily or exclusively defines them and bears interests and purposes overriding in cases of conflict with private lives and identities, were embraced or implicitly adopted by the most widely disseminated statements of feminist politics. As a feminist project this ideology required "the absorption of the private as completely as possible into the public."[5] Women, formerly private beings, would be "uplifted" to the status of a preeminently public identity to be shared coequally with men, already construed as public beings. What was conspicuously missing from the discussion was any recognition of the potential dangers inherent in calling upon the state as an instrument for sexual emancipation. In practice, what the demand for a thoroughgoing shift in the social identities of women involves is the full assimilation of women into a combined identification with the state and the ongoing terms of competitive civil society, terms that have permeated all aspects of public life given the close entanglements between government and corporations.

This process emerged in stark relief in an *amicus curiae* brief filed by NOW with the Supreme Court which argues that the all-male draft violates the constitutional rights of women. The brief asserts that "compulsory universal military service is central to the concept of citizenship in a democracy" and that women suffer "devastating longterm psychological and political repercussions" given their exclusion from such service in behalf of a militarized public identity.[6] Eleanor Smeal, president of NOW, is quoted as insisting that barring women from the military and from combat duty is based "solely on archaic notions of women's role in society."[7] Whatever one's position on women and the draft, NOW's stance and the stated defense for it embody the conviction that women's traditional identities are so many handicaps to be overcome by women's incorporation into already established terms for male public roles.

What all modes of feminist protest that inveigh against women's continued identification with the private sphere share in common is the conviction that women's traditional identities were wholly forced upon them—that all women have been the unwitting victims of patterns of coerced and manipulated exclusion from public life and forced imprisonment in private life. That is, women were not construed as agents and historic subjects who had, in their private identities as wives, mothers, and grandmothers, played vital and important chosen roles as neighbors, friends, social benefactors, and responsible community members. Though these latter roles and activities are not necessarily gender related, historically they have been more linked to women as beings who exemplified what is best called "civic virtue." Holding up the public world as the *only* sphere within which individuals made real choices, exercised authentic power, or had efficacious control, the private world in turn reflected, as a mirror image, powerlessness, necessity, and irrational tradition. The darker underside of the public world, with the notable exception of its exclusion of women, went unexplored just as the dignified aspects of women's private sphere got washed out in favor of often crude evocations of female victimization.[8]

Feminists who celebrated "going public" could point to the long history of the forced exclusion of women from political life and participation, whether the franchise, public office, or education and employment as evidence that women's private identitites were heavy-handed impositions by those having superior power. They could also recall a tradition of political thought in which great male theorists located women outside of, and frequently at odds with, the values, necessities, and demands of politics and the sphere of public action.[9] In contrast, another strain of feminist thought, best called "difference feminism"[10] (which comes in many varieties) questioned the move toward full assimilation of female identity with ongoing public male identity and argued that to see women's traditional roles and activities as *wholly* oppressive was itself oppressive to women, denying them historic subjectivity and moral agency. And rather than chastise Western political thinkers for their failure to incorporate women into their scheme of things, why not question that scheme of things with its implied or direct devaluation of the traditional world and ways of women—a subject to which I return below.

At this point in the discussion it is important to take the measure of that public identity into which "liberated" women are to be inducted. Contemporary American public identity is a far cry indeed from Jefferson's noble republican farmer or Lincoln's morally engaged citizen, the "last best hope on earth." Instead, we find a public life, political and economic, riddled by standards of bureaucratic rationalization and culminating in monopoly by the state of final authority in most vital fields of human activity. This process of rationalization and centralization aims at efficiency and control, and powerful bureaucracies have been set up to implement such aims. Individuals located in highly centralized and hierarchical bureaucracies operate in conformity to certain impersonal, abstract, and rational standards today; this is the "price of entry" into the *predominant* public identity available to anyone, male or female.

For women to identify fully with the present public order is for them to participate—and there is pathos if not tragedy in this—in the suppression of an alternative identity and way of being described by Dorothy Smith, a feminist sociologist, as "the concrete, the particular, the bodily," an identity with which women have traditionally been defined and within which, for better *and* worse, they have located themselves and have been located as social and historic beings.[11] This world, once taken for granted and now problematic, exists in contrast to and at odds with the abstracted "mode of ruling," the identity and ways of acting of the dominant and the officially powerful. Women's historic social identity, at odds with the extreme version of abstract individualism, exuded public-oriented behavior aimed at good for others not reducible to interest for self. The problem, as Jane Bennett pointed out in a recent study, is that women, as the "exemplars/defenders of civic virtue" were pressed to sacrifice individual goals altogether in order to preserve "a particular type of public good."[12]

Feminist protest that seeks the final elimination of this sphere of the concrete, particular smaller social world, viewing only the sacrifices forced upon women and not the good attained by women, is one response to identities and ways of being grown problematic under the pressures of rationalization and modernization. A second response, one whose growth in numbers is a measure of the felt anger and despair of its adherents, is the militant reaffirmation of a rigid "feminine" identity, one that aims to "leave" all the political stuff to men better equipped for the task —ironically, of course, such feminine women are actively promoting this passive end. Somewhat lost in the crossfire between these hostile camps is a third alternative, which I shall call "social feminism," that opposes the rush toward a thoroughgoing technocratic order and an overweening public identity and repudiates, as well, the standpoint of militant feminine passivity.

The third way, a feminist *via media*, begins with a female subject located *within* a world that is particular, concrete, and social and attempts to see it *through* her eyes. If one begins in this way, one cannot presume that this world is automatically one all women should seek, or need, to be wholly "liberated from." This latter presumption ignores the standpoint of the female subject in her particular social location and flows instead from the requirements of an ideology that has incorporated a devaluation of women's traditional identities, itself one hallmark of male-dominant society. The French feminist writer Julia Kristeva observed in an interview: "Feminism can be but one of capitalism's more advanced needs to rationalize.[13] Those feminisms that embrace without serious qualification the governing modes of consciousness and norms of social organization of the current public world serve in precisely this way.

To sketch my alternative requires that I begin from the standpoint of women themselves, within their everyday reality. Does that reality retain any vitality that women can tap to resist their total relocation as beings who identify fully with a predatory civil society and, as well, to counter female privatization? That is, is it possible to embrace the cherished ideals and precious human values that flow from the social world of women, yet to sever those ideals and values from patterns of male domination and female subordination? I am convinced this is possible, but I would have been closed to this possibility if I had viewed women's traditional identities as devoid of vitality, inexorably tainted by relations of domination. What follows is my effort to reclaim for women an identity that pits them againts the imperious demands of public power and contractual relations, one that might serve as a locus for female thinking, acting, and being as transformed by social feminist imperatives.

I mention a standpoint, yet I conjure up an image of fluidity, of intimations. The female subject I have in mind is an identity-in-becoming, not finally congealed and crystallized, remaining open to her worlds, inner and outer. Yet she is located historically and grounded in tradition. This female subject makes her own a tradition at least as old as Antigone's conflict with Creon. This powerful myth and human drama pits a woman against the arrogant insistencies of statecraft. Recall the story: The *dramatis personae* that matter for my purposes are Creon, King of Thebes and his nieces, Antigone and her sister, Ismenê, daughters of the doomed Oedipus. Creon issues an order that violates the sacred familial duty to burn and to honor the dead in the "higher" interests of state. Antigone, outraged, defies Creon. She defines their conflict with clarity and passion.

> Listen, Ismenê:
> Creon buried our brother Eteoclês
> With military honors, gave him a soldier's funeral,
> And it was right that he should; but Polyneicês,
> Who fought as bravely and died as miserably,—
> They say that Creon has sworn
> No one shall bury him, no one mourn for him
> But his body must lie in the fields, a sweet treasure
> For carrion birds to find as they search for food.
> That is what they say, and our good Creon is coming here
> To announce it publicly; and the penalty—
> Stoning to death in the public square.
>   There it is,
> And now you can prove what you are:
> A true sister, or a traitor to your family.[14]

Ismenê, uncomprehending, asks Antigone what she is going to do, and Antigone responds: "Ismenê, I am going to bury him. Will you come?" Ismenê cries that the new law forbids it. Women, she cries, cannot fight with men nor against the law and she begs "the Dead / To forgive me . . ." But Antigone, determined, replies: "It is the dead, not the living, who make the longest demands." Harshly, she orders Ismenê off with the words: "I shall be hating you soon, and the dead will too," for what is worse than death, or what is the worst of deaths, is "death without honor." Later, Antigone proclaims, "There is no guilt in reverence for the dead" and "there are honors due all the dead." This primordial family morality precedes and overrides the laws of the state. Creon must be defied, for there are matters, Antigone insists, that are so basic they transcend *raison d'état*, one's own self-interest, even one's own life.

Creon's offense is his demand that political necessity justifies trampling upon a basic human duty, an imperative that lies at the heart of any recognizably human social life. In her loyalty to her slain brother and to family honor, Antigone asserts that there are matters of such deep significance that they begin and end where the state's writ does not and must not run, where politics cannot presume to dictate to the human soul. In "saving" the state, Creon not only runs roughshod over centuries-old tradition but presumes to override the familial order, the domain of women. In refusing to accept *raison d'état* as thus overriding, Antigone sets the course for her rebellion.

Sophocles honors Antigone in that rebellion. He sees no need to portray a chastened Antigone, having confronted Creon but having failed to sway him, finally won over to the imperatives of *raison d'état*, yielding, at last, to Creon's fears of lawbreakers and anarchy. Strangely, Antigone has not emerged as a feminist heroine. Even as her protest has been silent to feminist thinking, a magisterial Greek thinker who would eliminate altogether the standpoint of Antigone is sometimes honored by feminists for his "radical" rearrangements without apparent regard to gender. I refer to the Plato of *The Republic*, a Plato dedicated to eradicating and devaluing private homes and particular intimate attachments, principally for his Guardian class. Such private loyalties and passions militated against singleminded, total devotion to the city. Plato cries: "Have we any greater evil for a city than what splits it and makes it many instead of one? Or a greater good than what binds it together and makes it one?"[15] (The preferred answer to each question is "no.")

To see in Plato's abstract formulation for rationalized equality (for that minority of men and women who comprise his Guardian class) a move that is both radical and feminist is to accept public life and identity as, by definition, superior to private life and identity. Indeed, it is to concur in the wholesale *elimination* of the private, social world to attain the "higher good" of a state without the points of potential friction and dissent private loyalties bring in their wake. Plato provides for women's participation under terms that deprivatize them and strip them of the single greatest source of female psychological and social power in fifth- and fourth-century Athens—their role in the household; their ties with their children. Effectively, he renders their sexual identities moot. In whose behalf is this dream of unity, and female public action, being dreamed?

What all this means is that the question of female identity and the state looks very different if one picks up the thread of woman's relationship to public power, in and through its changing forms in the history of the West, from the standpoint of an Antigone; or if one adopts the sanctioned, powerful viewpoint of the handful of thinkers whose works comprise the canon of the Western political tradition; or, even more troublingly, if one tells the tale through the prism of unchecked *Realpolitik*. From the viewpoint of the female subject, what one sees is a complex mosaic, layers of images of historic identities largely, but not wholly, "silent" to what counted as official political power and sanctioned sovereignty, excluded from "legitimate" statecraft unless she inherited a throne, yet an active historic agent, a participant in social life.

This sphere of the historic female subject secreted its own imperatives and inspired its own songs, stories, and myths. It was and remains for many if not all the crucible through which sustaining human relations and meaning are forged and remembered. If one can "see" any of this, it becomes easier to appreciate both the fears of traditionalists and the qualms of radicals at the suppression of this drama of the concrete and the particular in favor of some formal-legalistic, abstract "personhood," or to make way for the further intrusion of a rationalized, increasingly technocratic public order.

But how does one hold on to a social location for contemporary daughters of Antigone without simultaneously insisting that women accept traditional terms of political quiescence? The question moves to answer itself, for the standpoint of

Antigone is that of a woman who dares to challenge public power by giving voice to familial and social imperatives and duties. Hers is not the world of the *femme couverte*, or the delicate lady, or the coy sex-kitten. Hers is a robust voice, a bold voice. To recapture that voice and to reclaim that standpoint, and not just for women alone, it is necessary to locate the daughters of Antigone where, shakily and problematically, they continue, importantly, to locate themselves: in that arena of the social world where human life is nurtured and protected from day to day.

Through a social feminist awareness, women can explore, articulate, and reclaim this world. To reaffirm the standpoint of Antigone for our own time is to portray woman as one who resists the imperious demands and overweening claims of state power when these run roughshod over deeply rooted and particular values and identities. Women must learn to defend without defensiveness, to embrace without sentimentality, the perspective that flows from their experiences in their everyday bodily and material world, "an actual local and particular place in the world."[16] To see this world, simply, as the "private sphere" in contrast to "the public sphere" is to mislead. For contemporary Americans, "private" conjures up images of privatization and narrow exclusivity. The world of Antigone, however, is a *social* location that speaks of, and to, identities and values that are unique to a particular family, to particular mothers and fathers, sisters and brothers, on the one hand, but, on another and perhaps even more basic level, taps a deeply buried, shared human identity, for we are first and foremost not political man or economic man but family men and women. The family is our entry point into the wider social world. This familial standpoint, then, is the basis of a concept of the social for, as Hegel recognized, "the family is a sort of training ground that provides an understanding of other-oriented and public-oriented action."[17]

What is striking about political theorizing in the Western tradition is the very thin notion of the social world so much of that theorizing conveys. All those aspects of social reality that go into making a person what he or she is fall outside the frame of formal, abstract analyses. In their rethinking of this tradition, many feminist thinkers, initially at least, locked their own formulations into an overly schematic public-private dichotomy, even if their intention was to challenge or to question it.[18] Those feminists who have moved in the direction of "social feminism" have, in their rethinking of received categories, become both more "historical" and more interpretive in their approach to social life. One important female thinker "of," and activist within, "the social," whose life and work form a striking contrast to the classical vision and to overly rigid feminist renderings of the public and private, particularly those who express disdain for anything that smacks of the traditionally "feminine," is Jane Addams. A woman with a powerful public identity and following, who wielded enormous political power and influence, Addams' life work was neither grandly public nor narrowly private. Instead, she refracted the shared values of centuries of domestic tradition, the dense and heady concoction of women's imperatives, reflections, yearnings, joys, tragedies, and tears—and she brought these to bear on a political world that held, and continues to hold, human life very cheaply indeed.

What classical political theorists disdained as ignoble—the sustenance of life itself—Addams claimed as heroic. Rather than repudiate human birth and the world surrounding it as a possible source of moral truth and political principle, Addams spoke to and from the standpoint of the "suffering mothers of the disinherited," of "women's haunting memories," which, she believed, "instinctively challenge war as the implacable enemy of their age-long undertaking."[19] At one point she wrote:

> Certainly the women in every country who are under a profound imperative to preserve human life, have a right to regard this maternal impulse as important now as the compelling instinct evinced by primitive woman long ago, when they made the first crude beginnings of society by refusing to share the vagrant life of man because they insisted upon a fixed abode in which they might cherish their children. Undoubtedly women were then told that the interests of the tribe, the diminishing food supply, the honor of the chieftain, demanded that they leave their particular caves and go out in the wind and weather without regard to the survival of their children. But at the present moment the very names of the tribes and of the honors and the glories which they sought are forgotten, while the basic fact that the mothers held the lives of their children above all else, insisted upon staying where the children had a chance to live, and cultivate the earth for their food, laid the foundations of an ordered society.[20]

A feminist rethinking of Addams' category of "the social," resituating it as an alternative to the twin poles of self-absorbed privatization and thoroughgoing public self-interestedness, would allow us to break out of the rigidities into which current feminist discourse has fallen. Seeing human beings in and through the prism of a many-layered, complex social world suffused with diverse "goods," meanings, and purposes opens up the possibility for posing a transformed vision of the human community against the arid plane of bureaucratic statism. This communitarian ideal involves a series of interrelated but truly and importantly autonomous social spheres and activities. It incorporates a vision of human solidarity that does not require uniformity and of cooperation that does not quash dissent. The aim of all social activity would be to provide a frame within which members of a diverse social body could attain both individual and communal ends and purposes without, however, presuming some final resolution of these ends and purposes. A social world, then, featuring fully public activities at one end of a range of possibilities—writing a manifesto, organizing a protest, framing a law—and intensely private activities at the other—human sexual intimacy, a parent's caress of a child's sleeping face, a young woman's or man's dreams, the solitude necessary to reflect or meditate or pray or cry.

If this communal ideal, replete with its rich notion of "the social," is to be reclaimed as a worthy ideal for out time, a first requirement is a feminist framework that locates itself *in* the social world in such a way that our current public, political realities can be examined with a critical and reflective eye. Bureaucratic power, technological politics, and statist arrogance must be critiqued. One alternative feminist perspective, a variant on both "difference" and "social" feminism that helps us do this, is called "maternal thinking" by its author, Sara Ruddick.[21] According to Ruddick, women sexually and socially located as mothers have had a particular way of thinking that has largely gone unnoticed, save by mothers themselves. That is, women in mothering capacities have developed intellectual capacities that would not otherwise have been developed; made judgments they would not otherwise have been called upon to make; and affirmed values they might not otherwise have affirmed. In other words, mothers engage in a discipline that has its own characteristic virtues and errors and that involves, like other disciplines, a conception of achievement, those ends to which maternal efforts are directed. Most important for the purposes of feminist theory, these concepts and ends are dramatically at odds with the prevailing norms of our bureaucratic, increasingly technological, and centralized public order.

Ruddick's is an epistemological argument that ties knowing to ways of being. One can describe maternal practices, she claims, by a mother's interest in the preservation, the growth, and the social acceptability of her child. These values and goods may conflict, for preservation and growth may clash with requirements for social acceptability. Interestingly, what counts as a failure within the frame of maternal thinking, from inside this world looking out, namely, excessive control that fails to give each unique child room to grow and develop, is the *modus operandi* of both public and private bureaucracies: control being the key moving term, both ends and means. Were maternal thinking to be taken as the base for feminist consciousness, a wedge for critique of an increasingly overcontrolled public world would open up immediately. Beyond critique, for this notion of maternal thought to have a full and fair chance to flourish as it is brought to bear upon the larger world, it must be transformed in and through social feminist awareness.

Maternal thinking opens up for reflective criticism the paradoxical juxtapositions of female powerlessness and subordination, in the overall social and political sense, with the extraordinary psychosocial authority of mothers. Maternal thinking refuses to see women principally or simply as victims, for it recognizes that much that is good has emerged from maternal practices and could not emerge if the world of the mother were totally destructive. Maternal thinking transformed by feminist consciousness, hence aware of the binds and constraints imposed on mothers, including the presumption that women will first nurture their sons and then turn them over for sacrifice should the gods of war demand human blood, offers us a mode of reflection that links women to the past yet offers up hope of a future. It makes contact with the strengths of our mothers and grandmothers; it helps us to see ourselves as Antigone's daughters, determined, should it be necessary, to chasten arrogant public power and resist the claims of political necessity. For such power, and such claims, have in the past been weapons used to trample upon the deepest yearnings and most basic hopes of the human spirit.

Maternal thinking reminds us that public policy has an impact on real human beings. As public policy becomes increasingly impersonal, calculating, and technocratic, maternal thinking insists that the concrete reality of a single human child be kept, ongoingly, before the mind's eye. Maternal thinking, like Antigone's protest, is a rejection of amoral statecraft and an affirmation of the dignity of the human person.

NOTES

1. Betty Friedan, *The Feminine Mystique* (New York: Dell, 1974), p. 201.

2. Ibid., p. 325.

3. Betty Friedan, *The Second Stage* (New York: Summit, 1981), passim. Conflicts to be transcended include those between men and women; between individual "self realization" and "social good"; "the false polarization between feminism and the family"; and "the false conflict between volunteerism and professionalism." Although Friedan recognizes important cleavages, her leap to transcend is, finally, an avoidance that blurs real, not superficial, differences and blunts the edges of political conflict.

4. Susan Brownmiller, *Against Our Will: Men, Women and Rape* (New York: Simon and Schuster, 1975), 388.

5. Robert Paul Wolff, "There's Nobody Here But Us Persons," in *Women and Philosophy*, ed. Carol Gould and Marx Wartofsky (New York: Putnam, 1976), 140–41.

6. Linda Greenhouse, "Women Join Battle on All-Male Draft," *New York Times*, 22 March 1981, p. 19. We do have plenty of evidence on the devastating damage done men and women who served in a variety of capacities in Vietnam.

7. *Ibid.* My criticism of NOW's brief does not imply that I have ready, comfortable answers to the complex political, philosophical, and moral issues involved in the "right to fight" argument and in the arguments of those who finally oppose this position.

8. This should not be necessary but, alas, it seems to be: My argument should not be taken as a denial that women, historically, *have* suffered in specific ways. It is, however, a denial that this suffering has been so total that women are reduced to the status of objects—whether in the name of feminism or in the name of defenses of male supremacy.

9. This tradition can inspire at least two very different reactions. The first sees the problem as the "exclusion" of women from a particular theorist's definition of politics; if women were "included," presumably, the theory would no longer be problematic. A second possibility is for a feminist thinker to challenge, not only the terms of female exclusion, but the terms of male inclusion: Is this a vision of a public, political world women can or should share? Do I accept this theorist's implied devaluation of private social relations compared with his celebration of public or political relations? And so on.

10. Examples of "difference feminism" include Carol Gilligan, "In a Different Voice: Women's Conception of Self and Morality," *Harvard Educational Review* 47 (1977): 481–517; some of the essays in the volumes *Women, Culture and Society*, ed. Michelle Rosaldo and Louise Lamphere (Stanford: Stanford University Press, 1974); and *Discovering Reality: Feminist Perspectives on Epistemology, Metaphysics, Methodology and the Philosophy of Science* (Amsterdam: Dordrecht-Reidel, 1982).

11. Dorothy E. Smith, "A Sociology for Women," in *The Prism of Sex: Essays in the Sociology of Knowledge*, ed Julia A. Sherman and Evelyn Torton Beck (Madison: University of Wisconsin Press, 1979), pp. 135–88.

12. Jane Bennett, "Feminism and Civic Virtue" (unpublished paper, 1981).

13. Julia Kristeva, "Women Can Never Be Defined," in *New French Feminisms. An Anthology* ed. Elaine Marks and Isabelle de Courtivron (Amherst: University of Massachusetts Press, 1980), pp. 137–42, 141.

14. Sophocles, *The Oedipus Cycle*, "Antigone," trans. Dudley Fitts and Robert Fitzgerald (New York: Harvest, 1949), 186.

15. Plato, *The Republic*, trans. Allan Bloom (New York: Basic, 1968), Book V/460e–462d, 141.

16. Smith, "A Sociology for Women," p. 168.

17. Bennett, "Feminism and Civic Virtue."

18. I consider myself guilty on this score. See one of my earlier formulations on the public-private dilemma, "Moral Woman/Immoral Man: The Public/Private Distinction and Its Political Ramifications," *Politics and Society* 4 (1974): 453–73. I try to restore a richness this initial foray dropped out in *Public Man, Private Woman: Women in Social and Political Thought* (Princeton: Princeton University Press, 1981).

19. Jane Addams, *The Long Road of Woman's Memory* (New York: Macmillan, 1916), p. 40. This "instinct" or, alternatively, "impulse" of which Addams writes is a social imperative, not a crudely biological one, though it cannot, of course, be separated from female embodiment in the basic form in which she discusses it prehistorically.

20. Ibid., pp. 126–27.

21. Sara Ruddick, "Maternal Thinking" (typescript). A foreshortened version subsequently appeared in *Feminist Studies*, Summer 1980, but I draw upon the original, full-length draft.

19

Janet K. Boles

The Family Impact Statement: Ideology and Feasibility

Given the central role of the family in American society, government officials and policy analysts took note when demographers in the 1970s reported unprecedented changes taking place in families. Some observers linked this "crisis of the family" to inflation, the failure of the churches and schools, or general cultural stress stemming from rapid change in the larger society. But an increasingly common explanation among both government officials and the general public was that certain existing public policies have tended to disrupt family structures.

A survey in the March 1980 issue of *Better Homes and Gardens*, which drew 46,817 replies, found that 92 percent of all respondents felt that the "general effect of government policies on middle-class families like yours" has been harmful.[1] In a more representative poll, taken in 1980 by the Gallup organization for the White House Conference on Families, nearly half the respondents felt that the national government has an unfavorable influence on family life. Nor were state and local governments, the courts, or the legal system perceived much more positively.[2]

In an effort to quantify the extent of governmental involvement in family life (and, ironically, to counter the myth that there *is* no involvement), the staff of a family research center surveyed the (then) 1044 federal programs in the Catalog on Federal Domestic Assistance. They found 268 programs that had potential direct impact on families. The inventory also showed that a majority of these programs were administered outside of the Department of Health, Education, and Welfare and, as a general rule, were not limited exclusively to poor families.[3] Even this analysis was a limited one in that the programs of state and local governments and all court decisions were excluded, as were important areas of national policy such as defense programs and tax laws.

THE WHITE HOUSE CONFERENCE ON FAMILIES (WHCF)

The delegates to the 1980 White House Conference on Families (actually three meetings held in Baltimore, Minneapolis, and Los Angeles) reached broad agreement on a lengthy agenda to strengthen and support families. Issues addressed included most major national problems: housing, welfare, energy, inflation, unemployment, and economic and fiscal equity. Although 34 proposals were adopted at all three conferences, only 7 received the support of more than 90 percent of the delegates. The most highly ranked recommendations of the WHCF may not necessarily have been the most important but only the most innocuous. Three of the seven, for example, dealt with the special problems of the handicapped and the aging. Another called for new efforts to prevent alcohol and drug abuse. In contrast, consensus on the more explicitly family-oriented issues of child care, sex education, teenage pregnancy, family violence, and the Equal Rights Amendment was markedly lower.

Even so, one of the highest-ranked proposals was a relative newcomer to the public agenda. It called for a systematic analysis of all laws, regulations, and rules for their impact on families. Specifically, it was suggested that "every private and public agency be encouraged to write a family impact statement as part of every policy implemented; [and] that voluntary independent commissions for families be created by interested localities and states and at the national level, to insure that public policies impacting on families, including those of business and industry, be sensitive to the diversity of families and accountable to their special needs."[4]

THE CONCEPT OF A FAMILY IMPACT STATEMENT (FIS)

Although the concept of a family impact statement may have been new to many of the WHCF delegates, family impact analysis was first suggested in the early 1970s. It evolved from two dominant concerns of this period. First, there was a growing awareness among both policy makers and family advocates that many of the very expensive and well-intentioned social experiments of the Great Society had shown, to date, only limited success. Some charged that instead of seeking to strengthen families, these new government programs had attempted to substitute for them. Second, policy analysts, buoyed by then-prevalent optimism surrounding the Environmental Impact Statement mandated in the 1969 Environmental Policy Act, suggested that a similar process could and should be developed to assess the potential effect of policies upon families. Not only could such statements consider the possible spillover effects on families of proposed policies not specifically directed to families, but impact analysis could also evaluate overt family policies.

The concept of a FIS was given public voice in September 1973 when the U.S. Senate Subcommittee on Children and Youth held hearings on "American Families: Trends and Pressures." Former Vice-President Walter F. Mondale, then chairman of this subcommittee, said the hearings were "predicated on the simple belief that nothing is more important to a child than a healthy family. . . . We must start by asking to what extent government policies are helping or hurting families."[5] At these hearings, experts in the fields of child development, family sociology, and anthropology recommended that family impact statements be developed for all public policies.

IMPACT ANALYSIS PRECEDENTS

Interest in social accountability and policy analysis, however, exploded during the middle 1970s. Although a number of states and several federal bureaucracies have required other types of impact statements (e.g. economic impact statements, urban impact analysis, and the Human Subjects Review Process), the model initially adopted by those studying the feasibility of developing a family impact statement was that of the environmental impact statement (EIS).

The National Environmental Policy Act of 1969 (NEPA), as implemented, requires that all agencies of the federal government prepare detailed environmental statements on proposals for legislation and other major federal actions significantly affecting the quality of the human environment. Although from a political perspective the EIS has improved the sensitivity of policy makers to social and environmental factors, some feel that the EIS is not an integral part of the decision-making process but instead has become a formality prepared to support and defend a predetermined decision.[6] Others question the expense in terms of delays and dollars associated with the preparation of the statements; their misuse by interest groups to cancel, delay, or modify projects they oppose; and their usefulness and validity given the complexity of the task.[7]

RESEARCH IN FAMILY IMPACT ANALYSIS

Despite these ominous portents, the idea of an FIS attracted interest. Since fall 1976, the Minnesota Family Study Center has been engaged in a family impact analysis research and training program for pre- and postdoctoral students, funded by the National Institute of Mental Health. The primary group associated with the concept of the FIS, however, is the Family Impact Seminar, a policy project within the George Washington University's Institute for Educational Leadership. Created in February 1976 with a grant from the Foundation for Child Development, the seminar is composed of 24 scholars and public policy makers concerned with families who meet several times a year with the seminar's core staff.[8] To date, several books and reports have come out of the seminar's work. In 1980 the seminar conducted a nationwide field project in which 12 state and local government organizations assessed the impact on families of selected policies.[9]

FEASIBILITY OF THE FAMILY IMPACT STATEMENT

In 1976, in a report exploring the feasibility of developing and putting into operation a family impact statement, Sheila Kamerman stated the goals of the FIS as follows:

> A family impact statement would involve analysis of selected pending legislation, policies, regulations, programs, in order to make explicit:
> —the potential effects or outcomes, both negative and positive (with

> stress on the negative) of actions taken on pending (laws, policies, regulations) that might impinge on families (directly or indirectly);
> —the potential for unanticipated consequences (both negative and positive) of such actions; and
> —the potential lack of coherence or conflict with existing laws, policies, and programs.[10]

In 1981, after more than five years of serious efforts to develop and test family impact analysis, Bohen and Viveros-Long concluded that "the process of family impact analysis . . . is more of a generic outlook, or approach, than it is either a theory or methodology . . . the conceptual and measurement problems are so elusive and complex that it seems impossible to assess, in a comprehensive and exact way, the family impact of even a few of the multitude of policies that touch American families."[11] Yet even if conceptual and methodological problems could be surmounted, a plethora of political and administrative difficulties remain. My argument is that the feasibility of meeting the goals of FIS, as originally framed, is currently remote.

THE DEFINITION OF "FAMILY" AND "FAMILY POLICY"

Although in general those who have done research in family impact analysis have used a definition of "the family" close to that of the traditional nuclear family,[12] scholars have noted the hazards of adopting a narrow or inflexible definition of "the family." If the isolated nuclear family is adopted as the normal and universal family structure, indicators of desirable impacts logically fall under categories of intactness and normative role assignments. A family is thus viewed as deficient if the mother participates in the labor force or the father is absent from the home or does not function as a wage earner. Since a majority of American families would be considered structurally abnormal by this definition, family scholars have questioned its validity. They further argue that policy makers should look at how families function rather than only count family members. That is, policy makers need to ask whether family roles are being covered by *someone*. A narrow definition serves only to screen out adaptive functioning of major variant family forms.[13]

This critique of the normative nuclear family by those espousing the FIS has made it a popular target of conservative social critics. It is argued that if any voluntary association of people constitutes a family, and all forms of human cohabitation are equally valid, the policy maker has no real guidelines in formulating goals (positive impacts) for family policy.[14]

Even if a politically acceptable definition of "family" is found, difficulties persist concerning the differential impact of policies on families, whether conceptualized as an institutional structure, as an interacting group, or in terms of its individual members.[15] The appropriate level of family analysis has received relatively little attention despite its obvious importance in the process. Given the diversity of families, any one public policy may affect families in markedly varying ways, or the same policy may affect members of the same family in quite different or conflicting ways. Typically, scholars have been unwilling to break families down into their constituent parts. Yet family life, as we have known it to date, is often marked by discord and conflict of interest, not harmony and mutuality of interest. At a minimum, the present reality of the asymmetrical family must be recognized by the family impact analyst.

Finally, the subject of family impact analysis—that is, family policy—itself remains a "flexible and fuzzy concept," lacking a clear content or meaning.[16] As Kamerman has noted, without clear criteria for identifying which laws, policies, and administrative regulations should be reviewed by the family impact analyst, there are no limits to what could be considered as potentially having some effect on families.[17]

VALUES OF FAMILY IMPACT ANALYSIS

The idea of a family impact statement assumes that there is general agreement on what constitutes positive and negative impacts on families. Unlike environmental impact statements, for which there is a general agreement that less pollution is preferable to more, with regard to family there is no agreement on even the basic issue of whether intact families are good or bad for family members. In a pluralistic society there are many differences of opinion concerning what is, and is not, in the interest of families.

The politically cautious Family Impact Seminar has adopted as two of its key questions: Does the policy encourage or discourage marital stability? Does the policy encourage caring for family members by families themselves or by institutions? Whether explicitly acknowledged or not, "marital stability" and "deinstitutionalization of the elderly and handicapped" are values here.

The helping professions tend to question the validity of these assumptions. Family scholars argue that viable family life and emotionally healthy children are not dependent on whether parents live together or apart. According to this line of thought, it is only necessary that the family, however constituted, be able to meet the instrumental and expressive needs of its members. Thus psychiatrists and other domestic counselers tend to guide people through periods of transition and adjustment rather than concentrate on preserving marriages. Social welfare experts also tend to argue that families do not necessarily have the skills or the patience to provide special care for handicapped or aged members even when highly motivated by emotional ties. Deinstitutionalization, it is predicted, will make family life more stressful.

Marital stability and deinstitutionalization are also rejected by those who place a higher value on personal autonomy in social arrangements and familial roles. Feminists in particular are concerned that the costs of "saving the marriage" and providing home care fall disproportionately on women, given traditional role assignments within the family.

In theory, family impact analysis can proceed as long as the analyst makes clear the values implicit in the process. In practical political terms, however, the FIS cannot be implemented in lieu of consensual goals concerning desirable family impacts.

METHODS OF FAMILY IMPACT ANALYSIS

The theory and methodology of family impact analysis has been a topic of some attention in the past decade,[18] yet its research design and methodology remain an eclectic mixture of the qualitative and quantitative. Although multiple techniques per se are not a major shortcoming, policy makers may hesitate to embrace an analytical process in a state of apparent methodological flux.

Family impact analysts are still very much involved in the exploration and testing of alternative models. The general acceptance of a single model is complicated by the multidisciplinary nature of the FIS (with an accompanying lack of consensus on methods, content, and knowledge). More serious barriers to methodological convergence are the problems shared with other types of social impact assessment: available or readily accessible data, inadequacies of good measures of family functioning, limited knowledge of cause and effect relationships in family life, and difficulties in using experimental or quasi-experimental designs in field research.

Family impact analysis was originally conceived as a tool for both explanation and prediction. Because of the lack of data needed for forecasting and the inability to establish experimental controls or conditions, it is currently being used only for retrospective analysis of policies that have already been implemented. Even so, because of these methodological shortcomings, it often appears to critics as simplistic and impressionistic. The use of sophisticated models and statistical tools may only serve to promise more than the analyst can deliver.

POLITICAL AND ADMINISTRATIVE FEASIBILITY

In addition to conceptual and methodological problems, the implementation of family impact analysis in a governmental setting is surrounded by several other constraints. Like other social impact statements, the FIS is only one tool for the policy maker. Jurisdictional, budgetary, or political considerations may dictate that the "best" policy (in terms of family impact) not be chosen. Furthermore, as Druckman and Rhodes have stated, "the urgency of family-related concerns often demands immediate attention via policy legislation or social programs. It may not be possible to generate family impact statements quickly enough to meet these needs or to conform to the exigencies of political timetables."[19] Even if such confounding factors were not present, advocates of family impact analysis must overcome a currently hostile political environment without a solid history of policy precedents to assist them.

One difficulty presented by the political environment is the suspicion currently directed toward governmental bureaucracies in general and expertise in particular. Writing in reference to family policy, Gilbert Steiner has observed that

> the time is wrong. Family policy implies intervention, regulation, public assistance, manipulation of individual choice. . . . Yet family policy has been offered when, in nearly all respects, the national swing is to nonintervention, deregulation, fiscal restraint, reliance on market forces.[20]

Political conservatives have been skeptical concerning the FIS, seeing it as a means for the government to impose its own views of family life, contrary to those of citizens. Onalee McGraw of the Heritage Foundation has charged that

> family impact analysis is an empty bucket into which any concoction can be poured. The concoction will depend strictly on the values, ideology and political position of those who perform the analysis and write the family impact statement. In practical terms, family impact statements will be formulated by people in or under contract to the human services bureaucracies.[21]

Faced with this hostility toward intervention into the family by bureaucratic experts, and a certain amount of doubt concerning the ability of government policy to affect in any way the social forces responsible for the current changes in family life, advocates of family impact analysis are badly in need of policy precedents to bolster their cause. In Europe, where several countries have explicit family policies, there has been no interest in developing a formal FIS. According to Kamerman, most citizens and government officials do not feel the need for scientific validation of what they believe to be sound policies for families.[22] In the United States, the most visible policy precedent is the environmental impact statement, from which, given the political winds, FIS advocates have been careful to disassociate themselves.

In their recommendations to the White House Conference on Families, the Family Impact Seminar explicitly rejected the suggestion that the environmental impact process could be applied directly to family issues. Instead, they urged that laws *not* require analyses of all relevant policies and programs and that the process *not* be used as a legal weapon to prevent or delay programs.

A further indication of the political acumen of advocates of impact analysis (and especially those associated with the Family Impact Seminar) is the speed with which they have adjusted to the current hostility toward experts and bureaucracy. The family impact analyst, as originally conceived, was seen as a specially trained professional policy analyst, usually affiliated with a public bureaucracy (although private consultants and extragovernmental sponsorship were also recognized as possibilities). In its 1980 recommendations to the WHCF, the Family Impact Seminar clearly broke with this tradition by opposing the creation of government bureaucracies for the purpose of family impact analysis. Although conceding that at some level sophisticated research is necessary for answering family impact questions, the Seminar argued that a variety of organizations—such as PTAs, community action agencies, and interest groups—could engage in family impact analysis. Further, the process was said to not always require complex and long-term research. The seminar finally urged the creation of independent commissions for families at all levels of government. Such commissions would be composed of citizens, serving on a part-time basis, and would be advisory in nature, modestly funded, and be established at first for a time-limited test period. Granting the superficial brilliance of, at one stroke, repudiating expertise, bureaucracy, and costly government and endorsing the new federalism, volunteerism, and the sunset principle, the fact remains that the policy's most important ally—the policy analyst—is irrevocably alienated by the seminar's cavalier assertion of the simplicity of policy analysis.

EVALUATING FAMILY IMPACT ANALYSIS

Currently there appears to be little support among governmental decision makers, nongovernmental groups, and the general public for implementing family impact analysis. The politically damaging definition of the FIS as a "liberal" policy was not accompanied by increased commitment among liberals to this proposed process. Traditional members of the liberal coalition such as women's rights groups, social welfare professionals, child advocacy groups, and organizations that serve the poor were hesitant to vigorously support a policy that was neither conceptually and methodologically clear nor unambiguously in the interest of their respective constituencies.

The FIS has rarely been seriously advocated or studied by anyone other than those associated with centers receiving grants to engage in such research. Academic interest in the process faded as the complexity of the process (and the political problems) became evident. Scholarly literature on the subject, with few exceptions, has originated solely with the staff and fellows of the Minnesota Family Study Center and the Family Impact Seminar. Bureaucratic support has been undermined by the challenge to bureaucratic autonomy and expertise posed by the redefinition of the process in terms of citizen participation. Elected officials saw no political payoffs (but considerable liabilities) in adopting an advocacy stance.

Even so, it may be premature and irresponsible to discard the idea of developing family impact statements. Despite the schizophrenic packaging of the process — sometimes complex and sophisticated, sometimes simple — the social issues involved here are of great importance. The continuing incubation of the concept of a FIS within research centers may ultimately serve to sensitize policy makers in governments and corporations to the impacts of their activities on families. The scope of the process, although at present plagued with serious methodological, conceptual, and political problems, well illustrates the multiple influences on family life today.

The process, still in the experimental stage, is not without risk, particularly if captured by those committed to an ideal of family life that repeats earlier forms of female exploitation and oppression. A more optimistic scenario would suggest that as a growing body of studies utilizing the FIS framework emerges, it will become clear that no currently implemented or proposed family policy can have optimal impacts within present structures and institutions. Serious attention to the restructuring of work and home can then proceed. At the same time, the societal definition of the problems of work, family, and child care as *women's problems* must be recognized as the primary barrier to reform.

NOTES

1. Kate Keating, "Is Government Helping or Hurting American Families?" *Better Homes and Gardens* 58 (September 1980): 19–20.

2. White House Conference on Families, *Listening to America's Families: Action for the 80's* (Washington, D.C.: Government Printing Office, 1980), p. 183.

3. Family Impact Seminar, *Toward an Inventory of Federal Programs with Direct Impact on Families* (Washington, D.C.: George Washington University, 1978).

4. *Listening to America's Families*, pp. 18–19, 24–25, 54, 88.

5. U.S. Senate, Subcommittee on Children and Youth, *American Families: Trends and Pressures* (Washington, D.C.: Government Printing Office, 1974).

6. H. Paul Frieseam and Paul J. Culhane, "Social Impacts, Politics, and the Environmental Impact Statement Process," *Natural Resources Journal* 16 (April 1976): 339–56.

7. Eugene Bardach and Lucian Pugliaresi, "The Environmental Impact Statement versus the Real World," *Public Interest* 49 (Fall 1977): 22–38; Sheila B. Kamerman, *Developing a Family Impact Statement* (New York: Foundation for Child Development, 1976), pp. 13–14.

8. The founder and director of the seminar is Sidney Johnson, formerly the staff director of the Senate Subcommittee on Children and Youth (the Mondale Subcommittee). According to Gilbert Steiner, the seminar's members had grown rather disillusioned with the project by 1979, and over half declined to attend further meetings. See Gilbert Y. Steiner, *The Futility of Family Policy* (Washington, D.C.: Brookings, 1981), p. 30.

9. Family Impact Seminar, *Recommendations to the White House Conference on Families* (Washington, D.C.: George Washington University, 1980), pp. 9–13.

10. Kamerman, *Developing a Family Impact Statement*, p. 16.

11. Halcyone H. Bohen and Anamaria Viveros-Long, *Balancing Jobs and Family Life* (Philadelphia: Temple University Press, 1981).

12. The Family Impact Seminar, for example, uses both the census definition of the (household) family ("a group of two or more persons residing together who are related by blood, marriage or adoption") and the concept of a kinship family, identical to the preceding definition except that family members need not reside together. In neither definition are minor children required for "family" status. See Family Impact Seminar, *Interim Report* (Washington, D.C.: George Washington University, 1978), p. 1.

13. See Pauline Grossenbacher Boss, "Theoretical Influences on Family Policy," *Journal of Home Economics* 71 (Fall 1979): 17–21.

14. See Allan C. Carlson, "Families, Sex, and the Liberal Agenda," *Public Interest* 58 (Winter 1980): 62–79; Onalee McGraw, *The Family, Feminism, and the Therapeutic State* (Washington, D.C.: Heritage Foundation, 1980), pp. 5–8; Ellen Wilson, "Home Truths," *Human Life Review* 6 (Summer 1980): 19–29.

15. See Gerald W. McDonald, "Typology for Family Policy Research," *Social Work* 24 (November 1979): 553–59.

16. See Steiner, *Futility of Family Policy*, pp. 193–215.

17. Kamerman, *Developing a Family Impact Statement*, p. 5.

18. See especially F. Ivan Nye and Gerald W. McDonald, "Family Policy Research: Emergent Models and Some Theoretical Issues," *Journal of Marriage and the Family* 41 (August 1979): 473–85; Marcia G. Ory and Robert K. Leik, *Policy and the American Family: A Manual for Family Impact Analysis* (Minneapolis: Minnesota Family Study Center, 1978).

19. Joan Druckman and Clifton Rhodes, "Family Impact Analysis: Application to Child Custody Determination," *Family Coordinator* 26 (October 1977): 454–55.

20. Steiner, *Futility of Family Policy*, p. 205.

21. McGraw, *Family, Feminism, and Therapeutic State*, p. 14.

22. Kamerman, *Developing a Family Impact Statement*, p. 15.

20

Wendy Brown

Reproductive Freedom and the Right to Privacy: A Paradox for Feminists

This essay grew out of a nagging uneasiness with the existing political struggle for free and legal abortions. While the unqualified availability of abortions is at present indispensable to women's freedom, there are several profoundly disturbing elements of the contemporary political and legal formulation of the issue.

To begin with, fighting for "freedom of choice" and "self-determination" against those who call themselves "pro-life" is at best a paradoxical affair. There is more than irony in the unholy alliance the pro-choice slogans establish between feminists and right-wing libertarians. More disturbing is the fact that the extreme individualism underlying these kinds of pro-choice arguments is rallied in opposition to those seeking to stir collective conscience on a matter of public concern. While some feminist theorists and activists have sought to render the demand for a "woman's right to choose" in less libertarian terms, the existing pro-choice language still arrays feminists on the side of the individual against society while the Right-to-Life movement insists that community consensus on certain matters, such as the protection of nascent human life, must prevail over individual preferences.[1]

Moreover, while no one defends abortion as a positive or desirable experience, pro-choice activists have tended to ignore or trivialize the trauma of many women who undergo abortions. They have thus delivered into the hands of the pro-life contingent almost all concern with many women's tremendous emotional confusion, feelings of loss, and sense of complicity in a world forcing them to sabotage potential life in order to be, in some minimal sense, free.

Finally, it is difficult to reconcile a critique of our increasingly technological world with the fact that fighting for abortion rights involves fighting for the right to surrender one's body, its natural processes, and the potential life within it to cold technological intrusion. One does not lightly encourage such an instrumental relationship to our bodies and to nature. Nor does this treatment of our bodies and of life represent the values and conception of society that feminists and leftists presumably seek to shape.

For their contributions to this essay, my thanks go to Polly Marshall, Arnie Fischman, and Michael Brint.

In short, unlike most issues on which we are working—peace, ending sexual violence, democratizing our political and economic life—abortion is not a positive good but an unhappy necessity. But to call it a necessity is immediately to raise the question of how this "need" came to be. With very few exceptions, human needs are not given but created, produced by our own history, which is itself humanly produced. Because we create most of our needs, we also have the capacity to eradicate or alter them rather than devote ourselves to fulfilling them.

It is important to recall this feature of the human condition when considering the abortion issue because the very fact that abortions are such troubling and problematic things to fight for suggests that they may actually be a superficial response to a problem older and deeper than unwanted pregnancy. To put the matter starkly, women need access to abortions for their "freedom" because we currently live in a world in which having a child can represent the largest and most uncompensated burden a human being can bear. It is this which makes abortion an intensely political problem rather than a moral, religious, or technical one. But for this situation to be addressed and redressed, we must first discover how it has come about and then what fundamental restructuring of our values, institutions, and way of life will offer true resolution.

I. From its origins in Ancient Greece, Western politics and political theory have rested on the assumption that reproduction—the gestation, birth, and nurturing of children to maturity—is a demeaning experience for human beings and is not among the activities around which social and political life ought to be organized.[2] Throughout the tradition of political theory, reproductive work has been referred to as "prepolitical," purely "natural," or merely "necessary," all of which have been pejorative referents in most Western cultures in most epochs. Listen to Hannah Arendt's discussion of classical Greece in *The Human Condition*:

> The distinction between the private and the public realm . . . equals the distinction between things that should be shown and things that should be hidden. . . . It is striking that from the beginning of history to our own time it has always been the bodily part of human existence that needed to be hidden in privacy, all things connected with the necessity of the life process itself . . . [Greek] women and slaves belonged to the same category and were hidden away not only because they were someone else's property but because their life was "laborious," devoted to bodily functions. . . .
>
> What all Greek philosophers took for granted is that freedom is exclusively located in the political realm, that necessity is primarily a pre-political phenomenon, characteristic of the private household organization and that force and violence are justified in this sphere because they are the only means to master necessity.[3]

Thus women, confined to a realm conceived of as prepolitical and as existing to serve the political, "carried on an indisputably necessary function without any recognition whatsoever and without any power to shape other social institutions in ways which were compatible with this central process in individual and social life."[4] Moreover, because men repudiated any involvement with reproductive work, women became *the only reproducers*. And because creatures involved with productive and reproductive work were deemed unfit for public life by the Greeks, women's entire identity was subsumed under their reproductive function; in large measure, women were regarded as *nothing other than reproducers*.

Gestation and birth, of course, are a small fraction of the process of human reproduction; the majority of reproductive work rests in the long period of nurturance, protection, and socialization that follows birth. Yet, just as in Marx's account wage workers under capitalist relations of production come to be nothing but workers and produce for all, from the beginning of Western civilization women were assigned the entire burden of reproductive work and were demeaned in the process because public life and the freedom it embodied rested on top of this activity and devalued what it rested upon.

From the perspective of the citizenry in the polis, the private sphere encompassed the activities instrumentally necessary to the polis's existence and therein lay its primary significance. As the biological aspect of human existence was devalued and repudiated (with women and laborers as its repository), human capacities for other than productive and reproductive work were glorified as that which constituted fully human existence. Only the realm and activities free from necessity were imbued with the status of "meaning." As we learn from Aristotle, human life is polis life; private life is a mere animal existence, the life of an "idiot," cut off from the potential for achievement, recognition, community, and freedom.[5]

What established and cemented the oppressiveness of reproductive work—work that is inherently neither oppressive nor glorious—was the formation of the private realm as the realm of explicit unfreedom and inequality, the realm where issues of justice and democracy were literally irrelevant. Because productive and reproductive work were viewed by the Greeks as uncreative, unredeeming activities, valuable only in their provision of the material requisites of those engaged in higher pursuits, the organization of this work and those involved with it was not subject to the ethical or political standards applicable to citizen life. Arendt puts the Aristotelian conclusion sharply:

> Because all human beings are subject to necessity, they are entitled to violence toward others; violence is the pre-political act of liberating oneself from the necessity of life for the freedom of the world. . . .
>
> The "good life" as Aristotle called the life of the citizen, therefore was not merely better, more carefree or nobler than ordinary life, but of an altogether different quality. It was "good" to the extent that by having mastered the necessities of sheer life, by being freed from labour and work, and by overcoming the inate urge of all living creatures for their own survival, it was no longer bound to the biological life process.[6]

Of course the relationship of private to public, the structure of the household, and many associated values, practices and institutions have changed dramatically since the Golden Age of Greece. But some aspects of the Greek formulations have been remarkably enduring. Among these are the notions that reproductive work is prepolitical and lacking in real-world value, something from which it is appropriate for men to abdicate their involvement and from which they must escape if, in the world they have created, they are to realize their "full humanity." Also enduring are the ideology and practices allotting woman the full gamut of reproductive responsibilities, making this work into the entirety of her identity, and demeaning and cutting her off from public life in the process.

While early liberal thinkers insisted upon the purely conventional—humanly designed and constructed—nature of the state and a peaceful civil society, they continued to regard the family as a natural entity. Theorists like Thomas Hobbes and John Locke assigned the family a prepolitical status in the double sense that they cast it as existant prior to political society and as a natural, given, or nonpolitical institution once political and civil society are formed. This continuation of a view and treatment of the family as "natural" contrasts sharply with the new conception of politics and its relation to the rest of human life put forth by liberal theorists. No longer is political life portrayed as the ultimate in human meaning; to the contrary, politics comes to inhabit an extremely narrow, legalistic governmental space. For Locke, political power is "the right of making laws with the penalty of death"; and for Hobbes, "the end of Commonwealth (is the) foresight of (men's) own preservation and of a more contented life thereby. . . ."[7]

As political life is narrowed into the institution of government, civil society is the newly named sphere of economic and social life. And because individual liberty (rooted in a concern with self-preservation and material acquisition) takes on such primacy for the early liberals, the content of civil society is raised to a status hitherto unknown. Government, discussed in terms of the "publick Good," exists solely for the purpose of guaranteeing individual rights and liberties in civil society. Civil society becomes the realm of importance and "meaning" for individuals. Civil society is the realm in which one can theoretically use one's rights for individually designed purposes, which purposes, according to the liberals, epitomize and express our humanity.[8]

The questions we are given by this transmogrification of political, civil, and economic life are these: What bearing does the liberal conception and practice of rights and freedom have on the heretofore degraded, oppressively organized, and "rightless" activity of reproduction, for which women have been named responsible? Or, to what extent are the conditions for exercising one's rights in liberal society different for men than for women? Or, what is the relationship between woman's traditional place (the family) and the place where rights are formulated and exercised?

In order to develop and address these questions, I shall make use of Marx's critique of political liberty in the modern state. First, however, it is worthy of brief mention that Marx is no exception to the general themes we have sketched thus far in our consideration of the tradition of Western political thought and practice with regard to women and reproduction. Marx tells us that men are shaped by their relation to the mode of production. But we have seen that women (and men in a sense somewhat analogous to the bourgeoisie in production) are shaped by their relation to the mode of reproduction. So in the Marxian vision of freedom, realized when the means of production are collectively owned and controlled, the matter of freedom for reproducers and reproduction is ignored. Reproductive work is not regarded as work, and Marx joins the liberals in viewing the organization of this work nonpolitical.

The notion that reproductive work does not and cannot make one a useful member of society and that women as well as men will be free only when they escape it has persisted throughout the Marxist tradition, even in many "Marxist-feminist" writings.[9] Some version of Shulamith Firestone's "liberate women through test tube babies" has, until recently, lurked within most Marxist-feminist theory, presumably because the history of women's oppression through reproduction *appears* overwhelming, inherent, and immutable. From our considerations thus far, however, it should be evident that freedom *from* reproduction represents a purely negative version of freedom. As Lorenne Clark puts it, this is freedom only in the sense that women join men in securing the complete victory of the values of the dominant sex, the values that have historically stigmatized reproduction and reproducers.[10] Clearly, women's unique role in the reproductive process *can* be eliminated, but this is a highly unimaginative solution to the problem of oppressively organized reproductive work. When Marxists consider the oppressive and alienated conditions of productive work, they do not propose abolishing the work itself, but transforming its conditions. They seek to liberate and collectivize such work. Marxist feminists have only recently begun to propose similar possibilities for reproductive work.

Despite Marx's limited usefulness on the problem of reproductive work, his analysis of bourgeois politics and ideology can help us pinpoint difficulties in the liberal conception of women's freedom. In his essay "On the Jewish Question," Marx contends that eliminating the "property qualification" for citizenship *presupposes rather than abolishes* private property and its effects in political and social life. Abolishing the property qualification does not abolish private property but depoliticizes property relations, thereby allowing the state to constitute itself as a "universal" body above the divisions, distinctions, and particularity of civil society.

> The state abolishes, after its fashion, the distinctions established by birth, social rank, education, occupation, when it decrees that birth, social rank, education, occupation are non-political distinctions; when it proclaims, without regard to these distinctions, that every member of society is an equal partner in popular sovereignty, and treats all the elements which compose the real life of the nation from the standpoint of the state.
>
> But the state, nonetheless, allows private property, education, occupation, to act after their own fashion, namely *as* private property, education, occupation, and to manifest their particular nature. Far from

> abolishing these effective differences, it only exists so far as they are presupposed.[11]

Marx is making several points here. First, he perceives the ability to exercise the individual freedoms with which the liberals were so concerned as entirely conditioned by one's birth, occupation, and the like. Second, he sees that the very legitimacy of the modern constitutional state is predicated on the ideology that these distinctions are transcended in the course of political and legal adjudication; that is, liberal legal ideology presents these distinctions as *merely social* distinctions, independent of politics at their source and in their implications. Thus Marx called the modern state and bourgeois law "abstractions" because they abstracted from the content of individuals' actual existence, from actual daily life where birth, social rank, education, and occupation have tremendous bearing.

It should be obvious that no sleight-of-hand whatsoever is involved in adding "gender" to Marx's list of depoliticized social distinctions.[12] The *political* emancipation of women (suffrage, equal rights, etc.) leaves intact the fact of sexism with regard to reproductive relations just as "political emancipation from religion leaves religion in existence."[13] What better example than women to support Marx's claim that to treat an identity as "natural" rather than "social," to remove the political mandate from a given social role and leave its fate to the sphere of civil society and the free market, is not to emancipate individuals from the structural confines of these identities but to divide the individual into a public and private person, an "egoistic individual" and an "abstract citizen"? To provide a serf, a worker, or a woman with political rights does not alter the conditions of production and reproduction that make their lives unfree, but offers them only the opportunity to adopt a public persona abstracted from and alien to their everyday life.

Moreover, Marx reminds us, the right to individual liberty is curtailed whenever it comes into conflict with "public liberty," what Marx ironically called "political life" and what we know as "national welfare" or "national security."[14] This is significant for our purposes because so many Supreme Court cases entail adjudication of precisely this area of conflict between individual rights and the so-called national interest. By no means do all the decisions favor the individual, even when First Amendment rights are at stake.

Not only, then, does Marx criticize the abstract nature of freedom in the liberal state, but he has also identified the limits to even this abstract freedom, the point at which the rights of the individual are abridged by the state in the name of the national interest. As we shall see, both criticisms are important to our consideration of the abortion problem. Before moving to an analysis of abortion in the context now set out, I shall summarize the issues in liberalism and the Marxian critique central to the relation between women, reproductive work, and freedom.

1. While the emergence of the liberal state and commercial society created a sphere of political and civil rights for all citizens, the extent to which we can exercise these rights is strongly conditioned by our situation in society. Granting

women political rights does not mitigate the fetter on their civil and political freedom constituted by their institutionalized and degraded status as reproducers. Women's participation in civil and economic life and their acquisition of full citizenship bear a meaning of freedom and equality only in alienation or abstraction from their lives in the family, that is, when they are "abstract, artificial beings" in contrast to their "sensuous, individual and immediate existence" as reproducers.[15]

2. The rights of women in civil society are individual rights against other members of the community, rights to act in accordance with their private interests within the confines of existing productive and reproductive relations. For women, such rights have especially limited meaning because reproductive work takes place in the family, an ambiguous social realm that, since the time of the Greeks, has been "rightless" and unfree. While the status of maternity is, to some degree, protected by the state, and "reproductive rights" are on the current political agenda, reproductive relations remain generally isolated from the purview of rights because reproduction is viewed and cherished as natural, not as a social, political, or economic activity. While wage workers are "free," as Marx put it ironically, "in a double sense, that as free men they can dispose of their labor power as their own commodity, and that on the other hand, they have no other commodity for sale," women do not experience even the limited first type of freedom when they are engaged in reproductive work.[16]

3. Even the limited political and civil rights of women last only as long as they do not conflict with the state's determination of public welfare. And this is precisely the point at which we find the abortion question in the courts: It is so perfectly situated at the nexus between "individual rights" and "the national interest" that in the landmark *Roe* v. *Wade* decision, the term of pregnancy was literally divided between these two jurisdictions. (In *Roe* v. *Wade*, the first trimester of pregnancy was placed in the terrain of individual rights, the second trimester was put on a bridge between individual rights and public welfare, and the third trimester was planted firmly on the turf of "compelling state interest," which overrides individual rights.[17]) Still more bizarre, in *Harris* v. *McRae*, the national interest was construed as that which would *discourage* women from using the individual rights granted them in *Roe* v. *Wade*. In *Harris* v. *McRae*, Justice Stewart justified the constitutionality of witholding public funds for abortions by arguing that:

> . . . the Hyde Amendment . . . *places no governmental obstacle in the path of a woman who chooses to terminate her pregnancy, but* rather, by means of unequal subsidization of abortion and other medical services, *encourages alternative activity deemed in the public interest.*[18]

II. With the understanding of women's oppression through reproductive work and the critical perspective on the liberal legal tradition I have been developing, let us now look more closely at the formulation of the abortion controversy both in political debate at the grass-roots level and in legal considerations at the hands of the U.S. Supreme Court.

Personhood

For analytic philosophers, Supreme Court justices, and the Moral Majority, the concept of "personhood" or "when life begins" has been singled out as one of the most critical matters in the abortion controversy. Many argue that the abortion issue is so difficult to resolve because the terrain on which it could be resolved yields no definitive truths: "When life begins," Justice Blackmun remarks in *Roe* v. *Wade*, "is a matter of disagreement among doctors, philosophers, and theologians."[19]

When life begins is also a matter of disagreement among those who oppose abortions and those who support them. Yet both sides end up in what are, ultimately, paradoxical and unconvincing positions. Pro-life groups argue for the unqualified protection of "mere life," or human biological life, while they generally eschew concern with the meaning or quality of life *and* appear unruffled by the state's routine willingness to risk and sacrifice lives for national security (war) or national welfare. As one columnist put it, "it's . . . ironic for right-wingers to claim to be defending the welfare of the unborn when they so vigorously oppose public intervention to improve the welfare of the born."[20]

Abortion advocates, on the other hand, often end up arguing against the significance of "potential life," a move that involves decontextualizing and dehistoricizing the existence of individuals and humanity as a whole. For as numerous doctors and scientists on both sides of the abortion question have pointed out, in human reproduction biological life does not really begin at all but is part of a continuum:

> There is no period where life stops and later starts up again. Cells come only from living cells. If the ovum were not alive and mature, it would never be fertilized. If the sperm were not alive, it couldn't even reach the ovum, much less fertilize it. The continuity of life is a principle that both pro-life and pro-abortion scientists agree upon.[21]

If resolving the question of personhood and when life begins is so problematic, why do politicians, political activists, and Supreme Court justices persist in tying the abortion issue to this problem? A group of Right-to-Life scientists provide an answer: "Personhood is the source of rights that cannot justly be taken away by any individual, group, or earthly power."[22] In the liberal state, courts exist to adjudicate disputes on the basis of the rights of the parties involved. Now rights, as we all know, are things applicable to individuals, not to histories, cultures, or webs of relationships. Thus, despite Justice Blackmun's proclamation in *Roe* v. *Wade* that the Court "need not resolve this difficult question (of when life begins)," the Court really had no alternative but to decide the case precisely on the basis of such as resolution. The Court had to determine (1) when or whether a fetus has the individual rights to life, liberty, and so on accorded all persons, thus (2) when or whether the state is condoning murder, thus (3) when a woman is "no longer isolated in her privacy," when her right to do as she pleases so long as she doesn't hurt anybody no longer holds because she *is* hurting somebody.

Because the liberal state is predicated on and legitimated by the idea that justice must have the characteristics of universality, that is, the notion that social distinctions in civil society are transcended in the "illusory community" of the state, the Supreme Court justices are confined to viewing the abortion question as a membership problem: Is a fetus one of us or not?

The necessity of framing the abortion problem as one of determining the entities to which the Court must accord rights is made starkly clear in the last portion of Blackmun's summary of the "divergence of thinking" on the question of when life begins. Here, he reviews the rulings pertinent to the status of rights for the unborn and concludes that "the unborn have never been recognized in the law as persons in the whole sense."[23] Blackmun then proceeds to explain how and when fetuses are persons in a less than whole sense, where persons are construed as independent entities having rights. In the third trimester of pregnancy, the fetus is granted the status of "potential personhood," and with it the right to be protected by the state. The fetus is proclaimed "capable of meaningful life outside the mother's womb."[24]

Now it is patently obvious that no matter what one's "theory of life," as Blackmun refers to this matter, religious or other philosophical arguments need not even be invoked to remark on the utterly arbitrary character of the third-trimester determination. A baby born three months prematurely is no more or less capable of conducting a meaningful life than is a fetus that has gestated in a test-tube for four months or a ten-day-old infant delivered at full term. If the argument is based on a concept of self-sufficiency, then any life younger than three years is probably incapable of meaningful life outside the womb. If the issue is consciousness/self-consciousness, then biological movement (quickening) is surely not the indicator to use.

In short, the difficulty of establishing any given point in time as that at which a fetus is capable of meaningful life outside the mother's womb epitomizes the extent to which rights adjudication *requires* a denial of our complex interrelatedness and interdependence with others. Nowhere is this more obvious than in the question at hand: What could have a more explicitly dependent, historical, and interrelated or other-constituted character than "potential life"? However, since rights cannot be affixed to relations but only to entities, the entities to be accorded rights must be abstracted from their historical and omnipresent determination by things and persons outside themselves. Rights adjudication requires conceptually severing the fetus from its history, future, and relationship to what nurtures it and ignoring the network of social relations in which reproduction is embedded.

But let us, for a moment, place the accent marks on a different term in the phrase "capable of meaningful life." It is not easy to guess at what Justice Blackmun had in mind when he established the state's concern with lives of *meaning*, but we may presume the minimum connotation to be human life distinguishable from beasts and plants. What, though, if we assume that a life of meaning must encompass some measure of independence, some capacity for choice, for exercising rights and pursuing goals? What if this "meaning" is what distinguishes life from mere life, the "fully human" from those Arendt told us were "deprived of things essential to a truly human life"? Are we not then thrust back to the problem of the impact of reproductive work on the "meaningful life" of a mother? Consider Justice Burger's remarks on this issue in his concurring opinion in *Roe* v. *Wade*:

> Elaborate argument is hardly necessary to demonstrate that childbirth may deprive a woman of her preferred lifestyle and force upon her a radically different and undesired future. For example, rejected applicants under the Georgia statute are required to endure the discomforts of pregnancy; to incur the pain, higher mortality rate, and after effects of childbirth; to abandon educational plans; to sustain loss of income; to forego the satisfactions of careers; to tax further mental and physical health in providing childcare. . . .[25]

Clearly, the right to a meaningful life moves us no closer to resolving the abortion problem than does the right to mere life or the right to a potential mere or meaningful life. It is precisely the confrontation of rights with our conception of the distinctive characteristics of human life that illuminates the impossibility of attempting to legislate or determine social relationships via a legal framework incapable of recognizing them. That abortion is reduced to a "medical question" and meaningful life to a biological-technical one is not, as numerous commentators on *Roe* v. *Wade* have suggested, merely bad or unconstitutional law.[26] The problem lies in the blatent nature of abortion as a facet of historically shaped social relationships and processes as opposed to an isolated procedure applied to independent entities and static situations. It is this feature of the abortion problem that exposes the limits of the liberal constitutional mode of determining how we shall live together.

The "Right to Privacy"

> *The right to privacy encompasses a woman's decision whether or not to terminate her pregnancy.*[27]

One trouble with rights is that they isolate individuals in theory when they are not independent of one another in reality. Another is that rights tend to treat individuals in abstraction from the concrete historical and socioeconomic context in which people actually exist. Still another is that they tend to confuse us about the difference between equal treatment and genuine equality, and between abstract opportunity and concrete possibility.

The trouble with a "right to privacy" (besides its weakness as a basis for a Supreme Court decision since no such right is explicitly guaranteed by the Constitution) is that, traditionally, activities in the private realm have been sharply separated from the sphere in which rights are formulated, exercised, and where they can have any substantive meaning. We have seen that the historical treatment of reproduction as a private matter obfuscates its reality as a set of relations and a category of work whose conditions are determined politically and have serious implications for the status of the "reproducer" in society. Since reproductive work has been structurally and ideologically relegated to mothers, and motherhood has typically entailed exclusion from participation in the public world, it is clear that reproductive activity is less safeguarded from "public infringement" than it is considered irrelevant or insignificant with regard to politics or law.

In short, the "right to privacy" is a right to go back into the natural, "rightless" world from which women with unwanted pregnancies emerged in order to be considered by the political light of the state. In *Roe* v. *Wade*, the Supreme Court pushed reproduction and the issues associated with it back into this private sphere, the sphere, as Marx reminds us, where "depoliticized" distinctions between members of society are left to work in their own (oppressive) fashion. It is not the Supreme Court alone that has made this move. Almost all the diverse groups who come under the general auspices of the pro-choice movement cast the issue in a similar manner:

> On behalf of the National Abortion Rights Action League . . . I urge you to provide a truly comprehensive health care program for . . . families—a program which not only covers childbirth but also the termination of a pregnancy—a program which allows families to make their own choices based on their own beliefs . . . regarding this profoundly personal issue, unencumbered by governmental interference or influence." (*NARAL testimony to the Senate Appropriations Committee*)[28]

> We believe that it is the right of a woman to choose whether to bear a child and that restrictive or prohibitive abortion laws violate a woman's right of privacy and liberty in matters pertaining to marriage, family and sex. (*American Jewish Congress*)[29]

> ABORTION SHOULD BE BETWEEN YOU AND A DOCTOR . . . NOT A POLITICIAN. The "right to life" movement feels that your right to have an abortion isn't a personal issue . . . but a political issue. Your most important posession is being threatened: your freedom. (*Planned Parenthood*)[30]

Still another difficulty with the "right to privacy" argument is that it sets the stage for race- and class-biased policies like those sanctioned by the *Harris* v. *McRae* decision. For once the state has sent a problem or person back to the land of theoretical noninterference by politics or law, once a matter has been declared "personal" or "private," the individual truly is thrown back upon her or his own means to deal with the problem. The private realm, Justice Burger warned us in *Roe* v. *Wade*, is where "the right to be let alone" presides.[31] It should therefore not surprise us to find the justices who supported the *Harris* v. *McRae* decision insisting that they are not telling poor pregnant women whether or not to have abortions but are merely reaffirming the fact that abortion is a private, individual decision and that the state will have nothing—politically or economically—to do with it.[32] In 1973 abortion was deemed by the Supreme Court to be a matter of privacy and not of politics or public welfare.

One's economic status in liberal capitalist society, of course, is another one of those depoliticized distinctions treated by the state as a private, individual matter. And it hardly needs saying that there is a substantial connection between one's economic status and what one can do with an unwanted pregnancy—just as there is a substantial connection between one's economic status and the relative joy or suffering involved with bringing a child into this world.

Now it is true that the justices considering *Harris* v. *McRae* could have found poor, pregnant women to be a "suspect class," but the state interest all along, Justice Stewart tells us, lay in protecting potential life and not in supplying or advocating abortions.[33] Not that the state is necessarily against abortion—that is a private matter. The liberal state claims to exist only to guarantee everyone his or her rights. Period. Anything else it does for particular individuals is a bonus, which is why with perfect consistency, albeit without much integrity, Justice Stewart could say that the Hyde Amendment

> . . . leaves an indigent woman with at least the same range of choices in deciding whether to obtain a medically necessary abortion as she would have had if Congress had chosen to subsidize no health care costs at all.[34]

The State Interest

In *Harris* v. *McRae*, the majority opinion vindicated the contention at the heart of the Right-to-Lifers' concerns that the "legitimate governmental objective" is that of "protecting potential life."[35] Justice Stewart justifies the Hyde Amendment as follows:

> By subsidizing the medical expenses of indigent women who carry their pregnancies to term while not subsidizing the comparable expenses of women who undergo abortions. . . . . Congress has established incentives that make childbirth a more attractive alternative than abortion for persons eligible for Medicaid. These incentives bear a direct relationship to the legitimate congressional interest in protecting potential life.[36]

The state interest in protecting life was also the reason given by Justice Blackmun in *Roe* v. *Wade* for superseding a woman's "right to privacy" during the second and third trimester of pregnancy. (In the second trimester, the ostensible concern is with endangering the life of the mother; in the third, it is with killing a "viable" fetus.)

In both *Roe* v. *Wade* and *Harris* v. *McRae*, the Court presents the state as interested in protecting "mere life" so that we are free to pursue "meaningful lives." The Court, representing the state, establishes only that life has a right to exist, free from certain abstract impediments, but cannot confront the relationships making living and reproducing life so problematic.[37] By setting up the abortion problem as one of protecting privacy, on the one hand, and potential life, on the other, the Court has cleared the state of all responsibility for the politically shaped tradeoffs individuals find essential to conducting a life that is even minimally free. Because the Court, embodying "universality," does not deal with the particular *facts* of those lives, it refuses to acknowledge the vicious meaninglessness of the right to abortion when public funding for abortions for poor women is withheld. Hiding behind abstract principles and rights, the Court is now permitting the very thing it earlier asserted itself as being concerned to protect—the endangered health of a woman determined to abort an unwanted pregnancy. Thus, when Justice Douglas proclaimed in *Roe* v. *Wade* that the "state has interests of its own to protect," state interests are being explicitly distinguished from the cares, the condition, and the well-being of the individuals the state supposedly serves and protects.

Justice Stewart explains this move in a theory of the state that blatantly detaches government from the economic and social life of the nation:

> . . . although government may not place obstacles in the path of a woman's exercise of her freedom of choice, it need not remove those not of its own creation. Indigency falls in the latter category. The financial constraints that restrict an indigent woman's ability to enjoy the full range of constitutionally protected freedom of choice are the product not of governmental restrictions on access to abortions, but rather of her indigency.[38]

One could not ask for a purer (nor more mean-spirited) version of the liberal belief in the benign and autonomous function of the state in a free enterprise society: A woman's pregnancy, financial straits, hopes, and possibilities for the future are all her own individual doing. Stewart unequivocally denies the state's involvement with and perpetuation of the relations of production and reproduction that actually produce this woman's poverty, as well as the burdensome character of her pregnancy.

The difference between the Supreme Court declaration in *McRae* and the arguments of the Right-to-Lifers is that the latter promises to do something very concrete for and with all those unhappy pregnant woman and unwanted children resulting from the realization of Right-to-Life goals. Of course these intentions do not mitigate the fact that if abortion is either financially inaccessible or illegal, then illegal and/or self-induced abortions will once again become the norm. Equally obvious, even "taking care of" poor pregnant women and their babies does not in the least alter the existing relationship between women's freedom and reproduction, a relationship that the Right-to-Lifers have no interest in altering in any case.

Yet, as I have intimated throughout this essay, the Right-to-Life position strikes a resonant chord: Childbearing, potential life, bringing new life into the world, should be a matter of great concern and involvement for all of us. It is, sadly, the antiabortion forces who continue to insist on this and on the political nature of abortion; most proabortion groups defensively argue that reproduction is a matter of private choice for every woman and that abortion is a private, technical act so banal that were it not for the hysteria of the Moral Majority, no one besides a pregnant woman and her doctor would think twice about it.

Of course the context of the Right-to-Life position is a concern with preserving the traditional family and the "natural" function and status of women as reproducers. Pro-choice activists, on the other hand, are generally concerned with women's freedom through a broader spectrum of reproductive rights. (Some in the reproductive rights movement even view gaining abortion rights as little more than a first step toward the longer-range goal of revaluing and reorganizing reproductive work.) But I have argued that reproductive rights serve primarily to entrench women's isolation in their unique relation to the reproductive process. Insofar as rights are inherently *protective*, *defensive*, and *isolating*, these are three things that women-as-reproducers do not need more of. The most rights can do is to prevent the reproductive burden from being excruciatingly and inescapably heavy; they do not help us along the road to collectivizing reproductive work such that its extraordinarily burdensome character becomes a closed chapter in history.

III. So how does one argue for abortion without talking about rights? And what is the long-run solution to the seemingly inherent tradeoff between childbearing and economic, political, and social freedom? We can glimpse the answer if we start by treating these questions as inseparable, as two aspects of the same question: How must the institutions and values of our society be altered so that women do not find themselves in an isolated and defensive position (the position where rights appear relevant) with regard to their unique role in the reproductive process (their unique capacity for gestation and birth, for transforming potential life into actual life)?

We must start by repoliticizing the social relations and identities currently depoliticized by the "natural" character imputed to existing reproductive practices and by liberal legal theory and practice. This is the first step toward recognizing and dismantling the institutions that currently determine how we live together but *prevent us* from determining how we shall live together. Specifically with regard to reproduction, we must work politically toward a world in which bearing and caring for children is never a burden on one individual of one particular sex but is understood and organized as an indispensable and absolutely valued aspect of *all* our lives and work. The relations of reproduction that currently degrade and punish reproducers, that curtail their status in the political and economic order, must be replaced with collective responsibility for reproductive work.

Every successful integration of productive and reproductive work on the same premises, every workplace child-care center, every union struggle for a shortened workweek in the name of ending the tension between raising children and holding a job, every nonfamily structure that collectivizes child care—constitutes a contribution to the goals I have outlined. But none of these things are ends in themselves, especially insofar as they are located within or dependent upon existing liberal-capitalist institutions. And the point (God forbid!) is not to institutionalize reproductive work along the lines in which productive work is currently organized nor to place such work under the auspices of the state. Rather, we must persistently address the present invalidation and relative invisibility of reproductive work and incorporate a genuinely democratic approach to such work in *all* our radical visions and programs.

For many feminists, the most controversial aspect of this argument undoubtedly lies in my insistence that we must actively include men in this vision. Many feminists view the acquisition of reproductive rights as the means to women's full independence and view men primarily as impediments to our efforts to reclaim control of our bodies and lives. Whether individual women choose to associate with men or not, reproductive work as a whole will remain an insufferable burden for women unless men share in it fully. It will continue to be regarded as women's work and to be treated as less valuable and less deserving of compensation than other kinds of work. It will continue to be ghettoized. Nothing testifies more clearly to this fact than the contemporary phenomenon of many financially secure women who choose not to bear children because doing so would sequester them from the world they value and enjoy.

This is not to suggest that a political order in which productive and reproductive work are equally valued and shared by men and women would rid us of all our dilemmas about abortion, nor that we have no alternatives to *Roe* v. *Wade* or *Harris* v. *McRae* in our political order as it is constituted at present. The need for abortions and the sorrow and turmoil they entail can probably never be eliminated. What can change is their status and use as a desperate solution for women facing socially and economically desperate situations. Second, we can begin to develop the values and institutions that would free women not from their biology but from their isolated, degraded, and deprived status as society's chief reproducers. Free abortions upon request are undoubtedly a necessary element in beginning this work. It is not a matter of who has a right to live or when life begins but that as long as the relations of reproduction and production are what they are, unwillingly pregnant women are burdened by a weight unmatched in difficulty or longevity by any that is "naturally imposed" upon any other member of society.

The Supreme Court actions and congressional deliberations of the past several years, as well as the present strength of the Moral Majority in this country, all point to the limitations of the *existing* proabortion arguments. As long as we talk about rights and privacy, the rights of the unborn can never be definitively established as less important than the rights of the already living. It is in the nature of rights to be abstract; thus, the relative concreteness of either party is of little significance. But if we focus instead upon the needs of individuals, on the concrete prerequisites to truly living a life in common with others, where all have a recognized value and place in that common life, and if we take seriously that we are creatures of history who can also shape our world, our struggle for both short- and long-run justice can be pursued with greater conviction, consistency, and steadiness.

NOTES

1. See, e.g., Rosalind Petchesky. "Reproductive Freedom: Beyond a Woman's Right to Choose" *Signs* 5, no. 4 (1980).

2. In recent works, several feminist students of political theory have put forth and developed this argument. See especially Lorenne Clark's "The Rights of Women: The Theory and Practice of the Ideology of Male Supremacy," Lynda Lange's "Reproduction in Democratic Theory," and Mary O'Brien's "The Politics of Impotence," all in *Contemporary Issues in Political Philosophy* ed. William R. Shea and John King-Farlow (New York: Science History Publications, 1976). In this section of the essay, I have drawn quite heavily on Clark's argument and examples.

3. Hannah Arendt, *The Human Condition* (New York: Doubleday, 1959), pp. 64, 29.

4. Clark, "Rights of Women," p. 52.

5. Aristotle *Politics* I. ii. 1253a; I.v. 1254b; I.viii. 1256b.

6. Arendt, *The Human Condition*, pp. 30, 33.

7. John Locke, "Second Treatise," in *Two Treatises of Government* ed. Peter Laslett (Cambridge: Cambridge University Press, 1960), sec. 3, p. 308. Thomas Hobbes, *Leviathan*, ed. Michael Oakeshott (New York: Macmillan, 1962), p. 129.

8. While Hobbes and Locke sketch and justify the institutions of the liberal state at least partially in terms of a concern with individual liberty, it is John Stuart Mill who offers a full-blown and contemporary formulation of the relationship between individual liberty and our "essential humanity." See *On Liberty*.

9. See, e.g., August Bebel, *Woman Under Socialism*, trans. from 33rd ed. of the German by Daniel De Leon (New York: New York Labor News Press, 1904); Clara Zetkin, "My Recollections of Lenin," in *Reminiscences of Lenin* (New York: International Publishers, 1934); V. I. Lenin, *The Emancipation of Women: Writings of V. I. Lenin* (New York: International Publishers, 1975); Charnie Guettel, *Marxism and Feminism* (Toronto: Hunter Rose, 1974); and Shulamith Firestone, *Dialectic of Sex* (New York: Bantam Books, 1970).

10. Clark, "Rights of Women," p. 62.

11. Karl Marx. "On the Jewish Question," in *Marx-Engels Reader*, ed. Robert C. Tucker (New York: Norton, 1972), p. 31.

12. The difference between gender and the other social distinctions Marx lists is that gender was depoliticized long prior to the transition from feudalism and effective monarchy to capitalism and the modern state.

13. Marx, "On the Jewish Question," p. 27.

14. Ibid., pp. 41–42.

15. Ibid., p. 32.

16. Marx., *Capital,* trans. Moore and Aveling (New York: International Publishers, 1967), 1:169.

17. *Roe* v. *Wade*, *U.S. Supreme Court Reports* (35 L. Ed. 2d), 410 U.S. 164.

18. *Harris* v. *McRae*, *U.S. Supreme Court Reports* (65 L. Ed. 2d), p. 803.

19. *Roe* v. *Wade*, 410 U.S. 27.

20. "Right to Strife," *New Republic*, 6 June, 1981, p. 5.

21. Scientists for Life, "The Position of Modern Science on the Beginning of Human Life," in *1981 Department of Defense Appropriations Hearings*, pt. 6, DOD Nondepartmental Witnesses (Washington, D.C.: Government Printing Office, 1980), p. 146.

22. Ibid., p. 161.

23. *Roe* v. *Wade*, 410 U.S. 27.

24. Ibid., 410 U.S. 32, 33.

25. Ibid., 410 U.S. 214, 215.

26. See, for example, John Hart Ely, "The Wages of Crying Wolf: A Comment on

Roe v. Wade," *Yale Law Journal* 82 (1973): 947; or Bernard Nathanson, *Aborting America* (New York: Doubleday, 1979), pp. 206–13.

27. *Roe* v. *Wade*, "Summary," p. 148.

28. NARAL testimony before Senate Appropriations Subcommittee, in *Department of Defense Appropriations Hearings*, p. 183.

29. American Jewish Congress, Biennial Convention 1978 statement, quoted in pamphlet issued by Religious Coalition for Abortion Rights.

30. Advertisement placed by Planned Parenthood in The *New York Times*, 26 October 1980, Sec. E, p. 7.

31. *Roe* v. *Wade*, 410 U.S. 213.

32. *Harris* v. *McRae*.

33. Ibid., "Summary," p. 785.

34. Ibid.

35. Ibid., p. 810.

36. Ibid.

37. It is hardly necessary to recount the ways in which the state routinely sacrifices biological/meaningful life for "state interests." It is for "national security" that we go to war, engineer fascist coups in the Third World, escalate nuclear arms development, and respond to fiscal crises in cities by cutting social service programs that are often the lifelines of particular individuals. It is for "national prosperity" that we sanction the nuclear energy industry, manage recessions to slow down a racing economy, and permit carcinogenic industrial operations. What is left of the state's compelling interest in protecting the health of a pregnant woman and the potential life of a fetus when such lives are part of or born into a world in which they will not necessarily be cared for nor protected, when they can be made into an instrument of aggressive warfare, subjected to conditions hazardous to their mental and physical health at work, or reside in an environment where an industry's property rights are held in higher esteem than their right to breathe air, drink water, and eat food that won't kill them? The point is that the principles of the Constitution and the state in general cannot even fulfill their purpose in protecting mere life such that they provide the means to meaningful lives. Even mere rights to mere life are mutable because they are rights and principles applied out of context.

38. *Harris* v. *McRae*, p. 804.

21

Martha A. Ackelsberg

"Sisters" or "Comrades"? The Politics of Friends and Families

Sisterhood is powerful! Those words seemed to capture the intensity of feelings that did—and do—unite those involved in the women's movement. Yet the language of sisterhood, though effectively conveying the notion of connectedness, and of joy in that connectedness, also exemplifies an important paradox in the theory and practice of feminism, for the "sisters" referred to are not family members but friends.

We have been caught by the limitations of our own vocabulary. We have almost no language to express intense ties except that of family; we speak of "fraternity" or "blood-brotherhood" or "sisterhood." But that vocabulary denies the reality of many actual family relationships and shifts our focus away from the true nature of the relationships we mean to describe. It masks and reinforces a particular ideological use of "family" while enabling us to ignore—at least on a conscious level—the significance of friends.

That fact of language is reflected within the feminist movement itself. The strength of the movement, both during the nineteenth century and in the contemporary period, has been its base, not in family ties, but in friendship networks. Feminists have, in fact, severely criticized the practice of much family life in the United States, pointing out not only the failure of existing families to live up to the ideal but also, more specifically, the contribution of nuclear families to the subordination of women. Feminists have called for the creation of alternatives to the isolation of the nuclear family and for an end to "mother-monopolized" childrearing practices.[1] But few theoretical models have been offered that articulate viable alternatives.

Many friends—as well as families—contributed to the development of these ideas. I wish especially to acknowledge the help of Irene Diamond, Donna Divine, Philip Green, Jill Lewis, P. Lough O'Daly, Miriam Slater, and Verena Stolcke, as well as the inspirations and satisfactions I have experienced through the feminist movement and through my special relationships with Elana Rosenfeld Berkowitz, Elana and Jonas Divine, and Megan Hudson. This paper is dedicated to the memory of Jeanne McFarland.

In fact, on a day-to-day, a practical, or material basis, the beginnings of many models exist in the form of support networks, housekeeping "pools," communal living, or coparenting arrangements. And not surprisingly, given the origins and development of the feminist movement, many of these alternatives are based on friendship networks. But we have failed to integrate that existing practice adequately with theory. More significantly, we have failed to draw sufficiently on our experiences with friendship in developing alternatives to the nuclear family.

In this essay I attempt a modest exploration of some of these connections. I look specifically at the ideological uses that "family" has served and at the ways in which friends can provide alternative contexts in which to meet many of the expectations we have of families; and I speculate about some of the ways in which the ideology of family may have prevented clearer articulation of these alternatives. I do not intend, here, to propose fully developed friendship-based new social forms. Instead, I wish to reclaim in this somewhat new context what friendships have done and continue to do: to recognize their significance and suggest that attention to friendship might enrich not only our vocabulary but also our ability to envision alternative futures.

Families are highly political institutions. Kin relationships both shape and are shaped by the communities and the complex of social, economic, and political relationships in which they are embedded. And any actual family has an internal "political" structure of its own, characterized by particular patterns of authority, deference, respect, and support. The very meaning of "family" differs with the class, sex, ethnic culture, and social context of the definer. Within any family, for example, different members will have markedly different experiences—we can think of parents and children or of men and women.[2] Experience differs, as well, according to where families are situated within the larger sociopolitical context. Here we might note the difference between the experience of a child growing up in a dense urban extended family versus that of a child in a typical suburban single-family home.[3]

Perhaps the most perplexing policy implication of feminist analyses of "families" is their paradoxical quality. That which nurtures men in the traditional middle-class nuclear family, for example, appears to subordinate women. In addition, despite the emphasis—especially in the contemporary period—on the alleged centrality of the nuclear family and on nuclear family ties as *the* essential social bonds, extrafamilial ties have played a crucial role in the maintenance of families, at least for the last one hundred to two hundred years, in both England and the United States. More recently, impersonal institutions have taken over many of the functions (e.g., health care, care for the aged) traditionally performed by families or community groups.

Our conventional notion of the family ignores both the existence and the significance of these paradoxes. The "family," that is, is an *ideological* as well as a *biological* construct. First, the claim that the family is a "natural" biological unit masks the role of "family" in recruiting people into relations of production and reproduction.[4] "The concept of family is a socially necessary illusion which simultaneously expresses and masks recruitment to relations of production, reproduction and consumption—relations that condition different kinds of household resource bases in different class sectors."[5] The assumption of the naturalness of the nuclear family unit, for example, legitimates wage differentials between men and women, since the man is assumed to be "head of household," with primary responsibility for the financial support of the entire family. Gender assumptions also generate expectations about the role of the wife-mother in the household; she is held primarily responsible for managing the budget and assuring that her husband (and perhaps children) receive the support necessary for them to function in the paid labor force. Needless to say, these assumptions, and the socioeconomic patterns deriving from them, have specific and different impacts on those who do *not* live in traditional nuclear families. Thus it is impossible accurately to generalize about the family without specifying the social context of those persons whose experience is being considered. But the use of a single term "family" blinds us to the significance of these differences and thus serves important ideological purposes.[6]

Second, the concept of family is ideological in other senses. It serves to mask and thereby to maintain the particular subordination of women (and children) within patriarchal households. In addition, family ties—whether on the level of the individual family or on the level of the "folk" state—also have political uses. For example, such ties have been used to mobilize people for war. Plato's myth of origins—that all Greeks were brothers because all came from the same source—was designed to draw on "family" emotions in just that way: to legitimate a particular version of patriotism and to justify war against those who were not members of the same "family." Moreover, as any number of people engaged in insurgent social movements have pointed out, commitment to "family" often places an effective damper on continuing revolutionary activity, which might place "politics" in conflict with family loyalties or responsibilities.[7] All too often, the choice of activism (or, more properly, revolutionary activism) is posed as a choice *between* family/love/personal loyalty, on the one hand, and political ideas, on the other. In this respect, the ideological character of "family" can easily be seen as a factor critical to maintaining the status quo; relatively few people, especially in societies that socialize their members to place a high value on intimacy, would choose a life course that appears to make such intimacy impossible.[8]

It is interesting to note that, historically, non-kin-based living communities (based on friendship, ideological commitments, or life-style choices, for example) have reflected a sensitivity to at least some of these aspects of "family" life. Many utopian communities have attempted to challenge, or provide an alternative to, the family precisely along the lines just mentioned. Thus, for example, Owenite and Fourierist communes in the United States and Europe in the nineteenth century, Israeli kibbutzim, and many contemporary American communal groups have attempted to establish themselves as economically self-sufficient, a move that can be seen as a rejection of the role "families" play today in recruiting workers to production in the paid labor force, and actually seem to hark back to a period when all family members were engaged together in productive labor. Many have asserted control over sexuality—imposing celibacy or dictating the terms of sexual relationships—a move that can be seen as a rejection of the role families play in regulating sexual relations and in constituting units of reproduction. And many have attempted to initiate changes in the direction of greater sexual and, on occasion, racial equality, which can be seen as rejections of the patriarchal, and racist, nature of family relations under capitalism and a reflection of dissatisfaction with the levels of intimacy attainable within the traditional white nuclear family. In addition, as many of these units developed out of shared political commitment; some, at least, attempted to make possible opportunities for intimacy even within the context of insurgent political activity.[9]

Given the ideological roles "family" plays in sustaining most societies with which we are familiar, and the paradoxes and dilemmas of family life of the sorts described, can friendship provide models for any viable alternative social forms?

The question has particular significance for feminists. On the one hand, as we have seen, feminist proposals for alternative living-social relationships often take friendship (or extended kin networks) as at least an unconscious model. But the issue of friendship has particular importance for feminists in another sense as well. Despite the current popularity of the view that "women have a special aptitude for friendship because they are less fearful than men of emotional intimacy,"[10] the traditional view has been that those best suited to long-standing, meaningful friendships are men. The strongest images of friendship in mythology and legend are friendships among men (e.g., David and Jonathan, Damon and Pythias, Huck Finn and Jim); Plato and Aristotle elevated friendship to a place of considerable significance in the maintenance of a political community, but generally assumed that the friends would be male (not least, presumably, because women were more prone to be moved by "feelings," while men were presumably moved by "reason," this making possible a higher order of relationship).[11] Women, on the contrary, have traditionally been seen as unable to be true friends because they are perpetually (or at least potentially) in competition with one another for men. More recent examination of families has revealed, however, that these stereotypes of women are far from true. Extrafamilial, same-sex relationships have been crucial aspects of women's lives across many cultures and classes. In fact, there is evidence that these friendship networks have made possible the survival of the "nuclear family." But we jump ahead.

One further *caveat*: Friendship is almost as elusive a concept to define as is family. Generally speaking, the defining characteristic of friendship is taken to be its *voluntary* and egalitarian quality. Writers tend to distinguish friendship from the bonds that presumably characterize family relationships as a relationship based on choice and rooted in equality and reciprocity.[12] But the "voluntary" quality of friendship should not be misread in such a manner as to remove friendship from a defining, and in some ways constraining, social context. We may all *feel* as though we choose our friends on a completely voluntary or even impulsive basis, but a quick look at virtually any friendship circle reveals that factors of class, race, sex, age, life style, work roles, and any number of other structural characteristics play a major role in determining with whom each of us will be friends. In that respect, friendship is probably little less "constrained" than is so-called romantic love, supposedly the basis of family ties in "advanced societies," but which also exists within relatively clearly defined social norms.[13] Thus friendship—as is the case with family, love, or sexuality—exists within a particular social and historical context, and its very meaning cannot be adequately understood outside that context.[14]

Let us turn, then, to an examination of that which the ideal family is held to do. To what extent can friends perform these functions? To what extent have they always done so?

NURTURANCE/CARING/SUPPORT

Some contemporary scholarship on the family, particularly the family under advanced industrial capitalism, suggests that the family stands *outside* the standard exchange relationships of capitalism. In this view the family is an institution characterized by caring and nurturance—a caring and nurturance not "requited" in any way through the "cash nexus." As such, the family serves as both a critique of the exchange relations that predominate in a capitalist society and a haven from those relationships.[15]

Yet the family as institution and ideological construct is intimately connected to productive and social relationships, serving as a primary recruiting mechanism for the labor force. Beyond that, as feminist critics have pointed out, there is a paradox in the actual functioning of many nuclear families: "The bases of love, dependence and altruism in human life and the historical oppression of women have been found in the same matrix."[16] How can feminists continue to affirm the values of nurturance without affirming, at the same time, the subordination of women within the institution that can, under certain circumstances, provide that nurturance?

Here, I would argue, is where attention to the institution and practice of friendship can provide possible routes out of the dilemma. Whether we look historically or in the contemporary period, families have *not* been the only sources of nurturance within most social systems; nor, of course, are all familial relationships necessarily nurturant. On the one hand, there is the issue of domestic violence—generally directed against women and children within families. On the other hand, even in that majority of families *not* characterized by violent or abusive relationships, there is considerable evidence that while families may serve as institutions that nurture *men*, women have received much of *their* nurturance from extra-familial friendship ties. Thus, for example, Laurel Thatcher Ulrich found in her study of northern New England families, 1650–1750, that "self-sufficient households were atypical, and that relationships between women were far more crucial than most scholars have supposed."[17] While these networks offered much in the form of goods and services (e.g., sharing of scarce commodities, laundry, or child care), they also provided a more diffuse form of "nurturance," commonly referred to as "neighborliness." Associations among women may have facilitated the continuity of the family and the hierarchical distribution of authority within it, but they also protected women from abuse within their families: "Horizontal lines between housewife and housewife might form a counterweight to vertical relationships between husband and wife."[18]

The nurturing that women friends have provided one another is not merely material. Carroll Smith-Rosenberg's work on female friendships in nineteenth-century America points out clearly the ways in which those middle-class women received *their* nurturing, certainly emotional and sometimes physical, from other women—usually women outside the immediate nuclear family—rather than from the men to whom they were married.[19] Similarly, evidence suggests that women in working-class families in East London during the nineteenth century provided essential supports for one another across family lines. Women's associations based in the neighborhood provided a "safety net" for working-class families. Given the need to share laundries, toilets, and often kitchen facilities, opportunities for "intimacy and sharing were literally built into the housing."[20] Similar sharing and nurturance has been reported among black families in urban communities in the contemporary United States.[21]

Friendships, however, have done more than simply sustain and "nurture the nurturers" within nuclear (or even extended) families. Women (and men) have relied on friendships to provide support and nurturance independent of their family relations. In most Western societies, at least, women traditionally do the nurturing, and women's roles as nurturers and caretakers have often been seen to derive from their *biological* role as mothers. But one need not be a mother in order to nurture. The now popular concept of "mothering" may, in fact, be another of those powerful ideological constructs: We say mothering when we mean nurturing; and by identifying the two, we reinforce the role of women within the patriarchal family and relieve others from the responsibility to nurture.[22]

Male friendships, as well, have provided important sources of support for those who participate in them. It seems no accident that early associations of workingmen, which provided the basis for unions, were called "friendly societies." As factory discipline increasingly segregated friendship and sociability from work, a "differently organized male social world emerged in response, in which friendship and conviviality were part of the cluster of 'leisure' institutions, clubs, sports events, and pubs—which grew up as the industrial workday decreased. . . ."[23]

Thus, whether we think of nurturance and caring in terms of physical-material support or in terms of emotional support, it seems clear that families have not been, nor are they now, necessarily nurturant or the only sources of nurturance in an exchange-oriented world. Instead, families themselves have found important supports in networks of women. And many women (and men) have found sustenance for their own needs, not through families, but through same-sex friendships. If our goal is to revalue nurturance, to provide a set of standards other than utility and the market by which relationships and activities can be judged, then to limit our understanding of nurturance and caring to that set of activities performed by women in the "privacy of their families" is surely to reinforce the very phenomenon that is decried. Defining nurturance as women's work, or limiting its expression to the family context, only abandons the "public world" to utilitarian market values. Instead, we might well look to friendship as a model for the way people ought to behave toward one another—envisioning a society based on nurturant values of "community and caring" in the public realm as well as in the domestic.[24]

ACCEPTANCE/SUPPORT FOR SELF-DEVELOPMENT

We do, of course, look to families for other functions as well, some of them related to nurturance in the sense mentioned above. As we have seen, many recent critics and commentators focus on "mothering" and the value of the support and acceptance that ideal-typical mothers provide their children. In this view, mothers "must foster growth and welcome change . . . the 'being' that changes is always developing, building, purposively moving away."[25] It is in families that we assume that children and young people will find the support they need to develop themselves, to realize their potential as people, and to take their place in the larger communities of which they form a part.

But, once again, while some families facilitate the growth of their members, it is clear that we often look more to friends for that sort of acceptance than to family. Here, the voluntary quality of friendship may be relevant. Thus, as one discussion of female friendships of the nineteenth century in the United States suggested, "because female friendships were elective relationships with peers, they offered a young woman substantial freedom for self-realization compared to her family definitions as daughter, sister or wife."[26] Friendship, even more than familial relationships, seems dependent on *equality of respect* allowing room for the "creative development of personality, which is in turn dependent on seeing a person in her or his true self."[27] In Aristotle's words, "when friendship is based on character, it does last . . . because it is friendship for its own sake (in which each partner loves his friend for what he is)" (*Nichomachean Ethics* 1164a).

The point is emphasized further by the insistence of many "advisers" on friendship on the need for honesty, frankness, and trust. Thus, as Bertha Conde wrote in *The Business of Being a Friend*, "surely the greatest of all blessings is a truthful friend, for all of us are liable to fall into the snare of self-deception . . . a truth-speaking friend, who loves unselfishly, is the best cure for such self-deception."[28] And Lydia Sigourney's advice to young ladies said simply, "merit confidence by frankness, at the same time that you guard with fidelity whatever secret may be entrusted to you. 'Reserve wounds friendship and distrust destroys.'"[29] The distance between these admonitions and those of Adrienne Rich in our own day—that "an honorable human relationship . . . is a process . . . of refining the truths they can tell each other"—is short, indeed.[30]

Thus, while literature and life are filled with stories of people who feel unable to be completely open (or "themselves," we say) with their families, we hold much higher standards, in this respect, of our friends. Despite the *ideological* insistence that families provide the ultimate place of safety and acceptance, it appears that the "working hypothesis" for many is that the specific kinds of support for self-development that families are supposed to provide may be more readily found in friends. Families *seem* to demand one's fitting into prescribed roles. By contrast, friends seem to support us to "become the person I am."[31] The experiences and reactions of women who "come out" as lesbians, in the context of friends and families, for example, are markedly different. While it is true that many ultimately *want* the acceptance and support of families of origin, the process of becoming a lesbian is almost always carried out in a community of friends.[32]

Similarly, as we noted above, *family* relationships are more likely than friendships to hold people back from committing themselves fully to political and/or career choices that conflict with the maintenance of traditional family ties. Somehow we have the *expectation*, at least, that friends will support our moving off in such directions, even if that makes the continuity of the day-to-day relationship more problematic. Perhaps that is so because it is more often with friends than with family members that we engage in such activities. Ideologically, we assume that family bonds are stronger than those of friendship. But that assumption may well be related to the fact that, in these sorts of situations at least, we tend to experience family ties as restrictive and friendship ties as enabling.

SOLIDARITY/SOCIAL CEMENT

In addition to providing support and nurturance for their members, families are also looked to as the basic unit of society, the primary social bond on which social solidarity rests. Political theorists as diverse as Aristotle, Locke, and Rousseau have argued that the first building block of political community is the family.[33] As we have seen, the assumption that family ties are especially powerful is reflected directly in our language. We speak of "fraternity," "sisterhood," and "brotherhood" as values even when the relationships referred to are not familial in the strict sense.

It is, of course, important to recognize that the relationships implied by the use of such kin language are probably stronger than the reality of kin relationships. Ritual kinship structures use the language of consanguineal kinship, for example, "by analogy with the *idea* of brotherly love, rather than with the reality of brotherly behavior," which is fraught with sibling rivalry and the like.[34] Images of "sisterhood" and "brotherhood" are very powerful in politics and culture. Yet I would argue that nonkin friendships provide more frequent examples of the felt power of those terms than do actual blood ties. Those who have proclaimed the "truth" of the phrase "sisterhood is powerful," and have felt the power of female bonding, have not, for the most part, proclaimed it in the context of their own families. They have used a charged language of kin relationships to describe a relationship that is distinctly not one of family. The use of such terms is double-edged, however. On the one hand, their ability to move people suggests the power of networks of women to provide important contexts for social solidarity. On the other hand, the continued use of familial language reinforces, once again, the ideology of family as the ultimate social bond.

Nevertheless, it is important also to recognize that assuming the family as we know it to be the basic social unit is to assume and accept social inequality.[35] For traditional family solidarity is, in many respects, rooted in inequality—the inequality of men and women, and of adults and children, within the patriarchal family. Friendship, on the contrary—at least in theory—is rooted in equality. It is true, of course, that friendship patterns are themselves socially constrained. Often, friendship networks mimic or reflect patterns of relationship that derive from the experiences of families. And it is difficult to forge friendships across the lines of race, sex, class, or age. But such friendships exist. The fact of the friendship in such situations denies the relevance of socially defined inequality to the relationship. It is for this reason that friendship is sometimes seen as a threat to social stability, especially in authoritarian societies.[36]

Finally, many writers on politics and community have noted that friends, perhaps equally with families, are essential to social solidarity and the maintenance of a political-social community. Aristotle, for example, who in *The Politics* traces the development of political communities through families, clans, and city states, argues in the *Ethics* that "friendship also seems to hold states together" (1155a). In fact, he envisions the polis as a kind of "civic friendship" in which citizens imagine themselves "to be a group of friends, mutually bound to certain common purposes, responsible to one another."[37] Earlier in this century, Bertha Conde wrote, in opposition to what now seems the prevailing view, "the ties of friendship are more potent in fashioning the wills of individuals than the bonds of blood. One never knows where the life of love will lead. . . . The peace of the world will in the end depend upon our capacity for friendship and willingness to use it."[38] In our own time, much political theorizing explores the role (and limits) of friendship in sustaining democratic societies.[39] And there is considerable evidence that communities of friends and neighbors meet an important human need and are crucial to the development of identity.[40]

PROTECTION FROM ABANDONMENT AND ISOLATION

We often turn to families as those people who will "never let you down," those one can count on over time. Many observers have pointed out, for example, that especially in the modern capitalist world, characterized by geographical mobility, people are thrown more and more into dependence on nuclear families. Long-term friendships become increasingly difficult to maintain. Families, it is said, hang on.

Nevertheless, there is evidence that, instead of providing solace and protection from isolation, the ideology and practice of the contemporary nuclear family can increase, or even promote, that isolation.[41] That seems especially the case for women, for example, particularly in suburban environments. Recent studies of the impact of suburbanization on women and of the impact of sex-role expectations on spatial structure point out that the single-family homes that characterize suburban life increase the isolation of families, and of the women within them. Conversely, dense urban networks and the access to friends facilitated by urban life help overcome some of that isolation for women who live in cities. Increasing numbers of feminist architects and city planners are advocating taking precisely these sorts of considerations into account: advocating construction of living spaces that recognize the reality and significance of non-nuclear family-based solidarity.[42] The claim that "we have only the family to rely on" is probably reinforced by the very structure of our living spaces and denies the experience of many women. People *do* count on friends for support over time and, perhaps ironically, for overcoming the isolation they experience within the family![43]

SOCIALIZATION/REPRODUCTION

Another crucial function the family performs is the reproduction and socialization of children, which is related, of course, to nurturance. Although virtually all the primary socialization of children occurs in families, much recent feminist scholarship has pointed to some of the problematic consequences of the ways that socialization takes place. It appears that the single-sex ("mother-monopolized") model of nurturance and socialization that predominates at least in the ideal-type nuclear family serves to "reproduce" not only children but the subordination of women and the institutional practices that create and sustain war and other relationships of domination.[44]

Some of those same feminist critiques have also attempted to suggest ways in which that paradox could be overcome within the context of the family: Involve men, as well as women, in childrearing; attempt to develop qualities of nurturance in people of both sexes. Here, too, I argue, friendships have something to offer in the way of an alternative. Communal ideals from Plato's *Republic* to nineteenth-century communes in the United States to the contemporary kibbutz in Israel have proposed that friends can, in fact, play roles in the raising of one another's children; that the nurturance of children need not be seen as the responsibility of the isolated family but as the responsibility of the community.[45]

Such an alternative approach to childrearing could be valuable in two respects: in terms of its contribution to the development of the children and in terms of its contribution to the development of the adults. With respect to children, it seems clear that if a child forms strong, caring, nurturant relationships with other adults, specifically adults other than the mother, those relationships could relieve some of the intensity associated with mother-child relationships in the contemporary nuclear family as well as avoid the negative consequences of mother-monopolized childrearing. The child could come to see the world as a nurturant and caring community, rather than a competitive and individualistic place where competitiveness is relieved only in and through familial relationships. Friendship-based relationships could also provide other models of nurturance that should, in the view of Dinnerstein and Chodorow, help overcome the "reproduction of the subordination of women," which they see taking place within the structure of the nuclear family. A child raised in close relationship with a number of other adults (and children) would recognize that there are many ways to be, and many modes of being nurturant. In theory, changing patterns of childrearing in these ways should also make children more adaptable and sociable as they grow older.[46]

With respect to the adults, the benefits of involving nonkin adults should also be obvious. From the point of view of the parents, on the most basic level, it can make possible some easing of the tremendous responsibility and sense of isolation that now often accompany raising a child. The spreading of the daily "tasks" of nurturance can enable all who engage in them to give full attention to the children when it is their "turn" and to enjoy the activity of nurturing. It can also help create and cement strong ties of community and caring among the adults. Beyond that, any number of writers have pointed out the importance of nurturing others for developing a fuller sense of oneself. In a society organized around nuclear families, only those who give birth to (or adopt) young children, or who care for spouses, parents, or other relatives, have the opportunity to engage in that sort of nonexchange-based caring. If we were to extend our notions of what sorts of relationships are possible, adults would be able to engage in significant caring relationships with children and others not related to them by family ties. Those sorts of relationships could allow for the realization of what appears to be a significant human need (the need to nurture) without depending on ever-increasing birthrates.

SEXUALITY AND INTIMACY

Finally, of course, families have been the primary and officially sanctioned context in which people achieve intimacy and explore and express their sexuality. Yet, as Adrienne Rich and others have demonstrated, the patriarchal family allows only for the expression of one particular version of sexuality: compulsory heterosexuality.[47] Such an insistence on heterosexuality as normative affects everyone. Most obviously, it denies the legitimacy of sexual feelings anyone may have for persons of her or his own sex, relegating those who acknowledge and express such feelings to a category of "deviant," or at least "different." Less obviously, it denies or masks the element of choice and the element of coercion involved in heterosexual relationships. And compulsory heterosexuality locks men and women, whether they are engaged in heterosexual, bisexual, or homosexual relationships, into gender-divided patterns of behavior.

The contemporary insistence on the family as the only appropriate context for the expression of sexuality—expressed, for example, in the ideology of the so-called Moral Majority—reflects a response to the contemporary form of the disconnection of sexuality and intimacy. That particular disconnection is evidenced throughout our culture, perhaps most obviously in the sexualization of advertising, but also in the popularity of pornography, "sexploitation" films, and the like. In the same way that Lasch and others argued that family relationships are the only refuge from the cash-nexus relationships of capitalist society (while ignoring the oppressive side of those same family ties), so the contemporary moralists on issues of sexuality insist that the only way to preserve the "sanctity" of human sexuality is to limit and control its expression and development within the patriarchal, heterosexual family.

But if the problem is the disconnection of sexuality from intimacy, the solution is not the reassertion of the ideological family, but an assertion of the importance of the relationship between sexuality and intimacy that is *not* tied to the subordination of women. And the reconnection with a more communitarian, less individualistic world view. It may be that we see "valueless individualism" and traditional morality as the only options open for the expression of sexuality. What is essential, then, is a recognition that "sexual values and the positive, constructive experience of sex must be based in intimacy."[48] It is thus possible to agree with the Moral Majority that we suffer from a sort of moral vacuum without accepting either their definition of morality or their prescriptions for the family. Instead, as we saw earlier with respect to values of nurturance, there is a place for a "morality" of community, for a model of social relations based on ties *other* than those of utility and self-interest. That model, however, *cannot* be the traditional patriarchal family. Friendship can provide a context in which we can move beyond individualism to a recognition that "sexual intimacy, true sharing, is denied by the values of individualism whereby one is preoccupied with one's own needs.[49] Just as emotionally intimate relationships (whether with friends or members of one's family) are based not only on a concern for having one's own needs met but also on mutuality—a desire to meet another's needs—so fulfilling sexual relationships must be based on a similar mutuality. That is not to deny the importance of sexual pleasure, but to suggest that true intimacy requires both sharing and respect, attention to the context in which a relationship exists.

CONCLUSIONS: THE POLITICS OF FRIENDSHIP

To refer to sexuality and intimacy as "private" need not be to accept the legitimacy of the so-called public-domestic dichotomy nor to accept the conventional wisdom about the role of family (and friends) within that dichotomy. As many feminist scholars have pointed out, the very notion of two independent and autonomous spheres is misleading. Minimally, activities in each domain inform, affect, and are affected by activities in the other.[50] But the "family" has always been assumed to be located in, and in some ways definitive of, the private, or domestic, sphere. Some critics have argued that this is its strength: It is the location of the family in the private sphere, allegedly separate from the cash-nexus relationships of capitalism, that allows it to be the "haven in a heartless world." Feminists have argued, however, that the notion of a dichotomy is an inaccurate representation of reality and that the ideology and practice of the existence of a separate sphere in fact reinforces the subordination of women. Thus, feminists call for abolishing the dichotomy: The personal must be seen as the political, the implications of political ideology translated into the personal realm, and vice versa.[51]

This background may account both for the importance of friendship as a model for feminists and for the potentially "subversive" quality of friendship discussed earlier. For friendship challenges that dichotomy. While generally treated as falling within the "private" sphere, friendships can be intensely political. They can form—and have formed—the basis for radical political association. Friendship networks based on new assumptions about gender can provide contexts for childrearing that challenge traditional models of parenting and make possible the creation and nurturance of young people (and then adults!) who can experience a sense of their own wholeness. And, as we have seen, within certain contexts even the simple act of forming a friendship can be a significant political event. The separation of the private and the personal from the public or political has had important consequences for the isolation of people in the modern world; our meaningful political relationships are said not to be "intimate." Our intimate family (or friendship) relationships are said to stand in the way of our making full commitments to political action. But friendship itself poses a potential challenge to that dichotomization, and stands as a model of the unity of the personal and the public:

> The things that matter most about a person, his unique biography, his flaws and his virtues . . . are his most significant private possession. Yet every effort is made to prevent the intrusion of this private world into a person's public role system. Thereby the unique quality of the personal is suppressed. It is, however, precisely this personal quality on the basis of which friendships become possible.[52]

The basis for the formation of full and meaningful friendships, then, is the transformation of the alleged dichotomy between the personal and the political, the private and the public—the same transformation which, as feminists have argued, is essential to the liberation of women. While traditional families may have provided, and still provide, important sources of nurturance, support, and social solidarity, these human needs have been met at the price of the subordination of women. More significantly, families have not been able to provide these services without the support of friendship networks, nor have they been the only institutions in society to provide them. Families participate in, and reproduce, that same dichotomization of the public and the private that contributes to the subordination of women and to the high levels of alienation characteristic of life in the modern world.

While I have not attempted to provide a fully developed alternative to kin relationships, I hope to have demonstrated that friendship is central to the development of such a vision. Despite the ideology of the family, women throughout history have counted on friendships to provide them with the nurturance and support they have needed. Yet, as we have seen, although the roots of the women's movement are to be found in friendships, feminists and others have not thought seriously enough about friendship as an alternative social model, as a ground from which to respond to claims about the need for more communitarian and less individualistic values in contemporary life.

"Sisterhood" may, indeed, be powerful. But it is significant—and surely no accident—that the members of "old left" socialist, anarchist, and communist organizations referred to one another, not as "brothers" and "sisters," but as "comrades" or "companions." While those "political" terms may seem stiff or hackneyed to us, they convey an important conceptual difference. Rather than reinforce a particular, ideologically loaded view of family, those words allow their users to step back and take seriously those criticisms of "the family" that were essential to their identity as political-cultural activists. It is time that we accord sufficient value to our own experiences and analyses to take a similar conceptual leap.

NOTES

1. I first heard this term from Isaac Balbus, in his paper "A Neo-Hegelian, Feminist, Psychoanalytic Approach to Child-Rearing," presented at a Caucus for a New Political Science panel at the annual meeting of the American Political Science Association, New York City, September 1981. He develops his argument in *Marxism and Domination: A Neo-Hegelian, Feminist, Psychoanalytic Theory of Sexual, Political, and Technological Liberation* (Princeton: Princeton University Press, 1981). He draws, of course, on Dorothy Dinnerstein, *The Mermaid and the Minotaur* (New York: Harper & Row, 1976); Nancy Chodorow, *The Reproduction of Mothering* (Berkeley: University of California Press, 1978); Jane Flax, "The Conflict Between Nurturance and Autonomy in Mother-Daughter Relationships with Feminism," *Feminist Studies* 4, no. 2 (1978): 171–89; and others.

2. See B. Friedan, *The Feminine Mystique* (New York: Dell, 1963); Lillian Rubin, *Worlds of Pain* (New York: Harper & Row, 1976); and Jesse Bernard, "The Paradox of the Happy Marriage," in *Woman in Sexist Society*, ed. Vivian Gornick and Barbara K. Moran (New York: Basic Books, 1971), pp. 85–95, for example.

3. See, for example, Michael Young and Peter Willmott, *Family and Kinship in East London* (Baltimore: Penguin Books, 1962), for discussion of the effect of residency on urban networks.

4. Rayna Rapp, "Examining Family History: Household and Family," *Feminist Studies* 5, no. 1 (Spring 1979): 177.

5. Rayna Rapp, "Family and Class in Contemporary America: Notes Toward an Understanding of Ideology," in *Rethinking the Family*, ed. Barrie Thorne and Marilyn Yalom (New York: Longman, 1982), p. 170.

6. On this point, see also Ellen Ross, "Examining Family History: Women and Family," *Feminist Studies* 5, no. 1 (Spring 1979): 181–89; Barrie Thorne, "Feminist Rethinking of the Family: An Overview," in Thorne and Yalom, eds., *Rethinking the Family*, pp. 1–24; Carol Stack, *All Our Kin* (New York: Harper & Row, 1975).

7. One classic example from contemporary popular culture is the famous scene from Alex Haley's *Roots* when Kunta declines to join the slave insurrection because he cannot bring himself to leave his family. But similar conflicts were reported to me in recent interviews by those, especially women, who had been involved in the Spanish anarchist movement. And, despite my disagreements with his analysis, Edward Banfield's discussion of what he terms "amoral familism" in southern Italy points out somewhat related political implications of "family" ties. See Edward C. Banfield, *The Moral Basis of a Backward Society* (New York: Free Press, 1958); and Michael Walzer, "The Obligation to Disobey," in *Obligations* (Cambridge, Mass.: Harvard University Press, 1970), p. 14.

8. See, for example, Agnes Smedley's letter to Emma Goldman in which she writes of

a yearning for intimacy even in the context of working with people: "Why can I not find the person in whom I feel perfect rest and contentment—complete understanding? People are interesting, Emma, but I never find the person with whom I feel spiritually intimate." Agnes Smedley to EG, Sunday, Berlin, in *Nowhere at Home: Letters from Exile of Emma Goldman and Alexander Berkman*, ed. Richard and Anna Maria Drinnon (New York: Schocken, 1975), p. 135. I am grateful to Jill Lewis for bringing this letter to my attention.

9. For a brief survey of communalist experiments in the United States in relation to family issues, see Amy Swerdlow and Phyllis Vine, "The Search for Alternatives: Past, Present and Future," in *House and Kin*, ed. Amy Swerdlow, Renate Bridenthal, Joan Kelly, and Phyllis Vine (New York: Feminist Press, 1981), pp. 107–60; and Charles Nordhoff, *The Communistic Societies of the United States* (New York: Schocken, 1965; first published 1875). On the kibbutzim in relation to family issues, see Melford E. Spiro, *Children of the Kibbutz* (New York: Schocken, 1965); and *Kibbutz: Venture in Utopia* (New York: Schocken, 1966). The importance of the intimacy achieved in "political" cultural groups was stressed by many of those I interviewed about their experiences in the Spanish anarchist movement. On the Left in the United States in this context, see, for example, Barbara Haber, "Is Personal Life Still a Political Issue?" *Feminist Studies* 5, no. 3 (Fall 1979): 417–30; Barbara Ehrenreich, "The Women's Movements: Feminist and Anti-Feminist," *Radical America* 15, nos. 1 and 2 (Spring 1981): 93–101; Wini Breines, "A Review Essay: Sara Evan's *Personal Politics*," *Feminist Studies* 5, no. 3 (Fall 1979): 495–506; and Ellen Kay Trimberger, "Women in the Old and New Left: The Evolution of a Politics of Personal Life," in ibid., pp. 432–50.

10. Susan Jacoby, "Friendship," *New York Times*, 24 July 1980, p. C2.

11. I am indebted to Vicky Spelman for clarifying this point. See her "Woman as Body: Ancient and Contemporary Views," *Feminist Studies* 8, no. 1 (Spring 1982): esp. 111–19.

12. Horst Hutter, *Politics as Friendship* (Waterloo, Ontario: Wilfred Laurier University Press, 1978), p. 106; and "Friendship," *International Encyclopedia of the Social Sciences* 6 (1968): 12–18.

13. I am indebted to Verena Stolcke for making this point very forcefully. She discusses the social relations of romantic love in "Autonomia o soledad," *Dones en Lluita*, no. 2 (1982): 22–23, and also in *Marriage, Class, and Color in 19th Century Cuba*, Cambridge Latin (Cambridge: Cambridge University Press, 1974).

14. On the changing meaning of what constitutes family, much has been written. For an overview, see the articles by Rapp, Thorne, and Collier, Rosaldo, and Yanagisako, in Thorne and Yalom, eds., *Rethinking the Family.* On sexuality, see Ellen Ross and Rayna Rapp, "Sex and Society: A Research Note from Social History and Anthropology," *Comparative Studies in Society and History* 23, no. 1 (January 1981): 51–72, and sources cited there. Adrienne Rich's "Compulsory Heterosexuality and Lesbian Existence," *Signs* 5, no. 4 (Summer 1980): 631–60, has sparked a lively debate over what it is to be "lesbian" and what meaning that term has in historical perspective. See, for example, the articles by Ann Ferguson, Jacquelyn Zita, and Kathryn Pyne Addelson, "On Compulsory Heterosexuality and Lesbian Existence: Defining the Issues," *Signs* 7, no. 1 (Autumn 1981): 158–99.

15. Christopher Lasch, *Haven in a Heartless World* (New York: Basic Books, 1977). For a critical review, see Thorne, "Feminist Rethinking," p. 18; and Jane Collier, Michelle Z. Rosaldo, and Sylvia Yanagisako, "Is There a Family? New Anthropological Views," in Thorne and Yalom, eds., *Rethinking the Family*, pp. 25–39. Foucault seems to move beyond a concern with exchange relations to look at the notion of "family" itself, as a

construction of modern science. As a consequence, "the family" appears "natural" and to predate modern society. The criticisms are related, but I do not have space to develop this line of argument here.

16. Eli Zaretsky, cited in Thorne, "Feminist Rethinking," p. 19.

17. Laurel Thatcher Ulrich, "A Friendly Neighbor: Social Dimensions of Daily Work in Northern Colonial New England," *Feminist Studies* 6, no. 2 (Summer 1980): 392; see also Mary P. Ryan, "The Power of Women's Networks: A Case Study of Female Moral Reform in Antebellum America," *Feminist Studies* 5, no. 1 (Spring 1979): 66–86.

18. Ulrich, "Friendly Neighbor," p. 401.

19. Carroll Smith-Rosenberg, "The Female World of Love and Ritual: Relations Between Women in Nineteenth Century America," *Signs* 1, no. 1 (Autumn 1975): 1–29.

20. Ellen Ross, "Survival Networks and Domestic Sharing in an East London Neighborhood, 1870–1914" (Berkshire Conference on the History of Women, Vassar College, 18 June 1981).

21. Stack, *All Our Kin.*

22. I do not mean to deny, with this comment, the meaning or significance of what Sara Ruddick has termed "maternal thinking." Her claim is that there are ways of thought —combining appreciation and attention to the needs of a person, concern for that person's self-realization, etc.—which at least certain women who are mothers develop by virtue of being mothers. And further, that it is important that those ways of thought be generalized in society and, in particular, not limited to the domestic domain. But she also points out that "although maternal thinking arises out of actual child-caring practices, biological parenting is neither necessary nor sufficient. Many women and some men express maternal thinking in various kinds of working and caring with others." My own preference is for a sex-neutral term such as "nurturant" or "parental" thinking. The use of the term "maternal" in this context increases the likelihood that the concept will reinforce rather than challenge cultural stereotypes about men and women, and thus undermine what I take to be Ruddick's political goal. Sara Ruddick, "Maternal Thinking," in Thorne and Yalom, eds., *Rethinking the Family*, p. 89. Martha Fowlkes makes a related point about nurturance and nurturant values in "Katie's Place: Women's Work, Professional Work and Social Reform," in *Men, Women and Work*, ed. Helena Z. Lopata and Joseph Pleck in vol. 3 of *The Interweave of Social Roles* (JAI Press, forthcoming). See also Barbara Ehrenreich, and Deirdre English, *For Her Own Good* (New York: Anchor, 1979), pp. 321–24.

23. Ross, "Examining Family History," pp. 186–87.

24. Ehrenreich and English, *For Her Own Good*, p. 324. See also Ferguson and Zita, "On Compulsory Heterosexuality," on the need for "community" in self-identity, pp. 165, 175.

25. Ruddick, "Maternal Thinking," p. 82.

26. Susan Van Dyne, "Sisterly Pledges: The Importance of Female Friendship to Emily Dickinson and Adrienne Rich" (Alumnae College Lecture, Smith College, 22 May 1981).

27. This citation is from Jane Mansbridge, "The Limits of Friendship," in *Participation in Politics*, ed. J. R. Pennock and J. Chapman (Nomos XVI) (New York: New York University Press, 1975), p. 249. *Politics as Friendship*, p. 175. On equality of respect, see also Hutter.

28. Bertha Conde, *The Business of Being a Friend* (Boston and New York: Houghton Mifflin, 1916), pp. 31–32.

29. Lydia Sigourney, *Letters to Young Ladies* (Hartford: William Watson, 1835), p. 107.

30. Adrienne Rich, "Women and Honor: Some Notes on Lying," in *On Lies, Secrets, Silence* (New York: Norton, 1979), p. 188.

31. Elizabeth V. Spelman, "On Treating Persons as Persons," *Ethics* 88, no. 2 (1978).

32. See, e.g., Julia Penelope Stanley and Susan J. Wolfe, *The Coming Out Stories* (Watertown: Persephone Press, 1980); also Ferguson, Zita, and Addelson, "On Compulsory Heterosexuality." This is not to suggest that friendship communities may not also be repressive to "deviance." Pressure to conform to what is "politically correct" has led to splits in feminist communities throughout the country. But the at least somewhat voluntary nature of friendship communities would seem to leave open the possibility of moving on to another one when such conflicts occur. Still, within the context of the ideology of friendship, such "rejection" might be even more traumatic than the rejection of family.

33. Traditionally, we have treated family as the *strongest* social bond, superseding all others, perhaps even the state. There is, of course, much literature and political writing about precisely that conflict—the Greek myths of Creon and Antigone, for example. See Walzer, "The Obligation to Disobey," pp. 3–23; and Judith Shklar, *Freedom and Independence: A Study of the Political Ideas of Hegel's Phenomenology of the Mind* (Cambridge and New York: Cambridge University Press, 1976), pp. 57–95.

34. Julian Pitt-Rivers, "Pseudo-Kinship," *International Encyclopedia of the Social Sciences* 8 (1968): 412.

35. Verena Stolcke, "Women's Labours," in *Of Marriage and the Market*, ed. Kate Young, Carol Wolkowitz, and Roslyn McCullagh (London: CSE Books, 1981).

36. See Hutter, *Politics as Friendship*, pp. 10–11. Note, for example, the fear and anger generated by cross-racial friendships in the South in the United States, particularly during the days of civil rights activism. Or, in another context, the report of a woman who grew up in rural Spain at the beginning of this century that her father did not dare to be seen walking arm-in-arm—even with his wife!—within the limits of the village (interview with author, Barcelona, 14 February 1979). In a somewhat different vein, which highlights the potentially subversive nature of friendship, Walzer cites E. M. Forster, "if I had to choose between betraying my country and betraying my friend, I hope I should have the guts to betray my country." Walzer, "Obligation to Disobey," p. 14.

37. Michael Walzer, "The Obligation to Live for the State," in *Obligations*, p. 175.

38. Conde, *Business of Being a Friend*, p. 120.

39. See, for example, Mansbridge, "Limits of Friendship", Walzer, "Obligation to Disobey" and "Political Solidarity and Personal Honor," in *Obligations*, pp. 190–202; Carole Pateman, *The Problem of Political Obligation* (New York: Wiley, 1979).

40. On the importance of a morality and ethics based on human needs—and the centrality of community and caring—see Ehrenreich and English, *For Her Own Good*, esp. pp. 318–24; Ruddick, "Maternal Thinking"; Fowlkes, "Katie's Peace"; and Ferguson, Zita, and Addelson, "On Compulsory Heterosexuality." On the value of "community" as a need, see also Robert Paul Wolff, *The Poverty of Liberalism* (Boston: Beacon Press, 1968), esp. Chap. 5; Philip Slater, *The Pursuit of Loneliness* (Boston: Beacon Press, 1970); and Kathryn Ferguson, "On Liberalism and Oppression: Emma Goldman and the Anarchist-Feminist Alternative," in *Liberalism and the Modern Polity*, ed. M. J. Gargas McGrath (New York: M. Dekker, 1978).

41. See, e.g., Slater, *Pursuit of Loneliness.*

42. The demand from feminists, of course, has a long history. See Dolores Hayden, *The Grand Domestic Revolution* (Cambridge, Mass.: MIT Press, 1981). For contemporary analyses, see, for example, Susan Saegert, "Masculine Cities and Feminine Suburbs: Polar-

ized Ideas Contradictory Realities," *Signs* 5, no. 3 (Supp. 1980): 96–111; Dolores Hayden, "What Would a Non-Sexist City Be Like?" *ibid.*, pp. S170–87; Anne R. Markusen, "City Spatial Structure, Women's Household Work and National Urban Policy," *ibid.*, pp. S23–44. See also Frances Fox Piven, "Planning for Women in the Central City," in *Planning, Women and Change*, ed. K. Hapgood and J. Getzels (American Society of Planning Officials, 1974), pp. 57–62; Janet Abu-Lughod, "Planning for Women in the Central City," *ibid.*, pp. 37–42; and Suzanne Keller, *Building for Women* (Lexington, Mass.: Heath, 1981).

43. In the contemporary period, we might note the role of consciousness-raising groups in providing such nurturance. And we can also find in mythical traditions suggestions as to at least the *felt* potential of friendship. See for example, the friendship of David and Jonathan, which overcame even fierce interfamily rivalry; and that of Ruth and Naomi which, it seems to me, is better understood as a friendship relationship than as a kin relationship.

44. See, e.g., Chodorow, *Reproduction of Mothering*; Dinnerstein, *Mermaid and Minotaur*; and Balbus, *Marxism and Domination*.

45. Marge Piercy attempts to offer one possible vision of a new pattern of socialization: Three "co-mothers" (not necessarily all females), with no biological relationship to the child, take on the joint responsibility of rearing it, with the support of the community behind them. See *Woman on the Edge of Time* (New York: Fawcett, 1978).

46. The Israeli kibbutz was designed to accomplish a number of these purposes though it preceded, of course, the analytical contributions of Dinnerstein and Chodorow! There is some evidence that children raised on those early kibbutzim were in fact, more peer-oriented, more gregarious, and less dependently connected to their parents. Nevertheless, even the kibbutz did not abolish the family structure entirely.

47. See Rich, "Compulsory Heterosexuality"; also Gayle Rubin, "The Traffic in Women: Notes on the 'Political Economy' of Sex," in *Toward an Anthropology of Women*, ed. Rayna R. Reiter (New York: Monthly Review Press, 1975), pp. 157–210.

48. Kathleen Barry, *Female Sexual Slavery* (Englewood Cliffs, N.J.: Prentice-Hall, 1979), pp. 223, 227.

49. Ibid., p. 228.

50. See Donna R. Divine, "Unveiling the Mysteries of Islam: The Art of Studying Muslim Women" (manuscript, Smith College, 1981).

51. See, for example, Jean B. Elshtain, "Moral Woman and Immoral Man," *Politics and Society* 4, no. 4 (1974): 453–73. Markusen, "City Spatial Structure"; Hayden, "Non-Sexist City"; Ruddick, "Maternal Thinking"; Michelle Z. Rosaldo, "The Use and Abuse of Anthropology: Reflections on Feminism and Cross-Cultural Understanding," *Signs* 5, no. 3 (Spring 1980): 389–417.

52. Hutter, *Politics as Friendship*, p. 183; See also pp. 6–7 and 10–11 on the political nature of making friends.

22

Mary Lyndon Shanley

Afterword: Feminism and Families in a Liberal Polity

One of the lessons that emerges from the essays in this book is that it has been exceedingly difficult in the United States to lay the theoretical base for appropriate and coherent policies toward families, not only because of stupidity, ignorance, and misogynism, but in part because of the characteristics of the liberal ideology on which our political and legal systems are based. Feminists are confronted with a dilemma that, although intellectually intriguing, is nonetheless problematic: how to use the great potential of liberal ideas to enact changes important for women and their families and at the same time gain recognition for the fundamental failure of liberalism either to portray adequately family relationships and needs or to give a satisfactory account of the relationship between families and the state. This afterword outlines the past usefulness of liberal precepts in enacting feminist reforms, and the theoretical inadequacies of the widely used concepts of liberal individualism for a transformation of society along feminist lines. I suggest that any feminist vision of the "good life" must recognize the importance of sexual equality, meaningful work, civic participation, and nurturant activity for individuals and their communities and must put these at the center of public policies concerning families.

In the nineteenth century traditional liberal concepts of individual rights, natural freedom, and consent or contract were powerful tools in the hands of feminist reformers and provided an important part of the ideological basis of attaining women's rights. For example, individualistic and contractual ideas, particularly the notion that consent is at the root of all human obligations, were crucial to early divorce law reform. Ideas about contract were also at the heart of the battle against the common law doctrine of coverture, which took away a woman's independent legal status when she married. Consequently, a married woman's property belonged to her husband; she could make no contracts (nor even a will) without his authorization, and he had legal custody of their children. In procuring married women's rights, reformers argued that no other contract except marriage obliterated the legal personality of one of the partners. Similarly, the argument made by opponents of women's suffrage that women were adequately represented by their fathers, husbands, or brothers (who voted, in effect, for the "household") was for a while successful, but was ultimately doomed in a polity based on the notion that government was created by the free consent of individuals endowed with "inalienable rights."

Several authors in this volume argue that the successful battles to procure women's rights under marriage law and as citizens gradually substituted the authority of the state for the authority of the male head of household, replacing "family patriarchy" with "state patriarchy." They contend that despite women's formal equality in some areas, laws, judicial decisions, and administrative policies continued to assume that women's "natural" place was in the home attending to domestic and childrearing duties, while man's was in the paid work force. State actions thus tended to enforce the sexual division of labor and women's subordinate economic status. This is to some extent true; nonetheless, state patriarchy has also shown itself vulnerable to attacks based on liberal ideology.

In the 1960s and '70s feminists used liberal principles to secure legislation and court decisions undermining the sexual division of labor, for example, the Equal Pay Act of 1963, the enforcement of equal employment opportunity under Title VII of the Civil Rights Act of 1964, the Equal Credit Act of 1965, and the Supreme Court decisions extending the Equal Protection Clause of the XIV Amendment to sex discrimination (*Reed* v. *Reed, Frontiero* v. *Richardson*, etc.). In arguing for these measures feminists again insisted that public policy measures based on assumptions about the natural talents or proclivities of either sex were at odds with notions of natural freedom, equality, and rights of self-determination.

There was also a strong tendency to place traditional notions of individual autonomy at the center of feminist efforts to obtain contraceptive rights and sexual and reproductive freedom. The rights to contraceptive use and to abortion were both obtained by asserting the existence of a right to personal privacy, an area of life into which neither the state nor other persons could intrude. In the case of abortion, this area of privacy was clearly identified with bodily integrity, suggesting the phrase "woman's body, woman's right." I want to emphasize here the rather obvious fact that when women turned to the state to promote or defend their interests, the terminologies and conceptualizations they used were shaped to conform to the concepts with which our legal tradition is most familiar and best suited to deal.

But the reliance on individual rights, while clearly effective, created some paradoxes for those concerned with a feminist transformation of families and society. Extending to women equality under the law, whether through the Equal Protection Clause or an Equal Rights Amendment is a necessary but not sufficient condition for genuine reform. For one thing, as Ellen Boneparth and Emily Stoper point out in this volume, equal rights simply give women the opportunity to participate in the society as it is currently structured, but do nothing directly about altering aspects of those structures inimical to family well-being. The suit brought by several draft-age men in *Rostker* v. *Goldberg* (1981) illuminates this point. The young men charged that the male-only registration for the military violated their right to the equal protection of the laws because by excluding women it increased men's chances of being conscripted in the event of a draft. NOW supported the plaintiffs in an *amicus* brief, arguing that an all-male draft also denied *women* their full rights to serve in the military. Although the Supreme Court ruled against the men (deferring to Congressional authority to make regulations governing the military), the men were right in principle: If circumstances justified military conscription, sex alone should provide no justification for an automatic exemption.

But the draft registration case shows dramatically how foolish it can be for women to press for "equal opportunity" without also questioning the nature of the activity or office to which they seek access. Triumphs of equal opportunity in employment could prove pyrrhic victories. I think here, for example, of some forms of law practice that destroy members' chances of leading well-balanced lives of work, play, family, and friendship; or of industrial positions that routinely expose workers to harmful conditions or toxic wastes.

In addition, feminists must beware of falling into the fallacy of believing that legal reform will transform not only women's roles in the labor force and the political realm but also in the household. Several essays in this book mention the sobering and depressing fact that even after the attention the contemporary feminist movement gave to understanding ways in which "the personal is the political" and to uncovering the "politics of housework," there are still persistent inequalities in men's and women's contributions to domestic labor. Unless women effectively pressure men to undertake an even share of household responsibility, governmental action aimed at securing women's equal labor force participation will simply procure for women the "opportunity" to work at two jobs simultaneously.

Similarly, there is a temptation to accept individual solutions to deal with the problem of combining family life and work outside the home that are not "solutions" at all. Carole Joffe's essay in this volume mentions the day-care center that watches over an infant for nine or more hours a day and remarks that "a childcare policy may promote the needs of one party [the mother] at the expense of the other [the child]." But how many mothers truly wish to be separated from their infants that much of the day, five days a week? Joffe herself suggests that mothers may not regard this as a good arrangement but as an unhappy necessity produced by the organization of work in our society. Given the enormous difficulties of challenging as individuals the structure of employment, people are forced to make difficult adjustments such as placing a child for ten hours a day in child care, risking future unemployment by dropping out of the work force, or losing health and retirement benefits by going on part-time hours. I do not criticize those who make such arrangements; I simply contend that such ad hoc solutions are frequently painful and costly adjustment to a society that is fundamentally inhospitable to combining employment and human nurturance, and that they do not provide the basis for an adequate *public* policy.

The language of personal "privacy" is also a paradoxical basis on which to build a society that will encourage new forms of families or communal life and that will strike a new balance between work and family life. On the one hand, the right to privacy has been very effective in combating efforts both by the state and by men to control women's sexuality and women's bodies. It is probably the most effective tool feminists have used to undermine restrictions on contraception, abortion, and homosexual relationships. And yet, as Wendy Brown points out in her essay, reproductive decisions are of course anything but "private," involving as they do a number of human lives. Not only is it an error to deny or ignore the claims of the fetus (although these may be overridden), but feminists have long sought recognition of the fact that children are the responsibility not only of their biological mothers but of their fathers and, indeed, of society as a whole. It is thus ironic to speak of a woman's sole right to make decisions about pregnancy and abortion and at the same time to press for greater social involvement in and support for child care. As Brown argues, "reproductive rights serve primarily to entrench women's isolation in their unique relation to the reproductive process. Insofar as these rights are inherently *protective*, *defensive*, and *isolating*, these are three things that women as reproducers do not need more of."

While liberal ideals have been efficacious in overturning restrictions on women as individuals, liberal theory does not provide the language or concepts to help us understand the various kinds of human interdependence which are part of the life of both families and polities, nor to articulate a feminist vision of "the good life." Feminists are thus in the awkward positions of having to use rhetoric in dealing with the state that does not adequately describe their goals and that may undercut their efforts at establishing new modes of life. Martha Ackelsberg's fine essay on friendship implicitly recognizes that neither the language that traditionally has described the patriarchal family as a "natural" entity nor the contractual language of liberal political theory provides us with the range of conceptualizations of human relationships we need even to describe (much less to build) a polity that incorporates feminist values.

There are, of course, many feminist notions of what would constitute a desirable social existence, but in my view the most persuasive of these draw on a variety of traditions in political theory. First, despite liberalism's ultimate shortcomings, the notions of individual freedom and self-determination are important in establishing equal opportunities for men and women to develop whatever talents and to pursue whatever interests they may have. Second, one must recognize, as Marx did in the *Economic and Philosophical Manuscripts*, that a full human existence requires the opportunity to undertake productive and fulfilling work. This is the reason that "equal opportunity" alone cannot satisfy feminist demands, for *what* one is to have equal opportunity to do is critically important. Third, the good life involves citizen responsibility, some role in contributing to the discussions about public policy and about the distribution of goods within the community. For the Greeks, who bequeathed this ideal to us, only male citizens could undertake this role. Women were considered exclusively private or domestic beings, and mired as they were in the realm of "necessity," of reproduction, childrearing, and domestic management, they were thought incapable of the abstract and disinterested thought necessary to promote the life of the polity. Feminist thought not only asserts that women can and must (to share in the best life possible) take part in public life but also revises the traditional view that the repetitive and necessary work of biological reproduction and child raising is less fully human than the "free" activity of ratiocination and contemplation. Thus a fourth component of a good society would be a common affirmation of the importance of nurturant activity to a full and rich human life.

The basis for adequate public policies dealing with families, therefore, must recognize the importance to human beings of equality, productive work, citizen involvement, and nurturant activity. These seem to me to be the grounds on which to formulate the demands for adequate public support for child care whether in the form of day-care centers, tax deductions for child care, or tax credits for businesses that establish day-care centers; for parental leaves and flexible (and in many cases shorter) work hours; for adequate housing and community facilities; and for sexual and reproductive freedom; to mention some of the concerns touched on in these essays. From this perspective one can argue for public support for child care not just because women as individuals have the "right" to undertake nondomestic work, but because nurturant and productive activity are both important aspects of human life, which the polity should facilitate for parents and nonparents alike. Similarly, to insist that men and women share equally in childrearing is not simply a demand that women be released from domestic work (nor a ploy to bog men down in diaper changing) but an affirmation of a vision of life that includes human nurturance as well as material production, for all adults.

Increasingly, feminist writers are insisting that "women's work" has an importance and value of its own, not simply an instrumental value in sustaining life so that people can get on with the "real" tasks of human existence. Historians are producing a growing body of work on "women's culture" that shows how varied and extensive were women's activities binding together and sustaining the larger community; Sarah Ruddick's "Maternal Thinking" (B. Thorne and M. Yalom, *Rethinking the Family* [New York: Longman, 1982]) makes a compelling case that care of the young or infirm imparts a kind of knowledge unobtainable from other activities; Jean Elshtain's "Antigone's Daughters" in this book suggests that there is a particularly female sensibility (which comes from activity rather than from biology) that could be used to critique certain attitudes toward our understanding of the state itself.

The theoretical task facing those concerned with articulating the bases for public policies dealing with families is thus much broader than showing the inadequacies of liberal individualism to depict or account for the variety of human relationships, needs, and responsibilities that are part of living in families. The basis for adequate public policies must be the recognition that nurturant activity (which includes the care of the sick and aged, as well as caring for children) should be as much a part of a full adult life as productive work. These are tasks not only gratifying to individuals but centrally important to the common life of the polity.

About the Contributors

Irene Diamond received her Ph.D. in politics from Princeton University. She is the author of *Sex Roles in the State House* (Yale University Press, 1977), one of the first scholarly monographs on women in politics, and has published articles in such journals as *Signs* and the *American Political Science Review.* In 1980–81 she was a National Association of Schools of Public Affairs and Administration faculty fellow at the Department of Housing and Urban Development in Washington, D.C., and in the spring of 1981 she was a Fulbright Research Scholar at the Institute of Criminal Sciences of the University of Copenhagen, Denmark. She is currently working on a project that attempts to mesh feminist policy analysis with theoretical perspectives on cultural and political life in advanced industrial societies.

Martha Ackelsberg received her Ph.D. in politics from Princeton University. An associate professor of government at Smith College, she is a principal investigator with the Project on Women and Social Change. Her current work focuses on anarchist collectives in Spain during the Civil War and on protest movements in the United States. In addition to publications on these topics, she has contributed to *The Jewish Woman*, edited by E. Koltun (Schocken, 1976) and to *Response* magazine on issues related to Jewish feminism and political activism.

Pamela Armstrong received a master's degree in philosophy from the University of Delaware where she researched issues of violence against women and taught philosophy and women's studies. She is now a member of the Philosophy Department at Dowling College, Long Island. She has worked in rape crisis centers and battered women's shelters in Massachusetts, Pennsylvania, and Delaware, and has administered grants for Delaware programs for battered women.

Peter Bardaglio received his master's degree in history from Stanford University where he is at present a doctoral candidate. He is a visiting lecturer in history at the University of Maryland, College Park. He has published articles on Italian immigrants and the Catholic church and on pre-Civil War southern society. His dissertation-in-progress focuses on the transformation of family law in the nineteenth-century South.

Sarah Begus, a doctoral candidate in political science at the Johns Hopkins University, teaches women's studies at the University of Delaware. From 1976 to 1979 she was a member of the editorial collective of *Women: A Journal of Liberation* (published in Baltimore); she has also been an editor of *Quest: A Feminist Quarterly* (published in Washington, D.C.). She is currently researching issues in female psychosexual development.

Janet K. Boles is an assistant professor of political science at Marquette University and the author of *The Politics of the Equal Rights Amendment* (Longman, 1979). She has published articles on social policy and on women and politics in the *Social Service Review* and *Women and Politics.* Since 1980 she has been a member of the *Ms.* Magazine Advisory Board on Research, Scholarship, and Education.

Ellen Boneparth is an associate dean in the School of Social Sciences and an associate professor of political science at San Jose State University. She is the founder and director of the Aegean Women's Studies Institute and the International Institute of Women's Studies in Israel. She recently published *Women, Power and Policy* (Pergamon, 1982).

Eileen Boris teaches women's studies at the University of Maryland where she has acted as managing editor of *Feminist Studies.* An interdisciplinary scholar who received her Ph.D. from Brown University, she is the author of *Art and Labor: John Ruskin, William Morris, and the Craftsman Ideal in America* (Temple University Press, forthcoming, 1984). Her articles have also appeared in *Signs, Quest: A Feminist Quarterly*, and *Victorian Studies.* A recipient of Woodrow Wilson, Danforth, and Business and Professional Women's Foundation grants, she is currently writing a book on home production and women's lives.

Wendy Brown received her master's degree from Princeton University where she is a doctoral candidate in the Politics Department. She has taught political theory and feminist theory at Haverford College and Princeton University. An American Association of University Women Fellow, Charlotte Newcombe Foundation Honorary Fellow, and Woodrow Wilson Foundation Scholar, she is completing her dissertation on "The Agony of Virtu: Politics and Manhood in Western Political Thought."

Zillah Eisenstein is a professor of politics at Ithaca College. She is editor and contributor to *Capitalist Patriarchy and the Case for Socialist Feminism* (Monthly Review Press, 1979) and the author of *The Radical Future of Liberal Feminism* (Longman, 1981). She has also written several articles about the rise of neoconservatism and its impact on feminism for *Feminist Studies, Signs*, and other feminist journals. She is a member of CARASA and the Ithaca Task Force for Battered Women.

Jean Bethke Elshtain, professor of political science at the University of Massachusetts, Amherst, is the author of *Public Man, Private Woman: Women in Social and Political Thought* (Princeton University Press, 1981) and editor of *The Family in Political Thought* (University of Massachusetts Press, 1982). Her articles have appeared in many journals and magazines, including *Signs, Women's Studies International Forum*, and the *Nation.* In 1981–82 she was a member of the Institute for Advanced Study at Princeton University.

Steven Erie received his Ph.D. from the University of California at Los Angeles and is now teaching political science at the University of California, San Diego. He is a contributor to *What Reagan Is Doing to Us*, edited by Alan Gartner et al. (Harper & Row, 1982) and has published articles on blacks and the Great Society (with

Michael K. Brown) for *Public Policy* and the Irish and black experience of ethnic power for *Polity*.

Myra Marx Ferree is an associate professor of sociology at the University of Connecticut where she is active in developing and teaching in the women's studies program. Supported by a Woodrow Wilson fellowship, she received her Ph.D. in social psychology from Harvard University with a dissertation on working-class women's employment and attitudes. She has published a number of articles about paid work and housework, one of which will appear in *Sex Roles*. She is at present writing a book with Beth Hess on the women's movement, to be published by Twayne (a division of G. K. Hall).

Jane Flax is an associate professor of political science at Howard University and a practicing therapist in Washington, D.C. She has published articles in *Feminist Studies, Journal of Philosophy*, and *Journal of Politics*, as well as in edited collections. She is currently working on a feminist critique of Marx, Freud, critical theory, and object relations theory.

Joyce Gelb is a professor and chair of the Political Science Department at the City College of New York. She is a coauthor of *Women and Public Politics* (Princeton University Press, 1982) and has written many articles on women and minorities in politics. She has held awards from the National Endowment for the Humanities, the Yale University Project on Non Profit Organizations, and the Fulbright Hays Commission. She is currently writing a book, to be published by Longman, comparing the British and American feminist movements.

Jean Grossholtz received her Ph.D. from the Massachusetts Institute of Technology. She is a professor of politics at Mount Holyoke College, a member of the National Coalition Against Domestic Violence, and a member of the board of directors for Hegira, Inc.

Anne Harper did her graduate work in political science at the University of Michigan. She taught at Smith College where she was also a research associate and summer faculty fellow with the Project on Women and Social Change. She currently teaches politics and feminism courses at Virginia Polytechnic Institute and State University, Blacksburg. An article on human sexuality will appear in *Feminist Visions: Toward a Transformation of the Liberal Arts Curriculum*, edited by Diane L. Fowlkes and Charlotte S. McClure (University of Alabama Press, 1983).

Nan D. Hunter is an attorney with the Reproductive Freedom Project of the American Civil Liberties Union Foundation in New York. Formerly a member of a feminist law collective in Washington, D.C., she has litigated a number of family law cases. She is the coauthor, with Nancy Polikoff, of an article on custody rights of lesbian mothers that appeared in the *Buffalo Law Review*. She has taught law school and undergraduate courses in family law and women and the law.

Carole Joffe received her Ph.D. in sociology from the University of California, Berkeley. An associate professor at Bryn Mawr College's Graduate School of Social Work, she is currently a National Science Foundation Visiting Professor at the University of Pennsylvania (1982–83). Her publications include *Friendly Intruders: Childcare Professionals and Family Life* (University of California Press, 1977).

Shelah Gilbert Leader received her Ph.D. in political science from the State

University of New York at Buffalo. She has published articles on women and public policy and is the coauthor of *What Kinds of Guns Are They Buying for Your Butter?* (William Morrow, 1982). Formerly a policy analyst for the federal government, she is now a consultant and teaches courses on women and public policy at American University.

Ruth Nielsen received her LL.M. from the University of Copenhagen. She is currently a research fellow at the Women's Research Centre in Social Science, Copenhagen, where she is working on a comparative labor law project concerning women in northwestern Europe. Her publications include *Kvindearbejdsret, Copenhagen* (Juristforbundets Forlag, 1979) and articles in *Arbog for Kvinderet* (*Yearbook of Women's Law*). She is editor of European Women's Law, a mimeographed series published from 1982 onward by Kvindevindenskabeligt Forlag.

Nancy D. Polikoff is a staff attorney at the Women's Legal Defense Fund, Washington, D.C., and director of its Child Custody Project. In addition to her law degree, she holds a master's degree in women's studies from the George Washington University where she currently teaches feminist theory and women and the law. As a faculty adjunct, she has also taught women and the law at Catholic University and Antioch law schools. She has written several articles on women and family law issues.

Martin Rein received his Ph.D. from Brandeis University. He now teaches in the Urban Studies and Planning Department at the Massachusetts Institute of Technology. His most recent publications include *From Policy to Practice* (M. E. Sharpe, 1982) and a new edition (with Peter Marris) of *Dilemmas of Social Reform* (University of Chicago Press, 1982).

Jean Robinson received her Ph.D. in government from Cornell University. An assistant professor of political science at Indiana University, she is a specialist in Chinese politics, feminist theory, and women in comparative perspective. She served for five years as director of women's studies at Indiana University and has done research in the People's Republic of China. She has several articles forthcoming on Chinese politics, bureaucratic reform, and women in China.

Mary Lyndon Shanley is an associate professor of political science at Vassar College where she has served as acting director of women's studies. She has contributed articles to *The Family in Political Thought*, ed. J. B. Elshtain (University of Massachusetts Press, 1981), *The Artist and Political Vision*, edited by B. Barber and M. McGrath (Transaction Press, 1981), and *Women Organizing*, edited by B. Cummings and V. Schuck (Scarecrow Press, 1979), and has published articles in *Signs*, *Western Political Quarterly*, and *Victorian Studies*. She received her Ph.D. from Harvard University and is currently working on a book-length study of feminism and legal reform in Victorian England.

Margaret C. Simms is a senior research associate at the Urban Institute where she serves as director of the Minorities and Social Policy Program. Before joining the institute, she was an associate professor and chairperson of the economics department at Atlanta University. A former Brookings Economic Policy Fellow at the U.S. Department of Housing and Urban Development, she has written many articles and reports on public policy issues, including a monograph published by HUD, *Families* *and Housing Markets: Obstacles to Locating Suitable Housing* (Government Printing Office, 1980).

Emily Stoper received her Ph.D. from Harvard University. She is a professor of political science and codirector of the women's studies program at California State University at Hayward. She is a contributor to *A Portrait of Marginality: The Political Behavior of the American Woman*, edited by Marianne Githens and Jewel L. Prestage (David McKay, 1977), *Social Movements of the Sixties and Seventies*, edited by Jo Freeman (Longman, 1982), and *Women, Power and Policy*, edited by Ellen Boneparth (Pergamon, 1982).

Barbara Wiget is a Ph.D. candidate in economics at Harvard University. She currently holds a research appointment at the Center for Population Studies, Harvard University. She has coauthored *The Nation's Families* (Auburn House, 1981) and an article on the downturn in U.S. fertility for the Center for Population Studies' *Working Paper* (1978).

Index